The Divine and Demoniac

The Divine and Demoniac
Mahisa's Heroic Struggle with Durga

CARMEL BERKSON

DELHI
OXFORD UNIVERSITY PRESS
BOMBAY CALCUTTA MADRAS
1995

Oxford University Press, Walton Street, Oxford OX2 6DP

Oxford New York
Athens Auckland Bangkok Bombay
Calcutta Cape Town Dar es Salaam Delhi
Florence Hong Kong Istanbul Karachi
Kuala Lumpur Madras Madrid Melbourne
Mexico City Nairobi Paris Singapore
Taipei Tokyo Toronto
and associates in
Berlin Ibadan

ISBN 0 19 563555 8

Typeset by All India Press, Pondicherry
Printed in India at Pauls Press, New Delhi 110020
and published by Neil O'Brien, Oxford University Press
YMCA Library Building, Jai Singh Road, New Delhi 110001

Foreword

The originality of this book lies in the way in which it succeeds in combining a thorough, fully contextualized study—what the anthropologist Clifford Geertz would call a 'thick description'—of a myth-and-ritual complex with a vivid personal experience of the meaning of that myth and that ritual.

It offers a badly needed corrective to the present state of wildcat writings about Goddesses, a fresh new bridge between two camps that communicate far too seldom: on this side, in blue tights, the library of scholarship about various Goddesses, with its Indological branch (of which David Kinsley's *Hindu Goddesses* is my favorite) and its Western branch (of which Marina Warner's study of Mary is my favorite); and on that side, in red tights, the arsenal of feminist books of personal testimony to the magic of The Goddess (of which I have no favorite). *The Divine and Demoniac* is a book that, like Kinsley's (though with a far less technical scholarly background), focuses on the Goddess in a particular culture, indeed on one particular myth of that Goddess (the central myth of her marriage to and slaughter of the buffalo). But, like the feminist arsenal (though with a far less polemical stance), it interprets that myth in very personal terms.

The Divine and Demoniac also provides a bridge between another pair of cultures that often misunderstand one another just as badly as do the worlds of scholarship and personal feminism: the cultures of India and America. There are, of course, many good books about India written by Indians, and there are some good books about India written by Americans, and each genre has its virtues and its shortcomings. There are even a few wonderful books written by Indians who have lived abroad long enough to internalize Western ways of thinking without giving up their own, native ways of feeling. Among these, particularly brilliant contributions have been made by three men: A. K. Ramanujan, Sudhir Kakar, and Gananath Obeyesekere. The last two in particular, with their primarily psychological approaches, are an important part of Carmel Berkson's own scholarly apparatus.

Carmel Berkson's book represents the flip side of this cross-cultural personal assimilation: it is a book written by a woman who is neither a scholar nor an Indian but who has sojourned so long, and so well, in the worlds of scholarship and India that she is able to lend them the fresh insights of her own very individual approach to problems that they have been wrestling with for years. Carmel Berkson has lived in Bombay for many years because she loves it; and she has made it her life's work to photograph Indian art, and Indian reality, for the same reason. Her books of photographs of Indian sculpture, particularly of the great monuments at Ellora and Elephanta, have been widely praised. *The Amazon and the Goddess: Cognates of Artistic Form* (1987), her detailed and insightful comparative study of one particular rendition of the myth of the Hindu Goddess on her lion, fighting the buffalo, and another of the Greek Amazon on her horse, fighting Greek men, held within it a double seed of inspiration: it whet her appetite for a far more wide-ranging study of the myth of the Goddess on her lion, and it opened the way to a comparative, universalistic study of that myth.

The encyclopaedic study—for there is more in this book about the Goddess and buffalo than some people may want to know—is made possible by the focus on a particular myth, the depths of which are then plumbed in a number of different dimensions: textual sources from ancient India together with more recent retellings; renditions in classical Indian art and in contemporary reinterpretations; anthropological and psychological studies of the human counterparts of the mythical protagonists; and comparative insights from the study of similar myths in other religions throughout the world.

For although this book is ostensibly about an Indian story, the meanings that it draws from that story are universal. The arguments that Carmel Berkson makes explicitly for such universality are primarily Jungian, though she is no more dogmatic about this than she is about anything else, and her analysis of sexual relationships within (and without) the nuclear family owe more to Freud, I think, than to Jung. But the implicit assumption behind the book is that there is a common humanity underlying basic experiences such as motherhood and death, and that precious insights into that humanity are available to an American who keeps her eyes open in India. Indeed, the assumption (and, I think, demonstration, in this book) is that such insights are more readily available to her in India than in America, in part because one sees certain things better in other peoples' cultures and in part because Indian authors and artists seem to have been able to capture those experiences of sex and death more vividly and powerfully than any other authors or artists in the world.

Moreover, although *The Divine and Demoniac* grounds itself in a study of ancient Sanskrit texts and ancient stone monuments, the meanings that it draws from those texts and those monuments are entirely contemporary. The contemporaneity is supplied by Carmel Berkson's own observations of life in India, her personal anecdotes, her field notes not only on formal rituals but on informal relationships, her records not only of interviews with scholars and artists but of arguments with friends and lovers. The photographs of artistic renditions of buffaloes are flanked by photographs of the real buffaloes that one gets to know in an Indian village; the discussions of classical Indian ideas about yoga and asceticism are illuminated by notes on ascetics with whom Carmel Berkson has had dealings of one sort or another.

The analysis of old wives' tales in Sanskrit texts are enlivened by Carmel Berkson's personal interactions with old wives—and, indeed, by her experience of *being* an old wife, in the spiritual rather than chronological sense of the word: a woman who has been a wife and mother, and much else, and lived to tell the tale. She has met the buffalo, loved him, hated him, married him, mothered him, and, ultimately, killed him. But she came to understand that story only through her understanding of the ways in which the Goddess did it. It is my firm belief that this book will be of enormous interest to old wives all over the world, who will learn through it the many ways in which they are like, and, more important, the many ways in which they are *not* like, Hindu mothers, Hindu goddesses, and American women who make their lives in Bombay.

Wendy O'Flaherty

Preface

Various streams combine to encourage the perspectives presented here. Icons abound, and the texts provide ready data in rich language which saturates the core myth with emotional content and evocative symbolism. Amidst the innumerable oral variations from all parts of the country, there are enough constant motifs deducible from text translations to enable even the non-linguist to work with certain general assumptions in regard to the myth of Mahisamardini. These will only be useful, however, if the elusive nature of the work of art and of the myth is kept in mind. In the final analysis, meanings must be received directly, as insights, since their source is the undifferentiated seat of imagery, the unconscious, where projections are potentiated.

But the texts beg for interpretation, and as my own concerns have been primarily in the field of art, I have always relied heavily on the profound scholarship of Wendy Doniger (O'Flaherty). I adopted her as guru of myths, and in her inimitable generosity, she has never failed to offer encouragement and consistent ready support. I cannot be too grateful for the valuable criticism and attention, but above all, the unique Wendy spirit with which these many bounties are offered.

In 1976 David Shulman first telescoped many of the fundamental motifs which appear here. His subsequent analyses helped to clarify my own thinking. I value his penetrating comments regarding this book and our friendship which has developed out of our common concerns.

Sudhir Kakar, who leads the psychoanalytic field in India, opened avenues into the Indian psyche, and I wish to thank him for taking time out of his busy life to read the manuscript. These thanks I also give to N. B. Patil and Norman Sjoman, who generously gave of their fine abilities and time. They are responsible for the Sanskrit translations, except when Doniger's are indicated. Edith Chelimer Eisner, a friend of fifty years' standing, whose critical judgement I have always valued highly, read an early draft of the manuscript, made valuable suggestions and encouraged me to publish.

An earlier version of Chapter Nine, 'The Life Stages of the Hero', was published in *Roopa-Lekha*, Journal of the All India Fine Arts and Crafts Society, New Delhi, Vol. 50, 1994.

Thanks are also due to the Archaeological Survey of India and the Simla, Mathura, and Gwalior Museums for permission to photograph the images published in this volume. My own experiences as a student and photographer of Indian art and festivals during my travels provide continual corroborative evidence which virtually forces me into the Jungian camp. And although one must humbly confess to the limitations of being foreign born and foreign educated, the attempt to come to terms with the contemporary Indian personality in its protean manifestations is just as often enhanced by the revealing laboratory of personal relationships, enough to warrant the hope that a valid assessment of the power of this myth is possible. Truly, my debt to all the wonderful people who have entered my life here is immeasurable.

Finally, it was a happy circumstance which led me to my editor at the Oxford University Press. Working with her gave me much pleasure, and because of her very keen perceptions, we have a better book.

C. B.

Contents

Plates

19. The Goddess pierces Mahisa's body with her trident, holding him by the hind leg with her left hand. Fourth–fifth century AD. Gupta shrine, Ramgarh Hill, Madhya Pradesh.

20. The Goddess stands on the severed head of the buffalo. Fifth century AD. Gwalior Museum, Madhya Pradesh.

21. Mahisa, his front legs buckled under him, stands in front of the Goddess; he has more volume and stands within his own space; she breaks his neck. Sixth century AD. Ravana Phadi cave, Aihole, Karnataka.

22. The Goddess and Mahisa face each other as equals on the battlefield. Seventh century AD. Mamallapuram, Tamil Nadu.

23. As Mahisa emerges in human form from the buffalo body, the Goddess pierces him with the trident and is about to deliver the second mortal blow. Eighth century AD. Surya temple, Osian, Rajasthan.

24. The all-powerful Goddess slays Mahisa in buffalo and human form, reduced once again to a smaller size. Tenth century AD. Siva temple, Kitching, Orissa.

25. Mahisa in human form rises towards the Goddess as he emerges from the severed neck of the buffalo. Tenth century AD. Ambika temple, Jagat, Rajasthan.

26. The Goddess towers above Mahisa who has been brought to his knees; he is human, with buffalo head. Eleventh century AD. Chidambaram temple, Tamil Nadu.

27. Mahisa is now only in human form. Tenth century AD. Ambika temple, Jagat, Rajasthan.

28. Goddess and demon are nearly equal in size and importance. Twentieth century. Navratri festival, Calcutta.

Abbreviations

B.Can.	Bana, *Candisataka*
B.Kad.	Bana, *Kadambari*
BP, 4, LM	*Brahmanda Purana, Lalita Mahatmya*
DBP	(*Shrimad*) *Devi Bhagavata Purana*
DM	*Devi Mahatmyam*
EG	*Epic of Gilgamesh*
ERE	*Encyclopedia of Religion and Ethics*
GriS.	*Griha Sutra*
In.Vis.	*Institutes of Visnu*
KalP.	*Kalika Purana*
Katho	*Kathopanisad*
Khando	*Khandoya Upanisad*
KS	*Kama Sutra*
MatP.	*Matsya Purana*
QJMS	*Quarterly Journal of the Mythic Society*
Rg Ved.	*Rig Veda*
SB	*Satapatha Brahmana*
SivP.	*Siva Purana*
SkP.	*Skanda Purana*
SLA	*Sacred Laws of the Aryas*
TaiS.	*Taitireyya Samhita*
VamP.	*Vamana Purana*
VarP.	*Varaha Purana*

To Wendy Doniger

Introduction

The myth of Mahisamardini, recorded in the *Vamana Purana* and elaborated in *Devi Bhagavata Purana,* provides the structure for this study. The core story goes as follows:

The brothers Rambha and Karambha, Brahmin demon kings, performed severe austerities (*tapas*) with the goal of attaining sons. However, for fear of their growing power over the gods, Indra intervened and killed Karambha. Rambha threatened suicide but was stopped in the nick of time by the god of fire, Agni, who offered him a boon: the king would beget an invincible son by a female of his choice. When Rambha encountered a young she-buffalo, both were eager to mate. From this union a son in buffalo shape was born, although the father was very soon thereafter suddenly killed, and his mother, as suttee, plunged into the funeral pyre after him.

The son, Mahisa, grew to adolescence and withdrew to Mt Sumeru to perform penances; once again the gods were afraid, so Brahma placated him with a boon: he would not be killed by any man. Mahisa then conquered his own demon rivals, thereafter he vanquished the kings of all the world, and finally, after a prolonged battle with Indra and other gods, he wrested heaven from the gods, forcing them to roam the earth in misery. Subsequently, for the purpose of regaining their lost heaven, the conjoined energies of the gods were transformed into a Goddess, the parts of whose body and whose weapons were donations from each individual divinity.

The Goddess manifested as Durga, and as she sat on a mountain, she attracted the attention of the ministers of Mahisa, Lord of heaven. Awed and puzzled by her beauty and sexual attributes, they reported the news to their king, who then and there fell madly in love with her and commanded his ministers to bring her to him as his bride. The Goddess' ambiguous messages in response to Mahisa's offers spread confusion initially, but she soon entered into a protracted war with the ministers, killing many of them.

1

Nevertheless, still bent on wooing the lovely apparition, the buffalo
Mahisa turned himself into a magnificent, youthful human being.
During a meeting between the two, the Goddess even declared her
friendship for him, but she soon reversed her sentiments. There
followed a ten-thousand year battle with her erstwhile suitor and
his armies. In a grand finale, the Goddess first killed Mahisa by
decapitating the animal body; when a human emerged from the
severed neck, the Goddess killed Mahisa a second time, again by
chopping off his head.

Back in their abodes, the gods rejoiced; in heaven, the resurrected Mahisa was united with his beloved enemy. But the story
does not end here; Mahisa returns again and again, in cyclical
repetition of these life and death events.

Other enriching variants, reflecting changing times, interpretations and geographical and cultural conditions, especially the *Devi
Mahatmyam* (DM) for its focus on the battle, and the *Kalika
Purana*, for the fascinating story of the birth of Mahisa, are also
referred to here.

The Indian myth focuses attention on and then attempts to
mediate, integrate or reconcile oppositions and contradictions inherent in life, but in this study it is taken for granted that it is
virtually impossible categorically to classify the motifs in the
Mahisamardini myth. Continually jolted and propelled out from
fixed positions, qualities belonging to a single pair of polar
opposites attract others and form new ambiguous associations in a
perpetual interplay of linkages or combinations. Juxtapositions,
correspondences, correlations and mergings; oscillations, transformations, reversals and transcendencies are all only temporary.
Every effort to keep a single motif, theme or mytheme or indeed
the groupings of their combinations separate from and independent of all others is frustrated by their momentum; boundaries
hardly exist and elements are forever in transposition. As O'Flaherty's veritable 'ectoplasmic substance' ultimately resists systema-
tizing, it would perhaps be the better part of wisdom to rest
content with only an exploratory venture into its internal structure.

Yet we are fortunately not entirely in a chaotic situation, for
narrative does play an important role: while the details may vary,
and abrupt reversals and interruptions frequently take place, in all
the versions the key plot does not depart from its intrinsically

sequential, predictable order. This indissoluble core of the pro-
gress of events on the horizontal level magnetizes and is magnetized by the shifting relationships of the motifs; they hover around
the story and permeate it, always vibrating with the plot to form a
more coherent, larger unified synchronic construct. But it is a
dynamic construct, in a constant state of animation.

Our pragmatic approach will focus on the coalescences forever
in transformation, even while, as a matter of necessity and
convenience, it will also fasten on to these single points of
reference. There will of course be overlappings, reappearances in
new forms, repetitions and unconfinable items to add zest to the
unceasing quest for systematic clarity of the eventually elusive fixed
schema.

As embodiment of the controlling forces of nature, endowed with
absolute power and an insatiable appetite for the flesh and blood
offerings of humans and beasts captured in the hunt, the half
human, half animal (buffalo or lion) deity was only in late
prehistoric times split into two distinct, separately worshipped
components. But the memory of the shared heritage remained.

In the Indian context, as Durga, the descendant of this warrior-
protector, mistress of animals, confronts Mahisa, as descendant of
her primordial partner, and plunges with him into a fierce, wild
struggle. Both are of the forest. While the battle is between two
apparently opposed combatants, they are in fact consubstantial
and in many aspects analogous.

The forest/mountain conceptions were transmitted to agricultural communities where the Goddess was supreme authority for
millenia, not as symbol of the productive earth alone but as the all-
pervading, ever-present symbol of the phenomenon of human,
animal and vegetative birth, existence and death. Her animal
counterpart was only sometimes relegated to an inferior position as
associated vehicle.

In the West, in contrast, under the influence of Indo-European
and Semitic slow but insistent paternalization of the deity, it
seemed as though it was the Goddess who was now being
submerged. The hero slays the Goddess/monster; she was virtually
coerced back into the unconscious, but only to stir up turbulence
there. In India as well, when they confronted the terrifying
indigenous Mother Goddess, invading pastoral tribes in the second

millennium BC strove to demote the Goddess to the status of wife
of the gods of the male pantheon; a somewhat successful attempt
was made in the Rg Veda to suppress and harness the energy which
threatened to overwhelm:

> You, Oh, Indra, great (one), indeed you crushed that daughter of the
> sky (Usa), who was becoming too great.[1]

While Vedic sacrificial rituals honoured the male gods, occasionally poetic tribute was nevertheless also paid to the female presence.
A forceful Rg. Vedic statement hints at the ambiguities: it defines
the Goddess Vac (speech) metaphorically in her aspects as sus-
tainer of the gods, bestower of wealth and, prefiguring Durga, as
warrior. She speaks:

> I stretch the bow for Rudra so that this arrow will strike down the hater
> of prayer. I incite the contest among the people. I have pervaded sky
> and earth.[2]

Vac has the very same qualities later to be stamped on to the
Puranic Goddess, even though here the reference is to the
aboriginal deity.

In the succeeding centuries, during the period of the Brahmana
texts (c. 900 BC), priests claimed the devotion of the élite for the
male gods. The Upanisads (c. 700 BC) were suffused with the idea
of an Absolute, immanent in the self, and in the sixth century BC,
the rarified insights of the Buddha elaborated an atheistic ethical
system. But the potent female energy which had been the driving
force for millennia was never abandoned by the people of the
Indian continent—although ostensibly the Mother Goddess had
been kept under control, her virgin, independent, atavistic force
did in fact continue to dominate the consciousness of her captive
devotees. The efforts of Brahmanic sacrificial ritualists, the
Upanisadic philosopher-poets, and of the isolated Buddhist monks
(arhats) to transcend the human condition did not prove to be
efficacious or ultimately appropriate for the masses. The religious
need for intimate sensory experience was best served by the
resurgent Goddess, represented by a multitude of ever-present
symbols including mountain shrines, trees, rocks as well as the
evolving iconic repertoire. Inevitably these more concrete autoch-
thonous forms of folk religion were finally permitted entrance into
the new theologies, as Goddess worship was reabsorbed into the
faiths of the ruling classes who found it expedient, even necessary,

to accommodate age-old beliefs and rites. Slowly at the beginning, but gathering force by the fifth century AD, Hinduism and Buddhism welcomed the Goddess back into the fold, even as she continued her rule of forest and mountain where all had approached her in terror and servile devotion. As late as the seventh century AD, Bana described the Cabara tribesmen thus:

> [Their] one religion is offering human flesh to Durga.... The shoulders of those leaders of these forest dwellers were... rough with scars from keen weapons often used to make an offering of blood to Kali.[3]

A century later Vakpati wrote an ode to Vindyavasini,[4] Goddess of the mountains. Even kings searched her out in her remote mountain cave, devoted days of prayer to her, a feared and revered deity, and fasted in her honour.

By the time Cave 21 at Ellora (sixth century AD) and other major religious edifices were designed, the Goddess had regained her rightful place amongst the élite, re-emerging as the energizing power, either independent of and equal with or united in marriage with one or other of the male deities. Now that ancient Goddess of procreation and vegetation who was also a warrior was even put into the service of the king. It was his duty to battle with his enemies, and his conquests assured the growth of crops, as the earth demands her share of blood sacrifice. The Goddess rode before the troops, leading them to victory, and thus her aspects as nourisher/warrior, allied with the ruler, guaranteed the security of the realm. She permeated and controlled every sphere of life, and she was venerated and greatly feared, the recipient of sacrificial meat and the blood of men and animals.

Thus, the power which had been attributed for the most part to the Vedic male deities and to the Buddha and the *bodhisattvas* was reconnected with the prehistoric Goddess and shared with her in equivalent formal structures. In the separate cult of the *Saktas* she predominated over all. An extremely complex, all-encompassing system, communicated in lavish detail, assigned to the Goddess control over the entire range of human psychic drives, reactions and fantasies. Unconscious contents were recognized, externalized, isolated, organized and confronted with astonishing forthrightness in festival, text and icon, bringing a relaxation of the tensions which had been caused by the repressions. Now the Goddess was no longer denied nor subordinated; on the contrary, both her comforting and terrifying aspects were being faced head on, with courage and perhaps a great deal of resignation.

In India today, rituals and myths, enduring symbolic structures, still function vigorously, playing a primary, healing role in the lives of a great majority of the population. This is undoubtedly at the heart of the order which underlies all the multiplicities of the culture. Despite the multitude of perspectives regarding the Goddess,[5] ultimately, she is one and the same. Her existence is Indian in its particularizations, her imagery is vitally active in the consciousness, but she remains the persistent reflection of the ancient world view as well.

In fact, underlying the disparity of opinions and ability to verbalize and describe, a genuine belief in the real existence of the female deity is most likely the strongest element in the psychic make-up of tribal, villager and many urbanites in India today. Each individual conceives of the Goddess in accordance with his or her personal perceptions of society's complex and paradoxical definitions. The imagery is infinite; unique insights, emerging spontaneously from the unconscious, combine with inherited tradition, and are synthesized and absorbed in a variety of ways.

For her believers, she is neither all 'good' nor all 'evil' but a composite of nuanced, uncategorizable human drives. She is both feared demoness and symbol of rarified spirituality, and she also is all the intermediary stages. Her instantaneous momentary appearances, her transformations and disappearances are like the fleeting pulsations and lightning alternations of the reacting individual; immanent in all the transitory states, the Goddess is indivisible and whole. Each person is an inconsequential entity only until the Goddess enters the psyche; then he or she is invested with the sacred and shares her divinity—the personality is fused with the external symbol. Conversely, invested with part of the individual's inner processes, the Goddess appears as entirely separate. The longing for her would then indicate a longing for integration of all aspects of the self. For those who are adept, it is possible to internalize the Goddess symbol, but for most devotees, her externalized form offers the necessary defence, the means essential for defining and controlling forces not otherwise accessible to conscious recognition.

So great are the powers of the Goddess that traditional and

rigorous rituals, which have survived in primordial and adaptive forms, harnessed and supervised by priests, are necessary for mediating the danger sparked off by the Goddess's chaotic spontaneous eruptions. Those who dutifully provide her with vegetative and meat offerings in thanksgiving can expect a beneficent response; however, if the ritual is neglected or improperly performed, devastating consequences will be visited upon all.

In their efforts to define the nature of the Goddess, philosopher, poet, artist, musician and ritualist create an infinite array of structures within which she is manifested: for convenient propitiation, anthropomorphic models sometimes replace the animists' worship of all possible temporary physical habitations. Priests draw up ritual plans in prescriptive texts. At festivals, in paintings and lithic configurations, on temples and in caves, in mountain shrines and village sacred groves all over India, in verse, hymnal poetry, dramatic and dance performance, on two-dimensional *yantras* in daily use, during each hour of the day or night, what might very well be termed the scientific study of the *sakti* force, its differentiation into comprehensible symbols, is projected in ephemeral or permanent form. In fact, much of the history of culture in India may be understood as attempts at concretizing the concept and providing representations of the multifarious aspects of the Goddess, so as to provide the average devotee with accessible concrete symbols of the powerful internal pulsations each person is subject to. Cultural output in India is didactic and therapeutic, assisting the integration of psychic life.

The passionate, indeed obsessive, relationship of the devotee with one of the most potent aspects of the Goddess—Mahisamardini, the Goddess who slays the buffalo demon—runs deep and wide. Whether as focus of ceremonial litany and beloved tale, as iconic object of worship or living mental image, her cult is ubiquitous (see Chapter Nine). A legacy from the unrecorded paleolithic past, the earliest extant representations are preserved in the Kushan sculptures of the first and second centuries AD and in the DM text, a section of the *Markandeya Purana,* of the fifth. During two millennia, as Sanskritization imposed an entire corpus of formal structures on to the aboriginal intuitions, Brahmanical texts, rituals and statues spread in all directions, regardless of distinctions of language, caste and class. Today the DM is one of the most revered and popular religious texts in India, while the influence of variants, especially the eleventh-century canonical text of the Sakta cult, the DBP, is pervasive.[6]

The myth of Mahisamardini is re-energized during daily worship and the sacrificial festivals which have possessed the hearts and minds of Hindus through the ages. To serve the changing ritual requirements, a rich and diverse iconography and ever-evolving plastic imagery was continually being created and recreated. Even under the onslaught of modernization, the tremendous force of the inviolate, indestructible relationship of the Goddess (Durga) with the buffalo demon (Mahisa) provides meaning to the lives of some hundreds of millions of receptive devotees. An examination of this phenomenon with its ambivalencies and endless transpositions and shifting coalescences poses a challenge to the student of Indian culture.

The popular approach which would relegate the (buffalo) demon to the dark and irrational realm, the chaotic underworld, as symbol of evil who battles with a Goddess representing light, reason and order, is abandoned here entirely. That gods are not always virtuous and demons always evil in the general mythologies[7] for the Hindu myth has been demonstrated by O'Flaherty's thesis: it strips the battle of the gods and the demons (*daivasuram*) of its moral overtones, and, following Max Weber and Coomaraswamy (and the comprehension of a majority of Indians), positions demon and god on equivalent levels, and only in the final analysis as totally distinct.[8] This seminal concept stimulates our effort to reinterpret, and it leads into an analysis of each character of Hindu mythology, providing an instrumental guide to material for the most part lying hidden in the unconscious.

We are thus prepared to re-examine Mahisa, who is only temporarily killed by the Goddess. While certainly he cannot be entirely absolved of conventional demonic qualities (it will be shown that the Goddess shares them as well), it appears (if we focus on the relationship rather than on antithetical, fixed categories) that the complex symbol of the buffalo demon, reflecting human foibles and flaws but also the courage to struggle for survival and growth, is in fact, an attempt to come to terms with nothing less than the human condition.

We present the hypothesis that Mahisa is anthropomorphic hero—symbolic of the psychic struggles and fantasies of the mythmaker, the devotee and the artist—who dramatizes a predictable sequence of life events and rites of passage. Shulman's insight that 'Mahisasura may be a model for man'[9], 'that the human devotee identifies with the demon devotee',[10] and his concern with the 'divine identity of the heroes'[11] points in this direction. If this view is accepted, since the animal/hero is a common mythological motif, and Mahisa's buffalo form is in fact only a disguise, he can take his place with other mythological heroes as defined by recent general theories.

Rank stated the thesis,[12] and Jung, Neumann, Eliade, Campbell, Raglin, Samuels and others have agreed, that in diverse cultures and historical periods there are fundamental analogies and repetitive motifs in the life of the hero, allowing for regional and national variations of the theme. To designate the hero Mahisa as a representative of Rank's collective memory is to recognize therefore that he is a richly loaded symbol, and that the story of the buffalo demon falls into line with the cross-cultural material, without in any way contradicting the intuitive insights of the Hindu worshipper.

Mahisamardini is a functioning symbol. The symbol operates as a defence system which protects the individual from the ravages of dominating instincts liable to spring capriciously from the unconscious; it harnesses potential dangerous drives and the onrush of random discharges always at the brink of consciousness. Projected and organized into recognized interacting myths, ritual prescriptions and plastic and dramatic representations, the chaotic raw material of the unconscious is controlled, both releasing and protecting the person from the tyranny of the crushing forces within, even while the energy charge is conserved.

This encourages a systematic study of what is happening at all strata of the text, stage by linear stage. Thus a study of the birth, heroic exploits, contacts with the Goddess and, finally, death in sacrifice and resurrection of the buffalo demon, as recounted in the texts and re-enacted at the festivals may shed some light on the tremendous psychological force inherent in the complex network of projections in the Mahisamardini conception. The conclusions reached can then be observed to be implicit in the icons as well.

While it is true that Devi (Durga), the Goddess, and Mahisa, the demon, are an isolated inseparable dyad, the motif should be viewed within the larger framework of demon/god(dess) relationships which, in turn, cannot fundamentally be detached from the entire organism of Hindu mythology and rite. But for our purposes, we shall adhere rigorously to the skeletal progression of the single story, although sometimes imagery outside the specific context is referred to. Beginning with Mahisa's parentage and ending with his apotheosis, the narrative provides the organization for the chapters.

As threshold figure and bridge, the hero represents shadow and consciousness perpetually in tandem. The story opens with austerities, performed by a Brahmin demon king who seeks power through obtaining progeny. In the variants, the son, Mahisa, is begotten on a buffalo cow who is a sometime royal virgin, while the father is demon king, *rsi* or god; kingship or divinity is definitely part of Mahisa's heritage, usually as the result of an immaculate conception. His father is attacked and murdered, so into the sacrificial fires plunges his bovine mother as suttee, and the hero is born out of the pyre, pure, unharmed and whole. These unusual circumstances of birth produce an anomaly, a monster who is nevertheless a prince charming. Thus abandoned by his mother, little is known about his childhood, although the *Vamana Purana* implies that he was raised by the earthly *yaksas* and by the resuscitated father. The hero undergoes a series of initiatory trials, the first of which is withdrawal; his penitential austerities result in a boon being granted by the protective figure of the god Brahma. Father and son battle to strengthen the power of the youth; together they conquer all the demon kings. With his ability to transform himself magically Mahisa then battles with, defeats and kills all human kings, wresting global sovereignty and establishing himself as Cakravartin, ruler of the entire temporal world. In this capacity he marries many times over. His reign is violent, he prescribes laws beneficial to himself and his demon ministers, and thus he loses favour with men and the gods.

After a prolonged war with his heavenly adversaries, during which the father gods are deposed, the buffalo demon rules earth and heaven, and enjoys sexual excesses with the wives of the gods (implying incestuous conquest and outrageous conduct towards the deities). He also steals sacrificial offerings meant for the gods and comes to believe that he *is* indeed Indra, the bull, the sky god of thunder himself.

But into this wondrous male fantasy intrudes the Mother

Goddess who is, in fact, the one and only treasure Mahisa truly desires. Yet she is ultimately unavailable, for she is the opponent, masquerading as a beautiful maiden. She lures and entices him and, because she represents the power of the unconscious, the pull downward and backward into the protective womb and processes of nature, the demon unwittingly plunges into her dangerous orbit. In a throwback to reciprocal animal mating postures, they dance in mutual desire and dread. Lest he succumb entirely, and to overcome his ambivalent responses, Mahisa is forced into sacred, single combat with the fascinating but enigmatic, dangerous creature. On the battle stage the disguise of each is penetrated; then the demon and Goddess are reduced to their true nature; in the last analysis they are alike. Finally, like the ancient bull-kings who were themselves royal sacrifices, fecundators of earth, bearers of vicarious guilt, hero is transformed into victim and, having lost his position in heaven, now Mahisa loses his very life. He is decapitated by the Mother Goddess, but soon thereafter his resurrection reunites the two in heaven. On earth, paradise is restored, but only temporarily, for the demon inevitably returns to earth for the eternal cyclical repetition of the entire life process.

The life story of the hero is rooted in his own culture, set against a background of what might well be termed the Indian obsessional foci. As it both stimulates and reflects these motives, the myth defines the norms of society. Woven into the fabric of the narrative are primal drives which are operative in India even today. The myth is concerned with unconscious impulses resulting in suicide, cow worship and cow and widow sacrifice; birth, purification and death in fire; sibling rivalries; matricidal and parricidal wishes; fear and adoration of the Mother Goddess with incestual undercurrents and castration anxiety; the struggle for survival, and punishment by beheading. Most seriously it focuses on guilt and the human tendency towards self-sacrifice or for creating a substitute ritual victim.

A clue to the choice of a buffalo/human/demon to symbolize the hero lies not merely in his animal or demonic shape but in his magical ability to change himself instantaneously into a variety of forms associated with the changing human condition. Transform-ability is a fundamental law of reality in the thinking of the so-called primitive, and in myths. We are confronted at every point with mercurial metamorphoses: Mahisa is lion, elephant, buffalo, yet he is also demon, old man, magnificent human lover, warrior-king and god. Though he wallows in the muddy underground swamps as chthonic animal, he also reigns on earth, and, as Indra, in heaven. Like a human, he progresses towards rationality, light and divinity, yet he is always in danger of sliding back under the influence of somatic responses, and but for this mythologically-expressed portrait of multiple personalities, much of what is human nature would remain forever unrecognized in the mind of the devotee and would therefore play its destructive role in the repressions within the psyche. Ambiguities and fluid associations replace a fixed definition which would relegate the demon to only a *tamasic* (negative) position. In the unconscious, Mahisa can thus be many things to all men, as the imagery is always in flux.

For example, in the climactic passages of the DM, the Goddess combats not the single enemy but a series of aspects of Mahisa's personality. When Durga throws the noose, Mahisa quits his buffalo form; he becomes a lion, but the Goddess chops off his head; then he assumes a human shape, but even the man is decapitated with her sword; he becomes an elephant, she cuts off his trunk; Mahisa then resumes his buffalo form, and, trapped under her foot,

> Mahisasura half issued forth (in his real form) from his own (buffalo) mouth being completely overcome. Fighting thus with his half revealed form, the great *asura* was laid by the Devi who struck off his head with her great sword.[13]

But very soon thereafter he unites with his divine adversary.

Are these the lurid fantasies of the masochist? Or are the many forms the summation of all aspects of the human being, expressing the mythmaker's recognition of and struggle with his own condition? Mahisa is being put to death sequentially in all his aspects, and although as magician he is able temporarily to postpone his own destiny, he can do very little to alter the fundamental realities of his existence.

Certain demons are even today in the process of transformation, either moving upward or descending the demon/deity scale. Considering his ubiquity and long prehistoric existence, the buffalo and his fragmented qualities seem well suited to be among those symbols which defy permanent, static categorization. As stated earlier, one purpose of this study is to extricate Mahisa out of his fixed position as evil buffalo demon, to focus attention on the symbol as representing an amalgam of the unconscious contents of the psyche of mythmaker and devotee.

The myth is saturated with the potential for violence inherent in the male–female oppositions. As the story unfolds, the relationship between Mahisa and the Goddess is manifested at many levels: psychologically both demon and Goddess become what the other is, both behave like ferocious animals and one never knows what will happen in the next instant, as the constant alternations, which range from the bestial to the divine, are the only reality. Thus each of the antagonists can be symbolically interpreted as now the monster/dragon, now with feminine or with masculine attributes. Each can represent justice and power or evil and danger; and each contributes to the orgiastic disorder necessary for recreation.

The condition of the contemporary urban dweller who howls in fear in the dark as he confronts the bad animal of his nightmare differs little from the fright syndrome of the jungle dweller, forced into struggle with a live animal. Until the dreamer awakes, he is in the same situation as his prehistoric ancestors were. Pervading the deepest levels of the psyche, ready to spring at random, the residual animal, source of human energies, seeks recognition. The unfocused, floating primordial imagery, rooted in the biological heritage, is stabilized in culture. Externalized projections, first structured into dance, cultish animal rites, orgiastic fertility ceremonies and much later into literature, art, myth and ritual, provide the camouflage of human respectability and channel the anxiety into an acceptable form. Left to itself without organization, animal nature will surely erupt.

'Brahmin priests write the texts where myths appear.'[14] Mahisasura is a projection from the mind of the Brahmin priest, analogue for the sorcerer who painted the demise of the enemy bison on the walls of prehistoric caves. While the latter wears the skins of the bull and thus becomes the revered animal whose mask he wears, the former removes them from his own person but retains the identification via the symbolism of a buffalo-bull that he creates. The distinctions are still not always clear, as can be observed in ritual.[15]

We can take it for granted that the identification of the Brahmin with the buffalo/human/god as hero is not a conscious decision but a response to requirements to sort out some meaningful symbol from the mass of undifferentiated unconscious constellations. Out of the collective memory and his childhood experience, the Brahmin priest creates a symbol which functions for all. The force of the wild buffalo is retained in the unconscious while domestication of cattle reduces the fear and prepares the way for a positive identification with the now less awesome and more approachable animal.

The relationship of the pastoralist and also of the settled people with their cattle is mirrored in the contemporary experience of the village boy. One has only to travel around the villages of India to marvel at the complex of emotional responses and close psychological bonding which exists between the buffalo, who is very much part of the family, and his keepers. Both the prowess of the male animal and the nurturing female are accorded great respect, even as the skill to control them is gradually acquired. But this involvement is abruptly terminated at the time the animal is sold for flesh, or worse, for sacrifice. The village boy is in existential agony, identifying closely with his best friend, whose catastrophic fate he has himself escaped. Small wonder that after the trauma of consuming the flesh of his former friend, of having to offer it as well to the gods who control his life, the lower-caste adult will even today retain a vivid operative memory of the relationship, while the Brahmin priest, who no longer sacrifices animals, obsessively chants Vedic and Brahmanic sacrificial liturgy and relies heavily on the symbolic identification with Mahisa the buffalo demon.

In the folk conceptions, certain legends and rituals overtly reveal the buffalo/Brahmin connection. Buffalo sacrifice originated when a Brahmin refused to worship the Goddess Matangi. He was informed that he would be required to perform the Madiga (outcaste) rituals, and furthermore, as in the ritual of buffalo sacrifice, he would also have to be killed, his membranes made into drums, his arms cut off and placed in his mouth, and his fat spread over his eyes during worship of Matangi by all castes. When all was duly accomplished, the Brahmin was brought back to life and a buffalo was substituted.[16] In the 'flight of the milk drinker' ritual, to consecrate a new tank in North Bihar, a Brahmin was fed milk from various animals: he was the *asura* (demon), come to attack the gods. The devotees gave chase in mock battle and he was symbolically defeated.[17] It becomes evident that demons—in our case, Mahisa—may well be included in Shulman's remarks concerning 'structural weakness':

The major symbolic types in South India—including political actors, we have mentioned: King, Brahmin, even the bhakti god, ... are composite figures incorporating multiple personae, which come into view and then dissolve in relation to other such identities....[18]

In all cultures, children play at being animals, with aggression, sexual impulses and tenderness as yet not entirely differentiated. The children's fantasies are their realities, and so are the resulting feelings of guilt. In the modern context, in adult behaviour, the animal associations are repressed, the symbiosis being accessible only in the thought patterns of psychotics, in dreams, lapses of speech, or with conscious effort to retrieve the imagery.

The animal/child/adult triad continues throughout the life of the individual as the core framework of psychic processes. The tendency to deny the interdependence and the consequent distancing and hiding, may lead to dangerous sado/masochistic projections. When left unrecognized and unattended, under stressful conditions, animal impulses break through in random fashion, and blind fury re-emerges in full force. As repository for the archaic residue, Mahisamardini, the Goddess who slays the buffalo, is a therapeutic symbol.

Even though the hero Mahisa is popularly known primarily in animal shape, he is also *daitya chalamahisa*, he who

deceitfully assumed the body of a buffalo and is in the guise of the body of a buffalo.[19]

It is taken for granted in this study that as disguises are a universal feature of myth and rite, Mahisa's only 'real' form—the 'real' Mahisa—is human, which means he is part animal, part child and part god. In fact, as human he is more than ordinary, for he is exceedingly courageous and, concerning his situation, he deliberates with subtlety. He is a powerful leader, protective towards his followers, filled with enormous pride and almost never afraid. Compassionate with his own kind, ruthless with anybody who gets in his way, he is both self-indulgent and self-destructive. In the end, he suffers.

While sometimes displaying all the weaknesses of average men, he also rises to heights of glory, because those who identify with the myth attribute to him qualities which properly belong to an illusory god, and thus divinity is also an important aspect of

Mahisa's composite personality. As a result of his prehistoric and immediate paternal heritage, the blood of gods does in fact run through his veins, and his mother, the buffalo-cow, is often regarded as divine. It stamps him as other than merely demonic, animal, child or human. When he finally becomes Indra, he behaves precisely like Indra, that is, he becomes even more demonic, grasping at the divine prerogatives, voraciously consuming the sacrifices of the Brahmins, indulging in promiscuous sexual exploits and dreams of controlling the universe. As for death, Mahisa's activities eventually lead to his (temporary) demise, while even the gods occasionally succumb to Yama—the god of death—before their inevitable return to life in heaven.

In India, among the Saktas, the Goddess-dominated archaic constellations were retained in the psyche of the mythmaker. While the priest was able to create an ideated symbol, weaving his own fantasies with the exploits of Mahisa as a beautiful, god-like male, ruler of the nether world, earth and heaven, who stands for absolute power, who is immersed in sensual pleasures and has the physical strength of an animal, reality in the form of the Mother Goddess soon crashes through the megalomania and, in wrath, punishes with death the son mesmerised by his own dream-wishes. The original symbiosis of primeval times, when goddess and animal were conceived as one, is still in process, directing the buffalo who had been separated from the Goddess in the distant past back into herself. But now the reunion is preceded by the death of the king/god/consort, the hero.

When he encounters the Goddess, Mahisa, mired in animal/child responses, behaves compulsively and irrationally; he is the mother's son who yearns on the one hand for the two to be one and, on the other, for the one to be two. Similarly, as the devotee worships the idol of the Goddess, he is accentuating his separation from the mother whom he has succeeded in projecting outside of himself, but indeed they never are entirely separated. The magnetism of the ancient hierogamies continues to function in the seemingly irrational behaviour of both Goddess and demon. Even though he falls in love with the Goddess, she proves ultimately to be unavailable, and Mahisa never makes it to the bed-chamber. All the elements of archaic Goddess/consort connections are incorporated as latent material. He is the ancient royal sacrificed bull-hero, fecundator of the earth, and bearer of vicarious guilt. When

Durga the Goddess and Mahisa the demon individually contemplate marital union, they are merely carrying forward the tradition of the sacred marriage, the rites of coupling for fertility, the performance of which guaranteed rain, fruitful produce from the earth, and abundant human and animal progeny. The death and resurrection of the buffalo demon after sacred combat is the inevitable sequence in an inviolate tradition. As they had abjured physical congress of the aboriginal rites, so it was to the advantage of the Brahmin priests to focus on Durga's rejection of the marriage proposals proferred by the asura. But it was equally judicious to maintain the link, and thus the suggestive stances and mutual provocations which betray the archaic origins are overtly described.

The myth functions at these two levels throughout: there is the striving towards life apart, and then there is the desire to merge with the Mother Goddess. These are the contradictions with which the religions of India attempt to grapple. Emerging from a passive to an active state, Mahisa's task is to differentiate himself from the original matrix, to extricate himself from infantile dependencies, to battle against his brother gods—the associates of the Goddess—and to strive towards separation. But if he is to achieve wholeness, he needs also to stay in touch with the feminine roots of the unconscious. It is this paradox that is being faced in the myth, as the Mother Goddess is at one and the same time the magnet and the force against which the hero must pit himself.

Those in thrall to her require a handle by means of which to cope with their ambivalences. They will be submerged (merged) and remain in a passive submissive state in relation to the overpowering divinity unless they find an image which will serve as anchor symbol to encourage confrontation and thereby provide release from these destructive, maternal bonds. Only a youthful male, as beautiful, attractive and violent as she is, one who combines the prowess of a buffalo, elephant and lion, the perspicacity of the human and who is also divine can serve this purpose and challenge the terrible Mother Goddess.

In a society permeated by the force of the Goddess who, as protectress and nourisher, is beneficent, as castrator and killer is definitely malevolent and as seductress, confusing, the devotee is mired in her *maya* world, out of which he hopes to emerge, even though he simultaneously longs to succumb to her enticements. He also needs to rely on her as omnipotent receptacle for his murderous impulses, which he displaces on to the drinker of blood; she bears the responsibility for his violent drives, she is a hermaphrodite whom he placates with flattering hymns of praise.

In the battle it also becomes apparent that hero and Goddess operate, not on two different levels, with Goddess above and demon below—on the contrary, in slow stages, they are almost reduced to a single conglomerate entity. While in the West the animal is demoted to a low position in the hierarchical order and the highest status is accorded to the god, draped in the mantle of morality which seeks to control animal instincts, in the Indian myth, such vertical relationships are less applicable. As we have observed, neither the Goddess nor the buffalo demon can be conceived of as ultimately separate; their combat is, in the final analysis, an enactment of a many-aspected reality, reflecting a mode of thought which perceives seeming opposites as mere stages in a graduated spectrum of reality which has a minimum of definite boundaries. Instead of conceiving of an ultimate conjunction of opposites, which the evolved religious seeker who grasps the entirety finally understands, the average Indian sees the world as an infinitely graded tapestry.

The climactic event of the narrative is the sacrifice of Mahisa. He is beheaded after a long struggle, and not before the hero inflicts great harm upon his opponents, the gods. Even though they are deities who turn to the Goddess as protectress, Siva, Visnu and Brahma actually flee the field in fear, or they are transformed by the Goddess into females, or they imagine themselves to be infants. The mythmaker chooses impotency for the father rather than boldly face his own guilt-producing, destructive impulses. But this is not a story with a happy ending in the western sense, with the triumph of individuation. Mahisa never does manage to 'rescue the captive' or entirely to sever his relations with the unconscious.

The Goddess ultimately wins primarily because she is the more violent and rapacious of the two. Her phallic sword or trident, wielded during orgiastic, frenzied psychotic states after she quaffs her liquor, is the property of the masculinized mother at her worst. Her gender reversal hides the incestuous longings they both share, but only Mahisa is punished. His end comes to appease his own guilt, aroused as a result of the attempt to conquer the Mother. Nevertheless, ambiguity persists and pervades even the finale. The victim Mahisa dies, but as sacrifice he is resurrected, cyclically reborn like a plant, while in the ritual, the great and powerful Goddess is temporarily consigned to oblivion: she is taken over the boundary or drowned in the sea. Both will return to perpetuate the struggle. For the time being the demon becomes the medium for the salvation of the world, its Saviour; his death heralds heaven on earth, a millennium. This posits a tantalizingly unresolved solution for male–female relations.

In view of historical realities and the persistence of sacrificial rites in all cultures, most especially the monstrous perversions of the twentieth century, what is called masochism or introverted sadism would have to be redefined; not as distortion, but as a norm of human behaviour. If indeed the need to sacrifice/to be the sacrifice or to find a substitute for oneself is an inherent or perennial motivating force in the unconscious, how can it be dealt with in societies denuded of myth and rite? Mahisa's popularity would indicate that despite the inevitability of his ultimate fate as victim in the sacrifice, an ongoing emphasis on the confrontation before the end keeps alive his (perhaps illusory) hope for a partially separate existence. At all events, the battle permits a certain amount of self-recognition, accompanied by a tremendous burden of guilt for betrayal of the Mother. Thus sacrifice is the partial remedy for its elimination.

The Goddess still receives offerings of blood and buffalo heads in Nepal, and, even though buffalo sacrifice is outlawed in India, Gurkas and some remote communities still sacrifice buffaloes and substitution of the heads of goats is pervasive. When the reading about Mahisa's sacrifice transforms the awful deed into words, the myth turns out to be a most ingenious compromise, helping the devotee to confront and to attempt to overcome atavistic tendencies.

Chapter One Family and Society in Contemporary India

If the myth did not truly reflect the ambivalencies of generation after generation of worshippers, it would long ago have lost its importance. In this attempt to comprehend the role of the myth in contemporary India, it will be useful to refer to family and societal conditions which were operative in ancient times and are still in force today.[1]

The individual is fixed at a certain position within a complicated network of people to whom he or she is related by blood or by marriage. It is a closed system which subordinates personal development to primary family goals. For perpetuation both of the line and the economic status of the larger family by means of hereditary occupations, it is of primary importance to arrange appropriate marriages to ensure adequate male progeny. Fixed family hierarchies rely on the father, or after his death on the eldest brother, to direct and control economic, religious and community relationships. In turn, the family unit is involved in the close associations of the sub-caste. The *jati* (local endogamous group) members are linked to one another by means of common occupation, dialect, place of origin and traditional orthodox customs. To a large extent, the personality of each member is determined by these factors. As a result of the limitations on individual personal growth, thwarted emotional responses which, in a looser social structure or with greater privacy within the family, can be expressed more openly, are frequently redirected on to close relatives or their unconscious substitutes.[2]

Important for an analysis of the myth is a study of sibling rivalries, but even more of the son's close relationship with his parents, especially his mother. Symbiosis for life is the operative rule between mother and son; adolescent rebellion in the western sense rarely occurs, or is expressed much later in life, and then only weakly or in indirect, impulsive eruptions focused on unconsciously altered symbols far removed from the original stimulus.

20

One must naturally be wary of generalization, and there are certainly individuals who are able to escape the web of entanglements. But regardless of the welter of variations within the accepted social framework of thousands of communities, there is a remarkable basic consistency in the way a female spends her entire life. Her position within the family and her various changing roles virtually determine what kind of society her own child will create as an adult, although prejudice in favour of paternalism consistently tends to deny this.

In trepidation, the young, often ignorant bride, forced to leave her own family, enters the strange environment of her husband's. For them she exists merely as an economic asset (for she brings a dowry), as a vessel for procreation and not least. either as servant or at best as the one who relieves the mother-in-law of her most strenuous physical tasks. From infancy she has been prepared for this and is unaware that there are other life styles. For help in the traumatic adjustment, she can rely neither on her husband nor on the rest of her newly-adopted family members. The mother-in-law approaches the stranger with powerful feelings of prejudice, jealousy and fear concerning her now threatened primacy. Instead of compassion for a fellow sufferer there is often mutual suspicion; nor can the bride turn for support to her youthful husband, who is already deeply in thrall to his own mother. He finds it difficult to empathize with the stranger of the opposite sex whom his parents, not he, have chosen as his life partner. So far, he has come in contact with females only as mother, sister or close relative, and at this stage of his life he is too immature to be concerned about the fears of his bride. He knows he must make love to this wife, but a satisfactory sexual relationship seldom develops since in few homes is a separate bedroom available, and even if there is a curtain or closed door, maternal keyhole spectators are not unknown. To escape parental domination, the emotional complications of mother envy and the claustrophobic atmosphere of the home, the young man finds relief outside with members of his peer group. In this situation, the girl, alone and unloved, is bound to suffer from accumulated emotional stress for which she neither can account nor find appropriate outlets.

The young wife remains in this situation until the birth of a child. She is fortunate if it is male, as this gives her a modicum of status. But she craves affection, physical contact, release from her arduous physical labours and, most of all, for some control over her own existence. In desperation, she naturally tends unconsciously to manipulate and take advantage of her new situation as mother of a boy. It is at this time that a lifelong symbiosis with the male child begins to develop. He is the source of physical comfort and convenient object of her newly-acquired opportunity for self assertion, and thus she is unwilling to allow the baby boy the privilege of beginning life apart from herself. Even though a girl child, with whom she identifies as ally, will eventually provide the mother with genuine solace and affection, as antidote to her husband's indifference she turns unconsciously to her son. As the boy grows, the mother's demands on him increase, even while she gives in to his every whim with over-permissive tolerance, often at the expense of others. Wrapped up entirely in his successes, and 'sacrificing' herself to his every need, she thus sweeps him into her orbit.

There seems to be an accompanying positive sense of well-being in the child. For, in addition to his mother's love, he is the darling and centre of attention in the joint family, the recipient of constant though discontinuous, abruptly initiated and abruptly terminated, verbal stimulation and physical handling from all sides. During this early period of princely existence, he behaves well outwardly, is obedient and responds with charm and love. There is nothing more delightful than being in contact with a young Indian boy, full of intimacy, with a peaceful self image and affection. But the image is primarily spurious; his charm can be a means by which he persuades others to help him out of his sense of inadequacy and confusion. He clings to his mother and is encouraged by her to do so.

There is another shadow side; especially in the lower classes, this mother is a frightened, underdeveloped child herself, a cog in the wheel of the accepted family structures. Humiliated and unloved, she transfers her frustrations on to her son, the only possible object. While giving him an overabundance of love, she also simultaneously unconsciously attempts to diminish his masculinity. The result is often unbearable tension, as the apple of her eye is at the same time the sole recipient of her deep-rooted resentment against all males, for she sees in the little boy the prospective adult, female-demeaning male. She frightens him, is often unkind, domineering, angry and sadistic in her impulsive control over his movements and activities, stifling his initiative and inhibiting his psychic growth, so that his own infantile aggression seems to him now to be punished.

Thus while the son's adoration of the mother in response to her enticements is genuine, it is accompanied, in self defence, by its opposite. Ancient, tenacious and pervasive negative imagery which deeply permeates the Hindu psyche might be considered a significant emblem of the civilization. The female as harridan/ogre, cannibalistic devourer, bloody antagonist, the beautiful spider who consumes her prey—these images lurk in the boy's unconscious, the symbolic expression of his fear of the mother's unbridled sexuality and aggression.

> Underlying the conscious ideal of womanly purity, innocence and fidelity and interwoven with the unconscious belief in a safeguarding maternal beneficence is a sacred conviction among many Hindu men that the feminine principle is really the opposite—treacherous, lustful and rampant with insatiable, contaminating sexuality.... We must conclude that the sexual presence of the 'bad mother' looms front and centre in the unconscious experience of male children in India and is therefore critical to an understanding of the Hindu psyche.... The mine of collective fantasy around this theme is unusually rich.[5]

As Kakar suggests, the intense relationship of son and mother results in a polarization of the connections, as the overt love for the mother, which is very real, masks the revulsion and fear of the ever-present threat of regression.

In an effort to overcome his own responses to her loving/ destructive tendencies, the son compensates by means of narcissistic defences. This typical model is easily recognized and almost as easily categorized. To counteract his fears of sinking back into the mother morass, as though he alone were his own sole support and rescue, he is often inordinately lacking in humility despite his obvious shortcomings. Deflecting his faults on to others, he exhibits a childish self aggrandizement with the need to persuade others of his merits. The intensity is a symptom of his lack of confidence in his own ability to control impulsivity. His overvaluation and concern with self leads to arrogance and obstinacy, then envy and competitiveness, dissembling, even lying. The narcissist is unable to come to firm decisions or to adhere to principles. He therefore sometimes betrays friends and easily shifts extra-familial loyalties. Accompanying these outward manifestations there is passivity, submissiveness, anxiety and, in the last analysis, dependence on the mother imago, which leads to dejection and hypochondria.

Abbé Dubois, the offensively moralistic foreigner who was nevertheless a keen observer, might have exaggerated the fatuous and arrogant pretensions of the male, but his descriptions do not sound unfamiliar, and they are worth noting:

> Intense selfishness is also a common characteristic. Brought up in the idea that nothing is too good for him, and that he owes nothing in return to any one, he models the whole of his life on this principle. He makes it a point of duty not only to hold himself aloof from all other human beings, but also to despise and hate, from the bottom of his heart, everyone who happens not to be born of the same caste as himself.[4]

Kakar's more contemporary and objective view will give credence to the tenacity of certain age-old traits which the hero Mahisa so boldly dramatizes in his conceits:

> I would contend that among Indian men the process of integrating these archaic narcissistic configurations developmentally is rarely accomplished in the sense that it is among men in the West. This does not mean that Indians are narcissistic while westerners are not.

But in the West, there are fewer and less easily accessible outwardly manifested pathways back to 'archaic narcissim'.[5]

The narcissism is frequently the cause of intense rivalry between brothers for the love of the mother, and when the father dies, for the ascendent position in the family hierarchy, often the only authoritative position many men ever achieve. Sibling rivalries, hostilities and feuding which cannot be expressed openly within the family are either internalized into neuroses or externalized as struggles between one community and another, often leading to political antagonisms and violence. Ultimate authority is vested in the oldest in the family, in a *guru* or substitute at work and in political leaders. These stabilize the insecurities to some extent.[6]

As a Westerner, trained to prepare the child for equality and independence, I am as often as astonished at what I observe as are my informants in regard to western mores. A few typical fragments lifted from my rag-bag of personal experiences, in different parts of the country, provide verification of these statements.

The bath is the occasion for the male child's first struggle with the mother; she forcibly keeps her three-month-old prone on the washroom stone floor for ten minutes, while she gives him a good, solid massage, as though he were but clay, while he screams and fights to get away; the mother is amused. I contrast this with the delicate handling of a western infant, but this mother insists that what I would consider intrusive or smothering is the only way the baby gets properly washed. The child is certainly nursed until he is two and not infrequently until he is much older; often he even takes time out from playing with other children to stand close and imbibe a few sips of mother nectar before returning to his games.

In many communities, often until puberty, the boy sleeps on the floor next to his mother while the husband sleeps on the bed, if there is one. In most lower-class homes, the separate bedroom for parents is unusual; in the higher strata the child is placed between the parents and feigns sleep during the adult love making. If he sleeps alone, it is said, he would feel lonely and rejected.

A professor of Existentialism in a leading college deeply regretted his recent marriage to a Parsi lady, who, he told me (a perfect stranger), was 'just like a cold westerner'. 'How I long for my sensuous Hindu mother! When I think of her, chills go up and down my back!' Then there was the Nivea creme salesman who kept me awake for hours during a train journey describing his wonderful mother in adoring terms. She had died seventeen years previously, but the obsessive attachment remained unchanged.

The 'beloved' mother is everywhere to be found in physical proximity with the adult son and his family. A constant presence, she is reverenced and given priority of authority and attention after marriage, and even after death, she lives strongly on in the imagination. It is a rare Indian wife who does not resign herself to accepting the mother-in-law's authority in the belief that she is doing her duty; for there are fights if the girl begins to think for herself.

I have had male strangers speak too soon and much too frankly about their successes, with an inordinate amount of self praise. The 'I am behind the desk', 'I am the principal', or even 'I received the gold medal' (in college, twenty years ago) syndrome is the frequent fatuous intrusive defence, as though with these pronouncements the adult's right to existence is assured. If I finally object, there is the anticipated remark: 'But you are my *mother*', reflecting genuine respect, accompanied by a show of astonishment at being thus rejected. During long bus rides if my neighbour is a Hindu male, if he sleeps away the time, invariably my shoulder is used as a cushion for his head. Like the newborn duckling who follows any living being, closeness to mother warmth seems to be easily felt. Women manage very well to stay separate.

But the frightening aspect of the mother is not always masked, even in public. Parents have often made use of my presence to discipline their own children, saying: 'She will punish you if you don't behave', implying that this stranger, this female demon *raksasi*, is a dangerous mother surrogate. This can be an effective protective device against the inevitable hordes of children who follow one with intense excitement in remote villages; if I momentarily play-act the role thus assigned to me, children flee, some in terror.

These attitudes are the norm, but for a few who are aware and disturbed. A recent headline proclaims: 'Mama's Boy Syndrome Widespread in India',[7] and a rare analysis was voiced on the 'Opinion' page of a local Bombay newspaper, which no scholar could possibly improve upon.

> What is the tried and tested style in our country? Lick and kick. Lick the people above, kick the bleeding sods below.
> Why? Probably because of the patriarchal structure of the joint family system.... The son is dominated by his mother. He is her pride and joy, both *paneer* and *pakora*. He is also so obsessively over-mothered, that he is rendered incapable of adult relations for the rest of his life. In women he needs a mother substitute even when he is 45 years old. In subordinates, he needs a father who will condone his fits of temper, his giving with one hand, his taking away with the other. To his superiors, like to his father, he is a humble, obedient servant.[8]

The situation is exacerbated because during childhood, stern rules require the separation of the sexes. The boy, who is anyway in thrall to his mother, grows up fixated at an early stage; he dichotomizes women, unable to think of them except as idealized mother/sister or sexual objects. He stays very close to the females in the family but seeks sexual release with prostitutes and, in the upper classes, with a mistress, or he indulges in wonderful Maharaja harem fantasies. Young foreign travellers have been added to this list of desirable women. They are being harassed from all sides, and the new youth, who flock to American films and aggressively ride recently-acquired motorcycles, are no longer able to control the impulses resulting from pent-up family tensions. 'It is our weakness', so the men admit.

It is this person that Mahisa represents in the myth. Released from familial inhibitions and repressions, this symbolic rebel is the vehicle for feelings yearning to be expressed. It is no wonder that the myth, which invents a motherless hero who becomes king of the world and struggles with the Goddess, holds so much fascination. A courageous attempt at disengaging the son from the terrors of the dreaded but desired symbiosis, it offers perhaps the only solution for an impossible dilemma. The message is that he will forever be the victim of her whose primary unconscious goals are to extend his infantile life and to encourage his megalomaniacal tendencies by indulging his every whim in order to keep the son crippled and near. This suggests the probability that, lurking in the unconscious of many men is the wish to bring the longed-for satisfaction to the mother. Great shame and fear of her passion leads to death-wish fantasies, both for himself and for her. It is this desperate striving for autonomy that is the fundamental *raga* of the tragic story.

We shall hear more about the relationship of son and mother in the following chapters. The review of the contemporary male personality at this juncture serves to connect the obsessions of the childlike Mahisa who believes only in his own superiority, because he dare not do otherwise, with the hold the myth has on today's worshipper.

Chapter Two Birth of the Hero

Motifs

1. Mother is royal virgin with de-   *Varaha* and *Skanda Puranas*
   moness/Goddess associations
2. Father is king, rsi, descendant of   All versions
   a god, or a god
3. Born of a cow, animal ancestry   All versions
4. Father has bull connections   *Kalika Purana*
5. Circumstances of his birth are   All versions
   unusual
6. Born after struggle   *Vamana Purana* and DBP
7. Born after immaculate concep-   *Varaha Purana*
   tion
8. Survives death at birth   *Vamana Purana* and DBP
9. Born anomalous or extraordi-   All versions
   nary
10. Abandoned at birth (by mother)   All versions
11. Has connections with the under-   All versions
    world

Mahisa's Father Attempts Suicide

We can begin the study of the saga of Mahisa with the story as told
in the *Vamana Purana*, as it provides many hints and, indeed, overt
references, encouraging a frank analysis of the underlying motifs
which will later reappear in the main body of the narrative. Many
centuries later, the main outline was preserved in the DBP and
fragments entered into the *Kalika Purana*. While in the variants
Mahisa's parents differ from one another, all the pairs are united
by certain structural analogies. The language is succinct and spare,

with barely any flourishes or elaboration of the factual statements. Yet implicit in the simple words of a seemingly simple text are several layers of meaning that are not entirely masked, which we shall attempt to fathom.

Although the two sons of King Danu were blessed in lineage, they were poor in progeny, threatened with loss of power and even with annihilation of the royal Brahmin demon line. The brothers therefore abandoned temporal pursuits and barren wives in order to devote themselves to the proven path of the *tapasvin* (he who performs severe penances). Within the Pancha Nada (the five rivers of the Indus) Karambha stood submerged up to his neck, while Rambha hid in a peepul tree and then remained in the midst of Five Fires.[1] The deliberate discipline and depth of suffering undergone by Karambha can be realized fully only by contemporary ascetics whose lives bear out the potency of the myth. A legend at Ellora village explains the leg paralysis of the local, revered (recently deceased) Swami Janardan, as the result of the agonies he suffered during ten years of water penance, analogous to Karambha's. The soul which was healed for the benefit of thousands of devotees resided in a damaged body.

While thus lost in abstracted meditation and religious fervour, as self denial and mutilations of the body are intensified, dormant energies quicken and are kindled into fierce but contained body heat. A prolonged period of worship may even influence the deity to manifest; or it can transfer the power of the gods to the devotee. People, demons and sometimes even gods undergo severe austerities not necessarily for higher spiritual purposes but with mundane objectives: for prosperity, the well-being of the society, or for victory in battle and personal gain. The gods, jealous of the augmenting power of the demons, attempt to avert being overcome by demons more powerful than they.[2] Ignoring this danger of retaliation, the demon brothers Rambha and Karambha hoped to destabilize the status quo and achieve a favourable negotiating position so as to achieve immortality through the birth of sons. The cycle of Mahisa's life begins here.

But nothing is predictable. The myth often introduces disconcerting, jarring twists and turns abruptly: suddenly, with all the cruelty and deception symbolized by reptilian attributes, the bull/rain god Indra slithered under the waters in the form of a crocodile; from beneath he caught hold of the legs of the virtuous

Karambha, and then and there the demon-ascetic was carried away in the flow of the Indus.[3] God-become-crocodile introduces the motif of magical shape-shifting at the very beginning of the story. Guilt and the longing for punishment for sins is implied. Indra will never evade the dread and shame of killing a Brahmin, albeit a demon Brahmin, for even gods suffer for their sins. Formerly Indra had murdered another Brahmin half-demon:

> Indra became very much deprived of his energy and brilliancy due to the sin of killing a Brahmin... [and] was so terrified of his sin.[4]

Indra's punishment will come, not from the victim's brother but from his as yet-unborn nephew Mahisa.

As for king Rambha, even though he had recently lost the brother who had shared the same mother's womb, he did not respond appropriately to the crocodile. He did not kill him, or threaten revenge and retributive justice. Another leap off the track of the narrative finds Rambha prepared to commit suicide by self-beheading, as an offering to Agni, god of fire,[5] apparently having given little thought to the obvious consequences of such action: the progeny so longed for during the years of ascetic suffering would never see the light of day, and the hereditary line of *daityas* (demons) would disappear. The choice of suicide in place of retaliation is perhaps rooted in memory of the Vedic concept of Indra as father, the primeval sire:

> You indeed are our father, shining Satakratu, you are our mother Satakratu (who has done 100 sacrifices).[6]
>
> They made a dwelling for their Father (Indra). It was made well, with distinction.[7]

Somewhere in the dark cauldron of the demon's mind, fear and jealousy of the father god of lightning must have been transformed into thoughts of parricide, but he had not the courage to avenge the treachery. Anger rightfully directed towards the murderer was now being displaced upon his own head. Perhaps he half believed that since creation evolves out of sacrifice, as birth out of death, as a last resort his own suicide would bring forth the desired son, for the suicide often has utter faith in the invincible power of his act. But we must seek further answers to explain the bizarre turn of events.

King Rambha's self-destructive tendencies could also have been a resistance mechanism to an unconscious desire to be rid of a rival—his brother; Rambha has here become the bad brother of the folk tales. A thousand years of penances would certainly have resulted in sons for both brothers, all with equal claim to the demon throne. The evil accomplished by a convenient surrogate in the form of a father figure may well have aroused enough guilt to warrant the demon king's desire to escape into self-punishment. Indra's sin had been overt, and in the previous case he had become as thin as a lotus stalk, on the verge of death; Rambha's sin was unconscious but deserves the identical response.

The Brahmin text writer seems to project hidden wishes: the very father god whose assistance was only recently prayed for so ardently is now made responsible for the death of the rival brother. Guilt leads to dread in Rambha's demon breast. Moreover, because through death, Karambha has lost everything—his right to the throne as well as the much longed-for son—according to primitive thought, the dead demon will return in search of his real murderer (Rambha and/or the surrogate Indra) to avenge his own murder. Thus maddened, hoping for atonement, Rambha takes hold of the sword which shines with the light of virtue and seizes his own hair, symbol of life and strength (as the Goddess will later seize the hair of Rambha's son Mahisa to kill *him*). Now the wish to inflict pain upon his brother and on his father is reversed as he prepares to cut off his own head, the source of life and the container of the soul. Rambha wishes to become the sacrifice to ease the tensions caused by guilt, to restore order and to be rid, with the fallen head, of the terrorizing unconscious material.

According to certain ancient Indian dicta, giving up a life—one's own—is a perfectly acceptable free choice, helping the victim to acquire merit. Under particular circumstances, it is even required and encouraged by law. For adultery with the guru's wife, for example, the sinner

> shall cut off his organ, together with testicles, take them into his joined hands and walk towards the south: wherever he meets an obstacle (to further progress), there he shall stand until he dies. It is declared in the Veda that he is purified after death.[8]

The reader will not find it difficult to analogize 'the organ' with the head (a recurring association) which will be frequently met with during the subsequent tribulations of Mahisa. For Mahisa has unconsciously done far worse than slept with a guru's wife.[9]

But not all prescriptions encourage the suicide, for very good reason:

> According to Indian popular belief, wishes uttered immediately before suicide are fulfilled.[10]

As this makes the survivors liable to be cursed, laws against suicide are simple mechanisms designed to protect the living: 'He who cuts the rope by which the [suicide] has hung himself or who has been concerned with the funeral...or who sheds tears'[11] requires purification. This is Rambha's penultimate card. As he prepares for death he hopes to be the winner in any event.

Implied in his desire for self-sacrifice is recognition of his own role in forthcoming events. Since it is accepted that the heads of the Goddess' devotees or their animal substitutes are her due, Rambha's act could also be seen as an omen of the fate of his son, the buffalo demon, for Mahisa is the paradigmatic sacrificial victim. One may note that Rambha's ascetic exercises had been initiated not for reaching the godhead, not for transcending this temporal existence, nor as a seeker after truth, but merely to perpetuate his own race; however, the final outcome was precisely in opposition to his goal (which might be one of the many messages of the myth).

Now the god Agni, fire, the forgiving father, is called into service to oppose Rambha's destructive impulses. At the very last moment, acknowledging the long years of penance, the god offers a convenient reprieve. In what appears to be an act of sublime mercy, Agni advises Rambha that thoughts of suicide are entirely sinful and urges him not to commit the crime (the *Vamana Purana* favours the concept that there is no means of expiation for self-destruction.)[12] The suicide attempt itself relieved remorse to some extent, and Rambha now dutifully withdraws the sword in an act which prefigures the resurrection of Mahisa. However, Agni had his own reasons for intruding into Rambha's madness. Having been dragged into the situation by the tapas of the demon, like Indra, he judged that the gods could ill afford further defeats. Previously Rambha had practised austerities, and he had fasted and inflicted tortures on mind and body. But now, taking into account the facts of life (and death and rebirth), he was no doubt unafraid to die. It was in Agni's interest to prevent the self-sacrifice so as to protect the gods from the demon's ultimate objectives; to save the father's head so that Mahisa's could be decapitated at a more critical time.[13] Agni therefore offers Rambha a boon,[14] one that will change the whole course of the history of the three worlds.

By threatening self-punishment, the Brahmin writers (symbolized by Rambha) had proven their point, and now they were happily free from any further need to repent fratricidal and parricidal wishes. So, even in face of the hidden, brazen instincts revealed through the attempt at suicide, King Rambha very rapidly regained his love of life. The virtuous ascetic reverted to his natural character, with all its normal demon whims and fancies. For even when he had earlier humbly practised his tapas, he had set his sights on a mere demon for a son, for race perpetuation alone, and for that he had suffered agonies and burned his body within the circle of the Five Fires; but now, with the temptation to gain salvation through self-sacrifice so fresh in his mind, the original demonic greed re-emerged, and he upped the ante. He asked for a son who would conquer not merely the nether world (patala), nor even the earth, but heaven too; one who would be like god and would displace god. He asked that his son should have the strength of the gods in order to struggle with the gods; skill in weaponry;the ability for instantaneous transformation into a variety of forms[15] —to be, that is, like Indra, who had altered his form. The conditions did not seem too extravagant.

Now Agni proceeded to make amends for the demonic work of his brother god Indra. He added an extra blessing from the god:

> You shall have the son from that female to which your heart is attached.[16]

Good was now definitely emerging out of evil, dread and guilt were transformed into hope, King Rambha's agonies had not after all been suffered in vain; indeed, they were about to pay off, or so it would appear. But this, as we shall see, is only in preparation for the sequence of events in the life of our hero, Mahisa. Thus gods and demons play their useful roles in the lives of humans.

Lineage of Mahisa

At the very outset, in the variants, the Puranic writers are at pains to direct attention to Mahisa's ambiguous inheritance. By ancestry, he is not by any means unequivocally a demon; in all the versions, in fact, he is born of mixed parentage. Demon, animal, human and divine blood runs through his veins and, in most of the variants, his parents are who they are as a result of previous irregular alliances or transformations as well. As we have noted earlier, fluid transpositions between gods, men and animals and the non-fixed nature of the categories is characteristic of Hindu myths.[17] Mahisa is the paradigmatic hero who combines the triune qualities: the buffalo heritage comes from his mother's side, although she is only rarely purely animal; the father is a god or descended from a god, or he is a royal Brahmin demon. With so many sorts of relatives, the lineage is far from uncomplicated. From these roots, under divine influence, Mahisa is born. Since unnatural birth and the union of different species is dangerous, Mahisa is born fated to a perilous existence. His condition will have many ramifications, the most important of which will be his relationship to the Mother Goddess, who is no less enigmatic and aggregate a characterization than he is.

If they do not desire to follow the strenuous path of the tapasvin, demons revert to less direct but equally coercive methods to influence the gods. When subjugated and confined to the nether world, miserably nursing their wounded pride, they often aim to take advantage of the increase of power which results, not from their own austerities, but from those of the holy rsis. These are men and women who have left society to dwell in forests, under trees, or near water, exposed to the elements, torturing their bodies, nourished solely on nature's uncultivated bounties. They lead lives of contemplation, uttering *mantras* according to strict ritual, identifying with a chosen deity. As merit increases with intensified and long penance, they are favoured by the gods, but like the demon ascetics, they too pose a threat to the very gods whom they worship. With the logic of 'my enemies' enemies are my friends', it follows that the gods prefer not to interfere with the intent of the demons to acquire, by any and all means, some of the strength borrowed from the rsis.

Since there has never been a better way to achieve one's goals than to dangle a beautiful female before an unsuspecting enemy, it is just this device which initiates the connections between the future mother and father of Mahisa. Although rsis do not easily fall prey to temptation, since they are after all only human, eventually some do succumb,[18] as related in the *Skanda* and *Varaha Puranas*.

Skanda Purana *Father is rsi; mother is demoness turned buffalo*

The demoness Diti was the daughter of Daksa (father of the gods) and wife of Kasyapa. In the *Ramayana* she is a demon-cow.[19] She is the sister of Indra's mother Aditi. In this version then, Indra is the uncle of Mahisa. Diti instructed her daughter to assume the shape of a buffalo and then to practise penance in order to avenge the defeat of the demons by the gods. After long years of performing austerities, so great was the buffalo daughter's acquired power that she frightened all the gods. The sage Suparsva was forced to beg her to desist, promising 'the fair hipped one' a son, who would be born with the head of a buffalo and the body of a man, with extraordinary energy, enough to defeat the gods. Together the pair departed to the world of rsis.[20] In the *Kannyakumari*, a Tamil text, it is stated explicitly that Mahisa was born of this union.[21]

Varaha Purana *Father is rsi; mother is demon princess turned buffalo*

Like father, like son. Sindhudvipa, a king, manifestation of Varuna,[22] son of Suparsva, performed severe austerities: as ascetic heat was thus accumulated it was transformed into erotic energy.[23] Abandoning celibacy, the king united with the river Vetravati who assumed the form of a young woman. They had a son, Vetrasura,[24] who was an elder half-brother of Mahisa.

Sindhudvipa mated again when the mischievous demon princess Mahismati chanced to frolic with her friends in the penance grove. To play a trick on the sage-king, she turned herself into a buffalo with sharp horns. This transformation into a masculine mother figure hints at her son's dilemmas in a later part of the story as she frightened the sage sufficiently for him to curse her to be a buffalo for a hundred years. After due entreaties on her part, he promised that she would resume her own shape but only after giving birth to a buffalo demon son. He had his own reasons for this, and he made the best of this unexpected opportunity, for

He [Sindhuvipa] was performing penance in the forest with a view of begetting a son who would kill Indra.[25]

His son, Mahisa, would not kill Indra but would rout him from heaven, which was tantamount to death.

At this point, his former paramour, the river Vetravati, re-appeared; she came to bathe nude in the Narmada river, and seeing her, Sindhudvipa dropped his seed into a crevice in a rock in the river. In her buffalo form princess Mahismati came along and drank from this cup of life. The union between the sage and the buffalo–princess resulted in an immaculate conception—the birth of the infant Mahisa—'intelligent and valiant', and the mother was soon restored to her former human form.[26]

Vamana Purana and DBP *Born from fire; father is Brahmin royal demon; mother is buffalo*

King Rambha's austerities finally did achieve the intended goal; Agni promised 'an invincible son' who would have the ability to 'assume [various] forms at will'. So Rambha went about looking for a mate. Although he could have had his pick from among all the women in his kingdom, when he encountered 'the handsome three-year-old she-buffalo Syama' (plate 1), he offered no resistance to her advances:

> And she approached in haste the great demon, desiring union with him, and he too, as fate would have it, responded by co-habiting.[27]

Rambha did what his kin considered to be immoral:[28] he succumbed to Syama, and in consequence, she conceived.[29] (Later the son Mahisa would also be subjected to such seduction). Off they went to the nether world to start married life and 'the dark complexioned she-buffalo gave birth to a fair complexioned buffalo capable of assuming any form at will'.[30] But catastrophe followed soon after; suddenly Rambha was killed by a buffalo who appeared abruptly in the narrative.[31] In what may be a conflation of texts, another verse in the *Vamana Purana* describes Syama as being childless when, after the death of her husband, as suttee, she jumped into the fire. But the DBP clarifies this: 'When the she-buffalo died, the powerful Mahisa rose from his mother's womb from the midst of the funeral pyre.'[32]

Kalika Purana *Father is royal Brahmin demon; mother is Siva become buffalo cow*

The most intriguing version of the birth of Mahisa appears in a late medieval text, the *Kalika Purana*. According to this, growing megalomania spurred Rambha to dreams of even greater glory, which was for nothing less than to have the god Siva born to him as son in three births. Rambha pleaded:

> I am without sons, O great god: if you are kindly disposed towards me, you should be my son, O Shiva, in three births; a son who cannot be killed by all the living beings, and who will be victorious over all the gods; who has a long life, and who will be famous and fortunate, O Shiva.[33]

This might seem to be both disrespectful and arrogant, apart from entirely fantastic. In a lightning flash, the infantile wishes of the great Brahmin demon king come to the surface; the consanguinity of demons with gods is taken for granted. Even more amazing is the rapidity with which Siva replies: 'What is longed for you by you, be so; I shall become your son.'[34]

As for the reasoning of the priest–mythmaker concerning Siva's assent to the peculiar request and its accomplishment, it would appear that all austerities require attention; a king who has practised self-humiliation for so long cannot be ignored, lest the gods suffer dire consequences. On the consubstantiality and brotherhood of gods and demons O'Flaherty remarks:

> By nature, gods and demons are alike; by function however, they are different as day and night. In fact, one reason for their perpetual conflict is the simple fact that they only become distinct—and therefore real to the Hindus hearing the myths—when they are engaged in battle.[35]

This prepares the groundwork for the Siva/Mahisa connection, and, finally, for the Mahisa/Durga battle.

For the demon king, the situation was critical because of his desperate need for a son. Yet it was imperative that he place himself in a submissive position *vis-à-vis* the divine grantor of his wish. Rambha had always been a tyrant, never a supplicant and 'a dreadful demon ... who caused great disturbance in the world and [was] extremely powerful.'[36] It could hardly have been either easy or natural for the demon king to set aside his royal self-image and to bend the knee to another (Siva).

The childhood of both prince and pauper is spent in submissive and impotent identification with the father, conceived as god. Concomitant negative responses of hate are accompanied by self-reassurances through dreams of self aggrandizement, the fantasy of destruction of the god image and subsequently by enormous feelings of guilt. It is likely that Rambha (or the Brahmin priest who prepared these texts and projected symbolic patterns on to the mythical characters) had recourse to his own memories of father/son connections. So, after the many years of harrowing self-affliction, at this point, the boy in Rambha came to the fore. Worn out with austerities he wished fervently to be extricated from his dependent state. With a minimum of wiles, in all innocence, the child dares to make a straightforward request: that Siva become his son. (It is the fantasy of every ordinary boy who wishes to change places with the father, to enjoy the connubial pleasures that are the prerogative of the senior. It follows that when the father becomes the son, the son will become the beloved/hated father. This would require punishment for his evil thought. Mahisa also will be mired in hubris and Oedipal regressions.)

The request for the reversal of positions with the father is a love wish, even while unconscious evil desire simultaneously breeds fear and hate, a condition which will partially define the god/demon relationship. But for the time being, only positive thoughts are uttered. The Brahmin text writers speak about themselves, and the myth speaks for all; the different versions all lead to the same general conclusions, as the myth reflects the ambivalence of human nature. Rambha had already displaced the former king, his own personal demon father; so the son's guilt at usurping his father's position needs to be expiated.

The story shifts to Siva, who first assumes the shape of a cow and unites with the demon king. From this strange union Siva is born as Mahisa. Siva the father is now also wife, mother and son. This amalgamate figure should be kept in mind as the story of the life of the hero and his encounters with the Goddess unfolds. For, since the virgin Goddess with whom the adult buffalo demon will contend in battle often proclaims herself to be the wife of Siva, Mahisa as Siva is both husband and son of the Mother Goddess. Hero and deity, hero and mother are linked at birth.

It is to be taken for granted that the father/mother/demon/god/Goddess relationships are the metaphors for tensions related to unacceptable thoughts originating in the unconscious. The priest—mythmaker attempts to resolve conflicts by portraying son as father (Rambha=Siva) and father (Siva) as mother and son (Mahisa) thus providing temporary, if illusory relief. But the story continues, and Siva cannot remain the son of the demon king for long, as this situation would certainly give rise to renewed tensions, and so, as in all Indian myths, the beginning of the new relationship is the very moment of the start of its dissolution.

Buffalo Cow: Mother of Mahisa

Mahisa's animal ancestry is traceable primarily from his maternal side, although Siva's bull connections should not be entirely disregarded. Here it is useful to refer to the association of god/king/bull and Goddess/queen/cow in earlier western recorded traditions. As bovine/human relationships nourished and fostered the economic and spiritual needs of pastoral and agricultural societies, the bull and his mother cow were either conjoined, integrated, associated or juxtaposed to figures of prime authority. As buffalo/hero in theriomorphic/human shape, Mahisa is part of a universal pattern: he is partially buffalo/bull; his mother is partially buffalo/cow.

When too great an identification with animals appears to have become a threat to the civilizing process, an ascetic focus, functioning to control the animal nature in humans, becomes imperative. Religious systems seek to modify unrestrained instincts and extremes of lust and brutality associated with animal behaviour but basic to human beings as well. Indians had developed ritual formulations for the transformation of repressed atavistic impulses always threatening to break through to consciousness, at random, in explosive bursts. But as the source of energy and referring to the fundamental human condition, the indispensable animal imagery was retained, even while the sublimating and controlling processes of religion and myth were coming into being.[37]

Can the individual admit that he wishes his mother away? Can he cry out tragically about his fears that she will devour him as he devoured her breast as an infant? Even when he perceives his mother age and weaken, he feels the threat of impending destruction along with his need for her love, and this remains the dominant unconscious problem he has to deal with all his life. Hindu myths concerning cows are all about this, as O'Flaherty and

Shulman have observed. That milk is morally ambivalent and flows as a result of love or is withheld in hate and that the breast (or udder) can be an instrument of aggression, and blood equated with milk, are common Indian perceptions.[38] In the South, 'The depiction of the cow as violent and even murderous is common throughout the Tamil Puranic corpus.'[39]

When the tribal nomadic invaders assimilated to the Indian aboriginals, they were drawn into the morass of the primeval for which literature and idealizations provided only thinly veiled rationalizations. Buddhism, and later the *bhakti* movement, with its refined ethical theories, spread throughout India and animal sacrifice was abjured by philosopher, poet and priest. Then the dark wild and ferocious psychoid forces of nature, which no amount of wishing or intellectualizing could control, found an outlet in the story about the buffalo cow in the myth. By combining images of animal/demoness/princess/Goddess, and thus distancing himself from himself, the Purana writer created a metaphor to contain all aspects of the mother—the fear, the love and the awe she inspired. All are thus partially sublimated.

Hidden within the obfuscating imagery, primordial impulses are decipherable: erotic woman, dangerous virgin, mother, beloved nurturer—but destroyer; no single one of the projected responses to the cow as mother is entirely valid separately or definitely fixed, as the potency of the symbol relies essentially on its range of meanings. Like the enduring symbol of the cow in India, Mahisa's mother would appear to be the carrier of a particular pattern of unconscious responses which have been handed down from one generation to the next for millennia.

To return to our narrative:

> One lovely she-buffalo who was very maddened with passion fell to the sight of Rambha and he desired to have sexual intercourse with her, in preference to other women.[40]

The demon king was free to choose any female who met his fancy. Why then did he direct all attention to the beautiful, dark brown buffalo-cow in heat? In the preliminary stages, the priest/narrator had identified with an anthropomorphic symbol in the form of the Brahmin demon king, but the sage-like qualities, achieved by means of tapas, were contradictory to the original purpose, which was to perpetuate the race of demons. Rambha (or the sages) was in a difficult situation, and Rambha was depressed, a potential suicide. In order for the story to proceed, a breakthrough was required. Since asceticism is a defence partly against animal nature, the she-buffalo, introduced into a constellation of conflicting internal drives, now functions as antidote for Rambha's suicidal intentions.

The sight of Syama who is associated with the dark-brown, fertile mother earth,[41] ready as she was to assert her beautiful massive presence, aroused long-dormant animal passions in Rambha, now, after odious trials, all the more intensely felt. King Rambha is drawn irrationally and blindly towards this desirable object. She is a welcome contrast to the austerities performed in greed and guilt, and she is full with desire and happy to oblige.

Seduction of the virtuous male by a female with unquenchable appetites is a motif which runs through the entire myth and all the myths and is very little altered in the telling and retelling. Merely overture to the major theme, which will rise in crescendo towards a predetermined finale, Syama is a dim antecedent of her analogue the Mother Goddess. The intensity of the drives with which the myth is concerned cannot be overestimated; worship of the Goddess on all levels is imbued with great force, even at the highest spiritual levels, or, as in the case of Mahisa's mother, at the basest.

As the son of a mixed marriage, Mahisa inherits an entire set of ambiguities which play havoc with traditional hierarchical animal/human/god relationships based upon a fixed order of the biological species. A dynamic force operates in the narrative, ignoring custom and tradition, as the myth accommodates raw nature by displaying the contents of the unconscious to public perception; the laws of society simultaneously work to repress them. The myth confronts unconscious diffused forces which press toward recognition, yet are not accorded adequate attention in myth-impoverished societies.

The Cow as Sacred Animal

The role of Syama and her buffalo-demon son is illuminated in parallel idioms in the rituals and the literature of the ancient Vedic people and their descendants, and also in the contemporary lives of the buffalo-worshipping Todas of India.

Vedic and later texts

'Horses and cows are sacred in the Rg Veda; cows are more sacred than bulls.'[42] Vedic passages focus on characteristics common to both man and animal. The verses teem with imagery expressing deep emotions and the fullness of life, mirroring an intense identification with nature. The poet lived close to the elements, to water, earth, space and sky, to weather, colours, to proliferations. The cow is experienced as the rain cloud:

> Let the milk cows that have no calves storm down, yielding rich nectar, streaming unexhausted.[43]

She is dawn, light , nourishing mother and provider, and she is also the mother of god (Indra).

This animal imagery should not be confused with the incapacity to differentiate between self and object, as the highest peak of cultural attainment is achieved in the Vedas. The poems are characterized by a melding of imagery rather than classification by species, and adoration of all aspects of nature rather than taking her for granted. The sophisticated maker of hymns is stimulated to worship the cattle in the midst of whom he lives and upon whom he is dependent for protection, nourishment and therefore survival. As an adult he finds himself in the same state of dependency on the cow as he was towards his own natural mother during his infancy. These experiences are expressed in poetry. Even today, in the villages of India, the cow is kept in the home; often she sleeps with the old grandmother and the children in the same way that the cat and dog are welcomed into the modern apartment bedroom. In East and West archaisms function in daily life today as before, to the benefit of a human psyche energized by animal force.

Tribal legends are reflected in Vedic imagery which retains vestiges of the age-old widespread worship of the bull. Mahisa as hero, and as sometime deity, is born of the cow, as the Vedic Indra before him was born of the heifer Aditi. Syama will leap into her husband's pyre, leaving Mahisa an orphan; this is prefigured by Aditi 'who let her calf wander unlicked, to seek his own ways by himself.'[44] The storm gods (Maruts) were born from Prsni the cow; she mated with Rudra, ancestor of Siva.[45] In the *Kalika Purana* text of two thousand years later, Siva will himself assume the form of a cow to become the mother of Mahisa. As we have seen, the bull son, identified with the cow mother, is an ancient theme. Words, rhythms and chanting offer relief for the paradise of oneness.

Even as the Vedic tribes settled in India and some turned to agriculture, the sacrality of the cow did not diminish. The law books refer to cows as sacred auspicious purifiers; they alone produce sacred milk for ghee, without which the sacrifice is faulty. They take away every sin,[46] destroy guilt,[47] and the feeding of the cow procures exaltation in heaven. Land spread with cow-dung is thus purified.[48] In her urine dwells the Ganges,[49] and from the dust she raises as she walks and from her dung, prosperity is guaranteed. The penance for killing her is the same as for the murder of a Vaisya[50] or, when reborn in human form, the murderer will be blind.[51] He who partakes of the five products of a cow (*panchagavya*—milk, sour milk, butter, urine and dung) is purified.[52]

The belief in the purifying properties of the cow lasted for millennia and permeated the entire society. A golden cow was created by a ruler to undo the pollution caused by two ambassadors who had crossed the seas. They were placed within the statue and dragged out through the birth canal to achieve rebirth.[53]

Toda and others

The kernel of Vedic thought and the later codified Brahmanical ritual is found in tribal traditions. During the time of Rivers and Marshall (and later, when Emeneau produced his masterly studies), the Todas had been more or less undisturbed by outside contacts or influences. The research of these scholars encourages an attempt to search for deeper meanings in regard to the buffalo/human equation as it functioned in pastoral societies.

The two-line ritual couplets of the Toda poets reveal the depth of the relationship and yet acknowledge the obligatory separation, as ambiguities are confronted head-on and are not infrequently reconciled. With protean variations, the poetry expresses the symbiosis between the interdependent units but also the concomitant respect, awe and dread of a possibly dangerous antagonist. In sorrow they lament:

We are children in the lap; we are calves in the calf pen.[54]

For a dead wife:

You bore children filling the house, I owned buffaloes filling the pen.[55]

For a dead mother:

> Have I become an orphan, oh, mother's sister
> Have I become an orphan calf, oh, mother's sister?[56]

From this material it is not difficult to understand the lack of inhibition with which the Puranas approach the imagery of the demon/hero whose mother is a cow. The Todas even use bovine imagery to express erotic ideas:

> When the male buffalo Pilyar (the groom), gets upon the female's hind quarters,
> How beautiful it will be.
> When the buffalo, Sinmal-flower, bears calf after calf,
> How beautiful it will be.[57]

The pastoralist's own identity merges with the cattle upon whom he is dependent, and he perceives the she-buffalo as hierarchically superior to mother, wife and daughter.

Toda village life was entirely focused on the *ti* (sacred dairy), where selected cows and their products and ornaments were accorded the awe and respect due to a deity.[58] Purified celibate priests supervised the secret ceremonial;[59] magical properties were also attributed to the ti:

> Sacred place which gives a child to the barren woman;
> Sacred place which makes the barren buffalo to bear a calf.[60]

Among the Kurubas of Mysore, the commonest totems are the she-buffalo and the goat.[61] In most tribal cultures where cattle play a dominant role in the economy, the cow is accorded reverence, and there is usually a special festival in her honour. The Santals sing to her, kiss her and give her cakes,[62] and in South India at Pongal and during Dussera in the North, cows are taken out in procession, run through fires, painted and worshipped in the festivals of Go-puja (cow worship). Interesting festivals among the Newars of Nepal include the distribution of the head and skin of a sacrificed buffalo, masked children impersonating cows, revelry, dancing and music.[63] Thus is the cow image fused into the mental life of tribals and peasants.

Things still get mixed up all the time. In the street behind the five-star Taj Mahal hotel in Bombay the other day, some people called to me: 'Mommy, mommy, see Bhagwan (god).' They were leading the mutant five-legged cow, draped in beautiful textiles and ringing cow bells, who is often seen around the country walking in stately dignity. The incident seemed to sum up an entire cluster of responses, functioning as actively today for some as in the past.

Stranger Buffalo: Prefigures Mahisa

There another buffalo chanced to see her during her monthly course.
She approached the great demon to save her chastity.
The demon seeing that buffalo of elevated nose, took out his sword speedily and chased him.
He too in his turn struck the demon in the chest with sharp horns.
His chest rent, he (Rambha) fell on the ground and died.[64]

The stage has been set for the next episode. Rambha and Syama repair to the abode of the yaksas; there the nativity takes place. The trials of Rambha had finally come to an end, and he and Syama would presumably have lived happily ever after. But, as in life, there is an abrupt reversal, and the sequence of favourable conditions is rudely disrupted.

The demon king, who at first had simply wished for an ordinary heir, had now made the unreasonable request that Siva should be born as his son, sowing dangerous seeds. Fate, or the god Indra, in the form of a buffalo stranger, appears in the story veritably out of the blue, for a nearly wild buffalo bursts in and is about to seek lustful union with the mother-to-be[65] (or the new mother 'during her monthly course').[66] Syama's virtue is now put to the test. She comes through with flying colours by refusing the stranger's advances. In fear, she turns towards her husband who attempts to protect her with his phallic sword, but the horns of the stranger, symbolic of power and sexual potency, prove to be the more deadly weapon. Weakened by his years of penance, Rambha, unable to overcome the antagonist, is then and there killed.[67] (The fearless Asiatic savage buffalo who approaches domestic buffalo cows for mating is evoked here, introduced as the terrifying aspect of the primeval buffalo. The *bubalis/bubalus*, the heaviest and longest-horned animals in the world today, are a potent symbol of chaos and disorder.) Who is this intrusive stranger-buffalo? Although the Purana does not refer to Indra, the episode is analogous to the murder of Karambha by Indra in animal form.

Whether it was his self-destructive tendencies at work or whether it was truly a gallant act to protect his wife, Rambha is summarily killed and thus eliminated from the story, much to the consternation of the already pregnant (or new mother) buffalo-cow, whose protestations of grief loudly disclaim any provocative behaviour on *her* part. So much for Rambha's hopes to be the father of a super demon, or so it appears. Within an instant, ruthless, base instinct has destroyed the sentimental happiness of the pair united in blissful matrimony. The outraged yaksas, protectors of the moral code, attack the stranger, and he too is killed. He falls into the lake,[68] sharing the fate of Karambha, the recently murdered demon. Animal lust is punished by drowning in maternal waters.

The introduction of the wild buffalo momentarily puts gross, animal instinct on view, prior to the superimposition of mythic veils. The stranger buffalo in full rut also anticipates a component of Mahisa's character as it will later be revealed. It is a constellating symbol. He will be hero, lover, man, god, demon but, as buffalo, he is not unlike this wild beast who here approaches the mother and kills the father. This critical theme is introduced subtly; it will be amplified as the story unfolds. A hint is supplied in the *Vamana Purana:*

> Being thus prevented the buffalo who was lovesick fell into a charming
> lake and subsequently died. After death he became a demon, Namara
> by name, well known as possessing great might and prowess....[69]

At a later date, this very same Namara, as general of the *danavas* (demon) army, is again the *alter ego* for Mahisa, the son with incestuous intentions. As stranger-buffalo he lustfully approaches Syama; as Namara the general, 'he chases Durga violently.'[70]

If we assume that Mahisa, the buffalo demon, represents one aspect of the Brahmin priests and the male mentality, one reason for the introduction here of the wild buffalo becomes evident: he is full of sexual passion, and while Syama's attractions are her lovely appearance and certainly her undoubted virtue, it was nevertheless primarily her unrepressed animal energies which had already quenched the sexual thirst of the demon king Rambha, only recently released from ascetic celibacy. Writing the story, or telling it, the priests could not rest content with an entirely ideal image of the mother of Mahisa, any more than they could specify one particular image for the son.

The stranger-buffalo, who is the symbol of powerful brute force, understood by animal instinct that, lurking within the virtuous wife, was the lustful and impulsive animal. These two animals, representing raw instinct, are put on stage, if only for an instant, in hrder to reveal the truth about Mahisa's mother and about male fantasies in general. She is attractive, seductive and irresistible (dangerously polluted with menstrual blood, but thus doubly bewitching, doubly sinful), as is the mother to the son. He who writes and he who reads the story is permitted to fantasize an identity with the unrepressed image of a potent, strong, violent, conscienceless son who kills the father in order to conquer the mother. But morality prevails. The insight is immediately repressed, and the story is reconstructed to arrange for the Oedipal complex to be redeposited immediately into the unconscious. At this juncture, all the guilty parties must be punished— priest/writer/male, the intruding stranger buffalo for dreaming he is a master of potent manhood, and father Rambha for his megalomania and being a rival to his son.

Cow: Mahisa's Mother As Suttee

But what could be done with the mother, the sacred cow, whom tradition has treasured, sometimes elevating her to divine status? An apt solution, reconciling competing unconscious complexes, will put the mother to the torch, for nothing but total annihilation can be sufficient punishment to fit the crime of being a sexually provocative symbol. As in the fantasy, she must be eliminated, for the force of mother attraction having erupted into the myth threatens to overwhelm; here is the first hint of matricidal wishes, a core theme which reappears regularly even if not overtly in the subsquent narrative.

It is narrated that:

> The she-buffalo, seeing her husband laid in the funeral pyre, expressed her desire to enter also into that fire. The Yaksas resisted; but that chaste wife quickly entered into the burning fire along with her husband. When the she-buffalo died, the powerful Mahisa rose from his mother's womb from the midst of the funeral pyre.[71]

The buffalo stranger having been properly disposed of in a great battle with the yaksas, there was nothing for Syama to do but to plunge into the pyre of her husband. Like Rambha, she too ignored the obvious consequences of her actions: the son presumably would be stillborn. But Agni, the protective god, in the spirit of *sastric* injunctions which forbid a pregnant widow to commit suttee, preserved the infant. As the mother perished in the flames, her son was born, perfectly formed. At this critical juncture, with the elimination of the early protagonists—Karambha, Rambha, Syama and even the buffalo-stranger, and with the birth out of the flames of the hero Mahisa, the curtain is raised on the main drama. The premature, violent, gruesome deaths of the older generation will be seen to prefigure Mahisa's own unfortunate end.

The cow, as substitute for the mother symbol, sacrificed as suttee, is the focus for adamant, negative feelings. In a raw, blatant denial of incestuous longings, the adored mother is eliminated. In the ritual of cow sacrifice, the priest or tribal elder happily spears, cuts open, immolates and consumes the beloved mother substitute, even though he is always at pains to apologize to her for the necessity of so doing. He and those he represents wish to be rescued from the domination of the mother imago, for his very existence and growth depends upon removing himself from her overwhelming, malevolent influence. This is not an easy task: the story of Mahisa is the story of his Herculean efforts to overcome the longing for symbiotic union and return to the source, in a genuine attempt to confront and to set limits on the powers of the mother over the son. Ritual slaughter and immolation guarantees the severing of connections. Yet, notwithstanding her material disintegration, there is no escaping the mother/son relationship, and she will subsequently crash back into the life of the hero as Goddess, the dangerous female power. The myth repeats and amplifies earlier motifs, and as the structure becomes more complex, additional players and unforeseen events crowd on to an increasingly multi-dimensional stage.

The orphaned hero will at first attempt by means of penance to expiate the guilt arising in regard to the sins and the demise of his parents, but when he confronts the mother again, this time in the form of an incarnated Goddess, he struggles towards the development of his own individuality. Sacred as the cow is in the Brahmanical psyche, it is nevertheless imperative that she be ultimately destroyed, even as the Goddess is finally immersed in water after her festival. The plunge into the ritual fires is programmed into the story by the very same men who offer the victim hymns of adulation. (In another case, when the Goddess Sati was insulted by her father and her solution was to commit suttee, her husband, the god Siva, was driven to insanity. The male wishes to burn the female but because of his guilty fantasies he suffers impotency.)

The immolation of human beings was not unknown in ancient times. In India, theoretically, a leap into the fire was traditionally accepted as a purifying, beatific act, leading directly to heaven. It was occasionally practised in fact. A Brahmin immolated himself at Alexander's funeral, and another took his life in a public demonstration at Eleusis in Greece.[72] This was a male prerogative, highly praised but rarely performed. On the other hand, burning the female is a ritualized activity very deeply integrated into the Hindu religious system. Fire, deified element, purifies and protects from danger. Requiring a wife to join the deceased husband on the funeral pyre, although not generally encouraged by the early *sastras*, was later rationalized and accepted in custom. The collective unconscious erupted with vigorous strength, and it was the wife who bore the brunt of its tremendous force. The sacrifice of widows had already been institutionalized in Punjab when Alexander invaded India. Roman writers describe the Indian rite in detail, and societal attitudes and the rituals connected with it have persisted throughout two millennia, although not always with the same force.

Set upon the pyre by her own brother . . . the crowd ran to the spectacle; she heroically ended her life . . . laying herself beside her husband.[73]

Now the duties of a woman are: After the death of her husband, to preserve her chastity or to ascend to the pyre after him.[74]

The story of Syama's leap into the fire relies on a live tradition. It would serve little purpose if it did not. To prepare for the birth of Mahisa, it was expedient to assert that good emerges out of evil, as life out of death. The feared sakti force of the provocative, sexually dangerous female, imaged as buffalo cow, had to be entirely destroyed, for the priest gathered enough strength to identify with the powerful demon Mahisa only when the mother imago was safely eliminated. Syama is the cursed forerunner of her human sisters who, 'voluntarily' or not, became the sacrificial victim, violently eliminated to satisfy the psychic needs of the male.

In this view, the guilt derived from the belief that in consequence of her being a sinner in a former life the fate of the widow was deserved, was cancelled by the accompanying rationalization that she would be redeemed in the purifying fires. The family obeyed this custom with impunity, with the Brahmins at their side encouraging and even dragging the sometimes drugged, often reluctant victim.[75] This is not surprising, perhaps, as the priests were accustomed to receiving fees for their co-operation. They were also encouraged by the knowledge that they would materially benefit by large donations of the gold and silver ornaments removed from the body of the suttee immediately prior to the death ceremonies. A widowed queen was therefore taken more seriously than a woman of the lower classes. As a widow's right to the acquisition of her deceased husband's property was sanctioned by the laws of Manu, his family would naturally attempt by any and all means to protect themselves.

Moreover, after the death of her husband and before the immolation, the widow was believed to have enormous power for good and for evil. Her words and wishes would be fulfilled; she could bring even a kingdom to ruin,[76] and she was thus greatly feared. A literal outcaste with head shaven, hidden in white garments, it was imperative that she perish in the flames to ensure the destruction of her malevolent influence. But also, as the widow of a hero, she was seen as the courageous and devoted wife of a brave warrior who would forever be memorialized in suttee stones. As Colebrooke remarks: 'The compulsion was terrible, being the whole tremendous impalpable weight of familiar tradition and expectation.'[77] Honoured by being put to the torch, the suttee became the object of great admiration and veneration. The warrior caste gloried in the custom, especially in Orissa, Punjab, Rajasthan and Vijayanagar. In the nineteenth century, the Raja of Kota was secure in his rationalizations:

> The customs attended to have been handed down from the first father of mankind....In every nation of India... especially Rajpootana.... the queens, through the yearnings of the inward spirit, have become Suttees....It is not the power of a mortal to nullify a divine though mysterious ordinance.[78]

This Raja insisted that the act was entirely voluntary, claiming that even though she might be locked up in a room, the widow would press her way forward towards the pyre.[79] Thus royalty established its power. Splendid processions, sometimes accompanying multiple groups of wives in costly bridal dress, adorned with ornaments, riding in chariots to the sound of music, were staged at great cost, to satisfy the lust of the masses who, in an effort to climb the social ladder, often sacrificed lower-caste women simultaneously.[80]

The prospective suttee was accorded great respect but only if she made the decision to end her own life. Yet to 'volunteer' was merely a euphemism for automatic responses induced by centuries of injunction and custom; the entire history of widow burning influenced this choice and intensified a death wish lurking in the unconscious. For while the forces for life are strong, the death instinct will erupt when sanctioned and encouraged by society. Those medieval Christians who burned heretics are not psychically far removed from Brahmins and the families of suttees who did not permit the widow to change her mind.

At an unconscious level, society condoned the atrocity as a disguise for violent antagonistic drives in regard to the power of women. All emotions were manipulated in a grand design, a successful, barely masked effort to hide the murderous motives of the male towards the female. Love, devotion, respect and awe, revenge, lust for burning and for power and pride were amalgamated and institutionalized; in fact all of life's conflicting drives were shaped into a grandiose spectacle which often substituted women for the less potent, more distanced animal. Widows were much too powerful to have around, much too frightening and threatening, so there was nothing but to rid the world of them, not by means of mutilation, blood, and other guilt-arousing devices, but by the purifying fire, the god Agni, the conveyer of husband and wife to heaven.

Thus the suttee was glorified. As heroine, she acquired nobility, being sinner only until she died; her sins were now absolved, she received salvation, her husband and their ancestors as well.[81] With their ashes mingled, husband and wife live eternally in heaven, so say the mantras which accompany the soul of the suttee upwards towards heaven. Sometimes she even becomes a goddess; a number of South Indian goddesses had their origin when an ordinary widow followed her husband into the fire, and was deified soon thereafter.[82]

But there are consequences. As she burned, the widow left behind her a trail of destruction as retribution for the guilt accumulated by Raja and Brahmin. Even as Siva, maddened by Parvati's self-immolation, became utterly powerless, they too suffered severe psychic consequences. Mahisa participates in this mayhem.

It is hardly surprising then, that as legacy from this brutal past, the rite, largely modified by law and custom, has not been entirely overcome. It is reported that approximately three hundred widows are still sacrificed annually in Madhya Pradesh, Andhra Pradesh and Uttar Pradesh.[83] In a suburb of Bombay, in March 1990, a girl was burnt alive in an examination hall as she was writing her paper.[84] Daily in the homes of the families of their husbands, in altered form, the outlawed rites of suttee are perpetuated, now in a non-religious context. Often dissatisfied with the dowry brought by the bride, the husband's family burns the wife after dousing her with kerosene, setting her alight in her kitchen. The psychosis is rampant and associated eruptions are even today manifested in self-immolations only ostensibly for political reasons. Syama's is not an outdated fairy story but the unconscious life of Indians being externalized and put up to view for the world to ponder over the ways of the human mind.

Cow Sacrifice

Cows were sacrificed during the earliest period of recorded Indian antiquity by invading tribes and presumably, although no data survives, for millennia during a primordial age, by aboriginals. Among tribals as well as within the 'higher' religions of Hinduism and Islam, these rituals are still practised. Societal obsessions to perpetuate the sacrifice, despite the humanistic efforts introduced by Mahavir and the Buddha which continue till today, prompt an investigation into the meaning of the sacrifice of the Holy Mother and the subsequent sacrifice and resurrection of her son.

Texts

In her brilliant study of sacred cows (and bulls and horses) who are killed and eaten, O'Flaherty comments sardonically that 'the cows

are the *pièce de résistance* at the feasts of the Vedic gods.'[85] The
Vedic priest who idealizes the cow as Mother Nature also identifies
her as sacrifice:

> Just as the gods have released the cow whose foot was bound, about to
> be sacrificed, in the same way, release us from our sin.[86]

The earliest written prescriptions for domestic rituals include the
sacrifice of a cow when the bridegroom was received in the home
of the bride and again when the newly-married couple arrived in
their own home,[87] at the first-fruit ceremony,[88] and to honour the
deceased at his funeral.[89] A male relative or priest kills a barren cow
with a blow behind the ear. Her kidneys are placed in the hands of
the deceased, and the face is covered with a membrane.[90] Placing a
part of the dead body in physical contact with part of the body of
the cow is, as we shall observe, a vestige of a tribal rite which
Marshall recorded at Toda funerals. The ambivalence regarding
the mother continues up to the very end. For acquisition of
religious merit and worldly goods, every householder was required
to perform the *sulagava*, or 'spitted cow' sacrifice once in a
lifetime.[91] In the ritual of *gomedha* (cow sacrifice), in an ironic
inversion of her apparent benignity, as antithetical human drives
are reconciled, the victim provides the milk and *ghee* without
which the ritual cannot take place.[92]

In the *Sathapatha Brahmana* the cow is called *anubadhya* (to be
bound and immolated)[93] during the Soma sacrifice to Mitra and
Varuna and after the year-long sacrificial session:

> And whosoever gives a thousand or more (cows to the priests) he will
> slaughter all these: indeed everything is obtained, everything conquered
> by him who gives (when offered) thus in the proper order.[94]

During the *asvamedha* (Vedic horse sacrifice), and in conjunction
with human sacrifice, twenty-one barren cows were sacrificed.[95]

The general practice was to offer only barren cows. Sterility and
virginity, of itself evil, is dangerous and requires external counter-
activity. An unproductive womb is as problematic as one that has
not been fertilized. This provides the excuse to sacrifice the cow
with impunity. While the emphasis is on the cow whose womb is
either infertile or virgin, ambiguous verses put even this to
question:

> You are ours, Agni, Bharata, son of the sacrificers. We have sacrificed
> to you with barren cows,

> Dripping (flowing semen) and with pregnant *ashtapada* (eight-foot-ed) cows.[96]

With regard to a pregnant cow, the *Sathapatha Brahmana* gives very clear instructions for the preservation of the embryo, if indeed the priest should discover it during the sacrifice:

> They lay hands on the barren cow, and it having been quieted and the omentum having been pulled out... let him (the slaughterer) to search, probing for an embryo. If they do not find one, why need they care? and if they find one, atonement is made therefore.[97]

To kill a living embryo is forbidden: the embryo of ten months is kept alive, but the unfortunate mother is sacrificed.

Another text, the *Taittiriya Samhita*, eloquently describes the sacrifice of a pregnant cow. Here too, the priests were concerned to ensure the preservation of the embryo; if the cow was recognized to be with child, a barren cow was immediately substituted, but if her condition was not apparent, the *purohit* (priest) addressed the slaughtered victim thus:

Thee have I united with the gods, who has a tawny embryo and a womb of gold
Bring near, o bringer, remove away, O remover... (the slaughterer moves the embryo, *pradaksinam*)
I split apart thy urinator, thy womb, the two groins
The mother and the child, the embryo and the afterbirth
Let it be apart from thee... (He removes the embryo and pulls it down between the thighs)
The drop, far extending, of all forms, purified, wise, hath anointed the embryo. (He catches the liquids with his vessel)
With one foot, two feet, three feet, four feet, five feet, six feet, seven feet, eight feet may she extend over the worlds: hail.
May the two great ones, sky and earth, mingle for us this sacrifice. (He deposits and covers up the embryo with dead ashes)[98]

Manu rules that in a propitious ceremony a drink made of honey is first offered to kings, bridegrooms and returning Vedic students by the householder. A cow must be bound, slain, and then immolated, and these words accompany the ritual: 'My sin is destroyed, destroyed is my sin.'[99] The sacred or divine cow dies for the sin of the sacrifant who is absolved when the mother imago is killed. The guest is permitted to liberate the cow prior to her planned demise.[100] The mantras to accompany this provide the rationalization:

This cow is the mother of Rudra, Therefore I solemnly say unto all wise
men, kill not this harmless sacred cow.[101]

In the Mahisamardini myth the sin is Oedipal longing: later
Mahisa will attempt to eliminate the Mother Goddess, to actuate
matricidal fantasies, in order to obliterate the source of the conflict
which holds him back from gaining autonomy. But guilt intrudes,
forcing him to take the place of his intended Goddess victim. The
alternating ambivalent responses to internal pressures result now in
burning the mother and again in saving her when guilt accumulates
or when, with greater control over oneself, hostility towards the
mother is decreased and tender emotions are permitted to come to
the fore once again. Or perhaps, when all is said and yet not done,
the guilty sacrificer, still under the domination of the mother
imago, is too weak to perform what in fantasy he is free to imagine.

Toda ritual

The dependency, love and intimate involvement of the Toda
tribesman with the sacred she-buffalo did not preclude the
concomitant obsession to annihilate her profane counterpart. The
ti buffalo was deity: her opposite might have become a victim in
the funeral sacrifice. Even while she accompanied the dead person
into the next world, the funeral ritual included a reversal of the
manifest adoration of the mother cow, who was sometimes
described in terms which reveal hostility born of fear of the
'murderous barren buffalo'.[102]

The funeral provided an opportunity for the dramatization of
generally repressed inclinations. Here, insulated from daily life, the
cow was experienced in both her aspects. During the rites
performed for the dead in the sacred cow pen, sacred milk was
poured into the mouth of a human corpse, and the horn held by
the dead person was cornucopian, promising life in the hereafter.
In one instance, reported by Russell, the corpse of a girl was
brought out of the house with her feet resting on the forehead of a
buffalo.[103] At the final hour the Toda returned to the moment when
first he was put to the mother's breast at birth.

But simultaneously, the terrifying mother may turn violent: the
procedure of catching buffaloes for sacrifice entailed tremendous
skill, as sensing danger, they became wary, and once in a while a

cow or a bull would even gore the opponent. This skill carried great prestige, because the struggle was the responsibility not alone of the individual who was engaged in catching the buffalo, but of the entire society. The art is reminiscent of Egyptian and Cretan techniques: two men with arms interlocking seized the buffalo by the horns, bringing her to her knees. The animal was hit hard with severe blows and then 'with an axe deftly wielded', she was killed.[104]

This manifestation of the split cow imago may be conquered and butchered with impunity in the ritual, with little accompanying guilt, for the sacrifice is believed to be efficacious and the victim forgives as she and the departing soul go off together to the other world.[105] But not without appropriate lamentations couched in language which, in kinship metaphors, analogize the sacrifice and the deceased. 'As each animal falls, men, women and children group themselves round its head, and fondle, caress and kiss its face.'[106]

People wailed, touching each other's foreheads as they stood facing one another in pairs, showing signs of grief for the dead person and for the sacrificial victim. The mourners were enjoined to copulate in the fields prior to the funeral ceremony. Sexual excitement in response to the animal's cries and the mixed and merged energies released in the ritual helped achieve catharsis, with shame and remorse conveniently temporarily cancelled.[107]

By projecting his emotional conflict on to the buffalo cow and giving it expression in song and ritual, the Toda is able to be in touch and cope with the ambiguities of his condition *vis-à-vis* the mother, thereby modifying its effect to some degree. At the funeral, as in daily life, with obsessive repetition and intense adherence to custom, through the sublimation of conflicting drives, the individual is enabled to be relatively anxiety-free. One has only to experience the pathos of the poetry—its deep and true feeling—to comprehend its function as ritual therapy.

Other rituals

While in other tribal sacrifices the victim was male, which would suggest an operative taboo based on fear of a sinful impulse, there were also frequent prescriptions for the sacrifice of a cow. Among the Rengmas of Assam, the person who bestowed the Feast of Merit in celebration of a good harvest should first have had sexual intercourse with his wife, in the forest, during the day. Then, in the first of the big feasts, 'four or five or even more cows are killed...An old man of any clan kills the first cow by spearing it in the side...No prayers are offered.'

The victims' meat was distributed for feasting. On the second day of the feast, an unblemished cow was tied to a post, killed with a spear, the stomach slashed open, and thereupon the boys of the village staged a ritual battle for the acquisition of the intestines while others poured water over the boys.[108] In another instance, while the primary sacrificial animal of the Saoras was a male buffalo, cows were sacrificed to Jumtangbur Kittung, the spirit who steals cows and eats them, to protect the herds and to ensure the fertility of the crops,[109] very much in the spirit of the Vedic poetry which associated the cow with fecundity.

Birth of Mahisa Out of the Fire

As we have observed, while the particulars of the unusual birth, life and death of the hero differ in the variants, the story never departs from a consistent, underlying sequence. In the *Varaha Purana* the demon-princess turned buffalo-cow drinks water into which the seed of king/sage Sindhudvipa has accidentally been deposited. A valiant son is conceived and is then born. The *Skanda Purana* leaves the events of the conception in question, although the father is a rsi and the mother a demoness in buffalo form; Mahisa is definitely the son of the god Siva temporarily in the form of a cow in the *Kalika Purana*, with the Brahmin demon king in the paternal role, and presumably, the birth was a natural one, if one's imagination can be stretched to conceive of the god as mother cow.[110] Even though a female 'who is pregnant or where pregnancy is suspected is forbidden to burn herself with her dead husband,'[111] the writers of the *Vamana* and DBP defy these proscriptions by permitting Syama's leap into the fire while she is still with child. Phoenix-like, out of the burning womb of the buffalo cow, a healthy human infant emerges; the creatrix with the golden womb gives birth within the golden flames to a golden fair-complexioned son,[112] and simultaneously she perishes. Mahisa is born of the sacrifice and will die as the sacrifice.

When born he (the individual) lives whatever the length of his life may be. When he has departed, his friends carry him as appointed to the fire (of the funeral pyre) from whence he came, from whence he sprang.[113]

According to the DBP, as his parents were being engulfed in flames, Mahisa 'rose from his mother's womb from the midst of the funeral pyre.'[114] In the Rg Veda, 'the calf is the fire born of lightning', and 'fire and seed are equated in the Brahmana'.[115] This exemplifies a deeply pervasive concept; the destructive fire is creative; the seeds of rebirth are in the ashes of cremation. A cognate association interprets it as physical union: during intercourse the male makes an offering to the female ritual fires. Agni as creative heat is maternal. The sacrificer is assured that his soul, temporarily deposited in the body of the holocaust, will be resurrected.

In October 1990, certain events obsessively reflected the patterns represented in the myth. Children and young adults were burning themselves in a tragic eruption of an inherent, persistent elemental unconscious drive. Before they set themselves or their schoolmates alight, there are thoughts of sacrifice, and they speak of the immolation as a sacrifice. The rationalization to strike the match can come only from a cognate belief that life will arise out of the self-made pyre. The plague of burning, an atrocious contemporary perversion of the sacrificial traditions, seems to be as violently alive and active today as ever in the past. When traditional ritual and mythological sublimations have been forsaken, the unconscious drives emerge at random, spontaneously, regardless of social class or jati, time or place.[116]

To return to the myth, the miraculous birth of Mahisa is followed by the rebirth of Rambha:

> Rambha, too, emerged from the fire in another form out of affection towards his son. Rambha was known as Raktavija after he had changed his form.[117]

As the gods favour those who worship them, and Rambha had certainly paid his dues in overactive penances, he was rejuvenated by his *ista devata* (chosen deity) in an instantaneous transformation of death into life. His new form was as the demon Raktavija (blood seed), destined to battle by the side of his illustrious son during the travails the son would be fated to endure. Rambha's new name is not without symbolic significance. The mythmaker was surely aware that the son's function as sacrificial victim would be to furnish Raktadanta (Red-toothed), the Goddess, the blood of the sacrifice which she drinks for her own (and her devotees') revivification.

This late focus on the survival of the newborn does not entirely mask vestigial traces of the prehistoric requirement to sacrifice the first-born. The fire which is here midwife at the delivery of the infant is the fire which, in earlier times, consumed him. The rescue from death at birth might be a variant of the later layers of the myths, resulting from the slow ascent out of millennia of human sacrifice. As a victim must always be substituted for the original sacrifice, a ram for Isaac, Mahisa's mother could well be playing the role of suttee on the one hand and also be the oblation which redeems her son on the other. The guilty son is thus temporarily saved by the sacrifice of his mother and the rebirth of his father, whose death he had hoped for. If the boy actually wants his mother and to be rid of his father, the reversal is a perfect ploy to hide his true wishes.

The hero is born in the tragedy of destruction. He is only temporarily rescued, for Mahisa, the hero, part demon, part human, even part god, is destined to confront many obstacles but also to change the course of mythical history and eventually, after dismemberment as sacrifice, he will be resurrected and returned to the source. His birth is an especially appropriate symbol which will resurface in the final events.

Chapter Three The Labours of Mahisa

The First Labour: The Hero Withdraws

The *Vamana Purana* and the DBP offer hints about the little-known childhood of Mahisa. The fires which had destroyed the mother, miraculously and simultaneously brought son and father to life. Thus deprived of his mother, the orphan starts life under the protective guardianship of a powerful father who organizes a campaign against rival demons and vanquishes them all.[1] The charmed, favoured prince Mahisa inherits the danava kingdoms. But he suffers anxiety and guilt, longing for the lost mother for whose death he feels responsible. Moreover, he knows his successes are his father's, not his alone. In an effort to establish a separate identity, he must first undergo a severe initiation in the traditional ways.

The introduction by Brahmin priests of Mahisa's tapas into this late text (DBP) seems to be an attempt to come to terms with emotional ambivalences. Given Mahisa's situation at birth, nothing can be accomplished in regard to Rambha's wishes for a superson who will conquer the world, without offering a suitable sacrifice with hope for absolution and augmented powers. He therefore withdraws, recreating the same austerity conditions which had led to his own birth. The demon child is still the buffalo animal, not yet ready to engage in battle with the kings of the world and subsequently with the gods.[2] He is threatened by the forces of nature, but at the same time, in his struggle for survival, he is impelled by a will towards growth. As both instinct and the drive to become independent of instinct, he is the animal nature predominating in childhood, but simultaneously he represents the anticipated ontogeny energized by the tensions involved in the interaction of the *sattvic* and *rajasic gunas* (see p. 95). This buffalo energy will be useful to counteract the destructive effects of the tapas. The eventual achievement of a harmonious relationship of consciousness and the unconscious is implied in the austerities.

The period of initiation is the severance process in embryo, making it possible and encouraging the adolescent buffalo demon to reach adulthood.

For this period, the buffalo form is appropriate; it simultaneously symbolizes the sacrificer bent on expiating his sins and the victim of the sacrifice. By the time the Puranas were recorded, the Brahmins had abjured animal sacrifice for the most part. As the unconscious does not distinguish between the actual animal sacrifice and its mythological analogies,[3] the buffalo imagery is utilized successfully as metaphor to fix the identification.

Longing for the lost mother's breast, the orphaned child is still in a precarious position, entirely overwhelmed by memories of the consuming fires. As survivor, he associates himself with the death of his mother and believes that he was its cause; he neither saved her, nor died in her stead; in point of fact, he is conveniently relieved of the feared maternal dominance. Faced with this situation, he hopes for absolution by undergoing penances.

Also, considered from a human standpoint, Mahisa cannot avoid being steeped in guilt and shame in regard to his father's death as well. (Rambha had been gored to death by the horns of a lascivious rival during the attack on Syama, the provocative mother. In a momentary intrusion of the unconscious, the myth introduces a surrogate for the son who wishes to eliminate the father and to possess the mother.) The forbidden thought is immediately repressed when the yaksas, representing consciousness, law and order, conquer the stranger buffalo, but Mahisa nevertheless suffers the guilt of the parricide. The change in Rambha's name to Raktavija supplies a new identity and conveniently masks the dangerous intuition; Mahisa wins, as the eliminated father is reborn. But there is more: a parallel cause for guilt is antagonism towards the god Indra, the reptilian murderer of his kin. Moreover, he inherits the desire to retaliate against the father from the collective unconscious. But he is not yet ready to externalize these feelings of revenge; so, as penitent, at this stage he internalizes the anger by means of the tried and true method of ascetic exercises.

Mahisa also suffers the shame of his triune conception: he is grotesque monster, longing to rise to levels more appropriate to his divine inheritance, and like his hero predecessors, he is thoroughly misunderstood by the conventional order, which has a prejudiced view of him, one accentuating the aberrations. He is regarded merely as buffalo, who lives in the labyrinthian depths of the dark nether world, a demonic beast, and he is to be feared as the chaotic contents of the unconscious are to be feared. But as he is born of a royal line, the son of a human king, rsis and also of god, he finds his situation unbearable, his sensibilities repressed. To make matters worse, while the boon of transformability will prove to be useful in subsequent trials, it is also a veritable curse, as it increases the complexities of the already multiple heritage. Part animal, part demon, part human and part god, the potential for instantaneous transformations puts him in constant danger of dissolution, as he slides almost precipitately from one to another fluid condition.

By projecting one persona at a time, Mahisa strives to maintain a fixed role, but these are efforts in futility. When he is animal child, he longs to be human king; as human, he longs to be god; and when finally he convinces himself that he is god (Indra), he will long for reunion with the Goddess. The forces within the demon psyche are perennially at war with one another, forever locked in struggle; integration is precluded, with the result that he is trapped in slavish obedience to the conflicts within the self. This is the tragedy of the hero, the paradigm of the human condition, aptly symbolized by the buffalo demon.

The major problem is that there is no central core within his tormented soul. This fundamental agony will later drive him in frenzy and desire towards absorption into the Goddess who represents the fixed centre of the self for the hero and for her devotees.

The sacrifice after the battle, when he is killed by the Goddess, is prefigured when Mahisa withdraws to Mt Sumeru to perform tapas. Burdened as he was with guilt and shame, Mahisa may very well even have cut off parts of his flesh and undergone other mutilations in the manner of fellow demon devotees and of devotees of the Goddess throughout history, although the DBP does not specifically mention self-mortification (see Chapter Seven). Or his sacrifice may have been of the mind only, as in the Manasic Yajna. We are merely informed that he

> performed very severe and excellent tapasya, wonderful even to the
> gods.... Meditating on his Ista Devata (the deity for his worship) in his
> heart, elapsed [sic] a full ten thousand years.[4]

As Mahisa astonishes the gods with harsh and painful penances, Brahma calls him virtuous. The guilt diminishes; the bad demon becomes a good demon, and equivalent now even to the gods. This is possible for Mahisa because of his paternal lineage and also because

> asceticism hurts the gods, producing a challenge from men which breaches the basic Vedic relationship of human dependence on gods or demonic inferiority to the gods. Asceticism negates the distinction between categories of gods, demons and men.[5]

Long-term meditation and concentration should have resulted in transcendence and merging with his chosen deity, to enable him to renounce temporal greed and all desire, with loss of ego, with all his troubles finally eliminated. But things are seldom so simple. These preliminary tapas, it will be learned, are not a viable solution, for even severe penance to overcome atavistic tendencies will not lead to complete cure. Mahisa will change to suit the identification needs of the mythmakers; like pieces of a shattered mirror, his destiny remains fragmented right up to the moment of his death.

Internally a struggle arises between the increase of power due to tapas and fear and the desire for submission. Like the child who fantasizes, Mahisa is terrorized by his own growing independent strength. Other factors have become operative now as well: the impulse to possess the unavailable mother splits and is accompanied by guilt, and the motherless child's frustration over unrequited instinctual needs gains the upper hand.

No longer cowed into total submission and not having gained genuine courage either, Mahisa only now begins to be aware of his own identity; as he begins to live and to feel, he is on the way to becoming a full-fledged hero. Power accumulates, consciousness germinates and guilt diminishes in the heat of the concentrated austerities: now he is involved in establishing himself as an independent being, honing the steel of his character for the eventual fulfilment of forbidden wishes. Like the small child who tests god and finds him far from omnipotent, Mahisa begins to dream about outrageous goals. He no longer wishes for mere freedom but for conquest of the universe, for everything, including release from his buffalo form, defeat of the gods, and conquest of the world. Having established himself as partially separate, the child fantasizes his own deification. He believes that the great internal heat generated by tapas, like the sun, will produce a force strong enough to conquer even the gods. It is a child's psychology, born of violent aggressive feelings, in the beginning well repressed in the pressure-cooker body of the demon.

From this time onward, his actions will be related to the biological clock which determines the growth of human consciousness but also to the avoidance of counterforces, which in India are accorded serious consideration and given due respect as well. Always he is at risk of regression; the consciousness/unconscious equation will shift in weights and values as the lowly buffalo hero ascends and then once again falls prey to tamasic influences. So while the hero had grown to expect immortality as the reward for his virtuous austerities, he is very soon brought close to reality by Grandfather Brahma. Mahisa's first request for immortality is not granted, for demons are inevitably fated to die. Mahisa finds it impossible to accept the certainty that he is doomed, and so a crafty mind invents a ploy, 'Let woman be the cause of my death.'[6]

This request by the buffalo who wallows in muddy ponds and finds comfort in the maternal waters of the earth sounds more like a wish for final submission. Yet, he boasts, in a bombastic defence against anxiety rather than a statement of the way he sees reality:

'There is none among women who can cause my death. How can woman slay me? They are too weak.'[7]

In simplistic, childish denial Mahisa defines as 'weak' the very cause of his primary fears. And when Brahma instructs him that death will occur 'through a woman', Mahisa in all probability finds solace in the verbal expeession of a truth he has understood all along.

An underlying defeatism in his thinking is recognizable. He says what he really means and desires, as the statements suggest an unconscious incestuous wish to return to the mother who gave him birth. He may not be unaware of the futility of his boasts about his superior strength, as no amount of hubris can entirely conceal the fundamental and enduring original bonds of mother and son.

But there is a certain amount of power in these loud pronouncements as well, for they are the means by which his will to be separate is expressed. For the time being the hero will focus on his own masculine capabilities in the form of martial exploits, and he will thus be anchored safely to a level of development strong enough to withstand the ever-present tamasic pulls. His defensiveness is made evident by his vehemence, and a great struggle awaits him, as his longing for reintegration will paradoxically lead him into battle with a female whose masculine characteristics are even greater than his own. It will later become apparent that military prowess is not by any means a male prerogative.

The Second Labour: The Penitent as Cakravartin

Since earliest times, chief and monarch have been associated with a powerful bull deity which simultaneously served as sacrificial victim. The Mahisamardini myth is about animal/king/god dynamics. There was nothing startling in the transformation of the penitent demon buffalo into a monarch who ruled the world as, nourished and developed in local soil, the Indian version is a branch of the universal, ancient myth.

The demon rules in the underworld (or in the ocean city named Mahisa).[8] But as soon as he intrudes upon and conquers the *triloka* (three worlds), his reality changes. It is taken for granted in the myth that since he is descended from demon royalty or from the gods, the orphan Mahisa will temporarily regain his rightful status, either by virtue of his blood, as a result of success in conquest, or of his karma. So after Raktavija and Mahisa had overcome their demon rivals, Mahisa 'obtained sovereignty and brought the whole world under his control.'[9]

Buffalo demonhood is merged with universal Cakravartin monarchical status, and now sadistic responses emerge in full force. It matters little whether demon, god or human sits on the throne: the king seizes all authority, assumes all symbols of royalty—the title and the throne, the umbrella and the *Rajasuya*. Well guarded by loyal commanders, he lives in splendour with the unlimited wealth of his royal coffers. The army and administrative structures, the law, wise ministers versed in the sastras, palaces, queens and concubines are under his authority and control. The king is adept at *yoga*, he studies, has a charitable disposition, is devoted to performing great sacrifices, and above all, he supplies the Brahmins with 'profuse quantities of gifts'.[10] To maintain this position, he is accorded the prerogative of perpetrating acts of violence and savagery, encouraged, supported and extolled in the institution of war. This right to abrogate the laws of neighbouring kingdoms encourages conquests, theft of the enemy's land and wealth, and rampant self-interest. The monarch is thus led in a predictable sequence towards the sins of killing, stealing and even at times of excessive drinking.[11] Rapacious tyranny is made out to be justice, for the king is imaged as a faultless mighty protector, the conqueror even of the gods:

> The Pandya king, who wears rich ornaments across his broad shoulders, defeated Indra whose mighty arm was the dread thunderbolt.[12]

Shulman takes great pains to describe the rhetoric so frequently adopted by ancient kings in India, more fantasy and grandiloquent proclamation than historical reality. In fact the ruler is more often than not only a weak reflection of the rhetoric. For while he is theoretically virtuous and mature, actually, he is sometimes merely a figurehead or even a functionary of the priestly class who represent the gods on earth.

> The pattern as a whole suggests a conception of the king...as innately flawed, weighed down with an inescapable onus and always in need of healing by some outside power such as a temple deity, Brahmin or magician...He [the king] is the pivot of the whole system, but he lacks true power.[13]

The human ruler is omnipotent only in fantasy; his vast array of soldiers, weapons and armies of fighting men and beasts do not reflect his true character. But he tolerates no criticism and demands total allegiance.[14]

Because subjects are forbidden to express their perceptions of their emperor's clothes, intuitions about the true nature of the sovereign are neatly projected on to the demon, who is portrayed as the tyrant monster of myth and nightmare. In fact, Mahisa's rule is no more nor less tyrannical or demonic than the norm. The chaos of his reign is the routine chaos of perpetual war, pillage and rape, and the result of expediency. The goal is always the same: to sustain power. The demon is just as human as the human king.

In one dramatic scene the megalomaniacal fantasy is set in contrast to the tragic realities of life. A powerful demon king, Bhanda, analogue for Mahisa, eulogizes his fifty sons; they had been slain during the battle with the Goddess and her *saktis* (female warriors). He sheds profuse tears, he grumbles and babbles, and with broken heart, he falls from his throne into a swoon. Like David upon the death of Absalom, the demon king is reduced to his simple, pathetic human self. But immediately the real person is replaced by the image of the king. A minister warns him not to be 'a victim of sorrow like an ordinary uncultured fellow. . . . It is the righteous and eternal path [of heroes] . . . Death in battle should not be bewailed.'[15] Hubris will invariably over-power the genuine human emotions; Mahisa is similarly spurred on toward megalomaniacal dreams of conquering first the male gods and then the Mother Goddess.

A vestige of the annual struggle for the royal title which promises the winner the rival's queen or virgin is implied in Mahisa's conquest of all the Ksatriya kings of the earth. The unconscious expectation will germinate and re-emerge when Mahisa first confronts the Goddess. It will then become evident that it is not possible to prevail against the cyclical nature of a universally applicable psychic response system: the acquisition of world power will always turn out to be a mere illusion. Mahisa is always oppressed by the predictable sequential pattern, as one emotion follows another: unlocked infantile rage, the guilt accompanying it, and concomitant need for self-punishment; relief gained from externalizing fiercely aggressive emotions; further accumulation of guilt; again the need for expiation through self-sacrifice and death; and finally, the eventual return to the womb from which the hero has sprung.

The desperate nature of these stages within the recurring cycle can be observed in Mahisa's wild rush to conquer. Deprived in infancy of a relationship with his mother, the orphan feels res-ponsible for her death and carries the burden of guilt throughout his life. This stimulates an intense counter-reaction heightened to an obsessive level, spurred on by anger, insolence, and pride which hide the need to regress. Perpetually seeking release, having conquered his terrestrial rivals and established a new sovereignty, the king buffalo proceeds to conquer heaven.

The Third Labour: The Indra/Mahisa Battle

The battle between Mahisa and Indra is a multiform of traditional mythological motifs. There are echoes here of the ancient Indra/Vrtra struggle, and it also anticiaptes Durga's defeat of the buffalo demon. The hero seeks victory over a powerful antagonist in the

form of a giant, a dragon or a king. As monster, Mahisa is dragon;
as king he is hero; having tasted blood, the asura now dreams of
further conquests which will involve him even more drastically in
sundering the established order, with Indra, the source of his
primal rage, as prime target. For he remembers the god as
crocodile (dragon, instinct, repressed id and sin) who devoured the
royal demon uncle. Or perhaps Indra was the stranger buffalo who
approached his mother and killed his father, acting out every boy's
wish. In a convenient reversal fantasy, the buffalo demon wills
himself to be god (Indra, the father, the superego). He is the child
who dreams of eliminating his major rival and imagines himself to
have the strength of a bull. Until these identifications with the
father imago are challenged in combat, the individual is caught in
his own repressed, but not forgotten, fear and envy; growth is
crippled and development thwarted.[16]

The mania for personal omnipotence with the wish to be god
cannot be entirely separated from the common experience of being
possessed by the god. In India, where psychological boundaries are
unstable and elements of aggregate structures interact, there is
nothing at all remarkable about deification fantasies. Shulman's
term 'symbolic cluster', applied to the interdependence of Brahmin
and royal qualities,[17] suits the Mahisa/Indra relationship as well. Or
put another way, the Mahisa/Indra duality accords more accurately
with all the dimensions of the human condition than either one
when standing alone.

With absolute faith in his own military prowess and high
expectations, Mahisa sends a messenger to Indra challenging him
to battle, using terms of preposterous conceit:

> Offer your services to the high souled Mahisa; He is the lord.[18]

Indra is commanded to submit to the demon's protection or to
fight:

> The Danava never becomes angry with his opponents who become
> submissive like a servant; if you surrender and serve him, he will, out of
> mercy, grant an allowance to you.[19]

Rage has surfaced, and the tantrums begin. The dramatic battle
with the gods will serve to discharge the anxiety born of fear and
will exact vengeance for real and imagined wrongs, for Mahisa the
Cakravartin is the dependent child, still very much at the lowest

rung of the ladder. There is little subtlety in this portion of the narrative; the phraseology emphasizes the grandiose nature of the wish to usurp heaven, with the promise of worldly gratifications and displacement of the father. In heaven, Kamadhenu, the cow that fulfils all desires, will offer her sweet milk to comfort the orphan; he will achieve absolute power and sexual attainments of multiple kinds. To drink intoxicating *soma* and to receive Brahmanical sacrifices will be his prerogative. This is the impulsive, narcissistic child, unable to realize his true position and not yet adequately tamed.

The child wishes to invert his dependent situation, for the father to become the son and the son to become the father, but the dialogue is kindergarten playground talk, hardly the serious challenge of an evil demon. This ancient text is dealing with the universal struggle towards consciousness, as the intensity of the drive, the blindness of narcissism, the polarization of the pair of combatants who turn out to be more identical than opposed, the competitive insistence on superior sexual potency, is certain to prove that psychological states are common to different cultures and ages.

Prior to the battle, there is name calling, derisive sneers, imprecations and braggadocio: the licentious, hypocritical, treacherous demon projects these shadow traits on to the gods, in the same way that they had been projected on to him. There is also inordinate pride as he declares:

If hundreds of thousands of warriors like Indra come, I do not fear any of them at all.[20]

At first Mahisa, arrogant and dogmatic, insecure and fearful, is all bravado. But the primary thrust is a blatantly sexual one; in frank rivalry, Mahisa accuses Indra of impotency:

He is licentious and can only seduce others' wives... depending for his strength only on the beauties of the Apsaras or heavenly prostitutes.[21]

But Mahisa will soon delight in these very *apsaras* himself. Moreover, he will go to his father's bed and sleep in it: 'We will enjoy the Deva women in the Nandana Garden.'[22] Mahisa's sexual doubts are to be read in his defensive shouts regarding the prowess of his own hoofs and horns. To gain courage he falls back on the sexuality and potency which has always been attributed to his species. Like the conventional hero, he states: 'I alone can conquer the Devas',[23] needing no help from the army of daityas. He presents an invincible persona, and indeed, the outcome of this battle will temporarily justify this illusion.

But the buffalo demon's counterparts, the gods, retort in kind, for they share his characterological flaws and infantile responses. With unmasked emphasis on the sexual rivalry between the two, Indra matches Mahisa's aggressive language with equally derogatory comments:

> You are clever in striking with your horns: you don't know anything about warfare: therefore I will cut off your both [sic] weapons and render you powerless. Out of your horns, I will make a good bow.[24]

It is a warning to the enemy that sexual strength can be stolen. As Indra is plainly jealous, he will help himself to Mahisa's source of power, neatly reinforcing O'Flaherty's comment that Freud would have loved the Puranas.

Images of bull and horn, of fertility, sexual prowess and martial vigour, vibrate in the abuses hurled back and forth before the battle. To his dismay, the great warrior god of the Vedas, Indra, who himself had 'cut Susna (demon of drought) to pieces with his horn',[25] is now, in turn, threatened by the very same weapon. The horn is a common image in the fantasies of sadistic patients. One dreamt 'he is a bull who thrusts his horns into the bellies of a rival so that the bloody entrails gush out.'[26] Sex and violence in the Puranas! There will be more, much more, later, in Mahisa's battle with the Goddess.

Indra is moving into a mêlée of conflicting responses. He is constantly committing crimes; thus he is always followed by evil, for by Puranic times, the great Vedic god is no longer the king of the gods.[27] The mythmakers are thus happy to identify with Mahisa, who will mock the sinner and then defeat him, or perhaps Indra sees a good opportunity to displace his former sin on to the taunting demon.[28] Although when first challenged, Indra holds the demon in contempt, before the day is over he will flee the field, as Mahisa proves he is after all a master of warfare. Now, Mahisa is the paradigmatic hero: 'The heroes confront the gods as if they were their own equals, but their hubris is always and cruelly punished.'[29]

For the Brahmin priest who has Mahisa as his *alter ego*, the scenario is true to life. As buffalo, Mahisa is brute force, ever ready to kill the feared and hated father As child he fantasizes that he can do so, and as king endowed with godlike traits, he sees little distinction between himself and Indra. But the priests realize the danger, or they hope that the gods as superego will reverse evil wishes, and indeed, ultimately Mahisa will be controlled by the masculinized Mother Goddess who will punish him with death.

How can the demon dare to challenge the god? There are many in India today whose interpretations may be more Christian than a general Hindu viewpoint would seem to warrant. Some established scholars and even educators dichotomize the gods as good and demons as evil, ignoring the less obvious message of myth and art. Even the author of a recent volume, entitled *Mahishasurmardini*, maintains that the texts 'are full of heroic but impressive accounts of the periodic struggle of good with evil in the form of Devas and Asuras.... Time and again this beneficent Government of the Devas controlling the metabolism of the organizer of the universe, have been overthrown by the pride and ambition of some violent demon king, possessed of a reckless will-to-power.'[30] As a result of this view of gods and demons, they are frequently regarded as moral polarities, but sometimes two contradictory ideas are combined in a single expression—that demons are evil and gods are good and each has the qualities of the other!

Confronting the ambiguities inherent in the Indian demon/god relationship squarely, O'Flaherty cleared the air, dislodging the two forces from their fixed opposite positions and shifting the focus so as to return to the original meanings of the texts. The vacillations of demons as repositories of both good and evil are studied in all their complexity and the conclusion is reached that demons are 'ambivalent figure(s) to which the myth inevitably returns'.[31] Thus the Vedic gods and demons are opposed, as demons are expected to act according to their nature, which is to be evil,[32] but the Brahmanas, and then later texts, abstain from judgements concerning the morality of demon and god; and while there are some Puranic references to demons as evil, 'most of them are isolated reversals of more common patterns in which the demons are not responsible for the creation of evil.'[33] Nothing can be stated categorically, except that gods and demons are antagonistic.

By nature gods and demons are alike.... They only become distinct
when they are engaged in battle.... [there are] numerous Indian
texts... [about] the 'consubstantiality' of gods and demons, the
wickedness of gods, the virtue of demons, the brotherhood in actual
lineage as well as in behaviour. The strife is intensified by the sibling
rivalry of the brothers.[34]

It is important to note O'Flaherty's emphasis on family inter-
relationships. It is not a question of evil demons in opposition with
good gods, but rather of consanguine enemies locked in combat.

In one example, this viewpoint is explicitly articulated by one of
the most evil/virtuous demons. In the early texts, Prahlada is
'angry, lustful, opposing the gods',[35] but in the DBP he suffers
greatly at the hands of his father because of his loyalty to Visnu; he
pleads with Devi not to favour the gods alone:

We are your sons, just as the Devas are.·... There is no difference
between the Daityas and the Devas.... The Suras and Asuras all have
sprung from the permutations and combinations of the three qualities.[36]

With resignation Prahlada adds:

Every embodied soul possesses always cupidity, anger, covetousness;
how then can one expect to remain without any quarrels with others?[37]

Evil exists, but it is universal, not the trait of one or another group
alone. Later Prahlada recites the crimes of Chandra, Indra, the
priest of the gods Brihaspati, and of Visnu to prove that they too
have perpetrated acts of greed, lust and jealousy; indeed, that they
are criminals.[38] His argument that all are brothers, all sons of the
same Mother Goddess who causes their strife for her own pleasure
is a plausible point of view which acquires more and more validity
as the myths are examined carefully. Even Brahma is aware of this
reality:

You [Prahlada] will regain this kingdom in the Savarnik Manvantara.
Then Bali will come in your family as the grandson of Prahlada and will
conquer the Triloki and will get name and fame throughout his
kingdom.[39]

In another quarrel, Siva scolds the demon Sankachuda:

No need for further quarrels. Think that you all belong to the same
Kasyapa family. The sins that are incurred... the murder of a Brahmin,
etc., are not even 1/16 of the sins of hostilities amongst relatives.[40]

The medieval artists who created the great sculptured panels shared these perceptions and were intuitively aware of the constant struggle between equivalent forces in interaction. Two great masterpieces, the Narasimha/Hiranyakasipu panel in Dasavatara Cave 15, Ellora, and the Durga Mahisamardini panel at Mamallapuram, are the result of profound insights regarding the integration of conflicting drives (see Chapter Ten). Evil is an independent, iron-hard entity, invading at random now one group, now another, wreaking destruction with little regard for the moral state of its victims or for the systems they invent to avoid it.

Folk ritual and perceptions also lead us to understand the material ground from which the conceptions of god and demon arose. While at the village level today distinctions between good and evil *are* posed as polarities, as we have observed both gods and demons share the qualities of malevolence and beneficence. In fact, the entire social fabric of the people of India rests upon the premise that to propitiate the deity is to ward off that particular god's evil influence, always alert to harm a careless worshipper, while the demon is often seen as the protector, without whom survival cannot be guaranteed. As in the case of 'God is an elevated demon, as Satan is a deposed and degraded god',[41] in the East, demons often ascend towards godhood, and gods are demoted, as changing ideas blur divisions. Gods sin, demons are virtuous. The *sine qua non* of reality as understood by the majority of villagers even today applies to human groups as well: 'Those who were Raksasas (demons) before, they became the Brahmins in the Kali Yuga.'[42]

For a fuller understanding of Mahisa, we can refer to the arcane animism that lies deeply embedded in the Brahmanical texts. Mahisa will respond to the god Indra's taunts, marshalling his war machine, but not by any means as an evil demon intent on conquering the good gods. Both Mahisa and Indra are merely the sublimating symbols of animal/human aggressions, given name and form merely to identify the oppositions. The battlefield is the crucible within which traits are fused beyond recognition, in congruence with the floating symbolism of the folk tradition.

Familiarity with a few myths concerning Indra's perfidious efforts to inhibit the demons' desires to attain supreme power will help divest Mahisa and his fellows of the entire burden of guilt for evil.[43] Mahisa is merely another relative, and when the charts of comparison are aligned Mahisa the demon, if only by default, is less demonic than the father/brother god Indra. He is one of the malignant, life-hoarding ogre gods the hero tries to slay, 'god the avenger, the ventriloquized destructive impulse'.[44] Since all evil comes from outside, the primitive projects his evil thoughts sometimes on the god, sometimes on to the demons.

The architect of the gods Tvastr (Visvakarman), probably the father of Indra, married a demoness. Ambiguities introduced at the beginning of mythical history will perpetually plague the demon/god relationships. Loyal to both gods and demons, 'the maker of all' initiates the world by upsetting the ideal order of things. He fathers a three-headed son, the god/demon Visvarupa (or Trisiras, Three Heads), who, like Mahisa, is born an anomaly. He too practises very serious austerities. The real trouble started when Trisiras, in Indian fashion favouring his mother, uttered mantras for the demons; similarly Tvastr, permitting loyalty to override classification, fashioned weapons for his demon wife's people. Trisiras definitely can be described as a paragon of virtue; nevertheless, even in the Vedas, under the influence of soma, the revered god of thunder Indra committed a dastardly crime against him: out of sheer human, fraternal jealousy of the powers Trisiras had gained by austerities, he performed a triple beheading with his thunderbolt. This deed is a paradigmatic act, one that is repeated endlessly in later myths and history, and will be the unhappy finale of the life of Mahisa.

In fury, the bereaved father, the forger, created another son, Vrtra, born, like Mahisa, out of the fires. In the Rg Veda, he is the dragon who withholds the waters, but by the eleventh century we may suspect sibling rivalry to be at the root of the writers' concern. The father instructs Vrtra 'to kill Indra, my greatest enemy'; and 'as a son becomes then really a son when he obeys the commands of his father',[45] Vrtra is forced into agreement. By resorting to trickery, however, Indra also kills the second brother, but not before sibling fears and rivalry are dramatized in a bloody battle between the two, during which in an act of love and hate, Vrtra temporarily swallows Indra. There are others too, as early as the Rg Veda, whose heads were removed by Indra's thunderbolt.

A brave warrior who defeats his enemy (even if not by fair means), is termed virtuous, a convenient euphemism to cover a variety of protagonists. As god and demon each claim to fight for what is right, sibling hate and love in the texts know no bounds: in subtle form Indra entered into the womb of his pregnant step-mother, the demoness Diti; out of jealousy he sliced the embryo into seven and then seven parts again.[46] The half-brothers were consequently born as the forty-nine Maruts who paradoxically helped Indra to sunder Vrtra limb from limb.[47] Mahisa, desiring to re-enter into his mother, this time in forbidden love, cuts her into pieces with a sword when his love is frustrated, proving that gods and demons are morally indistinguishable.

If Indra is guilty of fratricide, at another time he is also the parricide. Tvastr the creator, who 'begets and feeds mankind,'[48] is the father of Indra. While in the Rg Veda 'a bull begat the bull for joy of battle',[49] other passages hint at dreadful events. That the father wished to kill the son and that the son killed the father, is plainly stated in the Rg Veda:

> By his birth, Indra conquered Tvastr, stole the soma and drank it from the sacrificial cup.[50]

> Who made your mother a widow? Who wished to kill you when you were lying still or moving? What god helped you when you grabbed your father by the foot and crushed him?[51]

O'Flaherty situates this mutual antagonism in the context of Indo-European mythology and of later Indian texts.[52] These allusions to the father who wanted to slay the son Indra and to Indra's revenge may be memory traces of the ritual sacrifice of the first-born until recently practised by some Indian tribes.

The mythmaker adapts each character to his own psychic needs: thus the god Indra enters his mother's womb and cuts up his siblings, but guilt is eliminated when all unite against common enemies, who also may be brothers. For parricide there is the appropriate excuse of the father's wish for infanticide, dismissing the convenient result that mother and son are left alone.

Rage prompts Mahisa to prepare a vengeful reprisal against Indra, the father symbol, but lurking beneath this justifiable motivation is the one that really counts: Indra and the gods, so favoured by the Goddess, must be eliminated before Mahisa can begin to face the intricacies of his (the mythmaker's) own complexes regarding the beneficent but terrible Mother.

Indra and Mahisa are therefore not unlike in regard to instinctual, treacherous and incestuous designs. They are part of what O'Flaherty has referred to as this 'incestuous caste'. It is not surprising that, even though Indra is the highest Rg Vedic god, in the Puranic literature, a now demoted Indra and the demon Mahisa are analogues, with their background, fundamental characteristics and essential qualities not easily distinguishable. They are alike, and therefore opposed. Their very symmetry results in conflicts.

This directs attention to the mutability of the myth, where fluidity, and the continual disruption and reorganization of symbols are the reflection of the unstructured unconscious contents of the mind. So, the positioning of Mahisa and Indra as opposites is a construct which can be maintained only in its ideal form, for neither the split nature of the demon in all his aspects nor the god's can be stabilized and fixed securely. Thus Mahisa is god who claims:

> I am now Indra, Rudra, and Surya. In fact, I am the lord of the entire world.[33]

And in the fantasy/dream of the myth, who knows if he really is or is not the god he claims to be? As living units of the unconscious psyche, subject to what Jung calls a 'high degree of disassociability', Indra and Mahisa are repositories for random unconscious fragments which erupt and fluctuate, so that their roles are often interchangeable; both are facets of a larger whole made up of transposable parts.

Indra was the all-powerful king of the gods in Vedic times when the buffalo sired cows, served as draught animal, was source of nourishment and sometime sacrificial victim. But in the lives of the indigenous tribal and agricultural communities, the constantly-feared and therefore revered buffalo was also often believed to be the deity. Indra is even referred to as Mahisa (buffalo)/Maha-isa (great man),[52] as the central role of the buffalo stimulated ambivalent imagery. Now, as the various negative but sacral projections are distributed between the two, Mahisa's is a force equivalent to Indra's.

Indra and Mahisa share bovine/godly parentage and abnormal birth: Indra emerges from the side of his cow mother[55] and Mahisa from the fire. Both were abandoned by the mother, Mahisa at birth and Indra at an early age, when he was still a 'calf'. Their common element is water; Indra, the god of rain and thunder, hides in a lotus in a pond to do penance for brahmanicide after the defeat of Vrtra and the release of the floodwaters. Mahisa rules in an ocean city or the underworld and, as buffalo, he is never far from muddy swamps. Both because of this and their association with the bull they are linked with animal, human and vegetal fertility, which is further associated with magnified sexual prowess and male promiscuity. They are like two great buffaloes, aggressive rivals for the female's favours; the weaker animal is driven off, as Indra and the gods will be after Mahisa has stolen *Indriya* (Indra's physical power) and has established himself and his demon peers in heaven.

Each is the sovereign ruler of his own domain, each the epitome of martial strength and heroic valour and endowed with magical powers; equally both are projections of the unconscious which carry remnants of animal ancestry. The Vedic Indra had consumed soma which flowed right through him, and from what came out of his nose, a lion sprang, from his ears, a wolf and from the lower opening, a tiger.[56] In our myth, he is a crocodile. The focus is on their transformation into animals, a trait they share with heroes of other cultures. As for beheadings, Indra is an inveterate head chopper, and Mahisa will have his own severed by the Goddess (suggesting that the claim to superior sexual prowess is born of fears of castration). The demon and the god symbolize all the terrors the mythmaker recognizes as lurking within his own psyche: they are common to god and demon alike. The most obvious is the mania for power, which makes of each a monster of self-aggrandizement and leads to immoral, even criminal behaviour. It is hypocritical and manipulative at best, but violent and rapacious as the norm; this is the underbelly of the adult human condition, the narcissism of the infant now in full bloom, exposed to view with little dissembling. The myth reveals the shadow.

Indra is licentious and addicted to others' wives, he is even a rapist; but he is also singularly jealous. He is avaricious, greedy, violent, a parricide and fratricide. Superstitious and impulsive, he rejoices in others' sufferings; yet cowardly, easily deluded and overwhelmed with terror, he flees the battlefield. He breaks contracts, swears falsely and instigates all kinds of trouble. Indeed there seems to be no evil known to man that Indra does not employ. Nevertheless there are certain manifest differences which ultimately set him apart from the demon.

While Indra is often the sacrificer, sometimes performing one hundred horse-sacrifices,[57] as deity he is more accustomed to receiving the sacrifices of others. Indeed Indriya, which assures success in battle, is gained by means of offerings to the god. This is the simple and crucial distinction, for although the buffalo demon steals Indriya and appropriates the sacrifices to the gods, his real karma is to *be* the sacrifice. No matter how many metaphors are mixed, ultimately he cannot escape his basic animal nature. The Vedic texts even require that as buffalo he be sacrificed to Indra himself. So, while Indra is even called 'buffalo' in the Vedas,[58] and once, to lie with the queen he entered the sacrificial horse himself,[59] he is never the actual victim. That is Mahisa's fate. The immortal god will never die, although he is subject to constant demotion and all kinds of transformation.

> Taking their weapons and riding on their battle v6hicles the gods accepted Mahisa's challenge.
> Then started the exciting battle between great warriors full of war cries from both sides.[60]

The antagonists face each other on the field of battle and plunge into a 'terrible fight'. (The description in the DBP bridges Indra's struggle with Vrtra, which Indra won, with Mahisa's with the Goddess, which he lost.) Riding on his elephant to face Indra, Mahisa is the standard-bearer and symbol for the countless silenced victims who served as substitutes for the sacrificer's compulsion to offer his own flesh to the gods for various purposes.

Each battles with a variety of similar weapons, but notwithstanding his earlier boast, Indra's *vajra* is ultimately no match for Mahisa's hoof, horn, tail and breath, energized to the peak of power by his rage. His transformations into lion and buffalo add fuel to his already intensified brute strength. Mountains shudder, the world trembles, and the rivers are swollen with blood. The two sides are equally matched at first, as Mahisa's army plunges blindly into war with Siva, Visnu, Garuda, Brahma, Varuna, Yama and the other gods; but after one hundred years, the demons emerge victorious. Mahisa who was one, becomes many:

> Hundreds and hundreds of powerful buffalo-like appearances resembling Mahisa became then visible on the battle field.[61]

These mere appearances of the wild buffalo surround the terrified

Indra, lock him within a circle of buffalo phantasms, mixing the memory of real danger from herds of buffalo with the fantasy of the myth. Visnu's *cakra* dispels the vision, and the battle continues 'normally', but only for a while. For soon Mahisa, who presumably was in human form when he gave the challenge to war, turns himself into a buffalo, hurls mountains with his horns and tail, then instantaneously becomes a lion with sharp claws. The transformations occur with lightning speed, serving the martial requirements of the moment.

There is hand-to-hand fighting between Mahisa and Siva and Mahisa and Andhakasura, who, in other myths, are related to the demon as father and brother. The struggle is very obviously a family affair. Indra cuts off the trunk of Mahisa's elephant and his arrows are like venomous snakes. Mahisa strikes off Indra's arms: his opponents are dismembered,[62] and in a symbolic but obvious reference, Mahisa

> violently destroyed the thousand eyes of Sakra (Indra) together with the assembly of the gods.[63]

Gods never really die, but there are frequent references to death which may perhaps be interpreted as the wish of the poet. In most versions the gods are only defeated; they are hardly ever killed. One by one, the higher gods, Visnu, Brahma, Siva and Indra, who abandoned his elephant Airavata and his horse, Uchchaisrava, flee the field, leaving the sturdier, lesser gods to go it alone. Finally the gods are conquered by the danavas, and they 'hide in deep cavities of the underworld, in waters of the sea, in corners of the cardinal points.'[64] Frightened and tormented, they abandon their wives and children for a long period. Mahisa gains heaven and rules the world from there:

> In no time Mahisa went to the abode of Indra deserted by all the terror-stricken Devas and got possession thereof. Then taking his seat on the beautiful throne of Indra, he made the other Danavas occupy the several seats of the other Suras.[65]

He receives the gods' oblations and 'the Asura Mahisa, after conquering all the gods, became the lord of heaven (Indra).'[66] At last the hero achieves his wildest dreams. He is the god, the young virile prince who, displacing the old king, assumes the throne, lord of all. Every possible fantasy has come true, including possession of the father's wives and all the apsaras; he commands and is offered sacrifices. For the moment (or the era), he rules.

The hero Mahisa has now completed three labours, all directed against various male groups. After performing severe penances so as to influence the gods, he successfully defeated the rival demon kings, and with the primal instincts of the buffalo who leads the herd aggressively in formation against a threatening enemy, and employing the war tactics of the Ksatriyas, he has now overcome the gods; thus far he has triumphed in the struggle for survival.

But as the story unfolds, the ambivalences of the Brahmin priests, identifying with Mahisa, catapult the participants into a whirlpool of conflicting fantasies. Residing in his heaven, the conqueror now carries a heavy burden of guilt for displacing the father and wishing him dead. A suitable way out is found, escaping the consequent agony: the story-teller splits the god image into two: while Indra and the others are condemned to roam the earth, Brahma, Siva and Visnu conveniently forget their terrible encounters with the demons who had tried to kill them, and each returns to his heaven to reign peacefully in grandeur. The myth-makers avoid confrontations and attempt to balance the wish (to eliminate the god/brother/father by defeating Indra) with the reality (the resulting guilt) by lifting the paternal authorities right out of the narrative and restoring them to their secure heavenly positions, keeping the scales in perpetual balance. The DBP describes the episode:

> Vasudeva Vishnu thus pierced in his breast with the horn, became confounded and fled away as best as he could till he reached his own abode, Vaikuntha. Seeing Hari thus fleeing away, Sankara (Siva) too thought him invulnerable and fled to his Kailasa mountain with fear. Brahma, too fled to his own abode with terror.[67]

Guilt thus rationalized, Mahisa should have lived happily ever after in the hard-won heavenly spheres. But his resistance to his male opponents and his spurious subsequent redemption from the sin of parricide are merely preliminary rites of passage, as all depends ultimately on the boon. In reality, he is nowhere, because even though the priests, by their legerdemain, indulge in fabulous exercises of self delusion, the attempt at parricide will not go unpunished, and Mahisa will certainly suffer retribution. But, even more perilously, his own deeply repressed obsession is soon to be released into his consciousness by the tantalizing provocations of the Goddess in the world. Even while, as in animal contests, his victory over Indra has gained for Mahisa full rights to all females, the myth defies biological certainties by introducing the Mother Principle (a female neither readily accessible nor easily won).

As for Indra, Mahisa has proved that the god is no match for him in potency. As the sacrifice, under Brahmanical control, is its source, Indriya emanates from Indra only so long as the gods are in a position to receive offerings:

> Thus when great calamities befell on the earth, the Devas became gradually weaker, not getting their share of the sacrifical Havis.[68]

By weakening the gods and conquering heaven, a wilful opponent is capable of intruding on the closed Brahmin/god orbit. Diminished in battle, Mahisa's energies require Brahmanical sacrifices for renewal. Identifying with the strongest, the mythmaker (Brahmin priest) assures himself that whether it is demon or god in control of heaven, the proffered energy will always depend on him.

Thus deprived of his own strength, Indra now turns for help to the original source. The gods on earth initiate action as a defence against disorganization, and terrified torpor gives way to a process of recovery. They go to Brahma, who takes them to Siva, and all together pay a visit to Visnu. The Goddess is forthwith created out of their combined energies. But as she makes her appearance, the closed system of god/Brahmin or demon/Brahmin energy in transformation is violently ruptured. Further complications, other alignments and devices for the elimination of guilt, and more competitive behaviour for the favour of the Goddess and for unmitigated power will constantly realign loyalties; Mahisa may yet regret the breach of the father/son nexus.

By recitation of the story of the battle with Indra, the priests accomplish two fundamental purposes. On the one hand, they identify with Mahisa and his desperate, valiant attempts to establish his manhood through victory over a male enemy, the father, the god. And for the time being, they hold a monopoly on sacrifice. But on the other, ironically, while he receives the sacrifice during his sojourn in heaven, he is also the future sacrifical victim.

Chapter Four The Demon/Deity Spectrum

As master of the universe, Mahisa, the new Indra, enjoys all delights in the former heavenly abodes of the gods. Immersed in the megalomaniacal fantasy life of the immature male, he has deprived them of their sacrificial privileges and has even stolen the deva women. For the time being he is entirely oblivious of any outside threat, but, as usual, he is deluded by maya and is unaware that he no longer is in sole control because the cosmic balance has again been shifted. For the gods, having found the situation intolerable, had only recently called upon the Goddess to save them—to manifest out from her Absolute state.

At this juncture it may be useful to examine why the concept of demon as god has so persistently been retained in the structure of the myth. This requires a digression from the main story line, as we look first at the historical role of the buffalo asura/divinity equation and then, in turn, for the Goddess, we observe the nirguna/sattva/rajas/tamas relationships.

The Buffalo Asura/Divinity Equation

It is taken for granted here that the vitalizing effects of primordial responses which do not artificially separate human from animal nor deny or ignore their common origins, are today still operative in India at the village level. Animals are closely linked with humans by the laws of karma which imply equivalent status.

Rituals, dreams, the reappearance of ancestors as legendary animals or divine powers, very commonly in motifs of transformability into animal shapes, and the imagery of psychotics—such projections of the primitive disposition are overt indications of what is hidden from consciousness. So the buffalo demon/king/

god/sacrificial victim symbol has re-energized the life of millions of worshippers in the past and does so today.

The equations in the Mahisamardini myth are the expression of the mystical relationship which existed for millions of years in the past when humans could barely distinguish themselves from other species of similar size and locomotive capabilities. Primitive man, puny and afraid, naturally aligned himself on the side of the powerful large animal and invested it with divine, magical powers. Often regarded by the early hunter as superior to himself, as father, or as god, the animal was thus incorporated into a unique hybrid animal/human/divine kinship system. In India, the Bhainsa, or buffalo, was a common totem. Although direct evidence of the consumption of the totem ancestor either as god or as clan symbol, or of identification in mystical blood exchange, is not available, traces suggestive of it exist, for example, in the worship of a clay image of the groom's animal totem and in its tattooed representation.[1]

The enormous and savage prehistoric aurochs which was hunted for food, hide and bones is the atavistic source of the buffalo/demon/god imagery. Then, distinctions between slayer and slain were not clearly defined; subject/object differentiations were vague, boundaries unclear and the fearsome aspects of the relationships were always still very real. As hunting societies were forced to confront, overcome and dominate the very creatures they worshipped, and since the deity, though deity, had nevertheless to be slain and eaten, terror in the face of this situation encouraged ambivalence. In India, the close relationship of the hunter with his prey continued until recently and experientially renewed and gave contemporary form to the inheritance.

In the Deccan, the Goddess Mahisamma (*Mahisa:* buffalo; *amma:* Mother Goddess) who controls buffaloes, in the Kuru region of U.P., Camunda Devi, a local Goddess of buffaloes,[2] and in our text Mahisamardini, cannot be entirely disassociated from their paleolithic predecessors. The male animal deity and the therianthropic Goddess, protectress of animals, held sway during the early periods of human development. Much later, the Goddess, now no longer in animal form, became the huntress who destroys, and the bull or buffalo, who had been *of* the Goddess, became her sometimes deified sacrificed lover. The prehistoric relationships lived on in the Middle East into the third millennium in Sumer and Egypt. Later, elsewhere in Mesopotamia, and in Anatolia and

Crete, among the Phoenicians and Canaanities, the bull played the central role in religiopolitical societies as source of energy, fructifier of the earth, consort of the Goddess (but equally as male defence system against the feared sexuality of the mother and as resurrected flesh-and-blood sacrifice). Mahisa, part animal, part human and part god, and the Goddess who behaves sometimes like a wild animal, are their legacy, far removed in time, but in the unconscious, very little altered.

In India cultivators were forced into association with the *bubalis bubalus*. At the end of the twentieth century, some two thousand still roam the jungles of Assam, and small herds are to be found in Bastar, M.P., in Bandipur sanctuary, Mysore District, and in other isolated areas. This is the feared wild buffalo with a shoulder height of at least six to seven feet and magnificent horns. The agriculturalist was always vulnerable to attacks by these herds emerging in their thousands from the jungle, especially as the crops grew. When, with a leader at their head, in square formation, they charged, only the tiger could withstand the violent onslaught. Because of its enormous size and physical force, expressed through frightening grunts and stampedes, the buffalo was greatly feared as an enemy who required direct propitiation, either as demon or as god. Various solutions were subsequently conceived in attempts to integrate conflicting urges—the need to be one with the animals but also to be separate from and to control them. The strength of the buffalo, lion, or elephant was often equated with power over nature and the acquisition and maintenance of absolute authority. Never is the god/human/animal a distinct entity. Pasupati, Lord of Animals, and the meditating male figure with buffalo horns on the Harappan seal, provide eloquent graphic expression of this.

In the Brahmanical rites and texts, at one level, the animal image is restated and re-emphasized at every turn. While it is true that Mahisa's divine traits are subordinated to his demonhood, the ambivalencies in the buffalo symbol suggest that belief in the strength and potency of the bull, and the ambiguity of the demon and god concepts as simultaneously beneficent and malevolent, are pervasive.

At the tribal/village level, god and demon/*bhuta* are an indefinable, numinous quality which exists outside of the individual. They are both a repository of the devotee's floating perceptions. While naming the spirits and specifying their locations helps to control

fear and to modify the consequences, their position in the
demon/god spectrum remains vague. Often the animal is associated with 'a religious principle that slumbers in winter and
reappears in spring, manifested in the harvest which sometimes is
represented as a spirit that guards over the earth and its fruits.'³

The cultivators' association of a fierce wind with the wild buffalo
herd hovering on the outskirts of the fields and with a sometimes
malevolent deity who requires propitiation with animal sacrifices,
links present-day god/demon-buffaloes or buffalo-bulls such as
Nandikona, Maysandaya, Bhainasura, and Mhasoba with their
prehistoric forebears, but also with the Brahmanical textual
ambiguities.

While his presence is ubiquitous in Maharashtra, it is virtually
impossible to confine Mhasoba, sometime buffalo god, within any
single specific classification. It is well to keep in mind the warning
of a long-term investigator of folk religion: even after many years of
study within the limited region of a former small kingdom ruled by
his ancestors, he and his scholar associates are not willing to make
any categorical statements-concerning the gods of Maharashtra.⁴
All Mhasobas do have certain traits in common, but frequently
these same traits are applicable to other bhutas.

Sontheimer's study of pastoral gods links Kalabhairava, Khandoba and Mhasoba/Mhaskoba, an interacting triad, with other
associative gods sometimes penetrating into this loose group.⁵ But
as we shall see, since today Kalabhairava is an emanation of Siva,
and even the Mhasoba/Mhaskoba connections are denied by some
local informants (see below), difficulties immediately present themselves. One cannot plot charts, because to enter the world of the
worship of folk deities is to encounter fluctuating boundaries, fluid
transpositions, precariously balanced horizontally along a malevolent ghost/demon/spirit axis and vertically downward and upward toward demons and gods. Yet it is possible to approach the
subject in the knowledge that all fresh data will serve to stimulate
ever deepening comprehensions.

Originally Mhasoba was a cattle deity primarily worshipped by
the Maharashtra herding and cattle-raising tribes. Sontheimer
emphasized the process of transformation: 'The history of Mhasoba shows how a herdsman's god develops into a god of all castes
and a god of established settlements...'⁶ 'In essence, the history of

the three gods, Biroba, Mhaskoba and Khandoba is to be found in the yaksas that populate mountains, rivers and trees and in spirits having the form of animals... These spirits, connected with the cult of the goddess (devi) became identified with gods of the high literate and sedentary castes.'[7] Finally, 'as a result of constant interaction with predominantly Hinduized societies, their (Kurubas') religion had been subjected to continuous Sanskritization, probably over the last three thousand years.'[8]

The Maharashtra district gazetteers of the late nineteenth and early twentieth centuries agree that Mhasoba is leader of the bhutas; he is also a deity who has the will and capacity to harm, but who, as the protector of fields and crops, is beneficent, and who is strong and brave. He is found in the form of a stone at the centre or edges of fields, on banks of free-flowing water or deep beneath and near wells, at the beginning and end of roads through the ghats, at the edge of villages, in the jungle, in cemeteries or under trees. While his shrine was formerly always located outside the village proper, this is no longer the case. Mhasoba demands something in return for his favours and receives offerings when, for example, a person who feels he has been wronged hopes to persuade the god to punish the enemy, or to prevent the god himself from harming individuals. He has been known to drag a victim into the running water and to bring on illness if the stones he inhabits are neglected. During epidemics, because of his relationship to the goddess of smallpox, Marai, and for his own sake, and during festivals, he is propitiated with goats, fowl and vegetal gifts.

Certain Brahmanical texts exclude Mhasoba because of his impurity, and in villages where caste differentiations are still inflexible, he may be considered to be dangerous, while in urban areas he elicits derogatory remarks from upwardly mobile clients. Mhasoba is today primarily the god of farmers, worshipped at the start of work, at harvest and at his own festivals; but this worship is by no means limited to a particular community, for in contemporary Maharashtra there is a good deal of variety in the locus of the shrine, the functions, the iconographical forms and vehicles, in his marital status, and in the myths. The fusion or contiguous positioning of Mhasoba with other bhuta gods, with Mahisa and also with Siva (Sankar) indicates the ever-shifting equations.

Mhasoba is usually found in the form of the largest of a group of five stones. The small ones represent four women whose sons were very ill, and who were directed to bring the children to worship him. The children thereupon recovered, and the mothers became devotees. Another version explains that the goddess of smallpox and cholera appealed to Mhasoba when her son was ill, but by curing the boy, Mhasoba proved his superiority over Marai; she too, having lost her dominating position, is a stone standing in a line with other goddesses: Satwai (Mhasoba's wife), Lakshmi and Joting. But Marai is still worshipped by the lower castes. She appears in dreams, and, like Durga, she demands and receives a buffalo sacrifice during her numerous annual festivals. Then the feet of the buffalo are bound, his head is cut off with a sickle, and his redemptive blood is spread on the Marai stones for the satisfaction of this goddess.[9] In various localities, government restrictions place stern limits on the sacrifice of animals, especially of buffaloes, but the practice nevertheless continues.

Enormous respect is shown for the power of Mhasoba. The god possesses people unexpectedly. When a professor in a local college was fourteen years of age, he suffered a convulsion. It was interpreted by the villagers as possession of a chosen devotee by Mhasoba. The local *devrsi* (priest/exorcist) asked him: 'Who are you?' He replied, 'I am Mhasoba.' To the question 'What does Mhasoba want'? He answered, 'I demand one coconut, a lemon (*limbu*) and a small *chapati*.' When these offerings were supplied, they tasted sweet and better than usual in the mouth of the boy who was, for the time being, a god. When he opened his eyes, he says, he was himself again. 'When I was in a fit, I was Mhasoba.' He had felt vibrations when the possession occurred; therefore the departure of the god was a relief.[10]

Fear is definitely a response to Mhasoba, even though the comments of informants around Nasik, Igatpuri and Aurangabad for the most part do not reflect this. But a primal worship, based on disturbing, undefined emotions, always dominates, no matter what the surface response is and which deity is being propitiated.

But what has all this to do with Mahisa? How does Mhasoba differ from Khandoba, Maruti, even Mhaskoba/Kalabhairava and other associated deities? Furthermore, how can the fact that Mhasoba is conceived as an incarnation of Siva by many contemporary worshippers be interpreted? Most peasants are puzzled by a question about Mahisa, or they deny the relationship, but there are nevertheless certain links between the image of Mhasoba with Puranic descriptions concerning Mahisa. Informants have two responses in regard to buffalo connections: Mhasoba as buffalo is the vehicle of Yama, the god of death, or that Mhasoba's own vehicle is a buffalo. In Nasik and Pune, Mhasoba is worshipped in the theriomorphic form of a buffalo, sometimes alone or with numerous or a specific number of 'wives'. So far so good. But even as buffalo, is Mhasoba Mahisa?

In the past scholars have associated Mahisa with Mhasoba [Marathi, *Mhas* (buffalo) and *Ba, Bapa* (father)]. Kosambi wrote:

> Mahisasura (Mhasoba) [is] the demon killed by that once independent goddess ... Sometimes, as at Vir, he is found married to the goddess Jogubhai, now equated to Durga ... The god still goes in procession once a year to a hillock adjoining the one on which his cult is located. ... The hillock is still called Tukai's pasture and her little shrine there contains a crude red-daubed relief which shows the goddess crushing a tortured buffalo—Mahisasuramardini.[11]

Sontheimer identified Mhasoba with Mahisasura, agreeing that, as Durga, Tukai is married to Mhasoba/Mhaskoba.

To follow up on these tantalizing hints, I visited the Mhaskoba temple at Vir, Pune District, Maharashtra, during Navratri 1991, in order to determine the present relationships of Mhasoba/Mhaskoba, Mahisa and Durga. To my surprise, I found that since Kosambi's report of 1962, as a result of the general Sanskritization, a shift away from the folk deities was in process here as well. The information recorded was supplied by local informants who agreed with one another, although they were separately interviewed. It became evident that today the villagers no longer identify their now more Brahmanicized god Mhaskoba with the buffalo demon Mahisa, nor his wife with Tukai–Durga, nor Mhaskoba with Mhasoba, whom they regard as a lower-order deity, on the level of the ancestor worship practised by farmers in the neighbourhood.

The villagers insist that Mhaskoba is Siva. In the two *sthalapuranas* (local temple tracts) of 1889[12] and 1984, Mhaskoba is merged with Kalabhairava, who was incarnated holding a trident and an hourglass drum in his hand when Sankar (Siva) pounded the ground in anger (1889), or when Kalabhairava/Mhaskoba emerged out of the angry scattered *jatas* (strands of knotted hair) of Siva (1984). The Puranic story of the argument between Visnu and Brahma, which elevates Siva (here Kalabhairava) as the highest god, is nicely incorporated into the account of the arrival of the pastoral god Mhaskoba at Vir and the neighbouring villages. A rise in status and widening distribution of his worship followed upon the conversion to Mhaskoba worship of a king of Satara; this permitted entrance into the cult by castes other than shepherds, *malis* and barbers. Today, although the priests are not Brahmin and the honorary rights in regard to the ritual are accorded to lower castes, all are welcome; even Brahmins come to worship Mhaskoba.

Jogubai (a folk corruption of Jogeswari), is definitely Mhaskoba's wife today, and she is disassociated from Tukai, Kamaladevi or Durga. The latter has been unconsciously separated from Mhaskoba, as a corollary to his being increasingly perceived as an emanation of Siva. It would seem that the malevolent aspects of the Goddess have been duly faced, overcome or ignored. The elaborate marrige ritual of Mhaskoba, not to Durga but to Jogubhai, is performed on the first night of the great ten-day Magh (January/February) *yatra* at Vir. Thousands of devotees attend this ceremony, which takes place within the shrine of the temple of the god. Among the witnesses is the icon of Mahisamardini. From her hillock shrine, she arrives on a palanquin on the day before the wedding, accompanied in procession by frenzied singing and dancing, and she is deposited in the courtyard with an excellent view of the proceedings within the shrine. But in the perception of the village informants, despite the literal depiction of the obvious iconography, the actual form of Durga as slayer of the buffalo goes entirely unrecognized. To them she is definitely Kamaladevi or Tukaicamal, attending the marriage as sister of the groom. Suggestions that she is Mahisamardini or the bride, or both, are met with adamant denials.[13] Another statue of the buffalo slayer in the *antarala* (vestibule) has subordinate ritual significance and is also known as sister Tukai. Other forms of the Goddess distributed at various locations in the courtyard of the temple are now also sisters of the god in what may be yet another step in the process of diminishing the power of the local independent goddesses, as the process of Sanskritization continues.

This is a rapidly accelerating trend, even in such remote localities. There is a definite increase in tension between the striving for upward mobility and subordination of the once all-powerful independent, unmarried local goddesses, in favour of a more compliant sattvic wife. Here the process is actualized by the insistence in the contemporary *sthalapurana* that the god is an emanation of Siva and the explicit separation of Durga Mahisa-mardini from any connection with a marriage to the demon/deity. And appropriately enough the yatra for the former folk god Mhaskoba conveniently slides into Sivaratri. Then, he is honoured and worshipped even as preparations for Siva's birthday are being initiated.

So while Durga and Mahisa can certainly be linked to atavistic sacred marriage rites, they cannot be considered to have literally been married, nor are they ever in fact bride and groom. On the contrary, because of the dangerous implications of the relationships between Mahisa, Durga and Siva, the mythmaker and the ritualist definitely (although unconsciously), strive to be free of the Great Mother's influence, and they avoid the marriage ceremony *per se,* concealing forbidden truths in more opaque layers of the myth, while emphasizing the struggle of two equivalent forces. If indeed Jogubhai and Durga were once one and the same, they have been properly bifurcated.

Jogubhai and Mhaskoba reside as one anthropomophic stone image in the shrine, but as ornately decorated metal masks, they are taken in procession in the court around the temple in a large palanquin a number of times a day throughout the year. Surprisingly, on the fifth day of Navratri, this *pradaksina* rite had nothing to do with Durga's celebrations, or so the people believed, and there would be no recognition of her here on the eighth or ninth day, as is usual elsewhere, even though the 1889 report indicates that Navratri was a time when special *pujas* were held for Durga.

Now during Navratri, the festival honouring the Goddess who slays the buffalo, celebrations are held only in front of a small, isolated shrine to the folk goddess Marai, situated at the edge of a field, approximately two miles away from the ever-busy Shri Nath Mhaskoba temple. Here, on Astami day, about fifteen or twenty goats are sacrificed to the goddess, and there is some music and dancing, and women are possessed. In the face of this constantly changing conglomeration of projections, the best we can do is record, with due respect for the complexities.

The worship of Bhagwan Mhasoba Maharaj continues at his

shrines throughout the year. He is the chosen god of a variety of worshippers in urban areas who today are no longer categorizable by caste or class, as acculturation seems to have removed many barriers. On the Nasik–Pune road, a small temple near the Nasik railway station enshrines the god in two forms. Literate and non-literate peasants and middle-class people come to pay homage to a buffalo image which fifty years ago was added to the much earlier aniconic stone; it had guarded the important highway for centuries. A Brahmin priest even conducts Vedic rituals here. A lady from Pune brings her one-month old baby for blessings. She insists (in English) that Mhasoba is Sankar (Siva), not Mahisa. Other devotees simply look puzzled when asked about the connection between Mahisa and Mhasoba. Some do not even realize that the later stone is in the shape of a buffalo.

It would appear from recent enquiries that Mhasoba, like Mhaskoba at Vir, is today often considered to be one more manifestation of Sankar. This occurs where pastoral/agricultural societies have come into close contact with Brahmins and their influence. However, the obverse is equally true: more sophisticated religions have had to accommodate to aboriginal practices in order to draw in and receive ever renewed energies from the people. Mhasoba is worshipped as an incarnation of Siva on his 'birthday', alone or in conjunction with other gods, who are also the incarnated Siva, as often there is general agreement that god is one, and the one manifests. Even the syllable Mha is now more frequently transformed into Mahadev, or Siva, as at Mhase, taluka Mubad, Maharashtra where Mhasoba is in the shape of a linga.

The Mhasoba shrines of Nasik are decorated with numerous bells hanging from the ceiling. Childless couples will vow to present a bell if Mhasoba will help them, or a bell is offered and tied when the baby is born. There is a connection here with the sacred buffalo bells of the Todas and also with earlier worship of the bull in India:

The people of this [Caveri] country consider the ox as a living god who gives them their bread: and in every village there are one or two bulls to whom a weekly or monthly worship is performed, and when one of these bulls dies, he is worshipped with great ceremony.
When a woman of a sacred caste has not a child so soon as she

wishes, she purchases a young bull, takes him to the temple, ceremonies are performed, and ever after he is allowed to roam at pleasure and becomes one of the village gods.[14]

Despite the Siva associations or also because of them, the unconscious fertility associations of ancient bull worship are still functioning in the psyche of people of all castes.

In the extravagant agricultural festivities in many parts of India, as the consort who ploughs the mother earth preparing it for seeding, the indispensable bull, ox or even the male buffalo (the one who has been fortunate enough to survive into adulthood and is harnessed against his will for work) is accorded enormous respect, affection and what appears to be a certain amount of awe. His potent horns are painted in bright colours, the body is gaily decorated with paint and profusely garlanded with flowers and then the animal is paraded, hymned to, offered reverence with namastes, to the inevitable accompaniment of music. But nevertheless, fearful of attack, certain communities still worship the animal with a spirit in it.[15]

Aniconic and iconic worship of bhutas is popular in the South Canara district of Karnataka even today. Out of the over one hundred identified spirit gods, approximately ten per cent are conceived as animals: the buffalo, tiger, pig or peacock are the most popular. At festivals the buffalo is incarnated in a ritual specialist, and in temple worship, as Nandikona (Nandi: Siva's bull; *kona*: buffalo), he is represented in large wooden carvings which are worshipped in conjunction with the other devas.

In the Folk Museum, Institute of Kannada Studies, Mysore University, Camunda sits on the back of a similar large wooden statue of a buffalo bull. Legend has it that as consort of the winged Nandikona, she is swept by him up to heaven to plead for the well-being of her sick devotees.[16] This may very well be an archaic remnant of the prehistoric buffalo/Goddess totem much later split and metamorphosed into Mahisa and Durga. As Siva and Nandikona have equivalent status and Camunda is often Camundesvari (and, even before recent Sanskritization trends, was considered to be the consort of Siva), we are confronted once again with the complex triple alliances, the consubstantiality (see Chapter Five).

But ultimately, the buffalo/bull is sacrificial animal, and it is then that his sacred status is definitely confirmed. The totemic origins, god as sacrifice and the consumption of the divine flesh and blood, must be taken into consideration when the paradoxical transformation of Mahisa from demon enemy into god and then into sacrificial victim and his subsequent apotheosis is being considered. In these rituals, we detect the perpetual exchanges of sacred power between bull and deity. Each depends on the other. Mahisa's feelings of longing for the Goddess are reciprocated by her. Neither Siva nor Nandi, Devi nor Mahisa is an entity isolated within a fixed category. The Saktas especially recognized the interconnections. Instructions in the DBP for worship of the Devi Yantra state:

> Then worship the attendant deities called Avarana Puja, Brahma with Sarasvati on the east, Narayana with Laksmi on the Nairirit corner, Sankara with Parvati on the Vayu corner, the lion on the north of the Devi and Mahasura on the left side of the Devi; *finally worship Mahisa* (buffalo).[17] (my emphasis)

All share sacrality as the powers are continually being interchanged.

The Goddess: Nirguna/Sattva/Rajas/Tamas

Defeated by Mahisa, the lost and wandering gods relying on traditional habits of worship turned for rescue to the Goddess. In the DM, the Goddess is created out of the light emanating from the male gods,[18] in the *Varaha Purana*, from their looks,[19] and her constituted parts from the gifts they bestow on her. While this is a popular version even today, the weakened state of the gods would seem to belie this male rationalization. This seems to have been understood in the DBP, where the gods borrow fiery energy from their respective spouses,[20] even while in their male pride they take credit for mothering the mother, who is born of her sons. In fact, it is the Goddess who chooses when and where to make herself known to her devotees.

Appearances of the Goddess: Bodhana

The Puranas describe the Goddess when she arrives as blazing with mingled red, white and blue light, and beautiful beyond conception. Great blinding conflagrations, the blending of billions upon billions of suns are brought to mind. The vision evokes the god imagery common to all cultures, but in India, for the Saktas, the light/female equation persists. The Goddess is like 'a burning mountain, a mass of intense energy'.[21]

Instructions to persuade the Goddess to appear abound in the sastras. With purohit as occasional intermediary, recitations, chanting of hymns and mantras, penitential performances, prayers to her iconic representations, offerings and sacrifices are the means by which a devotee becomes aware of her. These strategies provide multiple benefits: permission for temporary regression, the indispensable maternal support and, at the same time, help in the perennial struggle to ward off her malevolent, consuming powers. The terrible force is modified and kept well under control because it is objectified and confronted. If fear is actually conquered, creative energies are released.

The appearances of the Goddess vary according to the requirements of those who call upon her. She may arrive spontaneously, unannounced, like Venus, ascending from the 'northern shore of the milk ocean':[22]

> There appeared there out of the waters the great Goddess, a maiden wearing garlands and crown, clad in white cloth, with eight hands each holding a divine weapon.[23]

She appears in visions or in dreams, or she literally enters the physical bodies of her devotees: she entered the womb of Yasoda and gave birth to Krishna.[24] She possesses a person directly or the priests as intermediaries. All over India today, local priests are easily transformed into the Goddess, sometimes even at fixed weekly times. Through them the Goddess speaks to her followers. In Sri Lanka, the priests of the Goddess Pattini often dress the part by wearing female clothes.[25] In the demon-destroying wars, the Goddess may incarnate in human form, riding on her lion, as general of the deva army. Or the king relies on her support against the enemy. Women saints, worshipped even today all over India, are the Devi incarnate as well. (Sri Sarada Devi, for one, the wife of Ramakrishna, is believed by millions to have been the Divine Holy Mother, the Goddess in temporal form.)

The Non-Forms and Forms of the Goddess

The theory of the gunas may be useful for providing insights into the multi-faceted *saguna* nature of the Goddess. An inter-gravitational universal system of three reciprocally penetrating forces (gunas) is the perpetual process whereby either the sattvic (ascending), rajasic (expanding) or tamasic (downward tending) quality gains predominance in constantly shifting equations. At the individual level, the gunas are inborn in various proportions. While all human effort theoretically aims at ascent, life involves one in rajas and tamas too. Society and family do influence personal choices made in a former existence; but the implicit assumption is that evil actions will be avoided to ensure happiness in the future life. The history of Goddess worship, however, seems to indicate that most devotees need to project their free will on to the Goddess who represents all the gunas, thus distancing themselves from the rare adepts, those favoured few who devote years to prescribed ritual activity, the prerequisite for realization of the Goddess in oneself.

In the DBP, the Goddess *is* the gunas, even though, as Absolute, she is beyond the gunas; then, without beginning and beyond death, beyond name and form, she herself is supreme knowledge, unknowable, constant, unchanging, without gender.

> Before Creation, I, only I, existed.... My Atman is beyond mind, beyond thought, beyond name or mark, without any parallel and beyond birth, death or any other change or transformation.[26]

But nevertheless, in this state, the potential for eruption into life exists: the Goddess is poised at the border of the unconscious and the conscious, ever ready, at any time, to break through and to work at random for good or evil.

> I am Nirguna. And when I am united with my Sakti, Maya, I become Saguna, the Great Cause of this world.[27]

And then she is seemingly all that is good and pleasant: modesty, loveliness, faith, compassion, beauty, fame, enjoyment, fortitude, intellect, mercy and support, light and the light of the world.[28] As Sattviki she is the creatrix, not of the gods alone, but of everything, and this includes human beings and the demons they have invented as well. She is Cosmic Mother, the Mother even of the personal mother—the mother of all.[29] The world is a drama played on her stage:

> As a dramatic player, though one plays in the theatre, assuming many forms, so Thou, too, being one, playest always in this charming theatre of the world, created by Thy gunas, in various forms.[30]

Phenomenal existence is her maya, nothing in the world is real—it is her pastime, her *lila* (play in the world). She moves the world and moves within it; pervading all forms, she is immanent.[31] This is her rajasic form. She rules all beings, is the throne, the protectress who eliminates sorrow and brings wealth. She preserves, dispenses justice and removes sins.[32] She is invested with the idea of the sacred, and for those who worship her with punctilious care and without error, she dispenses welfare and reciprocates their love. She supports and nourishes, because she *is* the plants; 'the Goddess of vegetation dwells in the tree'[33] and is resident in the milky juice of the plants. She is the compassionate *mater dolorosa*, whose tears from her multiple eyes shed rain water on the parched earth. During droughts,

> when the body of the Brahmanas thus praised and chanted the hymns of Mahesvari, She created innumerable eyes within Her body and became visible. For nine nights continuously, the heavy rains poured down out of the waters flowing from Her eyes.[34]

These qualities she certainly has, but even though she appears as brilliant light, the epiphany will unfold, and her dark nature will be revealed to have been contained in her lustre. Projected on to the identical image are all the terrors of existence as well. For the purpose of the Mahisamardini analysis, it is especially important to come to terms with the Mother Goddess in her tamasic form. Associated not only with creation as female but with phallic horns and snakes, the androgyne is the dreaded warrior, fearsome and ferocious, with animal instincts all too easily aroused. The Durga/Kali imagery has remained permanently operative, for she receives energy from still functioning primordial sources, contained and harnessed in the Goddess symbolism. In a timeless, consistent pattern, as witch, demoness, vampire, she punishes with drought, barrenness and consequent death. During one ephemeral human lifetime, she voraciously demands for her own enjoyment of the lila, not merely offerings from fields recently harvested but sacrifices of blood, including parts of the sacrificer's body as well. Whether the Great Mother seethes in the underground darkness of the unconscious, or her appearances are externalized, the umbilical cord remains as a binding chain until the day the Mother takes the son back into herself at death. This is what Durga means when she later exclaims to Mahisa:

> For women are considered as chains to hold men in bondage. Men bound up by iron chains can obtain freedom at any time, but when they are fastened by women, they can never obtain freedom.[35]

The ritual is obligatory and must be correctly performed. Like a child, the devotee must aim for perfection, or at best the Mother will be displeased; at worst, she will punish, as when the father of king Janamejaya forgot his responsibilities toward her, and the Goddess entered into him as Kali.[36]

When, as mother of the gods,[37] she becomes horrible, the devas become immovable, senseless; she torments and terrifies, has large breasts, is wild and at the termination of life, she dismembers and disintegrates.[38] Thus made conscious, fears are modified. In all these respects, although her characteristics are especially Indian, there are general parallels with those of other Asian matriarchal deities who held sway for millennia in many parts of the then known world.

Although 'language forces thought into certain patterns', in relation to male–female categories, 'one begins to wonder whether they are true categories at all.' O'Flaherty believes in the categories, but she warns that in the myths 'things are mixed all the time.'[39] While manifestations and attributes are classifiable for the convenience of ritualist, scholar and the enlightened devotee, in the popular mind they are barely differentiated. Though each individual conceives of the Goddess in accordance with society's complex and paradoxical definitions combined with the inherited tradition, the imagery in fact springs from each individual's unconscious, and is synthesized and absorbed in a variety of singular ways.

With astonishing fluidity, when the gunas interact, the Goddess thus assumes a variety of seemingly inconsistent forms. Immanent in the world as protector, virgin, spouse, or warrior, the Goddess serves each devotee in his or her immediate need, like the personal mother, portraying the role appropriate for the moment. She is both feared demoness and symbol of rarified spirituality, and also all the intermediary stages. Her instantaneous, momentary appearances are like the fleeting pulsations and lightning alternations of the individual's personal responses.

As all her potential forms co-exist, she is ever the conglomerate and not the 'split' Devi, a term which implies separation and categories. The language that attempts to capture and fix is the language which is also part of her maya.

Her single specific, fixed characteristic is the suddenness and unpredictability with which she takes shape momentarily; the only constant construct is her potential for all conditions. Because both child and devotee believe that she contains within herself all possibilities, Mother is virtually the only appropriate designation for her.

Parvati (wife) creates Ambika (beautiful, nourishing mother) who instantaneously changes her name and form so as to terrify even the daityas with her terrible black appearance. In her battle with the demon king Sumbha

> Ambika got very angry, out of her frowny look, her eyebrows became crooked, Her face became black and her eyes turned red like Kadali flowers; at this time suddenly came out of her forehead Kali. Wearing the tiger's skin, cruel, covering Her body with elephant's skin, wearing a garland of skulls—terrible, with belly like a well dried up, mouth wide open, with a wide waist, lip hanging loosely, with axe, noose, Siva's weapons in Her hands.[40]

King Sumbha sees her in her multiplicity, but he would have preferred to 'slay her companion the Goddess Kali at the same time that chaste Lady [Parvati] is to be protected.'[41]

The 'incarnate of unpretended Mercy with a face ready to offer her grace, the Paramesvari' suddenly disappears:

> Thousands of fiery rays emitted from her form: She began to lick the whole universe with Her lips, the two rows of teeth began to make horrible sounds; fires came out from Her eyes; various weapons were seen in Her hands; and the Brahmanas and Ksattriyas are become the food of that Awful Deity. Thousands of heads, eyes and feet were seen in that form. Crores of Suns, crores of lightning flashes, mingled there. Horrible, awful. That appearance looked terrific to the eyes, heart and mind.[42]

But as her reality is always in transformation:

> Then, seeing the Devas terrified, The World Mother, the Ocean of

Mercy . . . withheld her Fearful Cosmic Form and showed Her beautiful appearance.[43]

Instantaneous, unpredictable alteration is the only reality.

'That Awful deity' is sometimes the beloved, emasculating enchantress who seduces and then destroys her lovers; she drinks their blood and consumes their flesh. She beckons the male back into herself via her magic vagina which destroys the phallus of the beloved, while, in sexual orgiastic bliss, he experiences the death throes of the masochist. He then becomes passive, inert, with no personality, overwhelmed by his animal instincts, in her total control, as he desires her desperately. Merely one of a great multitude of her victims, swept unknowingly into her maelstrom, Mahisa will deliberately expose himself: seemingly having no choice, he follows the non-moral rules of destiny.

Symbols are formed in infancy. The infant who sucks, bites, drinks of the flowing streams of milk from the nourishing breast is one with the mother. It is inevitable that guilt, caused by the aggressive feelings arising from lack of control over the milk, and sorrow in regard to the inevitable loss of the mother's physical bonding, will be projected on to the permanent Universal Mother imago, conceived as one who desires the male for her own convenience and satisfaction. The 'wild mother' is residual material incorporated into the myth. The normal child is involved in a profound fantasy life which often appears in dreams and phobias:

> It is the memory which appears in children's dreams and in infantile phobias where the mother may appear as a wild beast. Some children regularly dream that she is a terrifying animal, unmarried mother, dancer, coryband, maenad, nymph, pixie, water sprite: sometimes the Kore and mother figures slither down altogether to the animal kingdom. . . . There are bloody, cruel and even obscene orgies to which the innocent child falls victim. . . . Oddly enough, the various tortures and obscenities are carried out by an 'Earth Mother'. There are drinkings of blood and bathings in blood, also crucifixions.[44]

Memory traces of the mother's tender loving care but also of her fearsome aspect enter the conscious life only occasionally. That the power of the Goddess does overtly reside in the personal mother in certain societies was revealed to me in a conversation with a Christian, recently converted.

James is a twenty-year old Fijian whose mother is one of the five or so most respected witch doctors in her country. She is half European and half tribal. Her mother and grandmother were also witch doctors, and James was meant to follow in their footsteps. People come from all directions to benefit from her ministrations. They arrive at odd times, and her first loyalty is to her devotees. While exorcising demons, she becomes possessed and appears 'terrible, angry, awful'. She trembles and shrieks, and in these states, she utterly rejects her son. During his childhood, James felt great fear and finally, in late adolescence, became suicidal. Only the appearance of Jesus saved him, but he still feels the anxiety. Here the mother/Goddess identifications are blurred.

The genuinely felt, real, existence of the female deity, one of the strongest influences in the psychic makeup of a great many Indians today, is not confined only to illiterate tribals or villagers. But it is important to stress that generally the personal mother cannot be overburdened with the enormous responsibility implied in the Goddess symbol. Although the normal mother's influence is great, it is she who assumes the qualities of the Cosmic Mother in the child's mind rather than the opposite. This clear distinction is defined by a contemporary devotee, who like some others, is able entirely to repress the terrible aspects:

> While at home, I had loved my mother intensely, and she too had abundant affection for me. But could that love stand comparison with such unthought-of kindness and care as flowed from the Holy Mother? (wife of Ramakrishna). Nay, she is the mother of my innumerable past incarnations—the Mother of eternal time, the Mother of my being.[45]

For the very devout, the Goddess is ever present. Serious votaries cannot betray their need for total involvement; then there is no escaping her total domination. In the nineteenth century, Ramakrishna, the most famous of these, suffered greatly from her alternating blandishments and rejections, although he finally did achieve reunion. His struggle culminated in the solution inherited from his forebears. His way of being in the world, as we have seen, is experienced by multitudes of Indians, either out of conscious choice, which is rare, or more likely because they can offer little or no resistance to the persistent Mother Goddess, sakti force. Rolland recreates the drama:

> And the priest [Ramakrishna] was associated with all the intimate acts

of the day. He dressed and undressed Her, he offered Her flowers and food. He was one with the attendants when the Queen arose and went to bed. How could his hands, his eyes, his heart be otherwise than gradually impregnated with Her flesh. The very first touch left the sting of Kali in his fingers and united them forever. Having pierced him with Her love, the Wasp had concealed Herself in her stone sheath.... Passion for the dumb Goddess consumed him. To touch Her, to embrace Her, to win one sign of life from Her, one look, one sign, one smile became the sole object of his existence.[46]

In delirium, he thirsted, he almost died of longing, and then:

One day I was torn with intolerable anguish. My heart seemed to be wrung as a damp cloth. I was racked with pain. It seemed as if nothing existed anymore. Instead I saw an ocean of Spirit, boundless, dazzling. In whatever direction I turned, great luminous waves were rising. They bore down on me as if to swallow me up. . . . I lost consciousness. And in the depths of my being I was conscious of the presence of the Divine Mother.[47]

Much later, he awoke, calling: 'Mother! Mother!'

Others have identical experiences: a priest in the Chandi Temple in Cuttack, Orissa, describes his inner vision during meditation:

After performing meditation and the ritual for two or three hours, lightning flashes before my eyes. I am dressing the Mother. I am at the time the Mother myself. It is as though I were doing all of these things for my own mother. When I worship, I forget myself. I become the goddess. She who is Ma (Mother) is me. There is no difference between Ma and me. Water and coldness of water, fire and the burning capacity of fire, the sun and the rays of the sun; there is no difference between all these things, just as there is no difference between myself and the goddess.[48]

A fluid conscious/unconscious interflow permits the sensitive village priest and devotees easily to become possessed by the Goddess. With its western connotations, the term hallucination is not appropriate for contemporary Devi worship. As consciousness is easily lowered, millions have audial, visual and physical contact with the sakti propulsions emerging forcefully as concrete reality from within their own psyche, and for those so fascinated, the Goddess assumes name and form. For them her appearances are powerful, limited in time, and for fear of being engulfed by them, they must be controlled by ritual. The personality of the individual is fused with the external symbol, as subject/object distinctions become blurred. Longing for the Goddess can be interpreted as longing for the integration of all aspects of the self. For most devotees, the externalized form is the necessary defence, essential for defining and controlling inner forces.

The Gods are Infants; They are Females

According to the Sakta cult, the Mother Goddess controls the fate of all. Even though she makes her appearance when the male deities chnglomerate their respective energies, she is, in fact, not 'created' by them. All her incarnations are the result of her will to be in the world for the benefit of mankind; she chooses when and how to effect her lilas. In this situation her sudden arrival will spell doom for Mahisa, but only after a protracted interaction during which the confrontations between animal/demon and Goddess, male and female, son and mother, lover and beloved, equal combatants, victim and sacrificer, hero and deliverer, are given due attention as an exploratory venture into the dynamics of the laws of opposites, their reciprocity and repulsions, fusions and transcendencies. As metaphor for the adventures of the hero, the encounters of Mahisa with the Goddess provide useful material for the student of the collective unconscious.

The myth of the god Visnu who sleeps on his serpent Sesa while suspended in the ocean of eternity is the first episode in the Mahisamardini story in the DM, the *Siva Purana* and the DBP. It takes for granted that the Goddess of sleep, Yoganidra, is the sole moving force of the universe. Visnu is aroused for the purpose of rescuing the world from the demons Madhu and Kaitabha only at her bidding. It was she who really caused the 'night of destruction at the end of the world'[49] in the first place:

> During the time of Pralaya, she destroys all the Universe, draws within Her body all the subtle bodies (Linga-Sariras), and plays.[50]
> Thou swallowest forcibly all those that are seen.[51]

She consumes the entire phenomenal world. All earthly creatures and the gods are engulfed in the sleep of eternity, in darkness and stillness within a vacuum which is the full ocean/womb. Brahma becomes aware and tries to awaken Visnu:

> When I have praised Him so much and when He has not awakened, then it is certain that sleep is not under Hari but Hari is under sleep, and he who is under another becomes his slave; so the Yoga Nidra is now exercising Her control over Hari.[52]

But there is still resistance to submission, albeit weakly. Brahma reasons that in the Vedas Brahman is male. He then faces the ambivalence and the tremendous tensions involved by begging the Goddess to decide: 'Cut my doubts asunder.'[53] Immediately he is reassured by the benevolent Goddess: 'There is no difference at any time between me and Purusa (the male, the Supreme Self) who is I, that is Purusa; who is Purusa, that is I.'[54] Doubts will linger even as Brahma offers hymns of praise to the Goddess in recognition of her ultimate authority, but he adds: 'by the power of Yoganidra, Hari has been kept in prison.'[55] The prison is the womb of Yoganidra, the containing mother, the vessel, the mother of all Being.[56]

God and Goddess are not yet differentiated, and they are consubstantial. Consciousness does not exist, and there is yet no self or at most, a weak and ineffectual infantile self:

This all excellent Lady,...beckoned Me who was a baby then with greatest gladness. In former days, when I was sleeping on the couch of immovable fixed leaves of a banyan tree and licking my toe, making it enter within my mouth and playing like an ordinary baby, this Lady rocked my gentle body to and fro on the banyan leaves, singing songs like a Mother. Hear attentively that she is this Lady and She is our mother.[57]

And Brahma agrees that he was born of the Goddess:

Those who do not know thy character think that I am the Creator.... (but you) have created me as Brahma.[58]

The infancy stage is recognized; only the Yoganidra has the power to initiate mobility, which is the gift she offers to the new-born even while she is determining his fate for birth or for non-birth. Prior to reactivation of the world, before creation, Goddess and Visnu are one, so much so that in a convenient reversal Visnu does not emerge from the body of the Mother Devi; it is she who emerges from him:

...the goddess of darkness, extolled thus by the Creator there in order to awaken Visnu to slay Madhu and Kaitabha issued forth from his eyes, mouth, nose, arms and heart and breast and stood in the sight of Brahma.[59]

The Goddess is born from the maternal god, stirs from within and 'issues forth!' but a separation has physically occurred; and now the male experiences all the terrors and anger of the prisoner who had only recently been entombed. He is totally dependent, in a precarious position, but to rescue him from this terror comes the will to life.

The initial battle in the DM is between Visnu and the demons Madhu and Kaitabha; it is the start of the long struggle to reverse the dependency, to overcome the infantile fear of total annihilation and to emerge from the maternal waters, to enter into life. Like Mahisa's birth out of fire and his austerities, the defeat of the demons announces the conquest of life over potential death at birth. The right of the hero to exist, to be conscious, is established. But the tenuous nature of this first victory is soon made manifest. It is all maya; the controlling Goddess first offers the boon for victory to Madhu and Kaitabha, causing Visnu in his weariness, after the five-thousand-year battle, to feel like a child. The Goddess is called upon for help, and she uses her seductive side glances as weapons, to distract the demons so as to change the course of events. What these artful wiles were to lead to is of course not yet known.

Having thus re-entered life and with great difficulty defeated the opposing forces, as the myth unfolds the gods struggle to survive and evolve. As conqueror of demons, as symbol of consciousness, Visnu is nevertheless perceived by the mythmaker to be in mortal danger. All events are, after all, the mere play of the Goddess. The god finds himself in more or less the same dependent position as before, for now he discovers that the Trimurti (himself, Siva and Brahma) are mere emanations of the saktis Laksmi, Mahakali and Sarasvati, who in turn, are the Goddess manifested. Visnu instructs his co-deities:

> When the Shaktis become absent, you become inert, and incapable to create, I to preserve and Rudra (Siva) to destroy.[60]

Lest this advice be taken lightly, the male gods are without a by-your-leave transformed by the Goddess into females, to be, ironically, mere instruments accomplishing her work in the world.

> We looked beautiful and youthful women, adorned with nice ornaments.[61] We are transformed into young women before thee: let us serve thy lotus feet. If we get our manhood, we will be deprived from serving thy feet and thus of the greatest happiness, oh mother.[62]

And Brahma even asks forgiveness for his pride.[63] Even in their feminine condition the gods plead:

> May this relation as mother and son always exist between Thee and me .... Thou art omniscient.[64]

The Purusa is hermaphrodite and the gods accept their ambiguous gender status in relation to her. They are still undifferentiated infants, 'fastened by a [umbilical] cord',[65] they are dolls.[66] Deprived they are indeed! No sooner is the infant born, than fear drives him to imagine emasculation by a powerful Mother figure. They praise her, assuring her that their love is purely spiritual:

> Those who say that Hari, Hara and Brahma are respectively the Preserver, the Destroyer and the Creator of this whole Universe do not know anything. All three are created by Thee (Devi); then they perform always their respective functions; their sole refuge being thyself.[67]

In her (phallic) toe, the gods see the Goddess as the lustre of ten million suns.[69] Like Ramakrishna's 'ocean of ineffable joy'[69] they are full of *ananda* (spiritual exhilaration) and loth to separate. Echoes of the medieval text are heard in the words of contemporary devotees who are infants, inviting the incarnation of the Divine Mother Sarada Devi:

> One cry from her babe, and the veil is off! . . . The veil of the simple village woman [Ramakrishna's wife] . . . is too thin to hide that effulgence which is more brilliant than a million suns. Added to that, the baby which has the full freedom (which is its birthright!) to pull away that veil—the 'baby' in every one of us . . . is ever at it.[70]

In the retelling of the story of the gods transformed into females, the myth defines the stage of the infant child, and for now the devotees seem happy to be under complete, certainly masochistic, submission. Unless we remain content to think that this odd scenario serves only the masochist who virtually enjoys enslavement and castration, another explanation for the transformation of gods into women must be considered. This seems to be the imagery of the child in the man who may very well be relieved that even the gods are susceptible to the catastrophe he fears the most. By thus imagining the father god to be deprived of his powers, the child raises himself to a number one position *vis-à-vis* the mother.

At the time when the Goddess appears for the purpose of retrieving heaven for the gods, they are in precisely this condition: weak, without Indriya and aimlessly wandering. It is Mahisa, as Indra, who will take a stand and refuse the solution of castration. As both he and the gods are in fact entirely dependent upon the will and force of the female and cannot ultimately survive without her, the hero will be he who will risk confrontation in the attempt to emerge from the infantile state. While the gods are shown to be weak at one extreme, the mythmaker invents an *alter ego* in the form of a buffalo-demon whose powers may yet save the day. He is now featured as the polar opposite: young, powerful, strong and definitely male.

Mahisa is the real hero, since he will have faith in himself and will be willing to die for his cause. When the *pralaya* (universal stasis) episode comes to a close, consciousness has been established, but it is still in complete submission to the unconscious. Sustained only by his own will, Mahisa will also eventually succumb, but in the process, the dignity of the male ego will be given a certain amount of recognition.

Chapter Five The Mahisa/Devi Encounters

The Goddess Roars Like a Beast

Abruptly the Mother Goddess intrudes into the myth in the form of a threat which had been entirely hidden during the hero's rush to glory. She will prove to be both nemesis and ultimate salvation. Moreover, the divine female force is now destined to meet her match in battle.

The Absolute erupts into the universe as Devi. The Goddess has appeared, and she laughs a great laugh. Mountains tremble and the seas are agitated.[1] The tremendous elemental sound announces the cosmic crisis; the daityas 'took it as the great dissolution of the universe at the end of a Kalpa'.[2] And so it was, for at this instant, the pride and the fantasies, the hidden shame and the forceful attractions and fear of the Mother, until now lurking in the unconscious and totally denied, are suddenly blatantly revealed. In fury, the Goddess crosses the threshold into consciousness with the roar of the primeval Goddess/beast; all humanity is in dire risk when the Mother is angry. The grandiose claims and the overlay of rationalizations of the hero have come up smack against fundamental realities; dissembling is no longer possible.

Because her first appearance is in the form of a beautiful maiden, the hero Mahisa will have to deal with the 'love' impulsions which strike him out of the blue. Out of this will come the final drive to destroy the Goddess in battle and himself as well, until he eventualy finds release from his ambivalence through union in death with the object of his lifelong desire.

Mahisa and the Ministers are Confused

Magnetically drawn toward the Goddess, the mythmaker, whom we identify with Mahisa, reflects his dilemma in the narrative.

Thus, although sexual contact with divinity is dangerous, it holds the possibility of salvation. In yogic thought, duality is death and non-duality is the conquest of death; the merging of male and female is immortality. So, too, any contact with divinity—the closer the better—is an experience that promises a taste of immortality. The worshipper willing to risk this doubly hazardous encounter may achieve realizations and powers that can be won in no other way.[3]

Mahisa's encounter with the Goddess should thus be approached on various levels: when she is isolated as sacred power she will arouse both terror and magnetism. Eliade also points to the ambivalence:

> The sacred at once attracts and repels. The self-contradictory attitude is displayed by man in regard to all that is sacred. On the one hand he hopes to secure and strengthen his own reality by the most fruitful contact he can attain with hierophanies and kratophanies.

> On the other, he fears he may lose it completely if he is totally lifted to a plane of being higher than his natural profane state: he longs to go beyond it and yet cannot wholly leave it. This ambivalence of attitude toward the sacred is found even in most developed religious forms. (The repulsion may appear under many forms...hatred, scorn, fear, wilful ignorance or sarcasm).[4]

Anyone who approaches the deity without recourse to mediating rituals designed to modify the devastating *force terrible* is in mortal danger. Mahisa and his ministers had courageously faced enemies in fierce battle earlier and had emerged victorious, but they were now stunned and discombobulated as never before. The eruption into the world of this creature who roared and bellowed like a beast or an ogre, rending the air with thunderous clamour, but who appeared to be an exquisite adolescent girl as well, would make even the bravest of demons tremble: the *force tremendum* is an adorable lady! Because the circumstances evoked infantile memories of the feared and beloved mother, nothing could be more conducive to regression into terror, emotional helplessness and inertia; the reaction could only be an amalgam of uncontrollable emotions—astonishment, disorientation, fright, but, inevitably, also desire. Entirely unprepared for the profound impact of the sacred encounter, Mahisa can do nothing but succumb: all the joys of heaven conquered are mere megalomaniacal delusion, for while there is a Mother Goddess in this universe, subject to her every whim, Mahisa will be doomed forever to live the life of a psychic cripple, always begging for her attentions and endearments, fearing her anger and doing her bidding.

Before the meeting between the pair, each of his ministers and Mahisa himself holds, Rashomon-like, a single view of the Goddess, which, when combined, become a rounded concept of nuanced relationships and struggles between son and mother, male and female, worshipper and worshipped, animal instinct and human consciousness, all here compressed within the Goddess/demon metaphor.

When Mahisa's ministers first saw the Goddess meditating silently on the mountain, they rushed to convey the news to their commander. Astonishment is mixed with a fair amount of lascivious enjoyment:

> Oh chief of the Demons.... Come let us visit the Vindhyas immediately, there resides the most exalted Goddess, the most beautiful of celestial damsels. (3)
>
> She excels the clouds in her lock of hair, surpasses the Moon in her face, eclipses the three fires in her three eyes, and beats the conch hollow in her neck. (4)
>
> Her breasts, round in shape and with sunk nipples, excel as it were, the temples of an elephant. Knowing you to be the conqueror of all, Cupid has made the breasts his stronghold. (5)
>
> Her eighteen arms, round and plump, with weapons in them and appearing club-like and splendid, have been converted by Cupid, as it were, into your instruments, having known your valour. (6)
>
> O lord of demons, her waist also, beautiful due to the three abdominal folds, and charming by the series of hair, appears like the staircase built by Cupid, who, afflicted by fear, was not able to ascend higher. (7)
>
> O demon, the line of hair appears extremely beautiful due to the contiguity to the plump breasts, and resembles, as it were, the flow of sweat from the body of Cupid, out of fear from which he suffers due to your ascendence. (8)
>
> Her deep navel which curves to the right appears like the seal on this storehouse of beauty stamped by King Cupid himself. (9)
>
> The charming buttocks of that beautiful damsel adorned with a girdle on all sides appear to be King Cupid's extremely inaccessible city protected by high walls. (10)[5]

And so on. In the *Varaha Purana*, the sage Narada, son of Brahma, initiates the process which will draw the unsuspecting Lord of the universe into the murderous trap:

Like her we cannot find one among gods, demons or *raksas*. I have not
seen one like her in all my wanderings all over the world.[6]

All the sexual references can be interpreted as symbolic longing for
the divine converted into recognizable metonyms. Paganism does
not distance the sacred from the erotic, the erotic from violence,
violence from salvation. The practising Brahmacari priest experienced no shame and conveyed no disapprobation in using sensual
and sexually stimulating language to portray love of the deity. But
Mahisa hears only the erotic descriptions. The uncensored, frank
language of the ministers Canda and Munda was bound to enchant
an unsuspecting ruler of heaven who had tasted all the joys of
physical passion but, with a famished soul, still longed for the
mother love he had never received.

Impelled by their own ambivalent emotions, the priests invest
the text with such subtle ambiguity that the reader is drawn into a
maze of conflicting perceptions. The unstructured thought fragments of the ministers, faced with a traumatic situation, are
reflected in their conversations with Mahisa and with the Goddess;
they are the moment-to-moment shiftings and slidings from one set
of perceptions into another: disbelief and surprise, ambivalencies
and defensive postures, masochistic and sadistic revelation, hubris
and fear, follow each other in rapid succession, as the conflicting
provocative and belligerent messages from the Goddess are simultaneously received.

After confronting the bewitching apparition, Durdhara the
minister returns again to interpret his insights to the divine Lord
Mahisa. He reasons that her aggressive language is a metaphor for
invitations to love: 'I will pierce and kill you by arrows, face to face
in the battlefield. I will lay your Lord in the death bed of the
battlefield.'[7] By these words Durdhara understands that the
Goddess is requesting inverted intercourse, where the woman is
above the man.[8] When the Goddess announces, 'I will take away
the vitality (life) of your lord',[9] he believes that she refers to the
source, the carefully harboured semen, which in India is likely to
be preserved by the male as strength.[10] But when the Goddess,
entirely alone, plunges into a ferocious battle with each of the
ministers and his armies, defeating each in turn, Chiksura is
bewildered and asks the Goddess: 'Why have you desired to fight
instead of to enjoy sexual pleasures?'[11] Why indeed? We shall see
that her aggressive language is open to various interpretations. As

for Mahisa, he is now tender, now confused, full of unabashed pride and finally both mad with love and mad from the ambiguous rejection. As consciousness is charged with the Mother Force, maya overwhelms and confuses Mahisa and the ministers.

Subliminally, the ministers do perceive that she is the Supreme Principle, and this is actually acknowledged, although in a cacophony of dissonant messages, seemingly conflicting strands of the story are presented simultaneously. The fact is that at one level, the demon Mahisa is fully aware of the situation: he is about to become infatuated with a Goddess, for he is told so:

> The Devi is decorated with jewels and ornaments.... We are very much overpowered by the halo emitted from Her.[12]

> That woman is neither human, nor a Gandharvi, nor the wife of any Asura. Only to cause delusion to us, she, this wondrous Maya, has been created by the gods.[13]

But the king of heaven ignores the obvious. Has not the Lord of heaven, believing he is Indra, the right to hope for a deity as bride? He is being drawn unconsciously into her net.

Eventually, Mahisa does give battle, but not before declaring his abiding and total love, offering her everything. Although he has not yet even seen the object of his passion, he pants for her presence and feverishly begs the Lady to share all the wealth of his kingdom as his Mahisi (chief queen consort; also female buffalo), but at the same time he longs for total submission: 'I am your servant... grant your mercy.'[14] He will have this beautiful lady; he will woo her tenderly, even altering his buffalo shape to please her if necessary, but if this fails, he will take her by force. His ministers, who have all along counselled him to marry her, as she has no husband and is virgin, would even oblige by 'tying her down by a coil of snakes'[15] or 'make (ing) Her submissive like a slave girl'.[16]

The ministers grope for a way to solve the dilemma as they only gradually fathom the reality: this lovely damsel is horrific! Confused and shaken, they now begin to redefine the situation, especially as the warrior Goddess shows her true colours by defeating one minister after another in ferocious combat. For Mahisa the advent of the Goddess is the felicitous answer to all his wildest wishes on the one hand and a dire threat to his very existence on the other. Elation at the contemplation of ecstatic love, fear of the unknown and misunderstood, the sudden onrush of feelings of desire to submit but the need for power too, shame at his buffalo condition, but pride in past achievements, unnerves the hero/Lord/demon to such a degree that only the support of the loyal group of ministers helps him keep his violent passions in check. He sits on his throne in heaven, as the ministers run to and fro, declaring their conclusions after having first observed the magnificent apparition and then marched off to war against her to sacrifice themselves for the Lord Mahisa.

When he sees her riding on her lion, the minister Tamra is the first to realize that this woman is the Great Goddess, but while propitiating her by falling at her feet, still confused, he nevertheless entreats her simultaneously:

> O beautiful One, you would better be graciously pleased with that conqueror of the Immortals, the Mahisasura; O Thou of delicate limbs! Make him your husband and enjoy all the exquisite pleasures of the Nandana garden as best as you can.[17]

Even though Tamra then has a dream which signifies danger, of a woman wearing black weeping in the inner courtyard and birds hoarsely screaming in every house, he is still deluded and enchanted by the charm of the apparition.[18] Subsequently, further portents of doom are received by Mahisa, who is advised to take up arms and not to rely on Fate, the excuse of weaklings:

> It may be argued that there may be such a thing as Fate: to which it might be replied, what proofs are there for such an existence? Thus the weak persons alone hold it out as their only hope.[19]

The hero Mahisa will have to take the matter into his own hands; he has been persuaded that he should never acknowledge his inferiority before a woman for fear of disgrace: 'We ought not to show our backs.'[20] All the ministers advise action, buoyed up no doubt by memories of their victories when the defeated gods had fled the battlefield. And now, even though Mahisa is confounded and afraid, he decides to brave the dangers involved in the awesome moment of meeting with the Goddess. And since there is absolute confusion as to what has been learned from the single perspectives of each observer, the eventual encounter is all the more frightening and thus all the more irresistible. So Mahisa finally makes the most important decision of his life: he will go out to meet the Lady and accept the consequences. Poised now on the battlefield, aided by his surviving ministers, his warriors mounted and armed, he moves directly into the eye of the cyclone: confrontation with the beloved Mother, his worst enemy. In the light of the hierogamies of other cultures, replayed for millennia, and the persistent wish in the modern child's unconscious to marry his mother, obsessed with Oedipal drives, the universal king of heaven wants only to be whole again; for this he risks everything. Having conquered the brother/father, it is determined that he go now to the Mother.

Sex and violence, love and battle, are confused in the minds of the demons, dreaming of a Goddess who desires physical love and will be slave to a fantasizing male. While verses in the DM and DBP are designed to rid the devotee of sin in the reading, this perfunctory regimen reflects the thinking of the sadist who debases the female, desires to overcome her sexually by force and does not differentiate beauty from sex nor sex from violence. So used are the male authors to asserting their prerogatives of force that the intrusion of the Female Principle from the unconscious is met at first with sheer denial. The men want to believe that her advances are motivated by passion, to attract and arouse, and perhaps they have good reason to believe this is so.

The Goddess as Seductress

Mahisa's predicament is unbearable: the king of the universe has been infatuated with a delusion and is now vulnerable: but he is otherwise a rational ruler, versed in all the sastras,[21] one who patiently confers with his ministers and is ready to negotiate, to abandon pride and to behave like a humble and tender lover. These are not the characteristics of a 'beast', although the Goddess insists they are: as we shall see, it is a defensive posture on her part. Some of the confusion is more attributable to Devi's own puzzling behaviour and language than to the myopia of Mahisa and the ministers. The Goddess' words in fact reflect the mixed feelings of the mythmaker in regard to females in general, to sisters, mothers, wives or courtesans. When he beholds the beautiful Goddess poised to fight on the battlefield, Mahisa's demon analogue Sumbha cries out:

If you like to fight, better assume an ugly appearance, let your nature be ferocious and cruel; let thy colour be black like a crow; lips elongated, legs long, nails ugly, teeth horrible and let your eyes be ugly and yellow like those of a cat. Assume such an ugly appearance and stand firmly for the fight. O... Speak first harsh words to me. Then I will fight with thee; my hand does not get up to strike thee with handsome teeth, in the battlefield, who are like a second Rati.[22]

In this simple plea, the entire body of loathsome and repulsive Kali imagery is candidly revealed to be the drastic defence the son puts up against the overwhelming magnetism of the mother. Nothing less than an extravagantly monstrous personification of the beloved can serve as counter-offensive to the excruciating tensions set up by her presence. For even the vituperations and taunts that she spews at Mahisa's messengers leave one uncertain as to the true situation: are her responses meant only to provoke a war with the demons? Is she not truly as anxious for an amorous encounter with the hero as he himself is to love the Lady? While sex and violence in combination motivates males, it would appear from the texts that, along with her serious intent to murder him, Durga herself combines an only slightly-veiled erotic interest in the would-be demon lover.

The fear of the sexually threatening aspects of women in India has been amply discussed by Carstairs, Lannoy, Kakar, Brubaker, Shulman and Nandy, and as a general condition by Ernest Jones. This view is succinctly propounded in the DBP. An ascetic who had meditated for one hundred years complained:

The agile Apsara...has come to take away my precious fire of spirit acquired by my tapasyas. Alas! Why I who have practised for one hundred years the most terrible asceticism, have become so powerless by the mere sight of this Apsara?[23]

An ardent apsara will siphon off all the ascetic's hard-earned powers, and 'happiness will not occur... through her.'[24] As it is understood that the gods are often lascivious and exceedingly greedy, Devi cannot be dissociated from these characteristics either. But her 'side-long glances of love and amorous feelings which like arrows from the Cupid'[25] fascinate, enchant and agitate could also be artful stratagems designed to kill, or more accurately, to castrate.

In point of fact, her flirtations are not always manipulative, and her need for love is no less intense than the gods' or the demons'. Exactly like the males, the Goddess is an enigma; and the narrative is kept vague enough to permit the reader to interpret it in his or her own terms. If he is a bhakti devotee, he will hope for signs of love from the deity. If he is in Oedipal thrall, he will be magnetized.

As we have noted earlier, underlying the sparring of the Goddess with Mahisa's entourage are the emotional complexities inherent in the relationships of mother and son, lover and beloved, Goddess and devotee, female and male, warrior and enemy, and these roles are not clearly differentiated; we detect here incestual longings, sado-masochistic tendencies, vestiges of the sacrifice of the consort as germinater and, above all, the quest for sexual pleasure in love, for tenderness, acceptance, trust and security, common to both genders.

At first the Goddess is passively provocative, as she sits meditating upon the mountain; her appearance is beautiful, but then she proliferates into hundreds of potential female warriors, holding noose and rope.[26] On the other hand, when Tantric ideas prevailed, as Kamakhya,

> she has come to the mountain for the sake of sexual enjoyment (*kama*).
> For just as a man is a parasol bearer on account of taking a parasol, and
> a bather at the time he takes a bath, in the same way, Mahamaya's body
> when prepared for sexual enjoyment, coloured reddish yellow by the
> red saffron applied for the sake of sexual excitement is called
> Kamakhya. After abandoning her sword when it is time for love, she
> spontaneously seizes her garland; when she has abandoned love, she
> holds her sword.[27]

Mahisa might have guessed what was in store for him from the very fact that the Goddess was a virgin, a condition threatening and very dangerous in itself. But when she first meets the ministers, they most certainly would have been confused, because the warm, welcoming and alluring mother speaks in a voice 'deep like that of a cloud',[28]

> Tell me, without any embarrassment, the true message with which the
> son of Ramhba has entrusted you.[29]

Devi encourages the impression that Mahisa's desires will be fulfilled after he has defeated her:

> Hear the condition that has been laid suddenly in the family by the
> ancestors. He who conquers our daughter in battle shall be her
> husband.[30]

In the variant, the Goddess flatters the demon Sumbha. He is great, charitable, beautiful, a hero; and she states openly 'So I have come here from afar... with the desire of getting me a husband.'[31] Should the demon conquer her, she will have the marriage ceremony performed. She then blithely slaughters the attendants Canda and Munda on the battlefield and drinks their blood, after which she repeats her marriage proposal.[32]

It is a tribal custom for warring factions to mark the cessation of conflict with a bridal gift which is presented by the victors to the vanquished. Violence and sex are seen to be necessary and opposing factors which balance and maintain control. The challenge by the Goddess converts the 'difficult task' which is 'prerequisite to the bridal bed'[33] into a concrete physical contest between an ambivalent male and an equally ambivalent female. It can be reduced finally to the primal non-differentiation of gender. For, even while the sides of battle are being defined and aligned, the Goddess spells out her terms:

> Nature has ordained connection between two persons of like nature.
> Though I am not apparently a man, yet my nature is that of the Highest
> Purusa (Man). I show myself simply in feminine form.[34]

What is more, she refers to Mahisa as a hermaphrodite as well. Since they are both androgynous, they are both bi-sexual, beyond duality, and thus their nature is absolutely identical. Aggression then no longer is seen as 'male' or 'female'. In fact it is the Devi who initiates the action. In the *Skanda Purana* she sends envoys to provoke the demon with persuasive speech: 'Thus I will make him attack me in a moment.'[35] Her unwillingness to ignore Mahisa, her lengthy and over-emphatic aggressive statements hint that the truth may be the reverse of what she proclaims:

> I am not like your grown up mother, the she-buffalo, having horns,
> eating grass, with a long tail and a big belly.[36]

And again:

> Is there any woman in this world so stupid as to select Mahisa as her
> husband?... Can a woman like me ever indulge in bestial sentiments? A
> female buffalo has got horns; she, being excited with passion, may
> select your Mahisa, with horns, as her husband and come to him
> bellowing.[37]

With these barely masked pronouncements, the Goddess, who had only recently offered herself in marriage after having arrived bellowing like a beast, betrays herself. Devi continues: 'Do you think Me as deluded by passion?'[38] Her strong assertion that she is not a buffalo cow like his mother indicates the archaic material still operative in the myth. Even Siva likes to describe the Goddess as cow.[39]

While the Goddess denies consubstantiality with the demon at one level, she believes her union with him may be as dangerous as that of a mortal with an immortal. But for that very reason, it is all the more enticing: She claims

> The combination of similar substance leads to happiness; and if out of ignorance, the connection takes place between things entirely different in their natures, it becomes at once the source of all pains and troubles. How can connections become possible between us?[40]

But Goddess and demon are definitely consubstantial (see Chapter Six). Occasional and fleeting unconscious thoughts emerge: when the Devi is threatened by the sexual advances of the strong male animal force she often runs to the god Siva as her male protector, reminding us that the Goddess/Mother force sometimes yearns to abandon her dominating position. For even though Siva had declared his subordination to her in no uncertain terms in the DBP, the Virgin Goddess claims:

> And I too, though inert, owing to his [Siva's] proximity, work consciously.[41]

> He...the Siva...is my husband...I do not desire any other body than the Supreme One.[42]

Subsequently the Goddess wishes to test the demon's powers and weakness, but there is no indication that were the demon indeed to subdue her she would have abandoned her promise to marry. Perhaps this might have been the condition had the mythmakers been female, but the men appear to prefer a scenario of conquest by the Goddess, although there is doubt even about this. Bana, for instance, invests the Goddess' words with some hesitation in the *Candisataka*.

> What has a woman to do with the lust for battle? But this is not seemly, why did I undertake it?[43]

We are almost back to square one. If Siva has turned himself into Mahisa, and the Devi desires only Siva, we are getting rather too close to incestuous suggestions. The inevitable reversal of these forbidden thoughts follows immediately:

> I do not like to have Visnu, the god Sankara, Brahma, Kuvera, Varuna or Fire, how then can I select a beast?[44]

The denial has to be vociferous, to cover over what has already been admitted to consciousness. Soon her behaviour will turn out to be as beastly and as brutish as the hero's. We have noted earlier that in her aggressive pronouncements the ministers hear only sexual enticements, that they are confused by her threats and take them to be endearments, so their fear is modified. Now the Goddess will scorch Mahisa with her wrath: 'I would have burnt you to ashes by my fiery sight'[45] recalls the association in Tantric ritual of the female with Vedic fire.

'You [Mahisa] will go to the house of death, to Patala'[46] is interpreted by the asuras as the return of the demon to the mother, to earth. These signals, so suggestive of the incestual fears of the writer, are hard to ignore. Again, when she threatens to kill Mahisa, 'to make the soil muddy with his blood',[47] she invites him to the sacrifice which will unite his substance with hers, the earth. (Her threats are even converted into action; the virtuous virgin attacks the minister Vaskala, then Durmukha, Tamra and Chiksura, and vanquishes them and their asura armies.) But none of the denials of the Goddess can actually be taken too seriously; some are altogether spurious. Mahisa is born of a buffalo, but he is also born of god, he is even Siva who gave birth to himself as buffalo. She contemptuously declares Mahisa to be the worst of brutes,[48] a beast, stupid, a villain, and dull, but she herself very soon exhibits all these characteristics herself. Unconsciously, like Indra, she seems to recognize the similarities, but would fain hide this reality from herself.

Myths from many parts of the world, where the buffalo exists in the wild and is domesticated as well, often tell of buffalo/human marriages.[49] We are dealing here with imagery which has its roots in the common ancestry of the species. Antagonistic figures have always been and will be attracted to one another because of their common descent.

Mahisa's Love of Devi

Samuels' simple diagram, connecting personal and good and bad mother, and his assertion that each category 'has an ingredient of each other category'[50] can usefully be applied to the Mahisamardini myth. We have seen how the traditions of child-rearing in India reinforce the primary relationship. The son seeks relief from the symbiosis with the mother, not in detachment and transference of love to his wife, but in diversionary rites of sublimation which run parallel to the personal life. While Freud distinguishes between the 'normal individual' who 'has learned how to master the Oedipal complex' and the 'neurotic subject [who] remains involved in it',[51] in India such definitions are irrelevant. For with the aid of ritual and myth, the son can cater to the neurosis; this defines the norm. In the sanctum, the devotee conjoins himself to the image of the Mother (see Chapter Eight) and to some extent this helps to cancel forbidden longings and allows for growth into manhood and the establishment of the son's position in the world. But it also encourages him to remain in the domain of the Great Mother who is manifested in his own personal mother.

Mahisa is fixated at the pre-adolescent stage, reflecting the level of development achieved by the worshipper of the Mother Goddess in India today. While the DM text does not refer overtly to this response system, it is with astonishing frankness and psychological insight that the DBP spells out successive emotional stages. We may recall that the male gods in the DBP readily accept their position as sons of the Goddess: indeed Visnu welcomes being rocked in the ocean/cradle, basking in embryonic bliss. The pralaya episode describes the regressive wished-for integration. That is why in the DM and the DBP (and also, as we shall see, in the developing configurations of the Mahisamardini statues) descriptions of the symbiotic condition precede the main content of the narrative. The image of Visnu as infant slides into that of the pre-adolescent, who braves the overwhelming force of the unconscious even while the tremendous backward pull perpetually threatens him, as *nolens-volens* he is trapped in the orbit of the Mother Goddess.

How deeply infused with sado-masochism is the entire response system of the priest–mythmaker! Without batting an eyelash, Durdhara translated threats of violence into promises of love, taking for granted that the anger of the female would serve to arouse the demon sexually. Having envisaged the sexual partner in a punishing role, it appears the ministers are incapable at first of any other perception. Tamra finally sees the light and believes he recognizes the Lady as the Goddess who deserves the love of the devotee. In Chiksura the masochism is translated into hubris and he prepares for the struggle to overcome her power. Mahisa is confused because of these simultaneously interacting thoughts. His wish is to lie with the Mahisi, the queen, the buffalo cow, the earth, his mother, to be like the horse in the asvamedha to be 'dead', 'passive', 'inert', her obedient servant. He would seek unity and integration, a regressive return to the pralaya stage, but he is also willing to risk unbearable separateness, thereby to be released from the destructive predatory desires of the mother.

Having eliminated father and brother, as lover, Mahisa is now free to possess the mother. This illusory freedom, however, is fraught with great danger for the conqueror.

If Mahisa is to serve more than the 'source of urine',[52] he must struggle against his own instinctual desire to be merely the phallic fecundator, the buffalo-bull lover of the Goddess. If indeed he is to strive towards a certain degree of maturity, he must make an attempt to overcome guilt by undergoing the initiation of battle, implying both symbolic incest and matricide. Mahisa, like Hamlet, is slowly delivered by the mythologist to the realization that as the solution—albeit an illusory one—for overcoming the conflict, the source of the excruciating tension must be destroyed. One way to eliminate the danger of being drawn into the dangerous web is to kill the spider as she weaves it. At this stage, he believes he is analogous to the gods, and indeed manifestly, this is so; from this he draws courage.

The demon/god's compulsive rush towards the Goddess, wishing to ravish this female, to be her slave but to do away with her too, plunges him into an ocean of crippling guilt and depression for which the only atonement is death. But not without a battle, as the confused demon attempts to project the overwhelming guilt on to his adversary, she who had humiliated and demeaned him. The mother's scoldings and her insults are her own defence, designed for protection against her own wishes. By shouting her abuses to the world on the battlefield, she reveals her weakness—her unconscious desire for the son.

If the Goddess, mother, queen does not succumb to the fertilizing buffalo, the result will be barrenness; but should close relatives actually be wed, the order of the universe will be upset.

The only solution to this dilemma is the one presented in the Mahisamardini myth, where the union does take place but at a non-physical level. To rationalize the overwhelming impulse to 'love' the magnificent creature whom he has determined to eliminate in battle, Mahisa hides behind hubris, as he is least able to face the truth of his situation, steeped as he is in the maya of the Goddess. Conflicting commands are the indication of his confused condition. Dazzled by the sounds rending the atmosphere and by the beauty of the Goddess, he knows that he desires her and will have her, and at the conscious level he wants her alive. The chief minister is advised to win her over

> in such a way that Her life be not destroyed and bring that beautiful woman to me.[33]

But soon unconscious intentions are revealed:

> In case she does not come under your control in fight, kill her.[34]

Prior to the masochistic ending, the battle will provide plenty of sadistic excitement, permitting all kinds of unbridled fantasies their expression: terrible violence, directed against females; piercing, drawing blood, torture, tearing to pieces and heads chopped off will be described in gruesome detail for the satisfaction of the celibate priest whose asceticism was designed to hide his own sadistic propensities in the first place. By then, the wild and uncontrolled battle-drunk mother will compensate for the tremendous guilt accumulated during the onrush of forbidden feelings and the hate they engender.

Devi and Mahisa are Consubstantial

The texts go to great lengths to obscure the underlying meaning; at the same time, they do not fail, on almost every page, to convey the true message through numerous evocative references intended to arouse personal emotional responses, achieving thereby the appropriate therapeutic effect. The numerous metaphors suggesting individual characteristics reveal all the more that demon and Goddess have the same fundamental attributes, and that in their patterns of behaviour they are almost indistinguishable. When the Goddess refuses Mahisa's offer of marriage, what she is really saying to the messenger Tamra is that her intuitions must be publicly and firmly announced so that the forbidden wishes implied in the proposal will be immediately and properly repressed.

The assumption that there is a mother/son relationship between Durga and Mahisa requires textual confirmation. While we are never told that Mahisa is in fact the son of the Goddess, when the obfuscating language is examined, it becomes evident that an attempt to come to terms with the contradiction of love and magnetic attraction but also healthy resistance between mother and son forms the fundamental fabric of the myth. Conceived together in their relationship, the Goddess and the demon are constellated projections in continual transmutation, each barely retaining a nucleus of individual definable identity. Shulman recognizes this phenomenon even in symbolic types—the king and the Brahmin: 'It is all one can do to arrest these apparitions for a moment's scrutiny—nothing remains the same for long.'[55] How much more so with Goddess and demon! As they sink into the wild orgiastic mêlée of battle, the distinctions between them dissolve, and little remains to identify them as separate creatures. There is little doubt about the implications of the myth—the texts seem to strain backward towards primeval realities, when Goddess and buffalo were a single animal deity, and even today, the force of the symbolism is retained. At tribal and village level, demons and spirits are often not clearly differentiated from gods and goddesses, as so rightly stated by M.S.A. Rao:

> A good deal of confusion is caused by dichotomous division of different supernatural beings in the Hindu pantheon into god/spirit; god/devil; sanskritic/non sanskritic.... These are facile categories which do not take into account the people's perception.[56]

Even in Brahmanic ritual, the Goddess is believed to reside in the limbs of the sacrificial animal.[57] With this logic, Mahisa, who will end up on her altar as sacrificial victim, will *be* the Goddess.

The earliest extant statues of Mahisamardini, most of which are in the Mathura Museum, show the Goddess with a theriomorphic buffalo. But they are not battling against each other. On the contrary, the statue is a single volume, and the Goddess holds the large animal, almost equal in size, to her bosom, in a pose which can refer only to a mother holding her child or the merging of lovers. Many centuries would pass before this paradox of love as battle and the ambiguities of the relationship was altered. The styles evolved only gradually, and it was not until the Mamalla-puram seventh-century carving that the symbiosis was finally ruptured. We shall pursue this fascinating progression in Chapter Ten.

While the Goddess is all Goddess, she is also female demoness. Her close involvement with virtuous asuras is of primordial origin: 'I dwelt with them for many yugas, from (the time of) the creation of creatures', she claims in the Prajasarga of the *Mahabharata*. And in one instance, at the behest of Indra in the guise of a Brahmin, she emerged as Sri, the Supreme Goddess, from the body of the demon Prahlada wherein she had 'dwelt happily'. Although she has no fixed habitation, and her affiliations are with gods and rulers, she associates with whoever she wishes.[58]

Consubstantiality is precisely confirmed in a votive hymn in the DM where Brahma praises Devi as the Supreme Mother, with *asuri* (demoness) as synonym:

> You are the supreme knowledge as well as the great nescience, the great intellect and contemplation, as also the great delusion, the great Devi as also the great asuri (female demoness).[59]

Coburn links her power over the asuras with her condition of being an asuri,[60] and Agrawala describes her as the mother who creates both devas and asuras,[61] implying their consanguinity. A philological family connection can be derived from an epithet of Bana's: the term *gotrasya satruh* (foe of the family) is interpreted by Quackenbos as indicating that Mahisa is a member of an extended family which includes both gods and demons, since all are descended from Kasyapa and Diti the demoness.[62] Bana did not distinguish between species. Since Daksa and Visvakarman produced progeny by both demon and Goddess wives, this seems appropriate.

Sharing the same ancestry, the buffalo demon and the Goddess even share their name. In the case of the demon called Durga, he turned himself into a buffalo and then was defeated by Parvati-turned-warrior.[63] The Goddess says: 'My name is Durga, because I have killed this demon Durgama.'[64]

Stories about the birth of the Goddess and of the demon are structural analogues. Like Venus, she may be born of the waters.

Ruru asura and his armies also issued from waters.[65] More tantalizing and significant however, is the similarity of their common birth
out of the flames of sacrificial fires. Draupadi, Minakshi and Lalita
were born of fire:

> When all the flesh of the human victim had been dropped into the holy
> fire including feet and hands, and when Devas were desirous of offering
> the entire body, an excellent huge mass of brilliant lustre (of Devi)
> appeared in front of them.[66]

The mother of the world is born when asuras sacrificed humans,
while Mahisa the asura arises out of the sacrificial pyre of his
own mother! Although both appear as ordinary mortals prior to
the battle, both have the tendency to be transformed into savage,
bestial creatures although, for this to occur, Durga usually
requires her intoxicating liquors. Then she is no different from
ferocious animals and is capable, like her lion, of the most savage
acts. Her soldiers are boar-faced;[67] serpent deities accompany
her; her emanation Nakuli gives birth to the mongoose Goddess
for the purpose of slaying demons.[68] Visitors to the Tulsi Manas
Temple in Varanasi may contemplate the consubstantiality as
they examine an image of the Goddess-asuri with her necklace of
skulls, ferocious visage and long black tresses, who sports horns
and tusks.

When Siva is brought into the relationship, the situation
becomes increasingly complicated. In her aspect of slayer of the
buffalo demon, is Devi the wife of Siva or is she warrior, independent and virgin? This Goddess, who is also asuri, and to whom
Mahisa is related, is also the wife of Siva, mother of his sons. A
relationship with Siva is merely hinted at in the DM: Durga is
Isvari.[69] The *Candisataka,* describing the battle, recognizes all her
aspects: mother, wife, daughter and warrior. When she came to do
battle with Mahisa, she meditated on Rudra (Siva), who joined her
in order to give her support.[70] After the battle she is tired and flies
for refuge to her husband.[71] Prior to the battle with Bhandasura,
Lalita is wed to the young Siva in the *Lalita Mahatmya.*[72] Parvati,
wife of Siva, becomes Kali in the Sumbha/Nisumbha fight.[73] Siva
and the Goddess are definitely god and wife, even during certain
battles.

It would appear that the introduction, or rather the intrusion, of
the father god into the Goddess/buffalo dyad is part of an evolu-

tionary process in which Siva stands for the authoritarian superego, constantly attempting to force a separation. This effort is renewed in each generation by means of ritual aids at all levels of the folk/Brahmanical spectrum.

Mixing metonym, metaphor and simile, Bana artfully conveys his intuitions regarding the Siva/Mahisa relationship. This is recognized in the *Candisataka* by the father of the Goddess, by the Goddess and by Mahisa himself, who likes to associate himself with Siva. The poet's interpretation encourages a series of assumptions which definitely position Siva in a family relationship with both the slayer and the slain. Siva may be attempting to shield what will anyway become manifest over and over again. On the day his wife killed Mahisa, he announces:

> And since thy foe [Mahisa] has been quickly dispatched (by thee) to his long sleep, thou art not called Mahisi by me today (as generally).[74]

This is another instance of overstated protestations, in order to disassociate the killer from the slain. The name Mahisi would remind him of her close associations with Mahisa, whatever they are taken to be. Similarly in a South Indian local myth, Siva is jealous and feels rejected: when Parvati was thirsty, she killed a buffalo, drank his blood and wrapped herself in the entrails. With her power thus enhanced, Siva left her.[75]

Parvati's father Himalaya approached Mahisa in a friendly way:

> Since his [the Snow Mountain, Himalaya] relatives were mountains, he embraced Mahisa, who resembled a mountain under the impression that he [Mahisa] was the Vindhya.[76]

Even the Goddess' hints concerning the relationship are barely veiled: she prefers not to use the trident, the weapon shared by Devi and Siva, to slay Mahisa; since then

> he (Mahisa) would become Isa (Siva) and entitled to fame.[77]

Ironically, however, in a later verse, the Goddess does kill Mahisa with the trident, thus after all making Mahisa the trident-bearer (*sulin*), an epithet of Siva.

> She [Goddess] is intent on carrying out the sport [of battle] in the case of Pasupati Mahisa [lord of animals, Mahisa] just as formerly she had been intent upon carrying on the sport of love in the case of Pasupati Siva.[78]

As Pasupati, lord of animals, they are two sides of the same coin. Mahisa represents battle, and Siva love. The single split image equates love and battle here. These echoes of the Indus Valley seal showing Pasupati as yogi with buffalo horns keep intruding into the later differentiations into god and demon, or god and buffalo.

Chandika seems to remember the connection between Mahisa and Siva when derisively she begs Siva to exchange his rough elephant's skin for the soft skin of Mahisa,[79] and she also makes the comparison in a negative sense: she spurns Mahisa with her left foot as she spurned Siva in jealousy of his love for another.[80] Mahisa claims to be Mahakala (an epithet of Siva): he compares the noose of the Goddess with her hair, when she chastises her beloved Siva:[81]

> O lovely [Candi] pray do not thus repeatedly, with thy lovely lotus hand, throw at me thy noose of hair.
> That noose it is which is suitable for chastising thy beloved Siva when he has incurred a fault by indulgence in love's pleasures, and the like, with other women.[82]

By putting himself in the same position as Siva, Mahisa implies that the Goddess is also trying to hold on to him for erotic purposes. But like the guilty penitent son, he doubts that he should be summoning her in the manner of a husband.[83] However, he soon slips back into his comforting fantasy life:

> I am not Pinakin [Siva] making a mistake in [using] the name of co-wife while engaged in secret amorous play.[84]

Is he or is he not Pinakin (Siva)? That is the question. In two South Indian texts, analysed by Shulman, Mahisa is the devotee of the great god and later, as surrogate, he becomes the sacrificial victim: while doing penance on earth for displeasing her husband Siva, Devi killed Mahisa. To her surprise, she found a *linga* on the severed neck of the slain buffalo. When she tried to remove it, the linga stuck to her hand:

> If anything, Mahisa appears to feel devotion for Siva, and the horror felt by Durga/Vintai at the discovery of the linga stems from the sense of having killed not an enemy but an ally. In fact, this idea goes considerably deeper. Mahisa as bearer of the linga is said to partake of Siva's own form.[85]

O'Flaherty adds that Mahisa's head and Siva's phallus are identical.[86] Thus the killing of Mahisa by the Goddess is a double Brahmanicide, because Mahisa is both the son of the Brahmin demon Rambha, and he has the form of Siva. Now it is Devi's turn to play tapasvin in order to remove the linga and expiate the sin of slaying Mahisa, protecting Siva from polluting death. 'Mahisa carries the burden of Shiva's role in many of the versions . . . [He is] a useful victim . . . Violently disposed of so Shiva [can be] safely married to a less alarming maiden.'[87] Indeed, Siva has not succeeded in displacing the original Durga/Mahisa duo but merely in submerging it. Siva is Mahisa, implying the marriage of the Goddess to both god and buffalo demon. 'For the Goddess in fact marries twice, first symbolically the dead demon and then, officially, the loving god.'[88] And so the dyad of Mahisa/Goddess has been firmly transposed into a complex ménage-à-trois, and these late texts boldly state the newer reality:

> Therefore, the Goddess accepted the demon Mahisa who was actually the great god (himself).[89]

The son, the mythmaker, wishes so desperately to be father that he turns himself by slow, sure degrees, into the father (Siva). There are allusions, innuendos, hints, reversals and cryptic announcements, and further obfuscations, all revealing the hidden, ambivalent wishes of a son. The devotee dreams he is the demon who is the god who marries the mother Goddess. But he must solve another dilemma. He must do more than take the place of the powerful father; he has to eliminate him.

In the process this can be discerned as early as the *Candisataka*. Siva is seen by Mahisa as strong and virile, but often, when the god is frightened, he is rigid as a post (*sthanu*):

> Sthanu (Siva), upon catching sight, for an instant, there in the battle, of the enraged [Mahisa], became actually a post.[90]

As Biardeau has observed, the sami-tree, the demon Vanniyasura and the sacrifice of the buffalo to the Goddess on Vijayadasami day are associated with Mahisa.[91] In another ritual at Kannapuram, the Goddess marries a tree, loosely connected with Mahisa[92] (see pp. 191–2).

Sthanu (post) has multiple meanings. It refers to the god

> whose seed is raised up, whose linga is raised up . . . since he is fixed and since his linga is perpetually fixed.[93]

The god or father is in *urdhavalinga* (with phallus erected).
Presumably, 'fixed' refers to perpetual, contained energy. It is
chastity, not impotency. But simultaneously, on the contrary, the
ascetic who refuses to create—Siva as Sthanu—is by implication,
an instrument of death.[94] In the *Candisataka*, as in later literature,
puffed up with pride and thoroughly deluded, Mahisa makes the
most of these ambiguities. Siva's subordinate, even impotent,
status is brought into the open by an arrogant son: in the Mahisa
myth structure, Siva is weak, and it is Mahisa who bursts with
hubris at the condition of his father: 'For he [Siva] grew limp of
limb, languid in effort, with his [power] of speed destroyed by fear,
and the staff-life limb of his arm enfeebled.'[95] Making the phallus
into an arm to diminish the father fits in with one Indian tradition
which provides the antithesis to the concept of linga as power. In
the Sakta literature, as we have seen (Chapter Four), the power of the
gods is entirely dependent on the will of the Goddess. The figure of
Siva as corpse lying under the feet of the Goddess, inert until aroused
by the sakti of the Goddess, is a familiar image in Tantric art and
Sakta belief. 'If Siva be deprived of Kundalini Shakti, He becomes a
lifeless corpse. She is present everywhere, thus in everything in this
universe from the highest Brahma to the lowermost blade of grass.'[96]
Both Mahisa and Siva share the same fate of becoming a corpse,
unable to siphon off the energies of the Goddess until she negotiates
their resurrection. This seems to imply that Mahisa, who is literally
sacrificed in the battle with Devi, is surrogate for Siva, who, according
to medieval belief, is the true sacrifice.[97]

As though mirroring the fantasy life of the boy in the family
constellation, until the final moments of his life Mahisa far
surpasses the father in potency. During the four hundred years
which elapsed between Bana's *Candisataka* and the DBP, the strain
in the narrative which concerns the impotence of Siva is hardly
altered, as a result of the overwhelming power of the fantasy; limp
limb, post, flight—fearing his own impotence, the mythmaker
attaches himself to the buffalo image for support, enfeebles the
father and plunges into a head-on, fierce, love/hate encounter with
the mother. In his megalomania Mahisa had perceived the father,
not possessing power in an upraised linga, but stiff as a post and in
flight. So, despite all efforts to interrupt the demon/Goddess
symbiosis, its force is recognized, and its perpetual power˙ is
constantly referred to.

But Mahisa has got himself into an impossible quandary, for wishing the father away is inevitably followed by overwhelming guilt and the desire for just punishment, and so in the *Kalika Purana* the mythmaker poses a literary solution. Mahisa now believes he *is* Siva, and Siva readily admits it: Siva then turns to the Goddess and says:

> O Goddess, in whom the worlds are contained, my body which trained through yoga, being Mahisa, is to be killed by thee in previous as well as the following [birth].[98]

Competition with the father is a happy fantasy only until reality, in the form of the Mother Goddess, intrudes into the picture. In this text it is far more prudent to dissolve male rivalry and to restructure alignments according to gender associations in the face of the still greater threat from the female power. Now father and son become one, to prepare for the battle against the Goddess who exacts payment for her original gift of life as well as punishment for guilt over parricidal and incestuous wishes. Absolution will be gained only with sacrifice.

Even as Siva is born as Mahisa in three births in the *Kalika Purana,* in the *Siva Purana,* another story re-emphasizes the relationship: Mahisa's son Gajasura, the elephant demon, becomes Siva. Gajasura, seeking revenge for his father's death at the hands of the Goddess, performed penances so severe that the accumulated fires emerging from his head filled the whole world, and even the gods were again forced to abandon their heaven. When Brahma offered a boon, unlike his father Mahisa, Gajasura requested not to be killed either by men *or* women overwhelmed by lust. The poetic descriptions of Gajasura conjure up a combination of the refulgent sun, of power and enormous size. He conquered the heavens, but he soon became corrupt. The world was threatened so that Siva himself was forced to engage the asura in battle. They were two great forces in confrontation, and Siva was again at risk of losing his potency. But he managed finally to impale the demon with the trident and to raise him to heights above the world. (This had also been the fate of another demon, Andhaka, who was, in fact, the son of Siva).[99] We are led into another interesting revelation. Up there in the sky, out of necessity, Gajasura became a tamed and subdued, although reluctant, penitent. He offered his own beautiful elephant hide, symbol of great strength, to the naked Siva, implying the transfer of demon energy to an exhausted god. Siva accepted the elephant hide and thus was Krttivasas (one clad in elephant-hide), and in return, after his death, Gajasura became Krttivasvara (Siva who wears the elephant hide). Siva says:

> Your meritorious body...will be the foremost of all phallic images yielding salvation, destroying great sins.[100]

Now Gajasura (Mahisa) is Siva with all the powers of the great god to bring salvation, and like his father before him, he has been transformed into the Saviour. About these relationships we will hear more.

The same conglomerate symbol appears in a contemporary folk tale related to Marglin at the Orissan festival to Kali. As though they divined the Siva/Mahisa/Durga connections, the gods announced that Mahisa would die only after having seen the vagina of a woman, and although Devi/Durga was ignorant of this at the start, in mid-battle, she was told of the curse by her subordinate goddess. Mahisa soon found himself lying on his back between two adjacent hills, on each of which the Goddess had placed one foot. He saw, and then she conquered, killing the demon. We are not informed why the Goddess did not substitute one of her soldiers to save herself this humiliation. She became angry at the gods and transformed herself into a tiny Kali, wreaking havoc everywhere. Siva tried to stop her, lying prone across her path, but she placed her foot upon his chest (as she always manages eventually to do with Mahisa), and the two were joined in conjugal union in that position. Devi's anger disappeared.[101]

In these two episodes the Goddess assumes a position above the male. Siva acts upon what Mahisa observes, which sequence is again suggestive of the demon's role as surrogate for the god. Both are objects of Durga's unquenchable lust, for the all-knowing supreme Mother must have been aware of the curse all along. Her erotic compulsions are melded with battle and post-battle excesses of fury and violence.

The only constant in the multiple aspects of a changeable god, Goddess and demon in magnetic interaction would seem to be the Mother. Sakta worshippers prefer to think of her as Absolute, and she often insists on her inalienable position:

> I have no necessity for my Lord. I have got nothing to do with my Lord.
> I Myself am the Lord of all the Beings.[102]

The Meeting of Devi and Mahisa

Mahisa prepares for the awe-ful event of the meeting. The refulgence of the Goddess and her sakti power as she now appears on the field, stained with the blood of his ministers, should have left the demon stunned, but his disorientation serves him well. Because the Goddess clouds the situation in the obscuring haze of her maya, Mahisa does not recall the boon upon which all his victories depended, and on the conscious level he genuinely believes that blissful wedlock with the Goddess is his prerogative.

This serious flaw will ultimately lead to his demise, but for the moment, with the entire gamut of dialectical oppositions precariously balanced between Mahisa and Devi, the seeds of catastrophe germinate beneath the perceived surface. He puts his best foot forward in a deliberate final attempt to satisfy his obsessive desires. The Devi permits this brief period of neutrality in their energy fields; this heightens tensions and also reveals her own perplexities and confusions.

> Hearing the chariot had been brought, Mahisa thought the Devi might not care for him, seeing him ugly faced with a pair of horns, and therefore decided to assume a human shape. Beauty and cleverness are the delights of women: therefore I will go before Her, with a beautiful body and with all cleverness and dexterities. For I will never be delighted with anything but that woman looking at me with fondness and becoming passionately attached to me.[103]

Mahisa thought he was entitled to claim, 'I can supply all sensuous enjoyments.'[104] 'Thus Mahisa quitted the buffalo appearance and assumed a beautiful human shape. He put on beautiful ornaments, armplates, etc. and wore divine clothes and had garlands on his neck and thus shone like a second Kandarpa, the god of Love.'[105]

There follows a scene filled with irony. The knight woos the Lady, cajoling and instructing: the greatest pleasures are to be achieved when two equals of opposite gender meet. He speaks with affectionate and tender words, laying himself at her feet, arrogance abandoned for flattery, hubris turned into servility. He begs for mercy and confesses:

> I never showed my weakness to Devas; but today I acknowledge before you.[106]

With sincerity he promises everlasting subservience and faithful obedience if only she will marry him and become his Mahisi. On the conscious level he wants not death but life with the beloved.

While other cults did settle for the role of wife for Parvati and Laksmi, Durga will have none of it; her denials belie her provocative statements. But as before, she simultaneously initiates friendship:

> I tell you this very truly: I am satisfied with you by your words of friendship; therefore... When words are uttered seven times amongst each other, friendship is established between saints. That has been done so amongst us; so there is friendship now between you and me. I won't take away your life.[107]

It is not surprising that Devi is in no hurry to conclude the meeting, because she too is dazzled by the god-like demon, the epitome of chivalry; his commands and flattery are in precisely the correct proportion to satisfy an ambivalent female, intent perhaps on killing her lover but momentarily hesitant to do so. However, she is immediately frightened by the revelation of her own desires and covers her traces quickly: 'O hero, If you desire to die, fight gladly.'[108]

As for Mahisa, the efforts to resolve his sado-masochistic conflicts are merely exacerbated as the ambivalent mother entices and rejects, offers and retracts, to the distraction of the ensnared son standing on the battlefield, alone now, without the support of his bevy of ministers, facing the Terrible Mother. But as he is subliminally aware of the coming ignominious end, that he will never be her lover, but will find himself on the sacrificial altar instead, he reverses his approach, threatening that Devi will repent, should she refuse him.

The friendship was real, but the brief, tender episode lasts only an instant in time; then it is submerged by the dominant reality. Consubstantiality, incestual wishes, vestiges of prehistoric rituals, and the Mother Principle in confrontation with her son, overwhelm the momentary tryst. Devi's ire rises to a high pitch: the pair are now poised on the brink of a terrible battle.

Chapter Six The Battle

The Puranas often portray the dying demon as the tragic hero, who, unable to maintain his position as an independent son, is perennially at the mercy of the victorious Mother Goddess. But her conquests are merely temporary as, in an endless, repetitive cycle of events, the demons return to the struggle; and, although the Goddess always wins, nevertheless hope remains because the hero always re-engages in the struggle.

What accounts for the repetitive daivasuram struggle; what are its implications and what is its lasting impact as a religious symbol? To truly serve the purpose of being a carrier for human drives in conflict and confrontation, it must be appropriate for a particular time and place. But, lest it lose universality, its meaning cannot be too accurately specified or defined.

The devotee participates in the dynamic interaction and is thereby helped towards the integration of instinct, emotion and mind. The writer's descriptions of the vast multitudes of contestants in battle, of all shapes and kinds, agitate and vividly charge the imagination. Mesmerized by the vision, confronted with the objectified imagery now no longer entirely hidden from recognition, the devotee is no longer alone.

As we have observed earlier, the effort to maintain sharp distinctions between the protagonists becomes increasingly difficult as the details of the battle narratives are carefully scrutinized. The independent identities of Mahisa and Durga overlap, are blurred and confused. But a core of consciousness is preserved. Intoxicated-with-drink Durga and the equally maddened-with-pride hero recover their senses, if only for an instant; in the myth, this retention of the human potential marks the boundary between the daivasuram battle and animal jungle-combats, where physical might alone prevails. The demon who has been clawed to pieces by the Goddess' lion returns to the field in another form, either as elephant, human or lion. Durga retains the archer's skill, even while she is orgiastically inebriated. The battles are fought cun-

133

ningly and with expertise but also under a human delusion: each believes in the justice of their own cause.

It is best first to consider the distinctions that exist between them. These are limited to their location prior to the battle, to their vulnerability to wounds and to their final status as conqueror or conquered. Durga arrives from heights above the world; she is impervious to wounds and death (even though her saktis suffer from these human frailties, and the gods do too, although only rarely). Demons do die, but they are very soon reborn. Other than these differences, the various references in the texts justify the conclusion that while on earth, demon and Goddess share fundamental equivalencies, as their traits often cannot be distinguished one from the other.

Ultimately, when Mahisa is resurrected after death, they merge, as both are rooted in primitive nature deities, undifferentiated at the deepest levels of the unconscious. The battle narrative describes 'the slow descent of Durga and Mahisa, as they lose their specificity, into the sacred and highly charged arena in which life is dissolved back into the chaos from which it emerged.'[1] The deeper they penetrate into the individual unconscious and then even deeper into the symbiosis of mother and embryo, the more alike they appear to be. Together, Goddess and demon are a closed system. It is important to state repeatedly that one cannot associate demon or Goddess exclusively with unconscious shadow, evil or dragon; nor with its opposite, for, as we have seen, each forms only a section of an integrated system, in continual flux, continuously reorganized. This is the general constant theme apparent in the variety of versions. Mother/son, lover/beloved, Goddess/demon, female/male, warrior/victim, heaven/patala dweller—all such distinctions become diffused in the pugilists' arena where ecstasy, conquest, power, terror, uninhibited aggressive brutality, pride, pain and horror are abstracted, elevated from the particular and interchanged. If the ideal is the recovery of rta (cosmic order) which was upset by Mahisa's ascending to heaven, we are beset with a chicken and egg paradox, for the only order appears to be the perennial aspect of the conflict itself. The cosmic balance achieved by the victory of the gods is never permanent. Even though each side claims moral superiority, neither asuras or suras have right or good on their side, as they jointly share all that symbolizes life.

We must look for a different ideal in the battle between Mahisa and the Goddess: the meaning must be sought in regard to the internal conflicts of the individual. The battle is the paradigm for that brief period between birth and death. The battle is life, the struggle out of infantilism and into death. While there is no wholeness in life, or even in battle, there is glory in the struggle: because for this brief period, the contenders are equal.

Mahisa Poised on the Field of Battle

When it becomes inevitable that the mother/son symbiosis can only be severed by reversing the obsessional love, by risking physical pain and death in order to gain a separate identity, the hero has no choice but to brave the mother's scorching wrath; in short, to contemplate matricide.

His expectation of union with the beloved has been discouraged, not however, without much misleading ambiguity: thus the rage which follows upon the abrupt interruption of the cordiality and enticements. Mahisa's fixation encourages him to equate battle with love and violence with sex, which implies death. The battleground now becomes the locus for acting out his sado-masochistic drives.

However, the will for survival will imperceptibly but definitely turn into the will for self-annihilation, as guilt and shame, arising from the sinful wish for mother love and its concomitant desire to destroy her, overwhelm anger and pride. The sadistic responses slide into masochism and Mahisa longs to be a victim of the sacrifice. In the ordinary sense of the word, the hero can never in fact be victorious.

In the *Kalika Purana,* he is even confronted with his terrible fate in advance.

> When this demon was asleep at night on a mountain, the hero Mahisa saw a dreadful dream, which was horrible to look at; Mahamaya Bhadrakali cleft my head with her sword and drank his (sic) blood, her mouth widely opened and extremely frightening. Then the next morning, the demon Mahisa with his Daityas was scared, and together with his retinue he worshipped her for a long time.[2]

Mahisa propitiates the sadistic Goddess, and she comes forth as Bhadrakali: 'It has positively been seen by me in a dream that thou wast drinking my blood, after having cleft my head, O Goddess, with your sword. This drinking my blood shall certainly be carried out by thee, as I know from this evidence.'

The dream was a portent of the future: this was the 'woman' of Brahma's boon, destined to kill him. Since Mahisa's self-image depends entirely on his ability to conquer and even to kill her who will not leave him in peace, he resorts to great rage, which will ignite the powerful energies necessary for confrontation—pride, great physical prowess and blind anger. In her intoxicated state, as instrument of maya, however, the Goddess seals his fate. In all the versions, she must quaff her liquor before she can commit the dastardly act of slaying the son:

> She drank the beverage again and again. With eyes rolling, she laughed aloud.... With her face reddened as a result of the inebriation after drinking wine, and with her senses excited... (she killed Mahisa).[4]

Ironically, without her liquor, the Goddess seems to be as vulnerable as Mahisa, or even more so, although these may be tricks of maya, or of the human mind attempting to balance the drives of the unconscious. The Brahmacari priest invents a fanta- cized Amazon of superhuman dimensions, who will strike, kick, bite and devour, as a happy antidote to his own repressed sexuality.

The Battle as Festival

Continual daily recitations of the DM at the Navratri festival recreate the battle between the Goddess and Mahisa. On the eighth day at noon during the Tuljapur, Maharashtra ritual (see p. 207) a silver statue, half buffalo, half man, is ceremoniously transported into the shrine, where it is placeo near the Goddess. He enters as gallant suitor and there encounters a lovely, enticing female, dressed in red like a bride, profusely orna- mented, with a serene countenance. The Goddess and the buffalo demon remain together for many hours. But nothing is as it seems to be. By the evening, the veils of maya which have engulfed the demon since the time he received the boon have been removed. For the red of the bridal dress—the red blood of the marital bed—is the blood of war, and her many hands hold weapons in readiness for combat. The sanctum–wedding hall becomes a battlefield. On Ashtami night, festival and battle are synonymous, and the rapidly changing sequence of events dramatizes the climactic moments in the life of the hero. After a prolonged paradigmatic ritual combat, the opponent/lover/demon has been transformed by the many bloodied hands of the Goddess. The sanctum battlefield becomes the sacrificial altar, with Mahisa as victim. But in this same *garbhagrha* (womb house) the sacrificed demon will be reborn.

The Goddess had been benign at the beginning of the festival. On the seventh night at Tuljapur, she endows Sivaji with her sword, and her hair is dishevelled and black; on the eighth night, she finally cuts through the ambivalences and illusions that had plagued the interactions of the dyad. The dragon/monster Mother Goddess, erstwhile bride in red, beheads her husband or would-be-husband, and, as she consumes the flesh and blood of her asura enemies, the festival music plays on and on. Devi says: 'Today at my festival a buffalo Mahisa is sacrificed... let him be quickly dispatched.'[5] The orgiastic sexual rites related to the hierogamies, the narrative of battle and ritual combat at festivals ultimately serve the same purpose, and it is natural for the writers at times to mix metaphors.

The DM describes the battalions of the Goddess:

> Some beat drums, some blew conches and others played on tabors in the great martial festival.[6]

The martial festival *is* the battle, the rejoicing is the result of coming into contact with the centre of the self which craves release from conflicting drives, freedom from the bonds of maya of the Goddess. She *is* the unconscious. The tumult on the field of battle is the stage upon which ever wider aspects of the psyche seek expression.

To counteract the forces of destruction, another dialectical play is in process, affirming life forces inherent in the rhythms of nature, expressed in dance and music and the light always present in the setting of the battlefield. Music is the deity Mantrini, accompanied by *gandharvas*. Her role in the cacophonic disorder of battle is to provide the structure of an ordered universe by sounding melodious units of time, regular beats of the *mridanga*, and life-giving paeans of hope to overcome destruction. The Goddess of music represents the heartbeat—the wholeness of body, mind and soul which the intoxicated Goddess-gone-wild, abandoning herself entirely to chaos, threatens with dismemberment. The devotee is encouraged by Mantrini to rely on the predictable rhythms, the fundamental processes of nature, the hoped-for order which will return after the cessation of the furious battle.

And so it is music that announces the battle,[7] music that frightens the enemy,[8] that is played by both sakti soldiers and the army of the daityas,[9] and it is ever present, all pervasive during the battle. The entire field rings with the sound of mridangas, conch shells, lutes and other musical instruments.

As the battle increases in fury, arrows fly, flesh is pierced, all is in perpetual, violent movement, there are pursuits, flights, plunges and retreats, yelling and howling in pain. While limbs and bodies are being torn apart and flayed, while red blood spills like rivers, and heads roll, the band plays on, to encourage the deities and asuras in the struggle for survival. Until the very end the deity Mantrini, friend and supporter of the warrior, gives courage to the dying in moments filled with pathos and optimism.

> Headless trunks fought with the Devi with best weapons in their hands. Some of these headless trunks danced there in battle to the rhythm of the musical instruments.[10]

In one instance, when the saktis of the Goddess became thirsty, and they were no longer able to wage war, the ocean was called upon to supply them with an infinite amount of a variety of liquor, which they greedily consumed.[11] The incident provides the writers with the opportunity to combine the themes of sexuality, music, dance and war.

> The army of Saktis that had been stupefied before had been revived and gladdened by me (ocean).
>
> Some of them are dancing and singing with their girdles and waistbands tinkling sweetly. Some of them are clapping their hands in front of those who dance.
>
> Some are laughing with their beautiful breasts shaking and bouncing. A few of them lean on one another's bodies with laziness and slackness due to delight.[12]

The battle is a festival. Controls break down and secret doors of the unconscious are unlocked. In the wild frenzy the orgiastic activity is sometimes categorizable, but often instincts are melded under the intoxicating influence of drink and the fury of struggle. In battle, as in lovemaking, tensions are released through rajasic aggressions, participants are possessed by the unconscious; all is sunk in the mêlée and all to the sound of music. Even the drunken warrior deity herself, with bloodied hands and rasping voice, falls under the spell of the rhythmic beats:

> Seeing them (asuras) Durga took easily a lute and a nice damaru drum too in her hand and began to play on them smilingly.... the mother of the universe drank a good drink, playing all the while on the lute.[13]

We may recall that the 'stranger buffalo' who had intruded into the story had in fact been the symbol for an incestuous wish only momentarily brought to consciousness. Now, transformed into an asura general, this very same symbol, as Namara, suffered punishment for his unconscious desires:

> Grasping the Danava Namara in the middle, O Brahman, and whirling him with the left hand, the enraged Katyayani (Devi) beat him as if he were a drum.[14]

Poor Namara, like the Greek Pentheus in the post-Dionysian revelries, was paying the dear price of his life for his sins. As a result of her own ambivalent responses, the crazed mother attacks her son on the field of battle. Love, hate, combat and music, no longer separable, are all subsumed in the ritual of the battle festival.

In a therapeutic process, the festival unfolds an umbrella over that which is no longer under conscious control, and like war, it presses the stamp of justice on to amoral, unconscious drives. In this the Goddess is invoked: as she as well as the demons are equal participants, fully involved in the chaos of the prescribed ritual, human guilt concerning natural animal instincts (known in Christianity as sin) is modified. In that guilt-reducing system, Jesus died for these sins. In contrast, in Judaism, Adonai conveniently removes himself from these 'obscenities', and even ceremonials in his honour show little trace of his participation, as guilt is ricochetted back on to the devotee who is charged with obligatory readings of portions of the Torah dealing with tribal warfare. The Theravada Buddhist also relies entirely on the ability of the human superego to control instinct and on the rational individual to take ethical decisions and to stand by them. In both these faiths, the individual is required to carry the burden of guilt alone.

The festival to the Goddess on the other hand assures the devotee that she takes the guilt for instinctual drives upon her ample motherly bosom, and in a fortunate conceptual twist, unlike Jesus, she lives to tell the tale. In the battle with the Goddess, the father god assumes a passive role, while mother and son are plunged into the laws of the jungle which can then be realistically viewed.

The festival, as the superego, imposes a grandiose structure on to the instinctual confusion. The ritual enactment of primeval battle scenes was a regular feature of the archaic New Year rites to which the festival of Navratri is the direct heir. The recitation of the DM, the creation of magnificent pandals, and immersions bring into modern times the great traditions of the harvest festivities.

Reading the text, contact with the idol, and the dramatization of sacred stories and dancing is therapeutic and rejuvenating, as these devices help the devotee to cope with his inner conflict. Even though the goals may only be achieved temporarily, the cyclical nature of the battle which focuses, not on a final solution but on its temporary recurrence, paves the way for belief in an illusory permanence which seems to be far more satisfying for the Indian than an acceptance of death as final.

The Battle as Sex and Violence

Lust and violence are the result of powers in confrontation, and the two forces are linked, if not always interchangeable. O'Flaherty and Shulman lead us into the next level of the myth. O'Flaherty stresses the coalescence of lust and violence during the confrontations between the Devi and the buffalo demon:

> The demon lusts to marry the goddess and is killed by her in an ecstasy of sexual/martial confrontation.[15]

And Shulman states:

> If marriage can be described in Tamil myths as a battle (often fatal for the male combatant), war can be pictured as a marriage.[16]

In one instance, marriage is preceded by a brutal battle between the future bride and groom. The warrior queen, Minaksi of the three breasts, challenges the gods to battle during which she displays all her violent, horrific capabilities. But as soon as she confronts the god Siva, she is transformed into a shy bride-to-be, whose phallic aspect falls away.[17] If indeed Siva is Mahisa and Minaksi an aspect of Devi, we can assume a structural connection between the two myths.

Since the battle between Mahisa and Durga turns out to be a defence against and offers a therapeutic reversal of forbidden thoughts, the tension and dangers involved are greater even than the perils of marriage. At one level, the battle is an unconscious attempt at incestuous rape. Not for one moment does the wish leave Mahisa; he will kill the Goddess if necessary. He is confused about the love; at the same time he is terrorized, and he is only sometimes aware of the danger.[18] Imaging the Mother Goddess as the enemy has the effect of reversing the obsessive drive, and this encourages the demon hero to hope for rescue from the consequences of his own sinful wishes. No wonder the language of sex and the language of violence is often intermingled, even if the Devi indeed puts aside her weapons and dons the garland when she is ready to make love. In the midst of battle:

> As Candi dispatched her shafts, the joints of her corselet opened at the part where it bulges out from the bulk of her swelling breasts. Her rounded breast came into view, her girdle slipped down to her navel.[19]
>
> She crushed with her foot the buffalo every limb of whose body had been thrilled with her touch.[20]

Or in the *Brahmanda Purana (Lalita Mahatmaya)*, when the saktis are inebriated:

> Some begin to swagger as girdles and garments begin to slip down from their hips. They simply shake and shiver.... All their limbs and eyes became delighted with hairs standing on ends like the buds of the Kadamba tree. These Saktis annihilated the armies of the Crown Prince.[21]

Mahisa's generals were fond of directing attention to the distinctions between love and battle as well as to the vocabulary they had in common. Prior to the encounter on the field, as we have seen, the ministers attempted to persuade the Goddess that her war talk was, in effect, love talk. They believed that they knew better than she did (and perhaps, indeed, they did). In the confrontation of the Goddess with the demon Sumbha, for example, his minister Dhumarlochana remarks:

> The sentences uttered by Thee: 'He who will conquer me in battle' is full of deep meanings. 'Battle' means two different things according to persons for whom it is intended; it is of two kinds. One out of excitement and another out of sexual intercourse. With Thee, the sexual intercouse is intended.... The lord of the Daityas, expert in the science of love, will certainly conquer Thee engaged in amorous fight and will lay Thee stretched on a soft bedding and will make Thee tired; he will make Thy body covered with blood by striking with nails and he will bite Thy lips to pieces.... Those are certainly very unfortunate who like fighting with weapons.[22]

The symbolism of the sacred foot of Devi, which for millennia has served as icon for millions of devotees, is frankly analysed here by a wise minister. They knew the difference between making love and making war and did not relish the idea of mixing the two, although they already had intimations of associations between sex and violence. Tamra, the spokesman with the voice of reason, wishes to keep the impulses separate:

> O Thou of beautiful thighs...what is the use of holding ordinary arrows, when those two eyebrows, like bows, are existing with you. What need have you to take ordinary arrows when you are graced with those piercing eye sights, Your arrows.[23]

Analogies can be found between the language of the battle and instructions in the *Kama Sutra*. This suggests that the function of the battle in the Mahisamardini myth was indeed to allay the fears of Oedipal pulls which had been encouraged all along by the seductive Mother Goddess. That even in the height of love-passion identical Oedipal association are operative is suggested in the *Kama Sutra*. When making love, the participants are to exclaim:

> Amba, Oh Mother. O God! But sexual intercourse can be compared to a combat, on account of the contrarities of love and its tendency to dispute.[24]

The words are general enough to evoke both *vira* (battle) and kama sentiments in the devotee, as the following examples show.

Kama Sutra	Battle descriptions
When love becomes intense, pressing with the nails or scratching the body with them is practised.[25]	The lion too, by his nails, rent that Asura to pieces.[26]
There are various kinds of bites including *varahacharvitakam*: the biting of a boar.[27]	She ground them (asuras) most frightfully with her teeth... crunched them up with her teeth in fury.[28]
The biting which consists of many broad rows of marks near to one another and with red intervals is called the 'biting of a boar'. This is impressed on the breasts and the shoulders; and these two last modes of biting are peculiar to persons of intense passion.[29]	Potrini, the boar-formed Deity, 'had made all the revolving worlds her adopted children' but at the same time she had torn and pierced the haughty danavas. Her curved teeth resembled the crescent moon.[30]
As complementary to the Kama Shastra, the arts to be studied: Practising magic and sorcery... to augment... covert action, like sleight of hand and the arts of quickly changing and disguising appearances.[31]	The asura general Karalaksa was intrepid due to his mastery of black magic.[32]
At this time Hinkara, the nasal, and other sounds may be made, alternatively, or on the spur of the moment.[34]	He (Ruruasura) then discharged towards the gods a magical power which made them all fall into a swoon.[33]
	Mahisa made sounds in her ear. His (Mahisa's) bellow pierced the hollow of her ear.[35]
Blows with the fist should be given on the back of the woman... She should give blows in return, abusing the man. Striking is of four kinds, and the place of striking is the body.	Mahisa struck Devi with horn (and tail).[37] You will have to go... pierced by my mass of arrows, to your death.[38]
The use of the hands to form a wedge between the bosom, a scissor-like grip on the head and piercing with the fingers on the cheeks, and pincer motions on the breasts and side, may also be taken into consideration with the other four modes of striking.[36]	Devi pierces Durgama's heart.[39]
When a person presses the chin, the	Due to inebriation... All their

Kama Sutra	Battle descriptions
breasts...so softly that no scratch or mark is left, but only the hair on the body becomes erect from the touch of the nails.[40]	[Saktis in battle with Bhandasura] limbs and eyes became delighted with hairs standing on their ends like the buds of the Kadamba tree.[41]
When love play and intercourse lead to fatigue, the woman can take charge 'Purushayta Prakaran' (acting like a man)...she gets on top of her lover, should do in return the same actions which he used to do before returning his blows and chaffing him, should say, 'I was laid down by you and fatigued with hard Congress. I shall now therefore lay you down in return'....In this way she should act the part of a man.[42]	Mahisa's minister Durdhara states 'The saying of that lady, "I will lay your lord in the death bed in the battlefield" is to be taken in the light of inverted sexual intercourse, where woman is above the man.'[43]
The signs of her need of more enjoyment and of failing to be satisfied are: she shakes herself, does not let the man to get up...bites the man, kicks him.[44]	Therefore dost Thou make his heart bud forth by thy kicking.[45] And the great Mahisasura was killed by her with kicks of her feet.[46]

The Goddess' protestations about not associating with the would-be lover because he was born of a she-buffalo have a hollow ring in view of the *Kama Sutra*'s non-moral analogizing of animal and human energies. There is little self-consciousness or sense of degradation or shame in the free use of similes linking sexual intercourse on the human and animal planes. In an era which focused attention on exchange of energy and the power of the animal as a model for the human encounter rather than insisting on hierarchical, vertical relationships with superior human beings, all of nature—vegetation, animals and humans—functions as a morally equivalent interacting totality. Thus, in the *Kama Sutra,* male lovers are classified either as hare, bull or horse, and females as deer, mare or elephant, and various sexual activities have an animal nomenclature.

As the struggle between hero and Goddess moves towards its climax, lovemaking and battle, names and categories lose specificity, assuming an independent life. Now new sets of conditions reflect the constant tensions between rational control and unconscious force. The *Kama Sutra* advises: 'If a man and a woman are very much in love with each other, and not thinking of any pain or hurt, embrace each other's bodies . . . then it is called an embrace like a "mixture of milk and water".'[47]

The battle description goes thus: 'The close intermingling of Saktis and the demons was like that of water and milk.'[48] During the time of fighting it confused both of them.

The texts abound with phallic analogies: horns, elephants' trunks, mountain peaks, snakes, swords, dismemberment, blood from the demon's neck as semen ejaculated, extinguishing of life as loss of tumescence, ocular/vaginal symbolism; the birth of the hero out of his own buffalo body as reversal of his own birth, and devouring.

Even though the phrases can be interpreted in sexual terms, it is important to emphasize that Hindus prefer a multi-faceted view. If it is to be effective, the symbol will have the potential for many interpretations: the people who turn to Goddess worship today may not be able to analyse what is happening, but the relief and release they achieve as the undifferentiated instincts are projected on to a functioning symbol may well be all the greater for this.

Aggression

While a contemporary reader might be offended by the level of cynicism the *Kama Sutra* reflects, in its day, the didactic lessons may well have been the only means to harness and control rapacious impulses among the aristocracy, and warn them about the consequences of promiscuity. As it encourages pleasure, the *Kama Sutra* is, in the final analysis, about the triumph of life.

Conversely, the battle narratives are concerned with the everpresent threat of aggressive drives ultimately leading to death. Accounts of battles transport the reader into a nightmare world, within which horrifying images, a phantasmagoria of wild, floating associations, a host of frightening visions erupt. Undifferentiated repressions are catapulted in increasing frenzy on to the rubbish heap of the battlefield.

Like the dreamer who alone can interpret the meaning of his dream, the narrative can (and should) remain merely the potential repository, symbolizing what cannot be stated. Metaphors, allusions and analogies carry multiple meanings, now with one emphasis, now with a different focus, depending on the individual's internal responses to the common cauldron of the unconscious.

The Goddess and her saktis seem to have the edge on versatility and excesses of violence. According to the texts, Devi harasses, becomes enraged, slaps, smashes, strikes, delivers blows, pounds, drags, bites, kicks, ties down with a noose, injures, maims, mutilates, stupefies, paralyses, showers arrows on, breaks chariots, dismembers, swallows, blinds, tears and shatters bodies into a thousand pieces, severs necks, splits open Mahisa's breast and slays! But her lovely face is in no way perturbed. She accomplishes all this after having drunk wine, or blood, or having laughed, using both her own body, her cutting teeth, her multiple arms and all kinds of weapons to fight with. But true to form now and again there are reminders of her sattvic nature:

> The Lotus face of Kalaratri became softened in pity because of the stream of blood coming out before her eyes from his [Mahisa's] head which had been pierced by her dart.[49]

But while at times she shows weakness, seeking refuge with Siva or in larger and larger draughts of wine, these are only momentary lapses in her predominantly destructive powers. The Mother paralyses the demons and makes them mad; she eats their fat and flesh, but her speciality is the cutting off of limbs and especially the heads. 'Who can live after beholding the enraged destroyer?'[50]

At the height of her intoxicated state, Devi is the paradigmatic, primordial Goddess, repeating the eternal history of the human race. Giving her body to nourish the child in embryo form and at the breast, the Mother forever demands far more in return. She consumes flesh and blood, exacting payment for the miracle of birth of the creatures of the earth for which she alone is ultimately responsible. Because for the son union with the Mother is the only ultimate reality, what occurs on the battlefield is merely the inevitable processes of nature being compressed in Time.

For his part, the mythmaker is unable to dispense with the guilt he carries along from the day he realizes that, for his own survival, he must separate from the Mother, but he can make an attempt to come to terms with his situation. The Brahmacari sacrifices of sexuality are inadequate, and so identification with the demon has a salutary effect. It requires a great battle, and as the flesh and blood sacrifice, he will ultimately receive the longed-for punishment. To make peace with reality, each son born of a mother will have to wage this struggle, even though the hero will be he who dies in the struggle. The Goddess herself will gain strength from the offering, as the infant did from the mother's breast, and by the death of the son the books of life will finally be balanced.

Thus the demon hero's own aggression may be conceived as defensive: from their point of view, Bhanda's complaint that his asuras are being attacked by the powers of 'that sinful deity'[51] makes a good deal of sense. And so the buffalo demon fights for his life, primarily with his body: muzzle, hoofs, tail, teeth, feet, but the horn which pierces is his proudest weapon. With this phallic instrument, he wounds the Lady he rushes to penetrate. He and his fellows also pounce, smash, afflict the bodies of the saktis and lust for their blood; they split, immobilize, suppress, arrest, drag the Devi by the tresses, capture, hack down, massacre and crush, or at least they love to boast that they will. Often they have to resort to deceit to attack from the rear secretly at night, ever eager to strike at the weak points. Actually, as we have repeatedly stressed, during the battle the demon and the Goddess are but two sides of the same brutal coin, mother and son each striving for dominance.

This would account for the recitations about the regressions into primeval atavistic abandon; even today the priests consider it their sacred duty to teach these truths, to hand on to the next generations. For the very retelling gives courage to the devotee caught in this impossible situation. The rsi advises: 'Listen attentively (to) this ancient, holy sin-destroying fear-dispelling story which originated at the commencement of *Satyayuga* (the golden age).'[52] However unpleasant the reading of the events of the battle between Mahisa and Devi and of all the other daivasuram struggles, when the raw core of the human condition is put thus on view, the devotee gains cathartic relief. By recitation and worship of the icon, he renews himself.

Nature and Zoanthropic Imagery

The battle narratives are saturated with references to Goddess or demon equated with, controlling, or as fragmenting and destroying natural phenomena, so that the two often lose anthropomorphic identity. They return to their essence, as nature-related deities.

The texts of the battle use light and fire as metaphors more or less with equal weight in the descriptions of the Goddess and the demon. Both were born of fire or of fiery energy; the metaphors retain a memory of these birth events.

References to vegetation link Goddess and buffalo in battle and in sacrificial ritual. Always and everywhere at the festivals, the Goddess is either represented as a pot (*karakam*) planted with fast-growing grain, or as an ingenious form made from a variety of combinations of plants; or as icon she is garlanded so frequently and heavily that she is submerged in a plethora of offerings:

> One should worship the Supporteress of the worlds with... gourds, and coconuts, dates, breadfruit, grapes, mangoes and bilva fruit, and with *plihas* and citrons, with *kaseras*, betel nuts, roots, rose apples, Indian persimmons, etc.[3]

Similarly, the buffalo is copiously adorned with vegetation of all kinds and colours, often painted yellow with saffron; he shines with the light of his coming resurrection. Before the victim is sacrificed, he drinks a potion of consecrated rice and wine; after his demise, all share in his sacrifice by consuming his blood mixed with rice. At Tuljapur, in the Brahmanical ceremony, the victim is a fruit (melon), substituted for the animal victim.

When guilt becomes intolerable, zoanthropic imagery, as defence, is called upon. Imaging himself as a beast, the sufferer son is detached from an elevated, all-powerful and all-pure Mother Goddess; degrading himself, he puts himself safely out of reach. The Brahmacari priest who recites the myth is equally safely protected, forced into asceticism by means of his own fears.

Association with the power and strength of the buffalo provides a convenient release from conflicting human emotions. This permits the controlling female deity to overpower the brute, raw, infantile, dependent animal instinct, to ensure a certain amount of security, however spurious. While Goddess and buffalo demon as polar opposites have gripped the imagination of Indians for more than two millennia, there is simultaneously the continuing tendency for each to assume the characteristics of the other, as ample examples in the texts (and in the developing style of the statues), proves.

It is not unusual for gods and goddesses to assume the shape of animals. When Visnu cursed Laksmi to become a mare, he himself took the form of a beautiful horse. Union with his wife in animal form resulted in the issue of 'a beautiful well qualified child'.[54] Visnu's other animal forms are fish, boar and lion. Brahma turns into a deer to pursue his own daughter in animal form, and the Goddess herself is direct heir to the archaic Mistress of Animals. Mahisa's animal form, therefore, actually brings him closer to the Devi, for when she is on earth she usually rides on a lion, but at times she is mounted on a deer or horse and is surrounded by protecting animals. She shouts at her adversary: 'Even if through pride of strength you are anxious for battle, come then. Let my jackals be satiated with your flesh.'[55]

Sometimes, when she is the wife of a god, she has the body of a woman and the head of an animal. In regard to her emanations:

> From her laughter were born various strange spirits. Some were tiger-faced and terrific, and some looked like wolves, while others were horse-faced, buffalo-faced and boar-faced. Some had faces like those of mice and cocks, while others wore faces like those of cows, goats, sheep, having faces, eyes and feet of various kinds and holding multiple weapons.[56]

In the dreamscape of the narrative, on the battlefield, as Narasimhi, the sakti of Visnu's lion incarnation, precisely like Mahisa, she is in animal form. In this bizarre scenario who can tell the difference between Goddess and buffalo?

> Narasimhi arrived there, assuming a body like that of Narasimha, bringing down the constellations by the toss of her mane.... Narasimhi, filling all the quarters and the sky with her roars, roamed about in the battle devouring other great asuras torn by her claws.[57]

Or as Varahi,

> The Sakti of Hari, who assumed the incomparable form of a sacrificial boar, she also advanced there in her boar-form. Shattered by the boar-formed goddess [Varahi] with blows of her snout, wounded in their chest by the point of her tusk and torn by her discus, the asuras fell down.[58]

The metaphors uttered by the Mistress of Animals emphasize associations with beasts. In these terms she protests:

> Do you think that a lioness becoming very passionate would make an ordinary jackal her husband? or would a she elephant prefer an ass? or would a heavenly Cow like a bison?[59]

It can be assumed that this is a not too subtly masked identification with Mahisa's bovine mother Syama.

Chapter Seven The Battle as Sacrifice: Mahisa as Victim

Incorporating the entire gamut of possible response systems, the Mahisamardini myth would seem to be a late amalgamation of strands of belief and ritual that are also related to the sacrificial rites and mythologies of other cultures. They all end in the death of the god/hero/king/animal. Mahisa represents god and the son of the god; man as god, human or animal; and finally, animal as god or human who must ultimately die as a victim:

> Every sacrifice implies a solidarity... of nature between officiant, god and the thing sacrificed. . . . The idea of the sacrifice also bears within it the germ of a confusion with the animal, a confusion which entails the risk of being extended beyond man to the very god.[1]

As early as the DM (and perhaps earlier, although no textual records survive), god/human/buffalo as co-ordinate symbol for the sacrificial victim effectively united the parallel solutions. Mahisa as divine, human and animal sacrifice all rolled into one is a symbol of those victims whose death is required to satiate the permanent, persistent human propensity to deflect aggressive instincts on to the substitute sacrificial victim of one species or another. Now in recitation or dramatized form, Mahisa's death on the field of battle re-enacts, and thus recreates, the prehistoric but still living event.[2]

The buffalo demon's mother Syama performed her suttee rite in animal form; in the later imagery, the son's own demise was either in animal or human form, and in the texts and icons, during his transformations and in the final act, Mahisa suffers multiple beheadings as animal and as man. This ambiguity provides the great magnetic appeal of the myth and rites and the images connected with it. For the myth maintains conscious awareness of the animal nature in man (which the later religions attempted entirely to suppress) even while the demon/god analogue is

150

retained. The Mahisa symbol is reality oriented; it serves psychic needs effectively; it is confrontational and therefore human.

Durga shouts:

> Your king is born of a buffalo and is the worst of brutes. I will sacrifice him before the Devi for the benefit of the gods.[3]

At the start, the struggle with the Goddess takes the form of a conventional war, but eventually the battlefield becomes indistinguishable from the sacrificial ground, as during the prolonged ten-thousand-year war the would-be lover turned warrior is slowly metamorphosed into the analogue for victim in the Brahmanical sacrifice. Thus, the myth can be seen as one manifestation of the relationship between the cosmic battle and the ritual of sacrifice. Out of the chaos of battle Mahisa will return to his original state of union with the Goddess to whom he is being sacrificed on the field. The Mother stands ready; she has set the trap and is brandishing the sacrificial knife in preparation for the ritual battle, the ultimate dismemberment and resurrection, while the impetuous, infatuated hero rushes into the fray, totally ignoring her intentions.

Devi's saktis bear the brunt of the violence, and they do sometimes lose strength and lose heart,[4] but at the final instant, the Goddess emerges as what Maccoby terms the evil and righteous Lord High Executioner, who spills blood and dismembers the bodies of her consubstantial relatives, the demons. The references to the battlefield as sacrificial arena persist in the texts through many centuries:

> Kali, holding the heads of Canda and Munda in her hands, approached Chandika and said, her words mingled with very loud laughter; here we have brought you the heads of Canda and Munda as two great animal offerings in this sacrifice of battle.[5]

The meaning of this becomes clearer in Bana's poetry:

> Katyayani (Candi) had verily in person offered as an oblation the body of the great Daitya, the Foe of the Gods.[6] Mahisa . . . is brought as an oblation to Ambika (Candi) by the Gods with prostrated bodies.[7]

The all-powerful Goddess assumes all tasks: she is the slayer, the sacrificer and the recipient who shares her victims with her fellow warriors. Many centuries later, the DBP will reflect consistent ideas. After a furious battle with Canda and Munda, having 'tied down that Asura [Canda] by Her Pasa weapon [and] instantly fastened [Munda] down like his brother',

> Kali went to Ambika and said: I have brought the two beasts very auspicious as offerings in this sacrificial war.[8]
>
> ... Kalika spoke to her (Ambika) again: In this war-sacrifice there is this axe which is like a sacrificial post; I will offer these two as victims to Thy sacrifice. Thus no act of envy will be committed [i.e. killing in a sacrifice is not considered as envy]. Thus saying the Kalika Devi cut off their heads with great force and gladly drank their blood.[9]

Here is the entire sequence of the ritual of sacrifice. Canda and Munda are pursued, they engage in battle with the representatives of the Goddess, are caught, tied down with a noose, brought in front of the Goddess, chained to a post and slaughtered. Rationalizations to eliminate guilt, and consumption of the victim follow in proper order.

The *Candisataka* emphasizes the sacrificial meal:

> After Katyayani had verily, in person, offered as an oblation the body of the great Daitya (Mahisa), the ghouls (assistants to the Goddess) ate his large intestine.[10]

Like his counterparts both in the tribal rituals and in the texts, Mahisa is pursued, killed by means of blows and weapons, dismembered, and finally his soul is released in the longed-for return to the Mother.

Mahisa as Divine Sacrifice

The numerous textual references to the semi-divine status of Mahisa, descended from deity or rsi and the residual worship of the buffalo as god can be traced to times when in the forest, the hunter-gatherer propitiated the feared omnipotent animals of the wild. Both feared and exalted as totem deity, the buffalo was periodically sanctified, slain, dismembered, consumed and resurrected in prescribed rituals.[11] As buffalo and Goddess shared sovereignty of the forest, there must have been confusion about their relative or conjoined divine status. Later, the divinity is conceived as female in human form with animal attributes and/or with an animal vehicle, while the role of the buffalo becomes more ambiguous. With the domestication of cattle, as we have observed with the Todas, the buffalo retains the status of a god who is only occasionally sacrificed, while simultaneously serving a utilitarian function. Buffalo imagery is never far from the mind of settled people; thus Mahisa as god carries the weight of ages on his shoulders.

The rites established in a hunting–gathering society were preserved in somewhat modified form in pastoral and agricultural communities. Wherever in the ancient world the Great Goddess ruled, the universal belief in the death and resurrection of her consort, the divine king, was institutionalized in rites deemed imperative for the preservation of society. Only by means of appropriate mimetic rituals properly performed would life be restored to plants and animals otherwise inextricably subject to decay and death.

Primitive agricultural societies conceived of an in-dwelling spirit which suffered when scythes and sickles severed the plant at harvest. The spirit lived while the plant lived and periodically died when the plant died. Anthropomorphized or symbolized by a bull, as male god, it became necessary for the deity to be sacrificed, so that its fertilizing phallus, head and blood could be transferred to the expectant earth. Thus sacrifice of a live human or animal con-cretized the merged concepts of vegetative spirit, human god/king and Goddess/queen as fructifying agents given name and form. In the ritual, either king, priest or animal took on the divine male role as victim/sacrifice. The rites were cruel, involving the tearing to pieces of the victims and drenching the fields with the fertilizing living blood.

This was the quintessential creed which spread from Sumer and Egypt throughout the realm of the Goddess, and it was without doubt practised by aboriginals in India for millennia. During the festival the god-king united with the queen to fructify the earth, to the accompaniment of rhythmic music, prayers, lamentations, mimetic orgiastic revelry and a prescribed ritual system which culminated in the sacrifice and resurrection of the male and the triumph of the Mother Goddess. In historic times, to justify and explain the received rites, legends concerning the dramatis per-sonae of the festival developed and changed to suit local cultures, but the basic elements remained intact. This is Mahisa's heritage and this his function.

Mahisa as Human Sacrifice: Naramedha

A residue of primordial origin is the anxiety accompanying the persistent human impulse to sacrifice oneself, part of oneself, or a substitute for oneself, and it seeks relief through expression in myth and ritual. Violent emotions are diverted as 'the voice of the avenger within the self is ventriloquized within and heard as the voice of god. And this voice is persistent and allows no rest until, in despair, its hearer turns and rends himself, or finds someone else to injure in his place.'[12]

> It is tempting to remember that in the ideal case, humans and buffaloes are interchangeable as sacrifices to the Goddess, and that the ideal victim is none other than a composite of the two, the humanized Mahisasura.[13]

As substitute for the bloody rite, the myth has served to restrain what might have been even greater amounts of slaughter; embedding the sacrifice in the battle narrative is an effective means of masking the enormous amount of guilt connected with the slaying, not alone the guilt arising out of the act itself, but also because of the motives which are retained in the contemporary psyche. To imply that the death of Mahisa is acceptable because it occurs during a just war appropriately screens what cannot be faced directly. As victim of his existential situation, as inheritor of hunter instincts but as the son of a mother as well, the mythmaker deals with seemingly irreconcilable tensions and contradictions out of which he creates the fabric of his story. It could not have been otherwise: he is animal by nature, and he is born of his mother.

In struggling with these conditions the priests evolved functioning rationalizations. Revealing passages in the *Satapatha Brahmana* describe the transmission of sacrificial essence from the human victim, through a series of animals and into earth and grain:

> At first, namely, the gods offered up a man as victim. When he was offered up, the sacrificial essence went out of him. It entered the horse. They offered up the horse, and then an ox, sheep, goat etc. and as much efficacy as all those sacrificed victims would have for him, so much efficacy has this oblation.[14]

The prophets of Israel and, in India, the Buddha and Mahavir vehemently repudiated all blood sacrifices. But while this ideological stance successfully repressed the perpetual and troublesome unconscious drive to a certain degree, the impulse was by no means eliminated. In subsequent historical periods, in diverse cultures, the human sacrificial ritual took its horrifying toll.

To stem this bloody tide in the West, the concrete symbol of the sacrifice of Jesus Christ on the cross served as metaphoric substitute, returning the rite to the safe arena of consciousness. While this construct dominated the western psyche for two thousand years, Christianity paid little heed to the animal nature in man which seeks blood when threatened. The compulsion was transferred to religious wars, persecutions and crime. Since Judaism had long since come to conceive of human sacrifice as pagan and taboo, the re-emergence in Christianity of the human symbolic victim resulted in a bifurcation: Judaism and Christianity branched away out of the common tree, assuming different roles in history.

In India, a variety of solutions were sought to control the obsession for blood offerings which often overwhelmed reformist philosophies. Austerities, suicide, killing an enemy and animal sacrifice were written into the Brahmanical law, but the literature reflects the reality that the ongoing struggle can never be entirely ended.

Texts

The Indian texts preserve residual references to the sacrifice of the son: Sunahsepa, like Isaac and Jesus, is the first-born male human sacrifice, who first appears in the Rg Vedic hymns. As archetypal symbol, his story, with variations, is also in the *Aitareya Brahmana,* the *Ramayana,* the *Mahabharata* and in the *Puranas:*

> Bound to the triple yupa (sacrificial post), captured Sunahsepha called
>   out to Aditya (Varuna, son of Aditi)
> Tear off these bonds. Oh, Varuna, above, below and in the middle.[15]

In all the versions, a central core is retained: Varuna presented the childless King Harishchandra with a son, on condition that he would be returned as blood sacrifice to the god. However the king provided Varuna with a series of rationalizations for postponing the sacrifice, and when prince Rohita reached maturity, he fled to the forest; there he met a Brahmin who agreed to sell his own son Sunahsepa as substitute victim.[16] As potential human victims, both boys show their mettle by resisting what seems to have been

an established custom, and they do finally succeed in staying alive.
The story reflects the deep conflict between willing though
ambivalent fathers and unwilling sons.

In the *Ramayana,* when king-turned-saint Visvamitra desired to
offer *his* own sons as substitutes for Sunahsepa, they taunted him:

> You want to save another's son at the cost of your own ones. It is as
> good as to feed upon one's own flesh out of commiseration towards
> other creatures.[17]

In another case, in the *Taittariya Brahmana* and *Kathopanisad,*
the father was unwilling but the son wished to go, like a lamb, to
the slaughter. A Brahmin householder performed a Vishwajit *yajna*
prior to entering the *sanyas* state.[18] But when the father hesitated to
sacrifice his virtuous only son, Nachiketa, he thus goaded him:

> He said unto his sire, 'Father, to whom will thou give me?' He said this
> again and again, and again for the third time. [The father] said, 'unto
> Death do I give thee.'[19]

Compare this to what Isaac said in the Bible:

> Here is the fire and the wood, but where is the lamb for the sacrifice?[20]

Both sons endured the realization of their fate without a murmur,
although, as he does not doubt, Nachiketa is the greater martyr.
Neither does Markandeya, another potential offering to the very
god who gave him life, Siva; however, at the very last moment, his
faith saved him from Yama's noose.[21] In this regard, Mahisa's
struggle for his life on the battlefield can be likened to the attitude
of the rebellious Rohita and Sunahsepa. In all these cases, the boy
is saved. Nachiketa did go to the realm of Yama, but there he
learned:

> When all desires are renounced, the mortal becomes immortal and
> realizes Brahman.[22]

By making the problem explicit but also allowing for the reprieve,
the myth objectifies contradictory impulses—the need to sacrifice
and the need to preserve one's progeny. The insatiable gods and
goddesses can never be entirely placated—a single offering of
blood merely whets the appetite. The Brahmanas outline a veritable science of the sacrifice of human beings; humans are offered
to one hundred and seventy-nine different gods (the number
varies); the victim is analogized to each.

To a divinity of the Brahmin (caste), a Brahmana should be sacrificed; to the Maruts, a Vaisya: to Naraka (the divinity of hell), a Virahana (one who blows out the sacrificial fires)... to Gita the divinity of music, a Suta or musician... to the divinity of land, a cripple who moves about on a crutch... and to the Goddess of hope for attainable objects, a virgin.[23]

But after prescribing procedures for tying the victims to the stakes, a 'voice' commands:

Purusha, do not consummate [these human beings]: if thou were to consummate them, man (*purusha*) would eat man. Accordingly, as soon as fire has been carried round them, he set them free and offered oblations to the same divinities and thereby gratified those divinities.[24]

Even as the pastoral tribes invading from the West attempted to submerge the Mother Principle and claim the sacrifice for the male gods, in the early texts no amount of repression of the goddesses who continued to reign supreme at the village level could, in fact, more than modify their powers. The later Tantric texts and iconography accommodated this belief. In medieval India it was the bloodthirsty, carnivorous Mother Goddess more often than not who incessantly demanded the sacrificial blood of sacrilized human and animal victims. She was now conceived by her devotees to be an accountant, marking up the debits and credits. To summon her in times of peril, even the gods sometimes believed they could bribe her with flesh and blood, not their own, but of human beings. When Bhandasura had succeeded in conquering heaven, for example, the gods thought:

We shall then worship the great Shakti by means of Mahamasa (great flesh, i.e. human flesh).[25]

Blacquière's famous translation of the Rudhivadhyaya (Blood chapter) of the fourteenth-century *Kalika Purana* needs no further comment. After listing the animals for Candika's sacrifice, including the buffalo, the recommended sacrifice is:

Men, and blood drawn from the offerer's own body, are looked upon as proper oblations to the Goddess Candika... By a human sacrifice... Devi is pleased 1,000 years and by the sacrifice of three men, 100,000 years. Let a human victim be sacrificed at a place of holy worship or a cemetery, where dead bodies are buried. The victim must be a person of good appearance and be prepared by ablutions and requisite ceremonies, such as eating consecrated food the day before, and by abstinence from flesh and venery, and must be adorned with chaplets of flowers and besmeared with sandalwood. . . . Let the sacrificer worship the victim. When this is done, the victim is even as myself . . . then Brahma and all the other deities assemble in the victim and he gains the love of Mahadevi. . . . [26]

The motifs of birth out of fire and the sacrifice of the first-born linger on in the folk imagination: A wandering *sadhu* appeared suddenly in the home of a peaceful religious couple. He was offered a meal, but to the dismay of the man and his wife, the holy man replied that only the flesh of their son would satisfy his ravening hunger. He even insisted that the meal be served without tears and with devotion to god. Although the parents were 'both a little sad', the boy was duly killed, then cooked, and the meat was served by a smiling mother, who sang praises to the god. Satisfied with this show of blind devotion, the disguised god blessed the couple and forthwith brought the son back to life.[27]

Even today the bard of the Gond tribals sings about the war with the enemy in remembrance of the sacrificed Mana boys:

> They stole two small Mana boys and carried them off in their arms
> They came to the Penganga and hid the boys under a basket
> To their brothers they told naught of the boys
> At the ritual place they erected the sacred symbols
> Then went to the village and brought vermilion, incense, goats, cows and cocks
> Returned to the feast place and Tumram performed the rites
> So saying they went, and Here Kurma and Marapa
> Brought the Mana boys and sacrificed them before the god.[28]

As the Mana boys were the sons of the enemy, for them there was no reprieve.

Rites

There seems to be a continual struggle between efforts to satisfy an insatiable Goddess and the contrary abhorrence and revulsion which led to attempts to worship her in less sanguine rituals by providing scapegoats, human and animal. With the advent of the male desperate to free himself from the matrix, the Goddess is in danger of losing her pre-eminent role, as the paternal gods support the divine king's ascent to power. A human divine king, often now only symbolically associated with the fructifying bull, replaces the archaic passive consort and is no longer irrevocably submissive to the Goddess. Fertility can be assured by other means. Wars provide the earth the blood of the enemy as seed, or when his powers begin to fail, the king offers himself up as sacrifice, making way for a successor, the youthful monarch who ensures rich harvests and prosperity for the kingdom.[29] In this psychological inheritance, Mahisa, as king, retains memories of the attempts of both his father and of the divine king at suicide.

Two ninth-century Muslims described the ritual in the kingdom of Balhara in India. Before an assembly of four hundred courtiers, the king ate from a great pile of consecrated, cooked rice and fed those who had agreed to end their lives with him. Then he was paraded through the streets with a garland of straw, dry herbs and a potful of coal on his head, and when his flesh was on fire, without a change in countenance, he jumped into the fire blazing in the central square. One courtier preferred to cut himself from his own breast to the navel, then to remove his own liver, hand it to his brother and jump into the fire with equanimity.[30]

The sacrificial rites always included, with variations, the seizing of and favoured treatment for a chosen victim, anointment, tying to a post, the ritual murder, dismemberment, distribution of flesh or ashes to the earth, with the head and bones and intestines favoured as especially apotropaic.

To illustrate the connection between human and buffalo sacrifices on the one hand and the sequence of the sacrificial rite which has parallels in the battle between Mahisa and Durga, it is useful to cite a few examples. In 1917 R. H. Campbell estimated that among the Khonds (Khands) of Bengal an average of one hundred and fifty humans were annually sacrificed to ensure the fertilization of the earth Goddess Tari, increase of children and domestic animals, and to ward off diseases and other evils, including dangerous wild animals. The victim (todi) was usually brought from an outside village; as he was encouraged to cohabit with a female victim, their children shared their fate. These Mariahs were given special treatment and food over a prolonged period, often for years. Some ten days prior to the sacrifice, the victim was dressed in new finery and had his head shaven. The subsequent rituals included processions around the village to the Mariah grove, tying the victim to a post and anointing him with oils and spices. The devotees reached out, touched the victim and anointed themselves. During a three-day festival, amidst revelry, orgiastic activities and dancing to continuous music, the participants addressed the earth, asking for her behests and bounties.

Over the body of the victim, who had been drugged with toddy or opium, the priest made pre-sacrificial invocations to the earth. He ritually repeated the story of the Goddess who had shed her own blood to teach the people how to fertilize sterile soil. He entreated the victims to accept their role peacefully, protesting that the rites were being held according to custom and that no sin rested on the devotees. Then the sacrifice began. The victim was placed and tied with cords between the split branch of a tree, or he remained seated, tied to the sacrificial post, accompanied by the effigy of a peacock. In either case, the devotees then attacked his body with axes, severing pieces of flesh from all its parts until the blood flowed freely, and slowly he expired. In some ceremonies, a hog was killed, and its blood was released into a pit into which the Mariah's dead body was thrust. The flesh was distributed to the devotees and sent to other villages to be buried in the soil, or it was cut in pieces and strewn along the borderline, or the ashes of the burned carcase were made into a paste and rubbed on the walls of houses and granaries.[31] As these practices have been outlawed, the Khonds now sacrifice only buffaloes during their festivals in March and July, if at all.

Sometimes an ox (*gayal*) used to be substituted for a human in the rites of a wild tribe:

> On occasions of rejoicing they amuse themselves by dancing round a bull or Gayal tied down to a stake, and as the dance continues, the animal is slowly dispatched by numberless spear wounds aimed at every part of his body. The blood is caught in bamboo cups, and men, women and children drink it. The Koos have the reputation of torturing human victims in a similar manner.[32]

To fertilize the soil, human sacrifices were offered before the rice planting and again when the rice sprouted by the Rengma Nagas. After the death of the victim, his head and feet were hung on a central 'head tree'.[33] The Savaras or Sauras of the Deccan propitiated their malevolent female deity Thakurani with human sacrifice. They cut off the heads of captured strangers, and they also cut up their aged relatives and friends and consumed the flesh.[34]

Even by the mid-twentieth century human sacrifice had not been entirely eliminated. The Koyas sacrificed humans to Paleramma, and in 1939 a member of the Reddi tribe was tried for sacrificing a child for the purpose of achieving a higher yield from its blood poured on the paddy field.[35] The Reddis had a history of human sacrifice, and while there is ample evidence that human victims were still offered to Maveli Devta every third year, von Furer-Haimendorf thought that perhaps the strong belief may have been a fear inherited from the past.[36] Barua describes Dravidian customs of human sacrifice as a crude form of Saivism, and in the Naga Hills it forms part of the worship of the Mother Goddess.[37]

More recently, while the rite continues to be practised, human sacrifice does not take place. At Palya, in Kolegal Taluk of Mysore District, a person is kept in a house. At midnight, the priest and the village headman sprinkle holy water on him and immediately the priest becomes possessed by the Goddess. He puts his foot on the chest of the mock victim who is supposed to be dead, but by the grace of the Goddess, he is revived. A legend from the same locality relates that once upon a time the human victim escaped in the form of a buffalo, but later he was killed and sacrificed to the Goddess.[38]

Accompanying the sacrifice of thousands of goats and sheep, the various Dhangar (shepherds of Maharashtra) clans also offered a boy to Shri Nath Mhaskoba at his Magh marriage festival. A rationalizing myth restores the heads of four grandsons of the devotee Kamalaji after they were decapitated to satisfy the god's demand. In a substitute ritual today, certain holy men pierce their own tongues or stomachs with sharp swords, but there is no sign of their being thus mutilated.[39]

Urchins around the Gateway of India in Bombay still tell stories concerning boys who were kidnapped and taken to remote areas of Assam for purposes of sacrifice.

While girl infanticide is still prevalent today (and there is rampant misuse of amniocentesis for female foeticide), how much of it is connected with sacrificial rites to a deity is hard to know. Occasionally, a report in the press indicates that slaughter for religious purposes may still be practised: in 1986 a six-year-old girl was sacrificed: 'Suverna's blood was collected and with it *tikas* were applied on the foreheads of the four witch-doctors. The deity was also similarly marked.'[40] But contemporary murder related to the gods and goddesses is more likely to be a psychotic outbreak of the, by now, almost entirely repressed impulses. In Orissa, a man beheaded his four-year-old niece to appease the Goddess Durga. He then carried the head and buried it in a deserted place. It was the third case of suspected human sacrifice in recent months.[41]

The myth of the sacrifice of Mahisa as man on the battlefield provides a partial solution to the age-old dilemma faced by those driven by uncontrolled unconscious forces. The *Kalika Purana* gives instructions concerning the making of the icon. After the buffalo in animal form is killed by the Goddess, he is to be killed again in human form:

> One should further represent the buffalo under her, its head being cut off, just as it should be; and the demon is to be represented coming forth out of the spot where the head has been cut off, just as it should be, holding a sword in his hand, and his heart pierced by the [Goddess's] trident.[42]

Thus human and animal sacrifice is transposed into ritual art.

Mahisa as Animal Sacrifice: Pasubali

In an attempt to modify unbearable internal conflicts, the myth-maker reduces the demon from deified world sovereign to age-old traditional animal victim. Mahisa certainly had intimations of his fate and knew that he deserved severe retribution. At one level it was impossible for him to ignore the reality that his conquest of heaven had little to do with his personal prowess, that a woman was destined to kill him, that he was merely the manipulated puppet of the boon-bestowing grandfather Brahma, the representative of the gods who will go to any lengths to protect their right to receive the sacrifices. But this realization also provided fertile ground for hope, as atonement and salvation are cognate desires. And so the suffering hero plunges into battle according to time-honoured rites, offering himself, his flesh and his blood to the holocaust.

Texts

Established precedents paved the way. The links between the asvamedha and the ancient hierogamies were grounded in a living tradition. As consort of the queen, the horse was probably a substitute for the earlier human sacrifice of a priest who died after shedding fertilizing seed.[43] The ritual began with consecration of the horse. Accompanied by the king's courtiers it was then set free and permitted to roam for one year. The king and horse were again consecrated upon its return; then the victim was slain and the chief queen was required to lie near and copulate (or simulate copulation) with the dead horse.[44]

But the slaughter of a great number of buffaloes was a more common and more frequent event:

> Agni dressed quickly three hundred buffaloes... When you ate three hundred buffaloes' flesh... All the Gods raised a shout of triumph to Indra, praised because he killed the dragon (Vrtra).[45]

Brought into India by the invading cattle-rearing tribes, the asvamedha was actualized rarely, only when powerful kings celebrated conquests and established their authority by means of these imposing rites. When the newcomers confronted local Goddess worship, they were prepared to accommodate their beliefs to the rites of the conquered people. It seems that the buffalo as sacrificed divinity, or as animal sacrifice to the divinity or, most likely, as an amalgam of both, was a deeply-rooted indigenous practice long before the advent, with their horses, of the Indo-Aryan language speaking people; the availability of buffaloes would certainly have encouraged extensive use of this animal for sacrifice.

The *Satapatha Brahmana* recognized that ultimately, the queen, the Goddess, the earth, stems from a theriomorphic symbol:

> the invincible one... this earth... is a Mahisi (female buffalo cow), she who is taken to wife as the consecrated consort.[46]

> They cause the Mahisi (chief queen) to lie down near the horse, and cover her up with the upper cloth. In heaven ye envelope yourselves— for that indeed is heaven where they immolate the victim. 'May the vigorous male, the layer of seed, lay seed', she says, for completeness of union.[47]

Here she is described with buffalo symbolism.

Rite

A buffalo was sacrificed to the Goddess Mara in a South Indian ritual which is linked by analogy with the asvamedha. The buffalo was first sacrilized by water, purification, mantras and by rice sprinkled on its head, and the villagers chant 'Mara Kona' (Goddess Buffalo).

> It is then let loose, allowed to roam for a year, during which time it is allowed to eat crops without molestation, as the idea prevails that to interfere with the buffalo in any way would be sure to bring down the wrath of Mara. At the end of the time it is killed at the feast held annually in honour, or rather, to avert the wrath of Mara.[48]

The male and female, the buffalo and the Goddess, are associated by his name: Mara Kona (Mara: Goddess; Kona: buffalo). The Goddess Mara of the aboriginal rite and queen (Mahisi) of the horse sacrifice, are, once again, the earth requiring fertilizing by male seed.

We are dealing with gender reversals and fundamental features of the female/male/animal/god relationship in their changing equations. Mahisa and the Goddess represent one of these. His lust for her is one manifestation of the ancient, universal rites of coupling for fertility. In the finale of the Mahisamardini drama, the hero is like the horse of the asvamedha and the buffalo sacrificial victim. After an implied sexual union, as we have seen, he will be sacrificed on the field of battle, metaphor for the sacrificial ground, and then conjoined to the queen/Goddess/Mahisi. Archaic vestiges and continuities endure.

The sequence of catching, quieting, killing and consuming the sacrificial victim during the festival had the effect of stimulating usually dormant responses. This contact at primordial psychic levels reactivated savage eruptions of atavistic patterns of behaviour. Participants were catapulted back to an earlier period of human phylogenesis. In a 'civilized' society, these responses appear in dreams, reversions to infantile fantasies, in psychoses and, in India still, in the conscious thought of the folk when they are stimulated.

Each tribe and each community had developed its particular modes of giving controlled expression to unconscious forces. While the details may vary, a surprisingly consistent pattern emerges from the rituals. In many tribal areas buffaloes were (and sometimes still are) sacrificed during epidemics, at festivals, at appointed times during the year by an individual who would personally benefit and at rites of passage. Sometimes the buffalo was driven to another village as scapegoat. The number sacrificed varied according to the wealth of the community or individual—at royal ceremonies hundreds, and in villages during epidemics sometimes twenty or twenty-five.[49] During the present-day Navratri sacrifice in Nepal, as we shall see, the blood of buffaloes is spilled throughtout the long Astami/Navami night.

The ritual sequence is more or less standardized. Fat buffalo bulls were permitted to roam freely, then caught and led in procession—covered with plants or painted with turmeric, to the accompaniment of drums and trumpets—through the village or around the temple; villagers offered rice and worshipped it. Before it was killed, it was given some consecrated rice and wine. Mantras transformed the animal from a mundane animal into a sacred victim. Apologies and pleas for forgiveness by the priest and sacrificer preceded the ritual killing. Tied to a sacrificial post, the head of the buffalo had to be cut off with a single stroke. In one manner or another the blood and flesh of the buffalo were eaten, and flesh was distributed for consumption or offerings to the earth.

The animal sensed preparations for the sacrifice, and sometimes it engaged in fierce combat with young men of the tribe who showed skill and courage in confronting and capturing the threatened beast. They took pride in overcoming a dangerous opponent, liable to gore and seriously injure his captors. At the Toda funeral, the poet sings about the struggle:

You went to the horns of the barren buffaloes.
You went to the necks of the fighting male buffaloes.[50]

The captured females would be of the non-sacred herds. When Toda villagers tried to restrain a buffalo catcher from attacking his prey, he resisted, caught the buffalo and then composed a song:

Buffalo Osum is saying: 'I am uncontrollable . . . I am unmanageable' . . . Buffalo Osum was born for me, I will go; Release me! . . . Like the cane bee I will suck. Release me! I have blossomed like the Amaranthus flower. Like the stick bee, let (Osum) suck. Let me go there. I will leap the leap of a tiger, Release me. I will trumpet like an elephant. Release me.[51]

Once caught, the buffalo was felled, his four legs tied and sometimes the beast was even pounded with poles or the butt of an axe.[52] The Rengma Nagas even starved the *mithan* (bull) first so that it would fight desperately and 'give better sport';[53] or the buffalo was hamstrung to entertain the tribals or wounded on his nose.[54]

Even while thus humbled, the buffalo had the respect of the devotees. He was bathed in the village tank, garlanded, sprinkled with water, blessed with mantras and dragged through the villages, stopping at people's houses. Given this opportunity of identifying with the victim, in Whitehead's description the people bowed in worship as the low-caste priest announced: 'The buffalo devoted to the Goddess is coming.'[55] He had by now entered the domain of the sacred.

When the time came to sacrifice the animal, the Eastern Regmas separated the heart and even fought over the intestines.[56] The Mhars of Maharashtra struck off the buffalo's head with a sword in a single stroke and then tore him to pieces.[57] Other methods of slaying the buffalo were with blows or kicks, often the privilege of the priest possessed by the Goddess. Among the Khonds, the entire group of participants used to pounce upon the buffalo and cut it to pieces with knives while it was still alive.[58] And Saora devotees buried their heads in the body of the slain animal, drinking the blood, their lips dropping raw flesh,[59] a practice also reported in the late eighteenth century: in the hills of Rajmahal, those possessed of devils were seized and bound; then they 'are set at liberty and immediately [they] rush forward to take the buffalo's blood and lick it, while reeking. Thus they are exorcised.'[60]

Even very recently (1987) Chakrabarty described an agricultural ritual reminiscent of the buffalo sacrifice, still celebrated by Santals in the month of Kartik, as the paddy ripens, ready for harvest. On the first two days, offerings of beheaded chicks are made to *bongas* (local deities or spirits), there are pig sacrifices in front of householders' cow-sheds and worship of farm implements and ancestors, followed by merry-making. On the third day, a strong bullock is tied to a six-foot pole erected before every house, his horns and neck garlanded with paddy sheaves. While she circum-ambulates the animal, the housewife offers a new winnowing fan full of vermilion, grass and paddy and also the bullock receives a lighted lamp. Playing instruments and singing, youths and elders of the village panchayat march around the village, stopping at each house. Here the ritual takes an archaic turn: in order to arouse the fury of the animal, he is scourged with a leather piece to the accompaniment of ribald and savage cries. Fortunately for the victim the latter parts of the traditional sacrificial ceremony are cancelled, and he is left alive, the blood of the chicks and pigs having replaced his own in the obligatory rice and blood dish.[61]

The Santals' modification of the rite is a partial indication of changing times. Enormous upheavals have been suffered in remote communities during the twentieth century, even more so after Independence. In regard to buffalo sacrifice, central and state government laws, growing poverty, the relaxation and disintegration of established canons, the influence of reformers and the media and the general trend towards acculturation are some of the causes of the substitution of goat and fowl for the buffalo as victims of the sacrifice. But not infrequently, when the community can afford it, when officials turn a blind eye, or when the family desires to offer a male buffalo calf to a deity rather than let it starve to death for lack of food, the ancient compulsions surface.

Very definitely the impulse to sacrifice has not diminished; for an editorial in the Marathi newspaper, *Maharashtra Times*, as recently as April 1993, referred to a Tantric rite ('Sagara'), sponsored and directed by the Hiryyur Municipality in Karnataka. Twenty buffaloes, eighty sheep and one hundred chickens were sacrificed to propitiate the rain gods.[62] The bloody tide flows as before, and today it is said that after a major festival the earth remains soaked in blood for half the following year. Only now it is usually the blood of goats.

At the Devi Temple in Chamba, the Goddess entered the priest, and he danced wildly to the sound of turbulent rhythmic music; 'scourging himself all the time with the... trisula... [he] draws blood.' Possessed by the Goddess, he drank the warm blood from the head of a newly-sacrificed goat (formerly it was the head of a human being).[63] At the shrine of Gatodju at Bhuder village in southern Rajasthan, during the two annual Navratri festivals, the blood of a sacrificed goat was collected in a bowl by excited villagers; it was taken to the *bhopa* (priest) who, while sitting in a trance before the image of the Goddess, drank the blood and with it some liquor. He was the Goddess impersonated, receiving the offering.[64] And to satisfy the blood thirst of the Devi Ghairavi, in northern Nepal, the sacrificial blood was drunk at the festival of Devi Rath Yatra, and for another Goddess, the priests drank the blood, vomited it and served it as the *prasad* (offering) of the Goddess.[65]

Decapitation of Mahisa: The Goddess Cleaves

Almost a century ago, Freud and Rank recognized the psychotic content in the myth:

> This intimate relationship between the hero myth and the delusional structure of paranoics has already been definitely established through the characterization of the myth as a paranoid structure which is here confirmed by its contents.[66]
>
> Many analysts will have noticed that certain patients suffering from obsessions express an abhorrence of and indignation against the penalty of beheading, feelings which are far more pronounced as regards this than any other form of capital punishment, and will in consequence have had to explain to them that they treat being beheaded as a substitute for being castrated.[67]

In a seventh-century poem, King Yasovarman praised Vindhya-vasini, Goddess of the Vindhya mountains, thus:

> Thy arched gate is adorned with strings of bells (heads), as if they were removed from the necks of the family of the buffalo demon (Mahisa), brought away by thee as captives.[68]

Symbol for phallus, the head is also the seed and thus the essence greatly desired by the Devi. Furthermore, when Bana sings that Mahisa's 'head had been shorn of its horns. . . . melted by the heat of Candi's triad of eyes',[69] the temptation is to analogize the fire of the eyes of the Goddess with the fire of the sacrifice; again, in turn, the fire on the altar is often equated with vaginal fire:

> In many scattered passages of the Upanishads, the woman is conceived as the sacrificial fire, her lower portion as the sacrificial wood, the genitalia as the flames, the penetration as the carbon and the sexual union as the spark.[70]

With the result, as Shulman observes, that the male is drained.[71] As the woman accepts his seed, as the desire of the lover is extinguished, she acquires his strength.

This idea persists in contemporary India. Fathers advise their sons not to waste their powers frequently or indiscriminately. As fire, the Goddess will melt and make the male impotent. As warrior, during the act of killing Mahisa, the 'detachment' of the Goddess—'without any strain on her face"[72]—is merely a euphemism, because it is her knife that is the sacrificial weapon. Precisely like the sacrificer in the ritual, with a single bold stroke, she cleaves the head from the neck. Symbolically, as she cleaves (splits), she cleaves (attaches) herself to the head. In the Tamil myth, after Devi kills Mahisa, stand-in for Siva, the linga clings to her hand.[73] In the later texts and icons, the buffalo does not simply expire. Emerging live and whole from the severed neck of his own animal body, he gives birth to himself in the form of the human hero; this requires an instantaneous second decapitation.

Raglin provides examples of a type of story frequently found in other cultures: an animal or monster is beheaded, and a handsome prince emerges immediately from the severed head. He marries the princess and becomes a king.[74] Although, in their attempt to quell castration anxiety, these solutions fantasize a happy ending, in India, the lingering wish for the marriage of the hero to the Mother Goddess, the mother or her substitute, reappears here on the temporal plane merely for an instant; the spiritual union occurs only after death. It is worthy of note that in the Navratri rites in Bengal the instant between the two decapitations is actualized and crystallized in the pandals. Mahisa is invariably depicted as a beautiful hero in proximity to and almost of the same size as the Devi (see Chapter Nine).

In the myth, the event of their original coming together had included a friendship and an implied sexual relationship; in the ritual, the entrance into her shrine may very well be interpreted as a marriage. But the Goddess repeats her former back-trackings, using the phallic sword once again to kill her would-be lover who had recently emerged alive from his dead animal form. The sword and the Goddess are synonymous. It is to be worshipped by contemplating it and reciting mantras:

> Thou art Candika's tongue... having Kalaratri's nature; as being terrific, with bloody eyes and mouth, with a garland of blood and whose unguent consists of blood.[75]

Candika is the sword; in her second act of beheading with the sword, in gender reversal of her role as sacrificial fire, she is now the phallic executioner, castrating the male and even creating a symbolic vaginal likeness in the open neck of the buffalo, which bleeds.

Thus, to emphasize the already obvious situation that the Goddess lusts for the heads of those who adore her with the same intensity that the buffalo–demon hero lusts for her, the story ends with the demise of the hero. The perennial theme of castration anxiety is given its appropriate climactic attention. Now the Devi gets to keep two heads. In the rituals, she has received infinite numbers, although she is never properly satisfied:

> Then after one has carefully purified the blood of the oblations with water, salt, sound, fruit, honey, perfumes and flowers, one should put the blood and the head with the light on it in the proper place. Kausiki must be made swollen with blood.[76]

One would assume that the light which is always placed on the head of the buffalo victim[77] is the symbol which emphasizes the heat, power and regenerative properties symbolized by the victim. And in the icon, Devi stands on the severed head: thus petrified in stone, a permanent relationship is assured (see Chapter Nine).

As if unabashedly to proclaim the relationship between the Goddess and Mahisa, or with all those asuras whose heads she has acquired for herself, later rituals and icons carry the symbol one step further. In one of a multitude of examples, near Chamba, Kali as Chinamastaka, holding her *own* severed head in her hands, is worshipped for eight days before Diwali.[78] Blood spurts out of her neck. Now, in a mimetic response of absolute identification, the mother, not the son, suffers self-dismemberment!

As the climactic event of the narrative, the decapitation of Mahisa is the concretized universal symbol, arising from the deepest layers of the unconscious, repeatedly met with in tribal rites, in myths, historical events, dreams and psychotic outbursts. For one reason for another, in one or another contexts, the head must go.

Head-hunting raids, sacrificial rituals of human and animal victims or, as internalized aggression, self-beheading rituals have been known in India since historical times. At the height of the early Sakta period, the bloodied head re-emerged in full force. So persistent was the compulsion that it became imperative for evolving cults, even those with higher ideals, to incorporate earlier primitive practices into fresh rites and myths, either to avert disease and evil, or to acquire its fertilizing function. Since the story of Mahisamardini substitutes an appropriate symbol for the raw rite of beheading, and although substitution never actually succeeded in overcoming the obsessive unconscious force, it does suggest a humanizing effort to quell the still functioning atavism.

Human heads and those of bulls are frequent archaeological discoveries in caves, at altars, tombs and temples. As the seat of the soul, as source of power, as regenerative, skulls have had symbolic importance in ritual from time immemorial.[79] The Goddess participated actively in these fertility and power exchanges. Later anthropomorphized as protectress of wild animals, the original animal totem deity had never been entirely divested of her associations with her animal subjects. The continuity may be observed in Catal Huyak in the seventh millennium BC, where the Goddess appears in relief on the walls of shrines, frequently in association with bulls' heads or bulls' horns. . . . In several shrines one or more huge bull heads were placed just below the Goddess as if to assert and strengthen her powers.[80]

Seven millennia later, in India, identical beliefs are imaged in plastic representations of Durga standing on the head of Mahisa. Between these two distant geographical and historical points, on various continents, wherever the Mother Goddess held sway, the symbiotic relationship and mutually supporting functions of Goddess and bull/buffalo are re-projected in profuse and diverse forms; the buffalo's head and horns and the body of the Goddess are eternally bound to one another.

In the final analysis, after his great rebellions, his courageous efforts to escape the drag-net of the Mother, the hero's battle to recreate himself as a separate and individual entity is lost. The Mother's booty was his head, which in all the multitude of representations in India is never far removed from its proximity to the Goddess. (The gift of the head is the penitential offering for incestual compulsions: the male is terrorized by his own sinful aggressive response and willingly proffers his head as an act of penance and appeasement. The cultural substitutions are the cathartic pronouncement to the world concerning unresolved castration anxieties: Mahisa's beheading by the Goddess is an effort to come to terms with the consequences of inherent drives which concern the mythmaker.)

The final event in Mahisa's life is prefigured in the beginning. As if to prove that the sins of the fathers are inexorably visited upon the sons, the beheading motif had been introduced at the very start of the narrative, with Rambha about to sever his own head. It may have been Agni's divine joke to persuade Rambha not to die in such a cause simply to prepare for the grand finale when Mahisa becomes the heir to his father's hate and the associated festering guilt.[81] So the messenger Dundudhi informs the Goddess:

> For your sake, the chief of demons is ready to offer his head.[82]

In the context of Indian perceptions and ritual practices, this proposal might even be considered conventional, shocking as it may sound to the western ear. The DM is the earliest extant text in which 'the great asura was laid by the Devi, who struck off his head with her great sword.'[83] By the fifth century AD lithic representations show Durga standing on the severed head, for example at Gwalior (see Chapter Nine). Textual evidence from the South may be even earlier. A variety of South Indian texts instruct concerning the heads of enemies killed in raids or war, as well as the heads of devotees offered in propitiation.

The *Tolkappiyam* is the earliest extant grammatical text; it describes Durga as the Goddess of Victory who rides before the king's army as he marches off to battle: she carries a skull full of an assortment of seeds, grain, blood, intestines, other flesh, and a garland of skulls.[84] It is to be presumed that these are the donations of her devotees. In the *Silappadikaram* (seventh century AD),[85] Ilango-Adigal provides a vivid picture of the sacrificial rites of hill tribal hunters: they offer their own heads and their blood to the Goddess manifested in a young virgin dressed as the Goddess. Prayers follow the *avippali* (head sacrifice). The people are thereby assured of good fortune for themselves and their ruler.[86] When soldiers practise self-beheading as an offering to the guardian deity the process is graphically described:

> Stone slingers and different classes of soldiers who held shields stained with blood and human flesh, as well as lances, patted themselves on their shoulders, shouting exultingly, and cut off their dark-haired heads, containing such fierce red eyes as seemed to burn them upon whom they looked and willingly offered them upon the sacrificial altar (of the guardian deity) with the prayer that the conquering king might be ever victorious.[87]

During the first millennium AD these practices seem to have been common amongst non-tribals as well. In Vakpati's hymn to the mountain Goddess Vindhyavasini, the king reminds the Devi that she loves to walk on the burning ground covered with skulls and that her gates are besmeared with offerings of blood; her cave is dark and full of jackals who lick the blood-stained dark hair of the numerous offerings of human heads. The branches of her trees are red with blood and flesh hung from them. If a hero is slain and his head and flesh is proffered in front of her temple, all desires will be achieved, as she requires the daily sacrifice of humans.[88] The Parani literature, or later war poetry, is a rich source for the study of Sakta customs and rituals which include sacrificial offerings on the battlefield. In the *Kalingattupparani,* the poet fantasizes an entire temple to the Goddess, built from heads, flesh and blood, serving as brick, mortar and water. There the Goddess received, in her extended hands, three kinds of heads: peacocks', human infants' and those of heroic warriors who sing praises to the Goddess.[89]

The demand by the Goddess is so great that when heads are not voluntarily offered, she acquires them in the sacrifice of war. The Puranas are bathed in the blood flowing from the heads of decapitated asuric opponents, felled during her many battles. A few names in the long list of her victims are Durmukha, Vaskala, Tamra, Chiksura, Ruru, Canda/Munda, Sumbha and Nisumbha:

> Heaps of heads of the Danavas rolled down on the battlefield when the necks had beeen chopped off by the sharp edges of the brilliant weapons of the army of Saktas.[90]

Mahisa's head is a mere drop in the bloody bucket, but it stands for billions of other fallen ones.

> And others, though rendered headless, fell and rose. Headless trunks fought with the Devi, some of these danced there on the battlefield to the rhythm of the musical instruments.[91]

The battle provides the Goddess with ample opportunities for gathering to her bosom the severed heads of her adversaries for which she so desperately yearns. As both slayer (Durga) and receiver (earth), the Goddess is simultaneously instigator and beneficiary.

Hiltebeitel's remark that Brahma's decapitated head is a multiform of Mahisa's[92] would apply to other heads as well. In the DBP version of the sacrifice of Daksa the problem of incest is confronted and the guilt resolved: the father of the gods received a fragrant garland as a gift from a rsi, who in turn had received it from the Devi. He placed it on the marital couch of his daughter Sati to encourage her union with Siva, but, being intoxicated by the sacred flowers, the father substituted himself for the groom in the nuptial bed. For this sin he was punished by Siva who destroyed Daksa's sacrifice, cut off his head and replaced it with that of a goat, thus transforming sacrificer into victim.[93]

When the gods created the insect Vamri to gnaw away at the bow upon which Visnu was sleeping in order to awaken him, Visnu's head fell off. After appropriate propitiation, they asked the Goddess:

Why art Thou delaying in fixing again the head on Visnu's body?[94]

The fault lay with the Goddess manifested as Laksmi who had cursed Visnu out of jealousy. She killed two birds with one stone and directed Visvakarman to place the head of a horse on Visnu's trunk in order to fulfill her promise to the asura Hayagriva that he would be killed only by 'one who is horse faced'.[95] Horse-faced Visnu and buffalo-faced Mahisa are indeed products of like projections. The village god Sri Nath Mhasoba who was born of the jatas of Siva evolved out of Mhaskoba who in turn has a common origin with Mahisa (see Chapters Two and Eight). Once he cut off the head of Brahma who had lied about his journey to the top of the fiery linga, but he was later required to do penance to rid himself of the sin of Brahmanicide.[96]

While verbal sublimation may represent an advance in 'civilized' behaviour, the fears and aggressions it represents have not been obliterated.

Rite

Recently outlawed tribal rites attest to this. The Rengma Nagas seem to have been fixated on the head, as it played a crucial role in vegetative growth. After capturing an enemy they waited till the young rice began to sprout and its fertilizing influence would be most valuable. Then the enemy was killed and his head, hands and feet were hung from a head tree located in a central place in the village.[97] Among the Saoras, after sacrifice, the animal's head was usually placed on the altar, while the rest of the body was cut up and cooked. The head and stomach of the buffalo were placed in front of each house, so the spirits would know what had been done and sixteen buffalo heads, each with its own stomach balanced on top of it, were displayed to the public.[98]

Contemporary Vestiges

What may be a lightly veiled form of head sacrifice is called Shrishamranni (*shrisha:* human head). Here the heads of three persons thickly wrapped in wet clothing are placed in a circle on the ground:

> A *chulah* is then lit and rice is boiled in the earthen pot perching on it. The ritual meal cooked this way is then mixed with the blood offered by one of the three persons and given away as an offering. It is expected to appease the supposedly blood-thirsty evil spirits. As this bi-annual festival coincides with holi, or the coming of spring, it is most likely linked to the fructifying properties.[99]

That decapitation was not totally forbidden or designated as insanity is evidenced by a case which came to the court of Judge R. H. Campbell in 1917. A Khond tribal who had beheaded his older brother because he had handed the murderer over to a money lender as 'slave', was sentenced only nominally on the grounds that the homicide was justifiable.[100]

A performance of ritual dance by the Thangatha Martial Arts Troupe of Manipur accented the interrelationship of fertility requirements and castration, summed up in a single climactic instant of the dance. The final action came as one of a pair of male dancers, lying on his back in mid-stage, placed a very large gourd in a vertical position at his groin. A second dancer, blindfolded, slowly, but with sure steps approached his fellow. Suddenly, with a scythe, he cut the gourd off at its base. The rhythmic movements, mimicking copulation, were suggestive of the repressed atavistic impulses embedded in this ritual dance. The action of cutting the gourd represented celebration of the harvest; but it simultaneously also symbolized castration of the primitive consort.

Young recently-Christianized Assamese tribals today tell stories about their grandfathers' head-hunting raids, linking our times with the entire past, and explaining why the rites are still consciously operative. It also accounts for the psychotic behaviour which occasionally bursts forth in primeval force. One such incident occurred in Palghat, Kerala. There a teacher picked up the kitchen knife and went out of his house. A couple of minutes later, a loud 'Ha ha ha' was heard...Rushing out, the mother saw that her husband had cut off the head of the infant. He was drinking the red hot blood of his son. Later he took the head and held it to his chest. Then he went to his neighbour's house and cut off the head of two goats.[101]

These psychotic outbursts are unrelenting, as the violence in Sri Lanka has borne witness.

But a tremendous effort to counteract the dark nature of humanity is seen in the contemporary Ganesa festival which provides a happier ending to the decapitation theme. In the myth, the revered son of the divine couple, Siva and Parvati, had his head chopped off by his own father. It was later replaced by the head of an elephant. This son is one of India's most popular deities. Great festivals, in which millions of devotees pay tribute to Ganesa, the Lord with the symbolic phallus, the elephant's trunk (naturally so much larger than his father's), is a most ingenious way of literally thumbing one's nose at active parental involvements in the life of the son today. While Mahisa's victory comes only in death, the son of Siva seems to be holding his ground in Maharashtra, even while each generation of sons is beset with the same fundamental conflicts.

The monster Goddess makes insane demands which the Sakta devotee does his utmost to accommodate. However, except in the case of the severe masochist, the will to live interferes with the need to please the Mother. Even when the sadistic drives meant for the Mother are displaced on to oneself or a substitute victim, no society can survive if it has sadism at the heart of its rituals.

Blood

Blood is life; it is power, protection and consolation. In the battle, eternally flowing rivers of 'gushing streams of blood, carrying even elephants away in the current'[102] are shared by demon and Goddess. In its positive aspect, like semen, it is at the essence of psychic unity. Neither Goddess nor Mahisa can exist without the blood of the other, and they are thus engaged in a battle for that blood. In the O'Flaherty sense, fluids are shared, so much so that, saturated with common blood, as harbinger of the final union, the earth becomes the metaphor for dissolved individuality. During the battle and the sacrificial ritual, blood, as transformational medium, constantly alters the balance of power between Goddess, sacrificer and sacrificial victim.

Even though, like most of the major deities in the battles of the Puranas, the Goddess manages to keep herself above the fray and in perfectly healthy condition, when she is intoxicated she becomes ravenous, violent and dangerous. Sometimes it is the lion vehicle or her emanations which devour the flesh and drink the blood, but they are all multiples of the original, the Goddess herself, who craves the drink the most: she smote Raktavija with her weapons and 'Camunda went on drinking his blood.'[103] At another time she had by herself a drink of wine and blood in the midst of the demons in the same battle.'[104] Candika instructed her *alter ego* Kali: 'O, Camunda, open your mouth wide: with this mouth quickly take in the drops of blood.'[105] In many battles blood drinking follows the slaying of the daityas.[106] Instead of turning away from the blood, the Goddess Lalita's one thousand saktis wear garlands of skulls which serve as vessels for the asuras' blood.[107]

Because Goddess and demon are the often interchangeable qualities of the unconscious, demons show an equal interest in the blood of the enemy:

> Many Ramaptanas drink the exceedingly tasty and heartening spate of female blood of extraordinary nature, gushing out from the crevasses (open wounds) of your body.[108]

Demons lust for blood. While Mahisa will ultimately be entirely drained of his own, its acquisition is at the heart of the conflict, and often the Goddess and her emanations are in danger and lose strength:

> Nitya deities whose bodies were drenched in blood oozing from their wounds made by the weapons of the daityas, bowed down to Goddess Sri.[109]

The blood is also the comfort of the Mother. Having lost all his fifty sons and his brothers, thirsting for consolation, Bhandasura longs for the blood of the Mother to quench his pain: 'I shall put out the great fire of sorrow for my brothers and sons with the liquid coming out of the throat of that wanton woman the Goddess.'[110] He is like the infant who knows where to seek solace when he is upset. Both red blood and warm mother's milk are life-giving; they nourish and invigorate.[111] Blood also protects. In exchange for his throne, heaven and total power, Mahisa will be protected and will protect. Bana understood this:

> And the oceans of flowing blood issuing out from the holes of the wounds caused by the trident... May the oceans of blood protect you.[112]

The translator adds that boons for the worshipper are invoked through Mahisa's blood.[113] The troops of the Goddess and those of the demons literally share ties of blood, as each receives continual transfusions of the precious liquid from the others. Whoever wins will be redeemed by the blood of the conquered. The devotee/sacrificer, identified with Mahisa, is gradually transformed into sacrificial victim in the battle. In this system of exchange the devotee or priest shifts towards masochism and projects sadistic impulses on to the Goddess, thus procuring for himself redemption from sin (that of suppression of instinct). Then either 'Brahmanas and Ksaytriyas are become the food of that awful deity',[114] or partial offerings—heaps of rice soaked in blood, blood sprinkled on altars and idols, derived from the sacrificer's own body or from a substitute animal with which he identifies completely—are proferred in a desperate effort to atone:

> The king (Suratha) (and the Vaisya) began to cut off slices of flesh from his own body and offered them as oblations... Both of them were very much excited and began to offer their blood as oblation to the Devi.[115]

If the sacrificer identifies with the blood of the buffalo, he can save himself the trouble of self-mutilation, since the Goddess readily substitutes asuras' regenerative blood:

> And in the twilight, one should cause the bali (animal) sacrifice to be sprinkled with the blood of one's own limbs; after one has worshipped her in this way, one shall rejoice, being provided with blessings forever.[116]

By mixing his own blood with the animal's the identity of sacrificer and victim is physically actualized.

In these widely dispersed rites, animal, human and deity are no longer completely distinguishable. The rites differ in detail, but the ravening exchange of blood remains a constant. The slain animal is consumed by priest and devotees, either controlled by ritual or in chaotic orgiastic reversions to primeval behaviour. Both deity and devotee share a fundamental, wild need for the magical properties of the apotropaic life blood—it must be liberated from the victim and incorporated. The psychology of the rite is an attempt to divest humans of their animal nature.

The play of the Goddess in the world is a euphemism for the entirely successful self-delusion and deception within which priest and devotee operate. Included in this is identification with the buffalo demon who, like the Goddess, is introduced as medium and vehicle for containment of atavistic drives. The interchange of his blood, the dismemberment and consumption of his flesh, plays an important role in the narrative of the battle. The sacrificial ritual and/or the battle finale will satisfy the worshipper, because the dramatis personae are in actuality his conflicting drives vying for dominance in a see-saw of emotions.

While the Goddess and demon and their retinues are in the throes of desperate struggle, the priests manage their unbearable burden of staying separate and out of the clutches of the Mother. But when the Goddess consumes the blood of the demons, when she drains them entirely of their vital fluids, she is the ultimate conqueror. Whether this can be linked to the Hindu belief that the sexual act weakens the male, or whether therefore the male is ever in fear of castration, or even whether the concept of a female devourer is universal, the result in the myth or on the ritual field will always be the same. He who stands for the son will always lose all his blood, all his powers, and he will only gain liberation and union in death and resurrection.

Echoes resound at village level in real life. For example, when Tulaja's cousin died, she re-entered the body of Tulaja. Wildly she screamed at Tulaja's errant husband, Shivaji: 'I am Kaveri, Tulaja's cousin.... You brute, I will kill you. I will suck your blood. I will make you impotent because you have sinned with another woman. Behave yourself.' While thus enraged, Tulaja acted as though possessed, exactly like the Goddess when she drinks her draughts of blood. Later, the exorcist drove off the evil spirit of Kaveri, and then Tulaja returned to her normal state as 'good wife'.[117]

Mahisa as Bearer of Vicarious Guilt

Paradoxically, this very act of slaughter and sacrifice itself produces unbearable guilt and fear in the devotee. Atonement is the only hope.

Plaintive sentiments recorded in the Rg Veda differ very little from those expressed by the medieval or even the contemporary sacrificer. To the victim of the horse sacrifice, the priest announces:

> Indeed, you are not slain, you are not hurt
> Indeed, you will go by easy paths to the gods.[118]

Some two thousand five hundred years later, the plea has been very little altered:

> O sinless one.... The goats and other beasts offered as sacrifice before the Devas undoubtedly go to heavenly regions; therefore, in all the *sastras,* it has been decided that the killing of animals in a sacrifice is considered as non-killing.[119]

To add conviction to these emphatic statements, the sacrificer kisses, laments over, apologizes to, whispers persuasions into the animal's ear, or he averts his head from the final blow of the axe. Among the Todas, there was a 'frantic manifestation of grief and effort to salute the dead beast by placing a hand between the horns, weeping and mourning in pairs'.[120]

One swift stroke was the rule for beheading. A father and his son paid a tearful farewell to their pet goat, accompanied with caresses and kisses in the moments before the slaying at the Mahismal sacrifice (see p. 199). The guilt is universally felt and universally rationalized. Thus the *Satapatha Brahmana* assures the devotee that the victim's kin approve of the sacrifice.[121] Hemadri teaches that it is not a sin to kill the victim, as by this death, he is saved.[122]

If this is not entirely effective, the sacrificer attempts to avoid heaping further guilt upon himself. Now he abjures animal sacrifice altogether and relies on text, rite and tradition. By prescribing the reading of the narrative of the battle as a compulsory ritual, by substituting chanted mantras, gestures, and vegetative offerings for the sharp bloody knife, he lives the sacrifice in imagination, recalling the bloodshed, relying on the poet to bring the horrors back to consciousness. By shifting responsibility on to the Goddess as executioner in the narrated battle, being persuaded that it is she who accomplishes the deed under the just pretext of saving a threatened world, some kind of *modus vivendi* is achieved. Both priest and devotee benefit thus. Resurrection of the soul of the victim in the battle rounds off the defence mechanisms, for a risen demon/god, whose body is destroyed but whose soul remains intact as he returns to the Mother, is a fitting end for the drama of life; it mediates conflicting drives, desires and wishes. But only for a while, for the response systems are cyclical; they reappear and call for repeated expiation.

A society which provides substitutes—sublimating imaginative texts—to alleviate the torture of guilt is a compassionate society. Left to himself the individual introverts the destructive emotions, and damages his psyche. It is to Mahisa's credit that as the paradigmatic sacrificial victim of text and icon his death and resurrection through the centuries has been responsible for saving the lives of countless of his fellow creatures.

Text Comparison: Sacrificial Rite with Battle

In order to highlight the concept of the battle as sacrifice and specifically of the battle between the Goddess and the demon as the sacrifice of Mahisa, it is useful to point to the similarities between text and present-day ritual—the analogous sequences, the intensity and the final outcome. Like the rituals, the texts are about atavistic regressions which press for recognition, overwhelming unconscious human responses. This applies to the preliminary pursuit and struggle between two equal contestants, the Goddess with Mahisa in the myth, and the buffalo catchers with the buffalo in the ritual. There are processions, musical accompaniment to the horrors of killing, beheading, tearing of flesh, dismemberment, gorging on the blood and flesh of the dead or dying victim, lamentations and then the final demise, a preparation for the predictable ascent of the victim into heaven.

The parallel sequence of events can be tabulated thus: first, involvement of two distinct entities; pursuit, struggle and capture. This is followed by descent into climactic orgiastic convulsions, during which the antagonists lose identity, as powers are transferred from the weaker to the stronger; tying, pounding, beheading, hacking-off of flesh, tearing to pieces, drinking blood, devouring. Then follows redemption of the weaker, the sinner, in a happy ending which results in cathartic peace.

Some examples of textual descriptions of the battle evoking the sacrificial ritual are given below In descriptions of a particular battle, standardized phrases are applied equally to each of the asuras embattled with the Goddess.

Sacrificial Rite	Battle Text
Procession	While Brahma on his vehicle Swan, Visnu on Garuda, Sankara on his bull, Indra on his elephant Airavata, Kartikeya on his peacock, and Yama, the god of death on his *vahana* the buffalo, were on the point of going with the other Deva forces, the army of the Danava Mahisa met them on their way, all fully equipped with arms and weapons.[123]
Pursuit	Vaskala then pursued the Devi with a club in his hand to slay her.[124]
Struggle	Energized by the power of the Devi, these battalions fought with axes, javelins, swords, halberds and destroyed the asuras.[125]
Capture, Tying	Binding other asuras with her noose, she dragged them on the ground.[126]
Tied to a post	In this war sacrifice there is this axe which is like a sacrificial post.[127]
Lamentation	Crying 'Alas, Alas', loudly, his [Mahisa's] followers shouted 'Save us, O save us.'[128]
Slaughter pierced heart	Pierced in the breast by her trident, some fell to the ground.[129]
beheading	The Divine Mother hurled the Chakra; instantly that weapon severed the Danava's head.[130]
hacking off flesh with knives	Then the Goddess hit and struck the hosts of the enemies with her club (and) axe.[131]
drinking blood eating flesh	Kali, angry, began to drink the blood of the Danavas and ate the fat and flesh.[132] The Kalika Devi rent the asuras asunder and devoured them all.[133]
Possession	With eyes rolling, 'her face reddened', her senses excited...[134]
Music	Of those battalions, some beat drums, some blew conches and others played on tabors in that great martial festival...[135]
Praise and devotion	'Victory to you' exclaimed the devas in joy to her, the lion rider. The sages, who bowed their bodies in devotion, extolled her.[136]

Victim released from sins and reaches heaven.	The Goddess says: 'However, when you have been killed by me in the fight, O demon, Mahisa, you shall never leave my feet.'[137]

Ascension and Resurrection of Mahisa

His head was cut off with a sword. As he was killed by the Goddess, his soul went to heaven.[138]

The pairing of the Goddess with the dying god associated with a bull who is reborn after death, is reinterpreted in the Indian context. Even as he shared the circumstances of birth and the life struggle with earlier heroes, so Mahisa's death also has its mythic parallels: the victim is killed and dismembered and, to the sound of music and lamentations, he ascends to heaven, there to be united with the deity. Cosmic order and a paradisal era are ushered in as a result of the hero's resurrection.

At the time the Goddess was created from the energies of the gods they had suggested to her that, even though the asuras had committed sins likely to keep them 'long in hell', they might 'reach heaven by meeting death eventually at the battle'.[139] As the true relationship between the slayer (Durga) and the slain (Mahisa) is intuited unconsciously by the mythmaker, death as absolution can be the only defence; the mythmaker serves his own purpose by inventing an extravagant fantasy of purification in the fires of battle (which will permit the original sin to be re-enacted in heaven). Even Indra and the other gods are ready to admit that death transforms the daityas, and the Goddess promises sensuous enjoyments and life everlasting:

rebirth in Heaven, thus to enjoy the Deva women they could not have got in any other possible way.[140]

After death, asuras loyal to the gods have the right to enter into the 'heaven of heroes' (viraloka). This certainly implies indulging in relations with the wives of the father gods. (One wonders at the gods' willingness to share their wives with their former bitter enemies.) The unfortunate wives of the devas would seem to be the only losers in this male-dominated Nandana Garden.

These assumptions prepare the way for Mahisa's resurrection. The gods, and especially the Goddess, seem not to be opposed to the idea of accepting Mahisa's ascent into their magnificent mountain abodes. The wise poet defines the meaning through a simple but powerful simile:

> As the owner of any garden plants with pleasure the beautiful trees in his garden for his delight, and finding some of them not to bear any fruits or leaves or of bitter taste does not cut them off by the roots... so O Devi, thou has killed them off (daityas)... out of compassion.[141]

As usual her compassion is tempered with self-interest. The Goddess who only recently had chopped off the son's head is compared to the farmer who destroys the plants for food, retaining the seed and the root. She will prune, but, for her own survival, will ensure that the sinning son will find peace in heaven in union with the Mother. So, the Goddess grants life everlasting to the demon Mahisa.

These mutual dependencies were already suggested in the latent material of the *Kalika Purana*. In his terrible nightmare, the Goddess cuts open Mahisa's head and drinks his blood with her frightening, wide mouth[142] (see p. 135). The dream symbolism alludes to what is overtly stated in the DBP: the Goddess insists that she is really a man, showing herself in feminine form for the sake of expediency in this particular incarnation only.[143] Moreover, she considers him a hermaphrodite as well,[144] implying a feminine side. Nowhere is the sex and violence motif more sharply illuminated. The cleft in his head, slashed by the phallic sword as 'he slept on the mountain', is an only slightly masked metaphor for sexual intercourse in reverse. The Goddess drinks his blood (or semen) exchanging bodily fluids, quaffing the red liquor directly from his recently feminized head.

Under the circumstances, Mahisa can only wish for death as punishment leading to release, even though he is the passive feminine dreamer and she the guilty male/mother. But, unwilling to capitulate entirely and still hopeful of last-minute efforts to maintain a minimal amount of separation, he holds out for two boons: to share in the sacrifices and to serve at her feet 'as long the sun shines',[145] which the Goddess seems only too willing to grant. Mahisa asks simultaneously for power and for submission. In fact the Goddess recognizes him as Siva: 'Therefore the Goddess accepted the demon Mahisa, who was actually' the great god (himself). In three births the Lord Siva was Rambha's son.'[146] The transfiguration bestowed on him by the Goddess is a gift far more generous than even he had ever dreamed of:

> O demon Mahisa, you shall never leave my feet.... In every place where worship of me takes place, there will be worship of you; as regards your body, O Danava, it is to be worshipped and meditated upon at the same time.[147]

Both having achieved their heart's true desire, it has been so always in the worship of the icon of Mahisamardini in India.

The resurrection of the hero is the salvation of the world; as a result of his death, paradise will follow on earth in harmonious relationship with nature: it will come about that men will be virtuous and Brahmanas and Ksatriyas will fulfill their Vedic functions properly, without deceit. Wars, atheism, famine and poverty, plague, disease, and untimely death will vanish. Even women will return to good behaviour. People will be devoid of anxiety, fear and agony and will live in happiness and splendour. [148] So it is when Mother and son return to each other.

The kingdom of heaven on earth is gained by means of the sacrifice of Mahisa's flesh and blood. However, unlike his Christian counterpart, whose single sacrifice promises the permanent salvation of mankind, Mahisasura returns eternally for confrontational cyclical rounds. There is no final solution, only a continuing struggle with the Mother Goddess, so, for the Hindu, the millenial hope of the devotee is tempered by reality; struggle, not fantasies of paradise, is the hope for mankind.

For the more enlightened the ritual battles are analogised to those waged within the seared soul. Ramakrishna was able to explain what was happening internally prior to his submission to the ultimate Reality which overcame the power of the Goddess. As a *sadaka,* one who carries on the struggle within, he tempered the steel of his body and was able to detach his mind from all objects, with the exception of the too familiar form of the radiant Mother. She barred the way to the Beyond.[149] When he tried to concentrate, she intervened, but after prolonged meditation:

> I used my discrimination as a sword and I clove her in two. The last barrier fell and my spirit immediately precipitated itself beyond the place of the 'conditioned' and I lost myself in Samadhi.[150]

Here is matricide, the struggle against the Mother who perennially impedes efforts to find the Atman in oneself; or in our own terms, to reach maturity.

Chapter Eight Festival: Myth–Rite Equations

The relationship between myth and ritual is an interpenetrative one; there can be no real divide between the two because they arise from a common source. In the case of Navratri, as we have seen, in the myth the climatic event—the battle—is always described as a festival, and the events of the story are implied or dramatized during the ceremonies. While the priests chant the text of the DM and the votaries simultaneously perform the prescribed rites in contrapuntal conjunction, all experience the same guilt, penitence, sacrifice and then catharsis and psychic renewal.

The belief that the institution of the annual festival causes, stimultates, and perpetuates cosmic and world processes for the survival of the community, crosses cultural boundaries. This involves, *a priori*, unqualified faith in an authoritative deity, the blind acceptance of a particular system, and achievement of generally agreed upon objectives by means of traditionally pre-scribed sacrilizing rituals. In turn, these rationalizations give name and form to chaotic forces, and random, violent eruptions are thus kept at bay. The Goddess or god in the shrine is the calm, unmoving eye at the centre of the cyclone. During Goddess festivals the Devi is the centralizing presence towards whom all dangerous, recently released energies converge, powerfully draw-ing all the interacting forces towards her. From within the shrine, power is then transferred back to the now re-activated, highly charged festival atmosphere. In order to harness the danger, the sacrificial victim is made the repository and the new focus of energies. The multitude of devotees participate vigorously in the slaying on the one hand, and they symbolically identify with the slain animal on the other. Order and calm will be restored only where there is a consensus amongst the group to be thus symbio-tically involved in the act of violence and when the subsequent ejection of the deity from their midst at the end of the festival is assured.

The constant elements, the essence of the ancient festival, are very much in evidence today in a variety of manifestations. The permanent features include scheduling according to astronomical observations and agricultural cycles, coinciding with the new moon and lunar phases, the solstice or equinox, and with the specified number of days. The space is delimited and sanctified and ancestors are worshipped. The deity is aroused and approached with adoration and awe. Plants, grains, fruits, flesh and blood are offered in profusion. There are crowded processions and the public display of the image of the god or Goddess with symbols of organic plenitude. All-important is the proper handling of particular substances: oil, water, fire and the flesh and blood of the sacrificial victim by authorised religious practitioners. Sanctioned gestures, posturing and dancing, the chanting of magical formulae, hymns, prayers, the devotional singing of sacred texts are hypnotic and rhythmic. Possession by the deity is common. Devotees participate in ritual dramas and combats and identify with the concretized heroic divine narratives, miming the vagaries of human existence as well as the eternal cycles of life and death in nature. Music is the constant accompaniment, provided by the beat of drums and by loud wind instruments. As climactic event, if the divine marriage is celebrated at a sanctified place, it is followed by orgiastic outbursts and obscenities, sexual promiscuity and a mock reversal of the established social order. Animals or humans are sacrificed to the deity, accompanied by lamentations and pleas for forgiveness, and finally, when the festival comes to an end, the ritually dangerous deity is disposed of in a place outside the boundaries, over a cliff, or into the sea. Or it is simply sent back to rest in the darkness of the closed shrine.

In India contemporary festivals to the Goddess vary greatly in range and emphasis. Some differ very little from the archaic tribal rites out of which they have developed. Those connected with the important Brahmanical temples are intricate and highly structured, controlled and determined by traditional imperatives. While the gradations between the most primitive and most sophisticated and complex become increasingly more fluid, and there is a relaxation of regulations as to who may worship, general distinctions are still operative.

The lower castes and tribals still rely on their own priests, and, unless recently outlawed, there are animal sacrifices at simple outdoor shrines. Where the institutionalized Brahmanical rites have been superimposed on indigenous worship at the high temple complexes, in most cases, Vedic ceremonies and their concomitant textual readings are a substitute for the pasubali. Each festival place maintains its own traditions, even as it modifies and adapts them.

We are primarily concerned with the rites of sacred marriage, the propitiation of buffalo and Goddess in general, and of Mahisa and Durga in particular. The descriptions are of aboriginal, village and Brahmanical rites and a tale of sacred marriage; a folk festival to the buffalo god; festivals to Mhasoba/Mahisa in Maharashtra; festivals to the Goddess in aspects other than Mahisamardini; and Navratri.

Hierogamy (Sacred Marriage)

At the climactic instant in the Mahisamardini narrative, the Goddess, in the form of a beautiful young girl, but laughing thunderously, enters the universe. This myth is the Brahmanicized version of primitive rites of marriage of the gods to the Goddess or their substitutes. As surrogate for Siva, the divine husband, Mahisa is the dying god.[1]

While the New Year rites associated with royalty differ in detail, the basic concept of productive couples and the death, dismemberment and resurrection of the male partner has been altered very little: male/female coupling for the purpose of ensuring fertility is the inviolate central action. The procedures which take place on the eighth day (Astami) of the festival to the Goddess (Navratri), when the battle of Durga with Mahisa is commemorated, retain vestigial elements of the ancient hierogamies. Then, for example at Tuljapur (see p. 207), the image of Mahisa is ceremoniously brought into the shrine of Durga, and following their symbolic union, a goat is sacrificed to the Goddess as a substitute for the now prohibited buffalo. In structure, meaning and effect, the symbols representing the male/female relationships function for Indians today as they did for the people of the ancient world.

The sacred marriage rite during the festival of the New Year was earlier celebrated over land and sea: the fructifying phallus of the god/king/priest, often associated with the bull, symbolizing strength, the power of the plough, semen, seed, rain, *mana* or the Greek *zoe* or life force, in various equations, married the Goddess/queen/priestess or cow—the womb, earth, furrow, the nurturing mother.

During the festival, in which the entire community participated in mimetic orgiastic rites before the royal/divine/animal couple, 'it was the king's pleasant duty to marry the passionate, desirable Goddess of fertility and fecundity.'[2] Always the couple are members or symbols of an élite ruling power. Having established his position by means of military conquest, to consolidate his authority and to ensure the co-operation of the society, the king associates his sovereignty with the priesthood and through them, with divinity. Often, on the archaic level, he is represented by a bull. As Gilbert Murray has pointed out: 'The tremendous mana of the wild bull indeed occupies almost half the stage of pre-Olympian ritual.'[3] All over the ancient world to the west of India, in the realm of the Mother Goddess, the triad of bull/king/god, with priest as intervener, supported the image of the solitary, weak and vulnerable chieftain or ruler.

The marriage took place between a bull symbol or a man who assumed the attributes of the bull and a female representing the Goddess. The Goddess was often imaged as a cow who had given birth to a son, and at times son and lover were synonymous. In the case of Innana/Ishtar, Anath and Athene especially, the Goddess was, like Durga, primarily the Goddess of war. Nature depended upon, indeed *was* the constant tension and symbiosis between male and female.

Subordinated to the Goddess at first, by classical times the male consort, aided by the obsessive focus on the bull, under some conditions deprived the Goddess of superiority and overall dominance. While the Goddess receded into the background the bull was often personified as a beautiful lover; the deeply-engrained association with the bull continued to be the symbol of the heroes and gods of Sumer, Assur, Egypt, Crete and Greece, even, though for the most part hidden, of the Hebrews. There was virtually no way to inhibit intrusion of the atavistic imagery into the later rites; it retained its forceful power in the unconscious with absolute predictability.

Aboriginal, Village, Brahmanical Rites and Tales of Sacred Marriage in India

Before the necessity of male intervention in regard to human birth was recognized, the aboriginal Goddess reigned supreme. Later, marriage to a fructifying mate modified her absolute power, (although in Tamilnad even today male attendants are subordinated to the popular Tamil *gramma devata* or village goddess).[4] The love/hate tension between Mahisa and the Goddess may be studied in the light of ancient and contemporary sacred marriage rites and legends.

The male as consort/creative seed and the receptive female are represented in a variety of arcane forms, the divine husband being a material object, such as a stone, tree trunk, fossil shell, or icon; all imply the temporary tenancy of a spirit—or the role of the fructifying male is dramatized by a priest possessed by the Goddess. She in turn can be anything—a tank, a stone, a *tulasi* plant, the root or trunk of a tree or an icon; the combinations are seemingly infinite. In all areas of the country, these rites of marriage are celebrated with processions, anointings, rejoicings, dancing and music and easily-possessed priests and devotees.

The gramma deva Ellama was given a root by the godling Adijambuvu. It became a cock, she a hen, and then she laid three eggs. In an annual festival in Salem district in Tamilnadu, the god Shevarayan, in the form of a clay or brass idol, was married to the presiding goddess of the Kaveri river. Each was placed in a separate chariot and taken in procession. Afterwards, together they were marched down the hill in a triumphal car.[5]

At Chamundi Hill, near Mysore city, the goddess is taken to the temple of Mahabalesvara during the Ranna Kannada festival,[6] and at Visnupur in Bengal, during Siva's spring festival, Durga in the form of a sacred vessel is brought to the god in a secret nocturnal rite.[7] During the pre-threshing rites of the Warlis of Maharashtra, as plant dressed in a green sari, Kansari the corn goddess is married to Pandava, the god of vegetation in the form of an ear of paddy dressed in a white *dhoti*. Together bride and groom are taken in procession around the field and subsequently, to the sound of music, a chicken is sacrificed, the priests become possessed and *arati* is performed in the presence of other gods and goddesses.[8] During the Magh festival in Vir, Maharashtra, the wedding of the local god Mhaskoba with the Goddess Jogubhai (Jogesvari) is performed[9] (see p. 89).

We have seen that the Goddess, even though she remains unwed, longs for a mate in the same way that the devotee longs to unite with her. Thus another ritual interpretation attempts to satisfy her needs by providing a temporary human 'husband' in the form of a potter, washerman or barber of the Sudra caste. During the entire Pongal festival in some South Indian villages, such a person is brought to the temple, washed, clothed in new garments, is fed well and generally conceived of as bridegroom, while maintaining celibacy throughout.[10]

As Mahisa is a reinterpreted form of bull consort, of special interest for us are the vestigial practices which connect a goddess with a bull or buffalo in marriage ceremonies. Obeyeskere describes the marriage of two horns which represent the goddess and her consort in the Ankelia ritual in the Panama district of the east coast of Sri Lanka. The horns are intertwined with vines, ropes and coils, which provide the vegetal accoutrements, and the redemptive blood or its symbol, which is part of the ceremony, links this ritual to its original. A struggle between the teams of the goddess and of her consort ends when the consort's horn is broken. The author recognizes a combination of sexual and combatative symbolism including the participants' use of abusive language, generally with incestuous innuendos, nude dancing and humiliation of the opponent in a cathartic abandonment of propriety. Later, forgiveness songs cancel the temporary guilt.[11] Mahisa's desires, aggressions and final defeat can be symbolically analogized to these ceremonies.

In another celebrated festival at Bastar, Madhya Pradesh, bison-horned ecstatic dancers accompany a chariot with the insignia of the Devi as it moves in procession around the town.[12] Traces of the link between horned priests and the buffalo demon who will be slain by the Goddess are omnipresent; the suggestiveness of the universal horn symbol always lingers at the threshold of consciousness. These horns can in turn be linked to the buffalo who himself is led around the village before being sacrificed to the Goddess. In the Bellary district ritual, Whitehead believed him to be the buffalo husband (*gauda-kona*) of the Goddess.[13]

Beck (1981) describes the temporary marriage of a tree-trunk to the goddess Mariyamman in the form of a pot, and she sees the ritual at Kannapuram as being connected with the relationship of Mahisa with the Goddess who later slays him, although the 'husband' is also associated with the other demons, with the outcaste priest and with the animal victim. The equation, she asserts, should be left loose. 'One could not say that the tree trunk is a definitive lover/husband/demon/father/temple priest/local resident. There are enough correspondences to allow one to develop intuitions, patterns of associations and even a meaning. But nothing is so precisely explained as to lose its attendant paradoxical qualities.'[14]

The flexibility of these symbols is such that even gender association is not specific: among the Madigas, the Basavis (she-buffaloes) were virgin girls whose families had no sons. Dedicated and married to the Goddess in elaborate ceremonies followed by a marriage feast, they, like the male priests, danced as the buffalo was led to the sacrificial post.[15] It should also be kept in mind that Siva as post (see p. 127) would form part of the larger pattern when, as in some localities, Hindu worship has deeply inter-penetrated the aboriginal practices. Also in Karnataka, the Deccan and the Konkan, the Basavi was a girl married to the god Basavana (the Lingayat bull).[16]

At certain levels, as we have seen, the divine marriage of the Hindu goddess Parvati to the bull-riding god Siva is a construct parallel to the pairing of Durga–Mahisa. Like other marriages of the gods and goddesses in South Indian temples, these ubiquitous rites are late manifestations of the ancient originals. The Pangun Uttiram festival, during which the Goddess is married to the god Siva as Sundaresa, is observed in March–April at many important religious centres in South India.[17] William Harman has devoted an entire volume to the ceremony at Madurai.[18] In the Tamil *Tala-puranam*, the Sanskrit Puranas and throughout the centuries in art, the marriage of Siva and Parvati has been deeply entrenched as a model for all high-caste unions and is one of the most personally felt of Indian myths. In this way the contemporary psyche is linked to its primeval beginning, even though fertility associations may not always be recognizable as the prominent focus of the ceremony.

Whether or not the literal marriage is connoted, the buffalo bull as a victim with arcane consort associations is often a predominant aspect of the rite. In the texts Mahisa represents one of the many manifestations of the by-now remote ancestral progenitor. This explains his obsessive lust for the Goddess, for he is heir to the role of fructifier and sacrificial victim. Once this is recognized, the effort to situate the buffalo demon in relation to the Goddess works best if absolute assertions and categorizations regarding his status as husband are avoided, although one may point out certain broad associations.

A very popular folk tale, widely known and often published with variations,[19] was told to me in the following version: An outcaste shoemaker pretended to be a Brahmin and married a Brahmin woman. But after some years, the husband returned to his old profession, and even privately taught the skill to his own sons. Seeing the children's drawings of shoes, the mother became upset, took a chopper and started running after her poor husband. As he fled, a buffalo opened his mouth, so the husband jumped inside. In terror the wife cut off the buffalo's head. Her children tried to appease her, but as her lust for blood was insatiable, she then proceeded to kill both husband and children. Nevertheless, she ascended to heaven and became a Goddess.[20]

N. P. Shankara Narayana Rao[21] added that the Madiga shoe-maker observed all the Vedic rituals, and by the time he was fifteen years of age, he had assumed the Brahmin tuft, put on the *yajno-pavita* (sacred thread), left his position as servant in a Brahmin household and departed for a far-off place. There a local Brahmin became impressed with his knowledge and begged him to marry his daughter. They lived happily together for ten years and raised children. But the Madiga remembered his own mother and longed to see her. He invited her to live with them, but in order not to reveal her true identity, he bid her shave her head, cover it with a cloth, smear herself with *vibhuta* (ashes) and advised her not to utter a word. The wife liked her mother-in-law very much because she was so quiet, which prompted the husband to boast, 'Is not her quiet tongue like the tongue of a buffalo?' But the mother-in-law finally did speak about the wife's very tasty dishes: 'as good as the buffalo's tongue', she said. Since only outcastes ate buffalo meat, the wife first became suspicious, then horrified. She evicted the children and husband and put a curse on them, that they would 'become Madiga in the afternoon'. She then set fire to the house, killed herself and became a Mara.

In all the versions, a Brahmin lady marries an outcaste who is associated with a buffalo, kills the family and herself and is subsequently deified. Ritual, myth and folklore are all strongly suggestive of the intimate relationship, if not the actual marriage, of the buffalo to the Goddess.

Festival of the Buffalo God

Maysandaya, South Canara District

In the Tulu-speaking country of South Canara district, after harvest, at midnight, on full moon night, in April or May, the Maysandaya (*maysa* buffalo; *andaya* he, like a man) festival is celebrated. With a ritual specialist (*pambada*) clothed in vegetation, music, and excited dancing performed in a central open village space, it retains a pattern of worship of the buffalo god hardly distinct from its prehistoric antecedents. With a chosen elder as head, groups of five or six families co-operate in the preparations and in providing the money for the food and salaries of the musicians and the pambada, but only men may participate; the women are permitted only to observe the ceremonies from a distance. The ritual specialist is member of a hereditary caste: he becomes possessed and is the incarnated buffalo god for about fifteen to twenty minutes; during this time, with violent movements, he stamps around and charges, and emits the appropriate grunts and snorts. As the god is compassionate and helps his devotees, there is revelry throughout the night, but there is also the conviction that Maysandaya will curse if the festival is not conducted or if it is conducted improperly.[22]

Mhasoba, Nasik, Maharashtra

The traditional yatra rituals (pilgrimage festivals) have changed very little over the years in some areas. Held all over Maharashtra, they combine commercial transactions, relaxation and music with prayers and sacrifices. Many sheep and fowl were sacrificed to Mhasoba, the red-leaded stone in a shrine between Phulmari and Aurangabad one century ago.[23] On 29–30 March 1991, at the Purnima Chaitra at Siloor in Aurangabad district, participating in a two-day festival, thousands of devotees arrived from neighbouring villages in bullock carts or by bus with their families and sacrificial goats and chickens. The stone Mhasoba at Siloor, in the Sri Ksetra Mhasoba Maharaj Mandir, is in the form of a newly-painted orange stone of strange shape. It resembles a four-foot-high tree stump with a single thin branch, and has a small eye painted on to it; a cardboard crown sits on the 'head'. The idea that the vehicle of this god is a buffalo was often voiced. As at other yatras, the sale of sweets at many stalls, the wearing of new clothes and a festive atmosphere was combined with the worship of the god, and this included the sacrifice of over 600 goats, at a place some distance from the temple courtyard. The god was daubed with the blood of the sacrifice, although the heads were not brought to Mhasoba on his high platform—this it was considered would desecrate the sacred area; the meat was cooked on outdoor fires and eaten by the pilgrims.[24]

At Igatpuri on 14 April 1991, only a single goat was sacrificed to Mhasoba in the morning. In the form of a stone flanked by a few others, the god is alone in a newly-constructed small temple near a water reservoir—no longer in a forest far from the town. In the outer court, a shrine with seven stones, aligned horizontally, houses the 'seven sisters'. Only women and children worship them, and informants emphatically denied that they are married to Mhasoba, who here is definitely a bachelor. The local devotees comprise about a hundred families; they do not seem to connect their god with the buffalo image in the Mhasoba shrines of Nasik, twenty miles away, though here too the vehicle of the god is said to be a buffalo. All are well disposed to their god, or so they say. Devotees arrive with elaborate offerings.

In the contemporary urban environment, the Mahisasura legend is after all sometimes connected with the worship of Mhasoba. This was dramatically exemplified at Nasik in April 1991 at two contiguous shrines housing Mhasoba in theriomorphic buffalo shape (plate 2).[25] Now no longer outside the boundary, the god has been definitely incorporated within the precincts of the city. A popular story explains:

When Devi was about to kill Mahisa in human form he jumped into a passing buffalo to escape her. She went around slaying many buffaloes in order to determine where he had hidden. The buffaloes then complained to the Devi that they were being unjustly attacked for another's crime. Seeing their point she offered a boon. No one would be allowed to worship her until and unless they had worshipped Mhasoba (a buffalo).

The distinction between Mhasoba as buffalo god and Mahisa is made amply clear on the one hand, while the connections are also emphasized.

The celebrations at Nasik included an initiatory erotic dance to the rhythmic rousing beat of music by a man dressed as a female. While the dancer at Tuljapur (see p. 209) called himself Potraj (buffalo king) this was not the case here. A procession left the first Mhasoba shrine and proceeded to the second, about a furlong away. The main attraction was a magnificent live buffalo, resplendent in the light of the street lamps; he was covered entirely with turmeric, led by a rope, and was made to bow to his stone counterparts. Would he later be sacrificed? Was he a god? As the ban on buffalo sacrifice is enforced in urban areas, at the end of the month-long festival a single goat is substituted for the buffaloes sacrificed earlier. There was not a shred of doubt that these two small Mhasoba images were being honoured and worshipped as deity by all. During the entire evening, a steady stream of people brought offerings of flowers and vegetation and received the darshan of the god Mhasoba (plate 3).

Later that evening, the two Mhasoba shrines were visited by an assortment of other divinities in the form of worshippers wearing masks, but there was no sign of Mahisa. When I asked about Mahisa's mask, I received results beyond my expectations. I was directed to a nearby home where women of all ages were in the process of worshipping a magnificent pair of images: a beautiful, large, painted papier-mâché mask of Ganesa, and one of Mahisa with extended slim horns. In another private home a mask of the Goddess was being kept for the next morning's event. At Mhasoba's festival, Saptasungi Devi, the Goddess of the seven hills (see p. 198) becomes Durga who slays the buffalo demon.

Close to midnight a traditional Marathi entertainment (*tamasha*) took place, with first a male group singing religious songs (*bhajans*) in Marathi followed by the inevitable erotic antics performed by men dressed as women, to the blaring sound of cinema music.

On the following morning at 6.20 a.m. we were guided to the house where Mahisa and Ganesa had been worshipped the night before just in time to see a man, possessed, stamping around in the court like a bull. He was led into the main street to be fitted into an artfully constructed buffalo shell. The body, a simple iron armature, was covered with a blanket and flowers and the exquisite mask was placed in front (plate 4). This was Mahisa; we were about to witness his battle with the Goddess, whose mask was being fitted with difficulty on to the writhing body of another possessed man a short distance away. During the next hour, 'Durga' chased 'Mahisa' up the road, moving from the first to the second Mhasoba shrine. Each of the contestants had to be guided, as they were literally maddened with fury. Spurred on by provocative sounds from a man who was always one step in front of him, 'Mahisa' grunted, circled, charged and retreated with such force that five men had to hold him down. The 'Goddess' followed (plate 5); the distance between them gradually lessened. She swayed, turned, ran forward and brandished her swords. Neither was play-acting; they had lost consciousness, and, possessed by the demon and the Goddess, they *were* the buffalo demon/god and the Goddess. The accompanying music was shrill and rhythmic, stimulating some of the young men to fall to the ground on all fours, and also possessed, they too became enraged bulls in an overt demonstration of the fundamental assumption of this study—the bull–devotee identification. Others fell at 'Mahisa's' feet and worshipped him (plate 6). Finally, when both had reached the second Mhasoba shrine, and the devotees became more and more agitated, in an instant, the 'Goddess' slew the 'demon'. He faltered and staggered, then he fell in front of the stone buffalo image of Mhasoba. It took this impersonator of Mahisa about five minutes to regain consciousness. Then the constructed semblance of Mahisa was placed near the stone image of Mhasoba (plate 7), and both continued to be worshipped during that entire day. They were separate, equal, contiguous but not identical.

As for the 'Goddess', she was still in a frenzy; still wrathful and cavorting around, she was guided by the men back to the first Mhasoba shrine and finally, when she arrived, she made obeisance to two Mhasobas in buffalo shape there. One was a crude small buffalo, and a second stone had the face and horns of a buffalo carved in relief on it. The Goddess' mask, having been removed, was placed beside the stone images (plate 8). Here again was a hint of a marriage, this time following the battle, for otherwise the Goddess' mask would not have been thus offered to the demon/god. Together they continued to be worshipped with prayers and offerings during the entire day, and the closing ceremony of smearing a good amount of red powder on people's faces seemed to be the residual trace of the redeeming sacrificial blood which identifies the worshipper with the god.

On this day Mhasoba is the dominant deity and Mahisa's association with Mhasoba, if not his actual identification, was amply proven. All shouted: *'Mhasoba Maharaj Ki Jai'*, 'Glory to King Mhasoba'. This slogan bridges the worship of Mahisa/Mhasoba, as Mahisa had definitely been slain. But the youth of today persists in identifying with his royal likeness, Mhasoba, if only during the festival, as though to persuade themselves that they have the capacity to separate from the Goddess, to be both like the king and like the god (plate 9).

Festivals of the Goddess

Festival of Saptasungi, Goddess of the Seven Hills, Vani, Nasik District, Maharashtra

Until recently devotees climbed up the steep mountain on foot in order to reach the Goddess on the mountain summit—it would take days to do so. Today, a forty-minute ride in a minibus in winding ascent transports devotees to a halting station, approximately four thousand feet high. Then they begin a mile-long march along a path lined with the usual festival vendors of goods and fruits, naked rsis, and during my visit, there was even an ascetic who had buried himself in the earth. Only his hand and wrist appeared above the surface, fingers moving in slow rhythmic motion. He was still in the same position six hours later.

Reaching the steps, accompanied by groups of musicians and much crowding, we began the barefoot hour-and-a-half-long climb towards the Goddess in her recently-built modern shrine high in the rockface of the mountain. No single person hesitated, neither two-year-olds nor their great-grandmothers, as thousands upon thousands were magnetized or internally driven towards the goal. Having reached it, one found long queues, with a good amount of hysteria and possessed women awaiting the momentary confrontation with this ancient Goddess, now a very large painted carving on the rock face of the mountain. So anxious were devotees to approach the deity that police were continually directing the crowd out of the shrine. These moments in the life of the average Hindu take on sacred meaning and give hope and succour to the pain of existence. Vindhyavasini (she of the Vindhya mountains) of the medieval tract came alive, albeit Saptasungi is a mere shadow of her former self for she seems to be satisfied now with a single pasubali in the form of a goat sacrifice on *Purnima* (full-moon) of each month.

Spring Harvest at Mahismal, Aurangabad District, Maharashtra

The Girijadevi (mountain Goddess) temple in Mahismal, a remote mountain village, about a half-hour's drive up a steep incline to the north-east of the Ellora caves in Maharashtra, is one of thousands of other shrines where the Goddess has been worshipped for millennia. The Brahmanical overlay is a recent accretion. Even though the stone image of the Goddess in the shrine is the product of a trained artist, a more primitive icon with hardly more than an allusion to the human form remains permanently in a corner. It is the connecting link with her roots in animistic worship, as Girijadevi, very much the indigenous Mother Goddess, is as ancient as time, and her Brahminization is not completely effected even today. Still worshipped by the Bhils and primarily by peasants, the hill may have been a sacred place millennia before the temples at Ellora were carved out.

Now Brahmin priests conduct affairs in this recent small structure. It has a courtyard where many of the activities take place. On the north side of the shrine, within a rectangular recess, the Goddess' bed is permanently placed. Every night at 10.30 p.m. the doors of the temple are closed, and the Goddess is put to sleep. The bed doubles as a palanquin for the Goddess when she is taken out in procession on Purnima night. While the only reference here to Mahisamardini is a framed paper icon hanging on the inner wall of the shrine along with other representations of the Goddess, a review of the Magh Purnima festival and some thoughts about individual worship serve as a prelude to understanding the role of the Goddess in the lives of the people today and, by association, of her connections with the buffalo demon.

Magh Purnima is the spring harvest festival. Only peasants come to this mountain shrine for a combined celebration of yatra (pilgrimage), yajna (sacrifice) and market. About forty thousand pilgrims attend; they walk miles up the hillside, or they travel in ox-carts, rickshaws, buses and occasionally by truck or car. Each party arrives carrying a goat or two and their provisions for the week. After settling the family at a specific place on the land surrounding the temple, the new arrivals head for the temple and wait anxiously for hours in orderly lines in nervous anticipation of darshan of the Goddess. Inside the shrine, they offer prayers, incense, coins, sugar, plates with an arrangement of vegetative offerings and a mountain of saris; perhaps they touch the idol and then their own chest to incorporate the Goddess, or they prostrate themselves. Lamps are lit and arati (evening worship) performed; kum-kum is placed on the forehead of the Devi, and bells ring overhead. At any time of day or night, women are seized suddenly by the Goddess, and they easily fall into a trance amidst all the crowding and hubbub. A young man is possessed—he is in a fit for more than an hour; the music plays on and on through the nights and days, with only short periods of quiet. Tensions and atmospheric stirrings are the norm during the week. On the last day, a large fire blazes in the sacrificial pit situated in the court facing the Goddess in the shrine. No blood or flesh now, only coconuts and butter are offered, the air is filled with smoke and tense with heightened expectations.

On the morning of the second day, at a high place within sight of the temple, a slaughterer cuts the necks of about three hundred goats; the blood saturates the earth, and people lament and stroke the animal before the sacrifice. Each goat is then skinned; the innards are carefully removed by the owner. He keeps the meat for the family but saves the head and feet as offerings to the Goddess. Later, in the shrine, I see a large gunny bag filled with goats' heads and another with legs. It is then that I imagine the festivals of former times when buffaloes were sacrificed. The Mahisamardini myth and its final episode, when the buffalo demon is decapitated, comes alive with full force.

Aside from the religious duties, the atmosphere is gay, marked by a sense of relief after the hard agricultural labour that had preceded these celebrations. The recently-harvested cotton, wheat, lentils, grams and barley, staple crops of Maharashtra, are arranged aesthetically in the stalls set up along the pathway to the shrine. No doubt remains about the link between ancient agricultural rites and the sacrificial ritual. Women sing devotional songs; there is the ubiquitous loudspeaker playing cinema music. The *mela* (festival), which lasts for four or five days, provides a study in contrast between the anxiety and near hysteria of the proceedings at the temple and the jovial mood of the return to temporal pursuits.

Private Worship of Devi at Mahismal, Aurangabad District, Maharashtra

While the ancient connections dominate, this remote hillside has already been invaded by the middle class of Aurangabad, the nearby rapidly-industrializing town. On New Year's Eve, motorcycles and radios disturbed the peace I had hoped to find. But the temple offers city-dwellers the opportunity to stay in contact with the Goddess in the form which has been worshipped since time immemorial. On 1 January 1988, I had the opportunity of witnessing a fascinating private ceremony, one of thanksgiving to the Goddess. The devotee was an educated businessman from Aurangabad, whose family had worshipped here for five generations. He had arrived by car in the late morning with his entire family for the day of celebration, equipped with servants, cook and a very fine repast which I fortunately was invited to share.

I sat in the shrine and witnessed the procedures which illustrated how today ritual can be modified according to personal wish. A Brahmin priest chanted, and in complete disregard of orthodox Brahmin rules, the worshipper was permitted to conduct the bathing (*abisheka*) of the nude Goddess himself. Most impressive was the fervency and obvious devotion with which this modern gentleman approached the Goddess. With the palms of both hands, he rubbed the image with a good deal of force, alternately pouring water and placing large amounts of kum-kum on the idol for nearly an hour, while in the corner his own mother sat, also in some way involved in the procedure. He was totally absorbed, almost hypnotized by the activity. After the puja I asked him how he felt. He told me that when he is thus in contact with the Goddess, he loses all reason, and a feeling of ecstasy overwhelms him. 'You feel peace; I don't know anything else. I am alone with god.'

He had no trouble returning immediately to his role as head of the family, hosting us all to the delicious meal. At the end of the father's puja, after the Devi was dressed, the family entered the shrine; they stood, chanting the name of the Goddess, clapping hands, ringing the overhead bells. This lasted about ten minutes. I stood in wonder at all the levels of connection with the Goddess, as another ritual, Satyanarayan, was then performed for Visnu. I considered the effectiveness of the combined rituals which first permit regression on the part of the head of the family, while his personal mother looks on, and then provide a channel, by means of family identification with the male god, back towards the separation.

Here the Cosmic Mother merged with personally directed iconic worship. An American friend commented, 'I guess we don't like to separate ourselves from her who gives us birth.'

Navratri

During Navratri throughout India, the Goddess is worshipped in millions of large and small temples or merely in humble village structures. As beautifully-crafted stone, bronze or painted plaster icon, as pot or stone, residing in a tree or river, she is hymned, dressed in finery, daubed with powder or red paint, laden with flowers and saris and generally propitiated and adored. Swarms of humanity focus on this single idea. Each ceremony is unique, depending on royal traditions or place of origin and on the creative responses of fervent devotees. In some localities there is only devotional singing of hymns and silent worship. In others there is hubbub and excitement amidst the offerings; still other communities concentrate on a fixed ten-day ritual (with or without animal sacrifice) and final immersion of the Goddess. The variety of modes of worship is infinite, yet the skeletal framework is absolute.

In the huge temples rites are performed by priests, formerly in co-operation with royalty and today with government. Private groups sponsor celebrations, or individuals conduct worship at home, but during these nine nights and ten days, there is total and fervent attention on the Goddess, and this is ultimately the coalescing force of the people of India. During this sacred time, they forget differences of caste, status and economic level. Something much deeper happens, as the divisions and disputes of everyday life are obliterated.

The Hindu New Year is celebrated in Chaitra (March–April) and in Asvina (September–October). The sun begins its ascent from the southern to the northern hemisphere at the vernal equinox, the first day of *uttarayanam*, and on the first day of *dakshinayanam*, the autumnal equinox, the sun starts its movement in the opposite direction. Navratri is scheduled when the sun is in the asterism of Virgo. Virgo is Durga, and below her constellation in the skies, the centaur is Mahisa, half man, half buffalo; Leo is above.[26] The moon also determines the calendar. Texts vary as to the exact timing. The *Kalika Purana* advises that the celebrations should begin

> When the sun is in the sign of Virgo, my dear, from the first day of the bright half of the month onwards.[27]

As long as there are earth, air, heavens and water

> so long shall the worship of Chandika be observed on earth, for in ancient days, on the eighth and ninth days of Asvina, the autumnal festival used to be celebrated with great éclat.[28]

Even today, at the climactic event of certain festivals, the buffalo/bull Mahisa performs his perennial role as consort, fructifier, sacrificial victim and god resurrected. But the ferocious battle between him and the Goddess which precedes the sacrifice is the highlight of the ceremony.

The individual is urged to participate in the festival in order to avoid calamities but also to reap rich rewards. Both results are the play of the Goddess in the world as she imposes her will, but if the ritual is properly conducted it can influence her; a non-observer or one who fails to carry out the ritual properly will fall on evil days, but nothing is impossible for those who perform the duties scrupulously. Then all sin is cancelled, including that of killing a Brahmin, and superhuman power and salvation are attained. The ceremonies also help to control the passions, to counteract evil and purify the ambivalent heart. During these days, the merging of self with self and self with the Goddess becomes apparent as individuals seem to fuse into a single electrified organism. A *bhakta* (devotee)

> sings my name loudly and dances, being intoxicated with my Love, and has no idea of egoism and is devoid of his body idea, thinking the body is not his.[29]

All the goddesses of the Hindu pantheon, or the one Goddess with many names, are implied in the ceremonies. Not all Navratri festivals pay attention to the events of the battle, but the eighth and ninth days are recognized as the period of conquest over the demon and the tenth (*Dasami*) as the day of victory (*Vijaya*). In either case, whether seen as the prime focus or alluded to generally, the struggle with the Goddess is felt to be intense, real aod her victory cathartic.

At its most elaborate, Navratri was a royal celebration in honour of the warrior Goddess who influences the outcome of Ksatriya battles and gives courage to its participants. Like the royal suttee ritual, by displays of great material splendour, the ruler sustained and strengthened his own sovereign powers. Arab chroniclers described the annual ceremonies of the Vijayanagar kings of the fifteenth and sixteeth centuries, which were performed on a grand scale to mesmerise thousands upon thousands of subjects and to astonish foreigners. The bejewelled and ornately dressed ruler, seated behind curtains on an equally bejewelled throne, appeared before his thronging devotees at regulated times. Before him were paraded hundreds of painted elephants, dancing girls and musicians; vast amounts of food of all varieties were distributed. On the final day, two hundred and fifty buffaloes and four thousand, five hundred sheep were sacrificed at the temple of Durga.[30]

In Nepal, till today, the focus is on the sacrifice rather than on pomp and splendour, but the former king's appearance is awaited with excited anticipation, for he is the pivot of the ceremonies. Gurka regiments play a leading role. On Astami, at sunset, the sacrificial ceremony begins at the central square (*kote*) in Khatmandu. The animals are dragged towards the sacrificial post, tied to it and with a single stroke, decapitated. The agricultural mainspring of the festival is revealed when (rarely) the butcher fails to accomplish the task properly, for then the crops will suffer, and the angry crowd smears his face with the still warm blood of the victim. But he usually succeeds, and is then rewarded with a white turban. In 1912 Percy Brown reported that 'buffaloes were slaughtered in the thousands';[31] even today sacrifices are carried out throughout the night. To the sound of guns and the blare of trumpets, as the tower of decapitated heads grows larger and larger, the killing continues. All reports describe loss of consciousness on the part of devotees, an electrified atmosphere and flowing of torrents of blood.[32] There has been little change in these time-worn rites.

When compared with rites at other sites, a remarkable consistency is illustrated by James Preston's report of the Cuttack, (Orissa), Durga Puja held at the Chandi Temple in 1972, when seventy thousand devotees participated in the highly ritualized mêlée. There was the usual chanting of mantras, sanctification rites, trances and anxious anticipation prior to contact with the Goddess, who was dressed as Mahisamardini on the last night. Lamentations preceded the single-stroke decapitation of five hundred goats in front of the Goddess, and the sacrificial blood was offered to her in secret behind the closed doors of the shrine. Finally, the Goddess was taken in procession and immersed in two rivers outside the city.[33]

In 1990, in Mysore city, where the tradition of Durga worship has a long history, nearly a million people congregated to witness colourful folk arriving from various districts. Large tableaus were displayed, elephants paraded; in a blend of old and new, army, navy and air force exhibitions continued the Ksatriya/royal/military focus, but there were no sacrifices.

The ancient ritual of immolating a human being was until recently still practised in Assam on the ninth day of Navratri. Either the victims volunteered, or strangers were caught for the purpose.[34] Although some scholars have challenged these assertions the history of human sacrifice makes them plausible.

'The pillar to which the sacrifice is tied divides life from death.'[35] The sacrifice is justified on the grounds that the gods reside in the limbs of the victim: Goddess and victim are one, as the priest chants:

> Chandika in the chin, Ugrachandika in the sets of teeth, Chandaghanta in the tongue, Chanda in the neck etc.[36]

The spirit of the animal is freed, it receives salvation, and through its flesh and blood offering to the Goddess, the devotee is united with her, and he is released from the guilt attached to the slaying:

> Therefore I do kill thee in this yagna, though thou art unkillable.
>
> What was worshipped by me, O Goddess, let this be completed for me. Go thou into the river, into the water, and remain in thy home, in the interior of the earth... Thou hast been put into the water by me with a view to obtaining sons, a long life, wealth and prosperity. With this mantra the Goddess should be put into water for the sake of prosperity of all men.[37]

The Goddess and her buffalo consort drown together. Their joint potency, dangerous although absolutely necessary for annual recharging, is thus being controlled by the Brahmin priests. If the pair were to stay for too long, the devotee would be unable to emerge from the temporary regressions which the festival permits and encourages. The various means by which danger is averted— ejection from the boundaries outside the village, breaking the pots, immersion in water, and in Tuljapur, the implications of the *simolanghan* (processional and ejection ceremony) (see p. 214) and 'putting her to rest' for five nights in her bed within the closed shrine assures the priesthood total control over the Goddess, and thereby total control over her violence, lasciviousness, her devouring nature, her capacity for destruction of an erring devotee, in short, of the evil power of the Mother. Even while her coming is deeply longed for and crucial, her final exit from the life of the devotee is a great relief, celebrated with loud noises, sports, blowing of conch shells, games and songs.

Ambadevi temple, Amravati, Maharashtra

For the celebration of Navratri at Amravati in north-east Maharashtra, the Goddess Ambadevi (mother, nourisher) draws a seemingly unending stream of devotees from surrounding towns and villages. Here her tamasic traits have by now been emphatically subordinated, and she is associated with Radha and Krishna, although in a recent poem by Dasgana she is also called Kali, Chandi, Durga, the slayer of Canda/Munda and of Mahisasura.[38] In 1911, at the boundary of surrounding villages, a local Goddess, Mesakai, was still receiving many buffalo sacrifices. But by that time, the reformer Gargibarga had persuaded people to abandon animal sacrifice in the city temple.[39] Today substitute offerings in great profusion may perhaps compensate the Goddess for the deprivation of her cherished flesh and blood.

The first seven days of Navratri at Amravati are devoted to homage to two separate images of Ambadevi in her temple. Even while bhajans, prayers and donative rituals are actually accorded priority, there is also plenty of time for the purchase of supplies, and doodahs and baubles at the many stalls lining the path leading to the temple.

The most dramatic event is the huge fire sacrifice, performed at 4.30 p.m. on Astami in the temple courtyard when the DM is chanted in unison by about twenty Brahmin priests. Seated on the ground, they form a large oval surrounding the three huge raging fires. It is an emotionally charged, hypnotic ritual. As the sun sets and darkness envelops the three fires which shed a mystic glow, with modulated sounds and words precisely pronounced, the reading goes on and on, while some Brahmin members of the temple board, as honoured individuals, and the priests, continually feed the fires with vegetable, fruit and oil offerings. They would seem to be the contemporary substitutes for the king, who in Vishnupur, Bengal, still plays the central role in this ceremony.[40]

Surprisingly, the streams of devotees seem to ignore this climactic event, so anxious are they, as they have been all week, to enter the tomb-like temple to pay respects to and receive the darshan of Ambadevi. But on the way there each throws a small offering into the oval adjacent to the temple and, piled in huge mounds, these are later thrown into the fires; then, by means of the rising smoke, the fire god Agni transports these gifts, as ashes, to the Goddess. During the entire ritual, a doll-like effigy of Amba at the centre of the oval is the object of worship, as 'representative' of the two immovable idols within the shrines.

The reading about Devi's battle exploits at the *havan* ceremony has only recently been substituted for buffalo sacrificial rites. The motherly Ambadevi has shed her sanguinary attributes at the behest of a managing committee now controlled by Brahmins, with the fires acting as transformative medium to shift the emphasis. Thus at Amravati primal energies are conserved; while offerings of flesh are appropriately forbidden in accordance with Brahmanic conceptions, contact with the people is still assured. But in remote villages, if the government is lax, Devi can still indulge her fancy.

Tuljapur Bhavani, Osmanabad District, Maharashtra

From hundreds of miles around, half a million pilgrims arrive to celebrate Navratri at the Tuljapur Bhavani temple, District Osmanabad, Maharashtra, said to have been constructed by the great Maratha warrior-king Sivaji. Deviating from orthodox Hindu practice, the priests are not Brahmins but members of the Maratha caste, who claim that the Goddess is a Ksatriya because of her great battle with the buffalo demon.

The Goddess rests on her bed, placed next to her shrine but on the first day of the month of Asvina, she is installed on her platform inside. On Vijaya Dasami (the tenth victory day), after the Goddess has battled with and slain Mahisa, she is massaged with the contents of hundreds of bottles of oil and is again put to sleep, to recover from her strenuous efforts. Five days later, awakened at Purnima, she is replaced on her platform in the sanctum to resume her role as object of worship for millions throughout the coming year.

Between these two sleeping states, during the ten days of the festival, she is the central focus for the devout who are, in one way or another, in symbiotic relationship with the Mother figure. The Goddess has a terrible hold over hundreds of millions of people today. It seems as though her chaotic driving energies far outweigh the moderating influence of the complex rites designed to externalize and keep her powers in check. People are volatile, driven by a compulsion to enter the shrine, there to make offerings in return for her blessings. Many appear to be possessed; in most cases, this condition which subsides soon after contact with the Goddess has been achieved, can be described as nothing less than possession.

A preliminary bath in the Kallola *tirth* (tank) will wash sins away and cure diseases. From there the devotee enters the *gaimukha-tirth*, an artificial tank where Ganga water, said to come from Kashi (Banares), pouring out of the mouths of two silver cows' heads (*gaimukha*), purifies a perpetual stream of worshippers, already in a state of anticipatory fervour.

During the following hours and week it seemed as though all caste divisions had disappeared in the mêlée. (About Vishnupur, Ostor reports that 'the annual Durgapuja is the time for all jatis to participate'[41] although in the 1970s there were still some restrictions regarding participation by some lower castes). Thousands of votaries, peasant, middle class and also affluent, lined up for darshan of the Goddess. The courtyard was continually teeming with people, most of whom waited patiently but compulsively, determined and completely focused on their turn to enter the small *mandapa* (hall) which leads to the sanctum. It presented a scene of heightened energy kept under stern control, but the vibrations of

1. One lovely she-buffalo...

Mhasoba festival, Nasik, Maharashtra.

2. The god Mhasoba in buffalo form.

3. Woman worshipping Mhasoba in buffalo form.

Mhasoba festival, Nasik, Maharashtra.

4. A possessed man becomes Mahisa.

5. Durga before the battle.

Mhasoba festival, Nasik, Maharashtra.

6. Mahisa being worshipped.

7. Mhasoba is equal with Mahisa. Dindori Road shrine II.

8. Durga and Mhasoba in buffalo form, worshipped simultaneously.
Dindori Road shrine I.

9. Mahisa as Chakravartin/hero.
Chamundi Hill,
Mysore, Karnataka.

Navratri festival, Tuljapur, Maharashtra.

10. Potu Raja
dancing as
Mahisamardini.

11. Silver image
of Mahisa, shown
before he is taken
into Devi's shrine.

12. Interior of the shrine on Ashtami: Devi slays Mahisa.

13. View of the sacrificial pit before the
goat sacrifice.

14. Mahisamardini pandal being transported from Kumartali to street shrine. Navratri festival, Calcutta.

15. Hema Malini as Durga. Dance drama, Bombay.

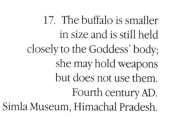

16. The Goddess and
Mahisa are carved
as a single volume,
expressing a
symbiotic relationship.
First century AD.
Government Museum, Mathura, Uttar Pradesh.

17. The buffalo is smaller
in size and is still held
closely to the Goddess' body;
she may hold weapons
but does not use them.
Fourth century AD.
Simla Museum, Himachal Pradesh.

18. The earliest known carving of Mahisamardini on a rock-face. Mahisa's body has been lowered; the Goddess breaks his neck and pierces him with her trident. Late third century, Ramgarh Hill, Madhya Pradesh.

19. The Goddess pierces Mahisa's body with her trident, holding him by the hind leg with her left hand. Fourth–fifth century AD. Gupta shrine, Ramgarh Hill, Madhya Pradesh.

20. The Goddess stands
on the severed
head of the buffalo.
Fifth century AD.
Gwalior Museum,
Madhya Pradesh.

21. Mahisa, his front legs
buckled under his body, stands
in front of the Goddess;
he has more volume and
stands within his own space;
she breaks his neck.
Sixth century AD.
Ravana Phadi cave,
Aihole, Karnataka.

22. The Goddess and Mahisa face each other as equals on the battlefield. Seventh century AD. Mamallapuram, Tamil Nadu.

23. As Mahisa emerges in human form from the buffalo, the Goddess pierces the buffalo body with the trident and is about to deliver the second mortal blow. Eighth century AD. Surya temple, Osian, Rajasthan.

24. The all-powerful Goddess slays Mahisa in buffalo and human form, reduced once again to a smaller size. Tenth century AD, Siva temple, Kitching, Orissa.

25. Mahisa in human form
rises towards the Goddess
as he emerges from the
severed neck of the buffalo.
Tenth century AD.
Ambika temple, Jagat, Rajasthan.

26. The Goddess towers above
Mahisa who has been brought
to his knees; he is human, with
buffalo head. Eleventh century
AD. Chidambaram temple,
Tamil Nadu.

27. Mahisa is now only in human form. Tenth century AD.
Ambika temple, Jagat, Rajasthan.

28. Goddess and demon are nearly equal in size and importance.
Twentieth century. Navratri pandal, Calcutta.

the human interaction, the sense of a common aim, is a sensation almost physically experienced. To fulfil their vows to the Goddess, devotees, mostly women, prostrated themselves, alternately standing and falling in rhythmic movements; some rolled on the ground or crawled in the direction of the shrine which they circumambulated. An informant reported that women started in their village performing these rites until they reached the shrine; others walk with stones on their head, an act of devotion which they hope will compel the Goddess to grant boons, or they do so in fulfilment of a vow.

In the courtyard, groups of people from the same village or family sang, danced and performed the *ghondhal* ritual. Families conduct private worship of the Goddess in vegetative form: an arrangement of five stalks, each two feet high, which meet at the top. Offerings of kum kum, bananas, rice, turmeric, betel nut and flowers were placed within. The stalks were hung with chapatis, coconuts, garlands and pan leaves. Devi worship included beating drums, family members circumambulating the image, and hymns being sung by the *ghondhali* (priest) as he carried a plate formed of chapatis laden with oil lamps. When the procedure was over, the family gathered up the 'Goddess' and took 'her' home.

Also in the courtyard, there was the frequent occurrence of sudden possession by the Goddess; women fell into a trance as they were gripped by her force. The concerned looks and comforting gestures of female friends and relatives indicated that the behaviour was genuine.

A professional entertainer who designated himself and whom others recognized as Potraj (buffalo king), dressed in colourful female garments, danced with seductive, erotic movements; with his accompanying drummer he was a constant presence throughout the ceremonies, entertaining crowds of amused and interested onlookers. When I asked him to dance Mahisamardini, he donned a veil, danced as the Goddess (not as the demon), with definitely suggestive, enticing prancings designed to please (plate 10). He told me that he was from a hereditary community of entertainers but knew nothing about connections with the buffalo king which his name connotes.[42] This Potraj probably represents the remnants of orgiastic rites accompanying the ancient sacred marriage ceremonies and thus was a potent connecting link with worship of the fructifying bull as consort of the Goddess. His dance as the Goddess seemed to be an invitation for revelry. (That sexually stimulating rites were programmed into the Navratri ceremonies in the past can be verified from the texts. According to the *Kalika Purana*, for example, in order for the rites to be efficacious, maidens and prostitutes had to accompany the image to its immersion, dancing, singing and using abusive or provocative language.)[43]

Within the very intimate columned mandapa, the worshippers first pay their mild respects to Siva represented in a small, lower shrine on the east, in view of the Goddess, but all attention and energy is directed toward her. First they grasp a very heavy iron 'health' chain, which hangs from an ancient (*c.* fourteenth century) carved column: they encircle their heads and touch their chests with it. My suggestion that it represented the anklets of the Goddess was not generally acknowledged, but the original meaning of a symbol is often lost to the modern devotee. As people approached the Goddess in the shrine, excitement heightened to near hysteria. They gesticulated, cried out plaintively to Mataji, with bodies writhing and expressions of deep emotion, and there was a general surge of masses of bodies no longer entirely under the control of the police—a desperate scramble to reach the threshold of the sanctum, while haunting chants by Brahmin priests, who sat on the high mandapa benches, blended with ringing bells and the general highly-charged atmosphere.

Within the shrine, in the corner, the sumptuous Goddess in the form of many small earthen pots, was surrounded by new growths of grain in soil which was piled high with offerings of multitudes of fruits, coconuts, leaves and coloured powders.

Every morning and evening, the Goddess was bathed in a private abhisheka ceremony attended only by the priests; they alone were permitted to touch the statue which was divested then of all clothing and ornaments. The public was forbidden, as no one may see the undressed Goddess. It was only after repeated entreaties to the manager of the festival that I was permitted entrance. My own interest was in the style and iconography of the statue, bared of its costumes. Indeed, it turned out to be an early twentieth-century carving of Mahishamardini and not the ancient idol people claimed has been there from time immemorial. This black basalt stone received respect and reverence from her priests. The Goddess was bathed in gallons and gallons of curd and with water from the gaimukha, which was applied vigorously to her 'body' for a period of about half an hour. A few favoured devotees, in postures of adoration, uttered mantras and lovingly touched the flowers and coconuts strewn at the base of the statue, and meat meals, duly cooked, were presented.

The celebration of Navratri here has traditionally been the responsibility of the family of a retired Colonel. He and his wife behaved to the Goddess as though the statue were a living child, with tenderness, with concern for the rites, offering her a delicious cooked meal, fruits, flowers, and saris. Their touching attitude of total submission is the customary approach of worshippers from all walks of life all over India. During the ceremony, the police were busy pushing back the crowds; children screamed in the crush as, in their instinctive rush towards the Mother Goddess, people jostled each other in great anxiety. These conditions prevailed every time I entered the shrine under police protection during the week.

The shrine is virtually a stage on which dramas are enacted. Each night, the Goddess is dressed to represent one of her aspects. She is beneficent for the first four nights, as Tuljabhavani. On the fifth night she is Krishna. Gradually she is transformed into the terrible Goddess; on the sixth night, she lies on her serpent Sesa; then on the seventh she presents Sivaji with his sword.

Finally on the eighth (Astami), she is Mahisamardini, she who slays the buffalo demon. This is the time when the battle between the Goddess and the demon is imagined, as the sanctum becomes a battlefield. Mahisa is slain by the Goddess exactly at the stroke of midnight, between Astami (eighth day) and Navami (ninth day). But during the morning of Astami, the demon, represented by a small silver image of a buffalo with a man emerging from the thorax (plate 11), is ceremoniously installed in a richly decorated, opulent setting within the shrine. There Durga meets her would-be lover (plate 12). It is here that vestiges of the sacred marriage ceremony of the ancient festivals may very well be indicated. For while Durga is shown in an elaborate stage setting, plentifully armed with weapons, in the posture of killing, paradoxically she wears a red sari and appears to be dressed not for a battle but for a wedding. Red is the colour she assumes when making love.[44] Fuller and Logan associate the red sari worn by the Goddess Minaksi at the Madurai temple Navratri festivities, only on the night she kills Mahisa, with a bridal gown, and referring to Biardeau and Shulman, they believe that a sacred marriage is in process:

It accords with the theme ubiquitously present in myth and ritual, that there is a marriage between the goddess and the buffalo-demon, as well as with the more specifically Tamil mythological theme that Mahisasura is Siva and that the goddess marries the god at the same time that she kills him.[45]

At Tuljapur, the procedures which take place in the courtyard before Mahisa's entrance into the shrine could substantiate the theory that a wedding, or vestigial references to it, is included in the ritual. There is no sign that Mahisa is conceived as a ferocious, evil animal demon. On the contrary, the statue, while small, is beautifully wrought in highly polished silver. Accorded the privileges of a groom on his way to meet his bride, it is garlanded and hymned, greeted with reverence, and then paraded slowly towards the Devi in the shrine. Once installed, the Goddess and the buffalo demon remain together for many hours, allowing plenty of time for both marriage and a battle. It is not difficult to associate the entire sequence of events with the archaic rites of sacred coupling and final death of the passive, subordinate consort of the great Goddess, even though no overt references are manifest.

Parallel motifs are to be observed on the ninth day of the famous Madurai wedding festival, held in April–May, when Queen Minaksi's battle with the gods is re-enacted on the streets of the city. On the tenth day Siva and Minaksi are wed in the Marriage Hall of the temple.[46] There can be little doubt that there is a structural linkage between the Siva/Minaksi and Mahisa/Durga couples, based on a similar association of sex and violence. The same may be said of the ceremony at Vishnupur, where the Goddess is similarly dressed as a married woman who kills the buffalo demon.[47]

At midnight on Astami in Tuljapur the Brahmin priests perform a Vedic fire sacrifice, chanting mantras and the DM for long hours of the night, as they sit around the *homa kunda* (sacrificial pit), a large, separate structure in the middle of the vast courtyard. The midnight prayers are important and are attended by the district collector and president of the temple trust.

The Goddess is tired and requires sustenance—animal sacrifice to revive her after her arduous task of defeating the demon. Perhaps she would have preferred a human head, or all the heads, but one informant hoped that the substitute goat's head would serve the purpose of re-energizing the Goddess and also aid the devotee to reach heaven. Other reasons given were that people become anxious if they do not follow traditional custom, as the Goddess may very well destroy the lax devotee. All through the ninth day, Durga is the receiver of the sacrifice.

At exactly twelve noon, perhaps half a million people, crowding the homa kunda, bring offerings. All consciousness is focused on the imminent act of sacrifice. I sit with hundreds of peasants under a massive peepul tree, not twenty yards away. It must have been a sacred tree long before the structural temple was constructed here. All is movement, colour; the bright midday light is dimmed by smoke rising from the sacrificial pit. Multitudes sit on the amphitheatre stairs or stand on roofs or peer down from any available space; the heightened but repressed tension, the outpouring of all energies towards the common centre are difficult to convey. An enormous goat is carried to the homa kunda, its legs held by the priests, belly facing upward. Then the animal is sliced through with three strokes of the sword of Sivaji by a slaughterer who may be from any caste; today he is attached to the office of the *tahsildar* (local government official). The two halves of the slain goat fall into the deep pit, now ablaze (plate 13); amid shouts and loud chantings, fruits and coconuts are thrown after it. In true desperation all try to obtain some of the redeeming blood as prasad from the sword.

The moment after the goat is slain, the slaughterer runs with the bloodied sword directly to the shrine of the Goddess, and with his finger, he either marks her forehead or her foot with the blood of the goat, or some say he puts it to her mouth so she may drink it. About this secret rite, opinions differed. (Perhaps Mahisa was being granted a last request, which was that he receive blood from the mouth of Devi. He must have been in human form.) The head of the goat is then given to the Goddess, as she loves to eat the head. All agreed that since the meat sacrifice is an ancient tradition of the Marathas, the Goddess would become wrathful if her annual tribute was to be withheld. As the sacrifice follows the battle sequentially, it can be assumed that a relationship exists between Mahisa and the goat who *is*, in fact, the sacrifice; or the sacrifice is analogized to his death in the sacrifice of battle.

The heightened anticipation which begins with the noonday activities is maintained throughout the day. Three thousand goats are sacrificed privately in Tuljapur homes. In the early hours of the tenth day the final and probably the most deeply-felt tradition is observed. Now people have a chance to see the Goddess in procession, again in the form of Tuljabhavani. K. B. Prayag describes the event:

> A very grand procession of this palanquin and the bedstead is taken out in Tuljapur at midnight on the Navami. Before setting out for the Shilangan (circumambulatory procession) the idol of the goddess... is wrapped with many garments. At this time the Goddess looks like a Ksatriya warrior who is going to the battlefield. From the inner door to the round seat of the peepul tree the idol is carried in many hands by the pujaris, which is a very responsible task, needing care and caution. The pujaris carry her safely to the palanquin and place her in it securely even at the risk to their lives. Then the goddess sets out for Shilangan. This spectacle is very grand to see and it rouses the latent war-like nature.
>
> At the time of the Shilangan of the goddess, the precincts of the temple are thronged with men and women.... As soon as the goddess occupies the seat in the palanquin, with the slogans 'Victory to Bhavani; Victory to Tulja Mata', the palanquin is rapidly taken out in procession. Before the palanquin, all the Ghondhalis start playing on the sambal and other warlike instruments with crashing sounds. At the time of Shilangan, many are inspired with warlike feelings.
>
> The palanquin comes around to the peepul tree, rests there for some time and then is returned to the shrine.[48]

All this is accompanied by loud noise, musicians' bands, cheers, blazing torches, the throwing of kum kum and general pandemonium which has to be controlled by police.

The *Silangan* (Marathi) (*simolanghan*: Sanskrit) refers to the act of crossing a border, as now the Goddess is symbolically ejected from the precincts of the shrine. But she soon returns to her permanent abode where she is put to bed for four or five days.

On the ninth night I found lodgings at the Aranyabuva Math. Early on the tenth day a ceremony was conducted by the Sivaranya Mahant and several Brahmin priests who chanted the DM in a traditional annual ceremony. This over, in a rapid succession of movements, the Mahant jumped up, was handed Sivaji's sword, hurried to the position near the homa kunda where a *kohala* (pumpkin) served as substitute for the goat. In a flash, it was cut in half and immediately picked up by a peon who ran out of the Math. I followed and witnessed him running down to a stream, and quicker than I could react with my camera, the pumpkin was immersed. For these Brahmin priests it symbolized the sacrificial victim.

Finally, the festival comes to an end, the excitement subsides, people start leaving. Within the shrine, the Goddess is exhausted. She must sleep, or to put it another way, her enormous power and dominance must be overcome by all who, for ten days, have been swept into her energizing maelstrom. As the ritual had first called her to come into the universe, it is now reversed to accommodate the needs of the priests and devotees to return to everyday life, a state they ultimately perhaps prefer, but which they can maintain only after giving the Mother Goddess due respect and devotion.

Durga, Calcutta, Bengal

During the last four hundred years, Bengal has been the central locus of worship of the Goddess as Mahisamardini. The next best thing to being at the ceremonies is to have at one's disposal the minutely detailed descriptions of the ritual reported by scrupulous scholars. Ghosha wrote in the nineteenth century; Preston, who described the Cuttack Durga Puja in 1972, and Ostor that of Vishnupur, Bengal, provide painstaking accounts of the ritual sequence, scheduling and general atmosphere so vividly that armchair participation in the sound and colour phantasmagoria of the festival is greatly enhanced. As reported by Ghosha, the order of the ceremonies as they are practised in Calcutta retains many of the ancient elements, although often the rites are transposed or transformed almost beyond recognition.

Only those aspects which refer to the relationship between Goddess and buffalo or associative effects will be noted, although its general relevance makes it difficult to view the dyad in isolation. Of special interest were the Rabindra Sarani, Kumartali Street studios of artists who hail from Thurni village. During the weeks prior to the festival, approximately fifty 'masters' with their assistants are busy preparing the large, individual statues to be co-ordinated into over-life size floats (*pandals*). They work according to sastra instructions learned from their forefathers, but now there is also much individual creativity. The Goddess is shown in a beatific stance, always above a slain buffalo; a beautiful, life-size hero/warrior (Mahisa in human form) represents heroic energy. The lion is there, chewing on the prone dead buffalo, and so are the figures of Sarasvati, Laksmi, Ganesa, Kartikeya, and Siva on the bull Nandi, who are also worshipped. But the Goddess and human Mahisa are given pride of place in size and focus (see Chapter Nine). Durga shows no emotion, but Mahisa appears to be fighting mad. There is a riot of colour of symbolic significance: brown for the dead Mahisa in buffalo shape but natural skin colour for him as heroic human. The Goddess is all pink, with jet-black tresses. There is plenty of blood but also gaily-attired figures in pastel shades and much subtle juxtaposition, so that the entire composition virtually shrieks out its messages, enhancing the festivities. When the festival begins, people come in trucks (it was formerly by ox cart) to take the floats all over the city to outdoor locations (plate 14). In the villages, a single float suffices.

As in ancient times, devotees first worship ancestors—the *pitrs*, during the fortnight before the Durga Puja and on Sarvapitri Amavasy, the day preceding the new moon of Asvina. On that day Devi arrives on earth. In the procession women, often possessed by the Goddess, bear on their heads the *ghatasapana* (large earthen pots) filled with newly-sown grains; these pots are ubiquitous and symbolize the festival, as they *are* the Goddess. In honour of Sakumbari, the Goddess of Vegetation, the processions transport a variety of symbols, including water, rice, banana leaves that have been dipped in the Hugli (Ganga) river and many other types of plant and fruit. Throughout the week, at the pandals and in homes, music and dancing, the lighting of lamps, chanting of mantras by priest and devotee is the integral and perpetually electrifying accompaniment to recitations of the DM. Reading about the battle between Goddess and demon replaces the mock ritual combats common to the ancient New Year festivals. All the elements of battle, weapons and chariots, blood, warriors and war animals, loud cries of distress, have been transmuted into verbal stimulants contributing to the chaotic but cathartic festival atmosphere. The battle *is* the festival, and recitations recall it in all its aspects.

Vestiges of the sacred marriage of the primitive tribes of India are implicit in the *Navapatrica* (nine plants) rites. Specific species of plants represent various aspects of the Goddess; tied together, they are consecrated with mantras. The bundle is then offered to the Goddess. The metaphor graphically tells the tale. A twig or three leaves in the shape of Siva's trident[49] from the bilva tree is placed on the Navapatrica; it is sprinkled with water, and the priest chants. The admonition which follows, to bring home a branch of the bilva tree, symbol for the male, to present it to the home idol of the Goddess, recalls the sacred marriage rites:

> On the seventh day, one should worship her again, after one has brought (home) a branch of the bilva tree.[50]

If we consider the connections betwen Siva as sthanu (post) and Siva as Mahisa, the ever-present but never actually stated Goddess/consort relationships can be assumed to be implicit in these rituals.

In Ghosha's time, on Navami, great numbers of goats, sheep and buffaloes were sacrificed. But today, hundreds of goats are sacrificed to Kali during her own festival, celebrated a month later. A prayer for presenting the blood and flesh of the buffalo sacrifice to Durga in a pot was formerly followed by an offering of the head upon which a light was placed. A drop of blood was applied to the forehead of the Goddess. Thus devotee, Mahisa (as buffalo sacrifice) and the Goddess were united in the sacrificial ritual. The limbs of the victim are the Devi, and the sacrifice is proffered to her, as all categories and differentiations are obliterated. A prayer which follows describes Devi as 'mother of Isvara, thou art Isvari and beloved of Isvara'. Siva (Isvara), Mahisa and Devi are fused in the flesh and blood of the sacrifice. Then, as the Goddess retreats behind closed doors, the priest completes the ritual with prayers from the sacred scriptures. The Goddess is praised and in addition: 'In front of the Goddess, on the left side, one should worship the great Asura Mahisa (demon) whose head has been severed by the Goddess and has attained union with her.'[51]

At Cuttack (Orissa) the fertility and terrific forms are still combined, as during Navratri the Goddess receives blood sacrifices (see Preston, Chapter 4), but the Calcutta Bengalis have managed to obliterate her ferocious aspect from consciousness during the ten days of the festival. Now she is the creatrix, a charming, nectarous, exquisite queen with long luxuriant black hair and apple-pink cheeks and bosom. For these festivities only, the treacherous, deadly nature of the Goddess has been entirely camouflaged, although only a month later, as Kali, she will demand and receive the blood sacrifices due to her in the form of hundreds of decapitated goats proffered at her own temple during her own festival. This permits Mahisa to come into his own. As the warrior aspect of the Goddess is hidden behind her obvious erotic and fertility associations, Mahisa plays the role of the ancient para- mour/lover, and as she looks down at the potent male, the Goddess sees the king/lover of the hierogamy and not the sacrifice he will become on Vijaya Dasami, the tenth and last day. Public processions, music and dance, a profusion of vegetative symbols, new attire and worship of the Goddess and Mahisa in the pandals recall the ancient fertility celebrations.

It is written in the texts that on the tenth day of Navratri, the idol is to be consigned to the water. On this Dasami day (Vijay Dasami) the Goddess is instructed by priest and devotees to depart to her 'proper place', to remain there until the following annual festival: 'I deposit thee in water, for augmentation of my life.'[52]

So, on the last day, all pandals are carried to the Hugli river. Amidst revelry and fond farewells, Mahisa and Durga are im- mersed, and they sink together into the great oblivion.

Bengalis who have settled in other parts of India continue the tradition of immersing the group float in the sea. The floats were formerly led through the streets on carts, and this mode of transporting the demon/Goddess duo still persists in the villages. In Bombay, traffic does not inhibit the gaity. On the truck, the images are covered with coloured powders, flowers, and even the image of the dead buffalo and human demon is decorated with garlands galore, in a final association of products of the earth with the implanting phallus. As the truck moves slowly through the streets, male devotees dance before the Devi to the accompaniment of music; often they seem to lose consciousness and sometimes become possessed, although urban conditions have modified the frenzy. Finally, as the sun sets over the Arabian Sea, the Devi/buf- falo pair is raised aloft and carried together to the sea. The crowds shout, the music gets louder, and the tension mounts. As they enter the sea with the pandal, the worshippers show a strong pained emotional response to the departure of the Mother.

Today opinions vary about why the Goddess and buffalo float are immersed. The Goddess will flow from the specific waters into the Ganga and hence to her Himalayan abode.[53] The more educated believe that they are returning the Goddess to her universal status. The peasants show fear if the Goddess stays around too long because she is capable of causing them great harm.

It would seem as though, in order for the post-adolescent male to go on with his life, to marry, have children and prosper, as he defensively explains to the Goddess in the final mantras, the overwhelming Mother figure must be violently desanctified and removed from his presence; his hostility is thus expressed. But he recalls her in the following year; the temporal year is but an interval, as guilt remains.

For urban theatre goers, stage dramas are enacted during Navratri (plate 15).

Chapter Nine The Life Stages of the Hero: Depictions in Stone

Icons of the Goddess and the buffalo flood India's artistic land-scape; some have fortunately been preserved for nearly two thousand years, while contemporary artists are still captivated by the symbol. The myth is also enacted in all the classic dance forms and in dramatic presentations at festivals; masks and costumes are created in infinite variety. Paintings, wood carvings, bronze figurines, portable metal two-dimensional icons, book versions of the DM, and posters, have always been and still are ubiquitous. An entirely separate study is required to do justice to these productions.

I have chosen to focus here on the development of style in depictions in stone from the time they appear in the first century AD, because this provides an opportunity to trace their significance for the life stages of the hero. As works of art, of course, they deserve an analytical treatment which does not concern this study. These stone statues were created as icons to be worshipped as prescribed in the sastras. They were designed for private worship, as well as for temple shrines, and are to be found on temple walls and in the cave temples. I have included the Bengali Navratri pandals, even though they are made of impermanent materials, because they represent a contemporary (and positive) frame of mind.

The statues of Mahisamardini fit neatly into categories within which, however, there are many variations and no strict bound-aries. The categories are distinguished by three important factors: first, the particular instant which is depicted in the story, before or during the battle, or after Mahisa is killed; second, the spatial relationship of the figures of Mahisa and Durga, ranging from symbiosis to total separation; third, by Mahisa's depiction as animal, as buffalo-headed human, as human emerging from the severed neck of a buffalo, or as human alone.

The Categories

1. In the first category, with instances covering the first–second centuries AD, the Goddess and demon are carved as a single volume, expressing a symbiotic relationship; their size is equivalent, and the demon in animal form is spreadeagled diagonally across the frontally oriented, flat, static body of the Goddess; his head, nestling within her armpit, is resting on her shoulder; his hind legs are on the ground; the Goddess may hold weapons but does not use them (plate 16).

2. In a transition from category 1, in the third–fourth centuries AD, the buffalo is horizontally placed, his front and hind legs are closer to the ground or already touching it, he is smaller in size and is still held closely to the body of the Goddess; she may hold weapons but does not use them (plates 17, 18).

3. In the fourth–fifth centuries AD and later, the position of the buffalo is reversed; the Goddess holds the tail, his head is on or near the ground; his body is smaller, usually positioned parallel to, and lower than the Goddess', at her left; the trident in her right hand pierces his body or head in a diagonal thrust (plate 19).

4. In the fifth century AD and later, the Goddess stands on the buffalo's severed head (plate 20).

5. In the sixth century AD and later, the buffalo stands in front of the Goddess; he has more volume and is in his own space; there is more distance between him and the Goddess; she either pierces him with her trident and/or breaks his neck (plate 21).

6. In specific creations, by the seventh century AD, the Goddess and Mahisa are of equivalent size; they are separated by the figures of accompanying warriors and they face one another on the field of battle; Mahisa is in human form with animal head; Durga rides her mount, the lion; both wield weapons (plate 22).[1]

7. By the eighth century AD and later, we find depictions showing that the buffalo has been killed; the body and severed head rest on the ground; out of the severed neck, Mahisa emerges in human form; the Goddess grasps him and is about to deliver the blow and/or the trident pierces (plates 23–4).

8. In the course of the eighth and ninth centuries AD and later, the Goddess appears towering above Mahisa who is human or human with buffalo head; she raises her sword, and/or pierces him with the trident and/or breaks his neck (category 8) (plates 25, 26, 27).

9. Finally, in contemporary depictions, the Goddess and demon who has emerged in human form from the slain body of the buffalo, are juxtaposed, of more or less equal size; while the Goddess is above, Mahisa is definitely the lover/hero in his own right (category 9) (plate 28).

As we have observed, the life stages of Mahisa follow in the timeworn footsteps of his predecessor heroes. I would like to suggest that the variations in the episodes depicted, the configurational relationships, Mahisa's transformations and the categories of statues thus established, may be approached from the point of view of their efficacy and value as symbolic expressions related to the structure of the myth. When statues of the Goddess with the buffalo demon are examined carefully, an interesting pattern emerges, directing attention to a correspondence between the sequences of changing forms and the stages in the individual's states of consciousness during his lifetime.

As the community of artists unconsciously projects its innermost comprehensions concerning reality on to the work of art, what is perceived and which stage of the life and death cycle is signified depends only to some extent on the inherited artistic norms and more largely on the inherent symbols which press towards recognition and predominance at a particular time in a particular place. Every artist must also confront and express his own inner processes and responses. Consequently, there can be no absolute chronological or formal limit, but certain general trends are decipherable.

From the first to the seventh century (categories 1 to 5) the changes in the lithic relationships subtly but definitely show a separation of the demon from the Goddess. In slow stages, they are entirely transformed with regard to the three factors mentioned above. In the statues from Sonkh in the Mathura Museum and others from Nagar, Achichchhtra and related sites (c. 1–200 AD) the two figures form a single, indivisible entity (plate 16). An assessment of these earliest extant stone statues reveals a great deal about the status of the relationship at this stage of artistic development. What distinguishes them from all later carvings is the deliberate symbiotic fusion of the two into a single more or less undifferentiated volume. The large flat body of the buffalo is spreadeagled diagonally across the entirely frontal, static, vertical figure of the Goddess, who holds weapons in her hands but does not use them. The back legs of the demon are on the ground, and the large head nestles against her left shoulder. The Goddess and the buffalo, carved from the identical matrix stone, are one, and except for the rough outlining of their essential forms, there is hardly any marking distinguishing one from the other, nor is there even any hint of mobility or warlike stance.

What are we to make of the artists' obvious intention to avoid any indication that the Goddess is slaying the buffalo but that, on the contrary, she is very definitely embracing, protecting and holding the beast close to her bosom, perhaps even carrying him to the sacrificial altar? This would seem to imply that the earliest extant sculptures are a reflection of the earliest human stage—the merely nascent consciousness of the dependent infant. Even though it may be assumed that the legend of the battle as found in the DM was already widespread in the Kushan period, the artists who, in the final analysis, express what is subliminal to consciousness, do not seem to have been either ready or able to portray the Goddess as the warrior she manifestly is in the narrative. At this time, the maker of the idol conceives of himself as a great big grown-up animal infant, the inheritor of the prehistoric imagery of the warrior-mistress of animals, not yet separated from her subjects. Perhaps he is her consort, under her total control, performing connubial duties. While the fifth-century DM is the earliest extant text, it is of course possible that something in the previous narratives would have given credence to this projection.

The barely defined, rugged 'style' is elemental, the externalized embryonic preconscious condition in the hold of the heavy downward pull into dark maternal containment. Consubstantiality and passivity are experienced as paradisal contentment, the pleroma, identical with the image of Visnu sleeping on the dark waters, depending upon Yoganidra to initiate reawakening into life. While the potential for release and growth, the beginning of separation, is dormant, some centuries will pass before a shift of focus can be detected in iconography.

In the third and fourth centuries, we see (plate 17) a slow disengagement, finer and more apparent modelling, with the now smaller, horizontally-placed buffalo only slightly removed and lowered, yet still not standing on his own feet, and as yet adhering closely to and under the motherly protection of the Goddess. Mahisa is in no way belligerent; in fact, the proportional relationship might well apply to the live model of a woman carrying, or embracing a buffalo calf. The Goddess always dominates here, and the buffalo-shaped Mahisa, while growing in prominence and volume, is a small, unequal, still passive figure. In these four centuries, the weapons held by Durga are the only indication of the forthcoming battle, but at this early period, the carving is an icon devoid of any narrative content referring to the struggle.

Therefore attribution of the term Mahisasuramardini, *She who slays the buffalo demon*, would seem to be inappropriate at this stage. Even though sometimes the Goddess holds weapons, there are no signs that in her state of immobility she either intends or even has the capacity to use them in a battle with the buffalo. The artist, with his infantile perceptions, creates a statue to mirror his comfortable symbiotic state. These can be connected with the battle only with hindsight, as breaking the neck of the buffalo and/or the virtual spearing is the necessary sign referring to struggle.

A profound change of style in categories 3–5 reflects an abrupt psychological transformation, that which occurs when the child emerges from the infantile stage. The perfect union with the mother has been shattered as the protective mother of categories 1 and 2 is relinquished, and Durga the warrior makes her first appearance as Mahisamardini. This can be deduced from the episode depicted in the more or less contemporary DM, the new creative positioning of the figures and their increased mobility, and finally by the introduction of the trident or the severed head.

As to how and why this change came about, it appears that the artist had realized enough strength and sense of self to be able to face the implications of the myth, to transfer the focus away from his absorption in the Goddess, even though the solution he now prefers is submission in death rather than the struggle itself. As the artist now seems ready to confront the core reality of his temporal predicament, the buffalo is shown being killed or already dead. In one configuration, in a throwback to the Tel Halaf mode of 7,000 BC, the robust, still immobile Goddess stands on the severed head of the buffalo (plate 20). A more popular early relationship at Udaygiri, Bharmaur, Bhumara, Badami and in the numerous scattered statues of the Gupta and post-Gupta periods, is the new convention of reversing the position of the buffalo, separating his body, placing it parallel to the Goddess, and reducing its size as the Goddess holds his tail/hind leg and pierces him with the trident (plate 19). It was popular during the fifth and sixth centuries but has a life of its own thereafter as well.

Simultaneously, at Ramgarh Hill (plate 18) and Udaygiri, the earlier composition (category 5) prevails, but now the buffalo, standing in front of the Goddess, has his feet firmly planted on the ground, and the Goddess wields the trident. While this carving is related to earlier ones, the trident, indicating the battle, shown in categories 2, 3 and 4, is a subtle though radical departure. This will continue to be very popular. In the following three centuries, bas-relief is abandoned in favour of an increasingly three-dimensional depiction with the separation of buffalo and Goddess becoming increasingly emphatic; by the seventh century at Ellora in Caves 21, 14 and 17, the buffalo stands at the feet of the Goddess, but they are definitely both powerful and independent figures, although they are not equal in size.

At Aihole, a masterpiece (plate 21) presents the interflow of energy between two dynamic figures with which the earlier western *Mithras Slaying the Bull* is imbued. Did the Aihole sculptor receive inspiration from Roman contacts? Mithras averts his head, and the Goddess is magnificently detached and places her bent knee on the back of the buffalo as she breaks his neck by a calculated backward thrust. But here, Goddess and demon are interlocked closely with no modification of tensions, which in the statue of Mithras is provided by the surrounding space. This compression of tension between two powerful antagonists involved in struggle, confined within a rigorous framework, is the contribution to the history of art by the Aihole genius who must have felt his own fighting blood boil, even while accepting his destiny. Later, in Orissa, interpenetrating energy will again be conserved in the double figures of Durga and Mahisa decorating the temple walls.

If the episodes in the life story of the hero Mahisa are retraced, categories 3–5 can be interpreted as describing his death after the prolonged battle—his punishment for the guilt arising out of the forbidden desires and fantasies of the child. The animal/child, in thrall to the Goddess but needing to challenge her, believes he can do so; yet he longs to return to his symbiotic state. He can escape punishment for his unconscious wishes only by defeat after battle—death brought about by the phallic trident, wielded by his Mother who slays him in a defensive denial of her own love for him.

The trident held diagonally, which from now on will be a constant component in the configuration, symbolises the victory of the Goddess over the buffalo. Hardly a statue in the fifteen hundred years following the fifth century is without it, notwithstanding all the other transpositions of style and changes in configurational relationships. It becomes an obsessive convention in the iconography of all later work, and today it still immediately identifies Mahisamardini. Its vital purpose in the relationship, which is only apparently limited to the Goddess and demon, is to signify the aniconic presence of the trident-bearing Siva. The paternal authority intervenes to purge the dangers of ambiguities inherent in the mother/son relationship which have plagued them throughout the entire legend. Durga relies on Siva to rupture and subvert the natural but perilous tendencies.

Three or four centuries passed before a new configuration evolved, imaging the periods of self-recognition of the individual as a distinct personality, who has the right to live unattached to the mother, with the duty to ward off her controlling tenacious hold (categories 6–9). When the adolescent has grown physically larger and more powerful than his mother, he begins to realize his own strength, and, struggling towards independence, he is able to challenge her. Now neither is passive any longer. They are depicted as force-fields in various degrees of attraction and repulsion, although the Goddess is always the conqueror. At Aihole there is strong compression; at Pattadakal, the demon is human but is not a vigorous opponent; at Orissa, the compact group consists of a strong buffalo or human with buffalo head, brought to his knees by the power of the Goddess, who breaks his neck. Only in the unique configuration at Mamallapuram is there a perfect balance between two equals (plate 22).

With preliminary studies and/or copies at Pattadakal and Salvankuppam in the seventh and eighth centuries, a complete rupture from the combined single stone configuration takes place. Although there were precedents for battlefield scenes at Nagarjunakonda, at Mamallapuram, for the first time, Durga and Mahisa, or for that matter any two antagonists, are carved as entirely different isolated volumes, separated by other figures (warriors). In the magnificent Durga panel, the buffalo-headed human-divine king as warrior and the warrior Goddess on her lion are poised, facing each other, of equivalent size, weight and stature, each accompanied by associated warriors in battle on the actual field. There can be little doubt that this complex configuration, which has no precedents in India, is the result of intrusive western contact, both in regard to inspiration and craftsmanship, perhaps even with co-operation between indigenous and Yavana artists.[1]

As indicated by the royal umbrella over his head, the demon is conceived as a human king with buffalo head, having the force of an animal but the status of a divine king. The narrative of the Mahisamardini cave relies on the DM, with Visnu's pralaya scene facing the Durga panel. It is only here that finally the Mahisa of the DM and the DBP, whose great armies challenge gods and goddesses and whose prowess matches and often overwhelms theirs, is mirrored by artists now consciously aware of the implications and dynamics of the myth.

As symbol for the adult, emerged fully from the matrix chrysalis, standing apart and alone, no longer dependent nor submissive, the hero realizes for the first time his potential as the masculine figure. Like the ancient warriors on Greek and Roman sarcophagi, he is of equivalent size with his antagonist; he is bold, heroic, with an assertive presence, well established as an individual personality separate from his beloved creatrix/enemy. He is now the true conquering monarch, entirely grown up, at the height of his male powers, not yet defeated.

Artists working during an expansive heroic age under the Pallava rulers in South India seem to have developed the powers necessary for this recognition and appreciation of their own potential, and thus they created one of the greatest lithic masterpieces of all time. It is a glorious moment in India's art history, the culminating expression of the spirit of the male fighting valiantly for his own liberation from the destructive maternal orbit. But this was a pinnacle arrived at after long struggle, and in India, it could not be sustained.

After this brilliant but brief episode, there was a return to the earlier conventions, ignoring the Mamallapuram innovations. The Goddess is now again always larger, with a scaling down of the size and position of Mahisa as buffalo, almost as if achievement of a totally independent status for Mahisa was overly threatening to those so perennially captivated by the Goddess. After the great leap forward, reverting to the former acceptance of psychological subordination, they now resumed their focus on the demon as victim. A renewed acknowledgment of the superior powers of the Goddess became the only appropriate functioning symbol, imaging the devotee's responses to the Mother Goddess both then and now.

But the counter effort which had taken place to modify the demotion of Mahisa seems to reflect a state of mind which could no longer entirely accept the original passive position of Mahisa solely in the form of an animal, nor the inevitability of his total annihilation. As an unconscious defence against the terrible dilemma, another innovation now introduced the popular cross-cultural symbol of the warrior emerging from the body of an animal. Now the demon is reborn in human form from his own decapitated body, sword in hand (plates 23–5).

> One should further represent the buffalo under her (Goddess), its head being cut off just as it should be; and the demon is to be represented coming forth out of the spot where the head has been cut off, just as it should be, holding a sword in his hand, and his heart pierced by the Goddess' trident... His body, red from blood, eyes tremble, (sic) he is strangled by the noose, face twisted.[2]

This death by Durga's phallic trident is the artistic reversal of his desired penetration into her; it results in resurrection, even if only temporarily. Mahisa as hero is given his due, although the recognition is neither bold nor unambiguous, for the warrior is instantaneously subjected to a second beheading. Mahisa is thus twice born and twice beheaded, but prior to his second death, his heroic self is alluded to momentarily, if only in truncated, dwarfed, transient form.

A later convention reduces the size of the buffalo-headed human Mahisa and reintroduces his subordinate status (plate 26). And finally, the buffalo allusion is abandoned entirely in favour of a demon/man who strains towards the Goddess; he has lost his equivalent status, is small and once again pathetically inferior. He is again in close physical contact with the Goddess at the instant of death (plate 27).

Not until modern times is there an indication again that the male artist is in control of his own destiny. Contemporary focus on the rights and responsibilities of the individual in Bengal seems to have been a factor influencing the creation of the pandals for Navratri there. Its roots in the ancient Pallava stone panel and displaying the battle spirit of the medieval Puranas, the heroic image of Mahisa has re-emerged (plate 28). Again he is the psychologically evolved adult, the temporarily resurrected life-size figure of a vigorous, powerful male, on equal terms with a now more feminine, quieter, though sumptuous Goddess. She stands at a higher level but no longer overwhelms the demon.

If one were not familiar with the story, the relationship might very well now be conceived to be the alliance of two correlated equal individuals. Durga's trident, the dead buffalo's body out of which the beautiful hero has emerged, and indeed, the variety of accompanying 'family' members are now merely minor details which serve to highlight the two protagonists. The male has certainly come into his own in Bengal, with the triumphant reborn Mahisa seemingly very equal to the task of withstanding both the blandishments and the emasculating tendencies of this maidenly version of the ancient Goddess.

Conclusion

Mahisa's role offers a single example of how myth functions as effective mediator between unconscious animal impulses and the behavioural requirements of an ordered society. It is an aid in containing and controlling conflicting drives, in harnessing still operative primordial instincts and in quieting fears of being overwhelmed by them. As mirror image of the unconscious and carrier of a load of projections in ever-changing constellations, the Goddess and the buffalo demon dyad is a defence against the threat lurking at the gates of consciousness, ever ready to erupt. Because of his threshold position, Mahisa can lead the individual in one of two directions. His presence guarantees connections with roots, with the matrix, the unconscious instincts, but with light, reason and consciousness too. His function is to guard and protect in the struggle with the incestuously dangerous Mother Goddess.

The myth is concerned with restructuring consciousness in the direction of the longed-for autonomy, for it permits identification with the buffalo as the antagonist of the Mother Principle. If the view that the buffalo demon is all evil were to be perpetuated, total submission of the male would perforce be implied. Emasculation and death and merging of the core self with a dominating image would be the definition of the triumph of justice. This perspective has been rejected here in favour of the alternative focus on two equivalent forces, fundamentally similar in nature and moral conduct. The buffalo demon and Goddess in battle are the appropriate symbols for the protagonists in the eternal male/female struggle and in the often fatal mutal attraction as well. By bringing the plight of the male out into the open, consciously focusing on it and revealing certain of the arcane realities, the myth is in itself a heroic attempt to overcome; as it describes the cyclical repetition of Mahisa's battle for superiority and of his repeated retrogressions, it comes to grips with the dilemma. It is a bold attempt to solve the unresolved conflict, even if for most it leaves the solution in question. Although the Goddess always conquers,

230

and the demon is always the victim in the sacrifice, predictably he will rise again to life, reflecting the round of creation/growth/maturity/death/creation. As Mahisa battles with the Mother symbol, he is the standard bearer for all would-be free men who (figuratively) accompany him and his huge armies of soldiers, elephants and musicians to war; with him as emblem they can still retain hopes of success, even though their temporal experience may forever belie their expectations.

The symbol expresses the complexities of male/female relationships. In Vedantic and Tantric practice, the possibility is held out for the spiritually advanced devotee to internalize the Goddess in the here and now. The icon or dyad is utilized to initiate the encounter with the divine; then the symbol, in fact all symbols, when they are no longer of use, are dissolved. However, the votary who is unable to reach *samadhi* (merging with the Absolute) but who does not submit to the manifested Goddess entirely either, will place his bets on the buffalo demon/hero as the source of power in his struggle against the inherent gravitational female force. For the savage force, the Goddess as dragon, she who quenches her thirst with human and demon blood, this animal/human/Goddess/monster will destroy, unless she is opposed strenuously. Thus the hero will battle bravely to keep his head above water, or to be more precise, to keep his head. The son will rely on the permanent and vital role the daivasuram symbol plays in the dynamics of his efforts to separate.

Perpetual confrontation, not demise and sacrifice, will be the hoped-for emphasis. Rather than rest content with reunion in death with the conquering Goddess at whose feet he is privileged to serve, an alternative choice is available to the one who can attempt to internalize the imagery of struggle. When his male and female aspects as beloved antagonists are recognized and accepted with compassion and self-respect, freedom, with all its perils, might possibly be achieved. Thus the Mahisamardini symbol will perpetually vitalize the self.

This is the true meaning of the myth, and its proper function. The symbolism of the battle through time may be regarded as the courageous effort to rely primarily on oneself for survival and inner sustenance, as internalizing the story of the battle is the cathartic means towards comprehending reality and living in harmony with it. This can occur only after the dyad is extricated from the unconscious, then projected, observed and welcomed back into a now integrated psyche. The symbol will sublimate and absorb aggressive drives.

Even though there is no defence against nature and eventual capitulation, and in the last analysis even the horns which move mountains and the tail that shakes the universe prove to be of no avail, the boy struggling towards a certain amount of autonomy will be helped to concentrate his powers on combating the annihilating tendencies of the Mother.

Appendices
Congruent Motifs in Myth

In regard to stories of heroes in other cultures, we take note of the congruent motifs which are consistently found in all the Indian versions and in many of the foreign myths. In others, ideas are strongly emphasized, encouraging comparison. The coincident birth events provide a prelude to the later comparative material concerning the life passages, struggles and death of the hero.

Heroes of those cultures which might well have had early contact with India are chosen because they are well known, but the shared motifs may not necessarily have been transferred. The central events of Mahisa's rites of passage provide a surprising parallel to the list Raglin proposed for western heroes. There is no need to play Procrustus, as the analogies fall easily into place, as is indicated in the charts.

Appendix I Birth

Common Motifs

Mahisa	Dumuzi/Tammuz	Enkidu	Gilgamesh	Osiris
1 Mother is royal virgin with demoness/Goddess associations	Mother is either goddess Innana/Ishtar, or Sirtur, wife of god Ea or Enki	Mother is Goddess	Mother is Goddess Ninsun or Goddess Aruru; or royal princess	Mother is Nut/Hathor/Isis (Goddess)
2 Father is ṛsi, king or god	Father is God Ea or Enki	Made in the likeness of Anu, god of heaven	Father is deified ancient king, king, high priest or demon	Father is earth god Seb or Geb
3 Born of cow	Mother is either Innana/Ishtar, 'the cow of Sin', shown on seals with cow horns, or she is Sirtur, 'as good as Ishtar's mother'; Ningal, who as cow was 'mounted by a bull'		Mother is 'wild cow' who 'was as strong as a wild ox in the byre'	Mother is Nut/Hathor/Isis (cow)
4 Father has bull connections	Father is Ea or Enki, 'the restless young bull'... 'a rampant bull'	Made in likeness of Anu, the great bull god		
5 Born in unusual circumstances		Created out of clay	Born in tower	In mother's womb for only five days
6 Born after struggle		People of Erech in struggle with king	King locks daughter in tower	Born after symbolic struggle between Ra and Thoth
7 Born after immaculate conception		Born after being modelled in clay without male intervention	Born in tower without male intervention	
8 Survives death at birth		From inanimate clay, he emerges alive from the fire (kiln)	He is caught by eagle in mid-air after being thrown out of tower by guards	
9 Born anamolous or extraordinary	Described as 'young calf, 'wild bull'	Represented on seals with horns, tail and hindquarters of bull; he is covered with hair and looks wild and primitive	Aruru was told, 'thou hast created an impetuous son, like a wild bull, high is his head'	
10 Abandoned at birth (by mother)		He grows up alone in the wilderness without his 'mother'	He is raised by a gardener, having been separated from his mother	Nut entrusts the infant to nurse Pamyles
11 Has underworld connections	Descends to underworld for half the year	With Gilgamesh he enters the forest to slay Humbaba	Gilgamesh searches for eternal life in the world beneath the mountain	Osiris will be the god of death and rule the underworld

#	Mother is Isis (Goddess)	Mother is goddess Aditi	Mother is goddess Asherah	Hera, heifer-eyed Boopis is his mother; mother is goddess	Mother is mortal virgin
1	Mother is Isis (Goddess)	Mother is goddess Aditi	Mother is goddess Asherah	Hera, heifer-eyed Boopis is his mother; mother is goddess	Mother is mortal virgin
2	Father is king/god Osiris	Father is god	Father is Shor-El, (bull god)	Father is god Zeus; Mother is heifer-eyed Boopis	Father is god
3	Mother is Isis (cow)	'The heifer has brought forth the strong' (Indra); born a calf	Mother is wife of bull god; mother of Anath, sometimes analogized to cow		Born in a manger, the usual birthplace of animals
4	Father, Osiris, is 'bull of the underworld'; worshipped as Apis in the form of a bull	'...a bull begat the bull'	Father is Shor-El (bull god)	Father is Zeus who is often transformed into a bull	El Elyon was originally a bull god. Father has only vestigial connections with bull
5	Posthumous birth; his father was already dead when he was conceived	Born from his mother's side after a prolonged pregnancy		Sometimes said to be born as elemental fire	
6	Born after Set murders Osiris				Born during massacre of innocents
7	His mother conceives after she breathes into his father's corpse or flaps her wings			Hera and Zeus rarely meet; perhaps the birth is from an immaculate conception	Mary was visited by the 'ruach' (spirit) of Elohim
8	He is killed by Set in the form of a scorpion but is revived by Isis or Thoth	'Then up he sprang...' as soon as he was born his mother deserted him		Hera and/or Zeus attempt to kill him at birth; Thetis saves him	
9	Born with falcon head; with solar disc	Born as bull	Born with horns of bull; born divine; his symbol is the head of a bull	Born weak and lame	
10	Horus is hidden in bul-rushes; later he is put in a boat and floats down the Nile. Isis leaves him in the care of goddess Buto	'...deeming him a reproach his mother hid him'.		Mother throws him off cliff	The family flees to Egypt to avoid death of infant Jesus
11			Will travel to underworld as vegetation god		Born as Imanuel (God is with us)

The numbers in brackets in the foreign narratives below refer to analogous motifs listed in the tables.

SUMER, AKKAD, AND BABYLONIA

Dumuzi–Tammuz

The Goddess Innana was born of the union of Sin 'The Brilliant Young Bull' (4) 'the moon god and the moon Goddess Ningal (1) in the form of a cow'[1] (3). Innana (Babylonian Isthar) may have been the mother of Dumuzi (Babylonian Tammuz) (1).

> Only 'cow of Sin', Maid of Sin, is her name.... She rules over the plants as she waters them.... In the secret place of the herdsmen, where shepherds see not.... The restless young bull mounted the cow, taking her virginity
> When her days were ended, her months completed, The cow was in agony, she quivered in pain

> When for the third time she touched her
> The calf fell to the earth like a gazelle
> 'Amarga' she created, the name of the calf
> As the Maid of Sin gave birth happily[2]

Innana/Ishtar is often conceived as a cow (3), depicted with cow horns in seals.[3] Perhaps the actual mother of Tammuz is Sirtur,[4] 'as good as' the mother of Innana/Ishtar.[5] The hero is the son of the god Ea or Enki[6] (2); he is 'seed begotten to a king',[7] 'the divine Ushumgal of heaven'.[8] His epithets are 'wild bull' or 'young calf'[9] (4). Legend has it that he was put into a boat to die but was subsequently rescued, surviving death at birth(8).[10]

Enkidu

Burdened by the cruel taskmaster, King Gilgamesh, the people of Erech appealed to the Goddess Aruru (1) for help. Out of clay baked in the fire of the kiln (8) she created (7) a challenger in the likeness of the ruler of heaven, the great bull god Anu (2, 4).

> Aruru washed her hands, took a piece of clay and spat on it (7)
> Enkidu she created, the hero, lofty offspring
> Covered with hair was his whole body
> He wore his hair like a woman (9)[11]
> He knew not men and the Land (10)
> He was clothed like Sumugan (the god of cattle) (3, 4)
> Eating grass with the kids,
> Drinking at the watering place with the cattle (9,10)[12]

Enkidu survives death at birth out of fires (8). It would seem that the Mother Goddess Aruru had nothing more to do with him, as he survived alone in the wilderness, being cared for by animals (10). He drank the milk of the animals

and water at the trough, and ate grass, implying he had been nursed by them
(3). Represented on seals with horns and tail, covered with hair, he appears
wild and primitive, like a beast (9).

Gilgamesh

His mother is Goddess Ninsun (1), 'wild cow' (3)[13] who was 'as strong as a
wild ox in the byre';[14] or he is, like Enkidu, formed by Aruru (7).

(She) created an impetuous son, like a wild bull, high is his head[15]

Gilgamesh sometimes claims to be the deified ancient king of Erech[16] or
'Lillu', king, or a high priest or demon (2) is his father.[17] In another version, as
a result of a prophecy, because he feared a rival son would be born to his
daughter, the king locked her in a tower, but somehow she became pregnant
(7). There Gilgamesh was born (5). The king's guards threw him out of the
tower; he was rescued by an eagle in mid-air (8) and delivered to a gardener
(10) who reared him.[18]

EGYPT

Osiris

As sky, Nut was personified as cow (3), her four legs formed the pillars of the
cardinal points. She gives birth to the sun in the morning (3), protects him in
the day and each evening he dies in the embrace of the cow. The sun is the
'bull of his mother' (9).[19] Even though names change in various periods, the
Goddesses are related to each other in their aspects. As Nut, and later as
Hathor, Isis, often depicted with horns in icons, as cow gives birth to Osiris,
'the bull of this mother' (3). As late as Herodotus, Isis was represented as cow
who was taken out in procession once a year at the commemoration of the
death and resurrection of her brother/husband/son Osiris:

> The female [cow] they [Egyptians] are not allowed to sacrifice, since
> they are sacred to Isis. The statue of this goddess has the form of a
> woman but with horns like a cow, resembling thus the Greek represen-
> tations of Io; and the Egyptians, one and all, venerate cows much more
> highly than any other animal.[20]

The cow Goddess unites with the earth god Seb or Geb, but only after Thoth
nullifies the curse of Ra: Nut should not give birth on any day in the year.
Thoth won five extra days, and Osiris remained in the womb only for this time
(5). After his birth, Nut entrusts the care of the baby to the nurse Pamyles
(10). The bull Apis becomes Osiris only after his own death, but it is
interesting to note that the bull is born from a cow who has been struck by fire
which comes from heaven (8). The lightning/rain/bull god is thus evoked.[21]

Horus

After Set murdered his brother Osiris, he set him afloat in a box on the river

Nile. Isis, his mother/sister/wife searched for and found him; she breathed into the mouth of the corpse and later gave birth to Horus in an immaculate conception (5). Or she beat her wings and then conceived (5); or Thoth gave her power and she conceived (5). Horus is born with a sun disc ('the bull of his mother the cow/Goddess'), as falcon (9). She transforms Horus into a bull.[22] Horus is hidden in the bulrushes or hidden in a boat and sent down the Nile (10),[23] but he is rescued by his mother. In the form of a scorpion, Set enters the house where Horus is concealed; he kills Horus but Isis or Thoth bring him back to life (8). Isis leaves Horus in the care of the Goddess Buton (10).

INDIA

Indra

> A bull gave birth to a bull for battle. Indeed, that very one, a woman, brought him forth as a man (in human form) (9).[24]
>
> Let me not go from this way—the passage is hard; therefore I will go from the side (5). v. 2.
>
> What contrary [forbidden] act did he do that his mother carried (him in the womb) for a thousand months and many autumns? (5). v. 4.
>
> The mother, considering him as it were like something unspeakable, made him be placed in a cave [womb] (10) on account of valor (*virya*)... He became erect, becoming lustrous; being born, he pervaded heaven and earth. v. 5.
>
> The heifer chose to produce Indra, a sturdy child (3) made for wandering [the earth], according to his will (10). That Indra, whose strength was equal to a full grown man's, who was unconquerable, a veritable bull (Vrsaba: who has testicles, capable of fertilization)...(9) Still a calf, a child, he wanders himself, desiring his own body [independence from mother]. (10) v. 10.[25]

The motifs sung in the Vedas include Indra's birth from a Goddess, Aditi with cow associations (3), and from the god with bull associations (4). Indra is born in unusual circumstances (his mother's long pregnancy; birth from her side) (5). He survives death at birth as the infant calf was allowed to wander (8, 10). He is abandoned by his mother.

CANAAN: PHOENICIA

Baal/Hadad

Baal/Hadad the Canaanite and Phoenician god was born as the son of Shor El (bull god) (2), (4), and Asherah his Goddess wife. He was born with horns and is depicted in the statues with horns (9).

CRETE AND GREECE

Hephaestos

The heifer-eyed Boopis-Hera (3), wife of Zeus (1), shares bovine characteristics with her Mesopotamian, Egyptian, and Indo-European forerunners. 'Hera wrangled with her husband and because of anger, untouched by him (7), she bore glorious Hephaestos.'[26] The son Hephaestos was born weak and lame (9) not too long for this world, and consequently, in some versions Hera, and in others Zeus, attempted to rid themselves of the newborn (10), but he survived death at birth (8) and lived to become the great god Fire:

> (Thetis), the very one who saved me from anguish that time I had fallen so far on account of my bitch-hearted mother, who wished to get rid of me because of my lameness. Then I would surely have suffered much more than I did, if Thetis had not been so kind...[27]

Zeus / Dionysos

Every time Rhea gave birth, out of jealousy the god Kronos 'gulped down his own children, to Rhea's endless grief', but when Zeus was born she tricked her husband by wrapping a stone in the infant's swaddling clothes.

> He took it in his hands and stuffed it into his belly—the great fool! It never crossed his mind that the stone was given in place of his son thus saved.[28]

Zeus (2), (4) made love to a lovely maid, Io, when Hera came upon the scene; then the god, ever the dissembler, turned Io into a cow (4), doomed to wander the earth.[29] She was the ancestress of Dionysos (3). In a variant from Thebes, Zeus in bull form married Io in the form of a cow. From their line, many heroes were born, including Dionysos.[30]

In yet another love affair, in a subsequent Theban epiphany, Zeus came to Semele, the daughter of king Cadmus. This mortal woman insisted on beholding the god face to face, but the effulgence struck her with great force (6). She perished in the divine fire, like Syama, but the unborn Dionysos was snatched from within her burning womb by Zeus, who sewed the embryo into his thigh, later giving birth to the boy himself (5), (8). The bull ancestry reappears in Dionysos (4), the Bougenes, 'cow's son (3) and worthy bull', who was expected to come to the Dionysian maenads 'with riotous bull's foot'.[31] He is the horned infant (9)[32]. Other variants of the birth of Dionysos from Brasiai in Laconia tell how Cadmus had his daughter Semele thrown into the sea with Dionysos (10). They were subsequently washed ashore in a chest (8)[33]. Or Zeus visited Persephone and she bore him Zagreus (Dionysos).

> It is precisely the wild and raging bull whose image the devout have before their eyes when they summon Dionysos. The women of Elis cry for 'Lord Dionysos', 'Noble Bull', 'raging with the bull's hoof' to come (9).[34]

Asclepios / Aesculapius

The god Apollo loved a mortal woman Coronis (formerly the Great Goddess), but she was unfaithful, as she loved a mortal. In his wrath and jealousy, he cursed her to be burned on a pyre, but as the mother died in flames, Apollo saved the infant (8), who was sent away to be reared in the cave of Mt Pelion by the kindly Centaurs.[35]

The Epidaurians say that Coronis came there with her father when she was pregnant by Apollo, but when Asclepios was born, the mother exposed him on Mt Titthion (10). A bitch suckled him (8), and a goatherd hailed him as the newborn king. Apollo protected him and taught him the healing arts.[36]

CHRISTIAN
Jesus

The Virgin Mary conceived after the Semitic god (2), in the form of the holy ghost, 'came upon' her (7). Elohim/Adonai retains vestigial remnants of the fertilizing consort/bull (4). Rejected at the inn, the family moved to Bethlehem where the birth of Jesus took place in a manger (5). But the massacre of innocents was being carried out, and to avoid the wrath of Herod, Joseph and Mary fled to Egypt (8). Jesus is born as an extraordinary infant: his name is Imanuel (god is with us) (9). We hear nothing of his childhood.

Appendix II   Sacred Marriage

Dumuzi/Tammuz, Enkidu/Gilgamesh, Osiris/Horus, and Zeus/Dionysos are the outstanding examples of the bull/king/god, descendant of primeval bull/Goddess associations, preserved into historic times. Other heroes who have similar origins and parallel life events with Mahisa marry the Goddess only by implication or not at all.

Common Motifs

Mahisa	Longs to marry the Goddess; Siva as buffalo/cow unites with Rambha, father of Mahisa. Siva mates with the Goddess as Parvati at a festival.
Dumuzi/Tammuz	Is royally received into the quarters of the Queen of heaven and earth; at a great festival, a woman mates with the god (Marduk?) in the Ziggurat.
Gilgamesh/Enkidu	Innana/Ishtar invites her brother Gilgamesh to be her consort. Enkidu throws the bull's thigh at Ishtar in symbolic copulation after he kills her heavenly bull.
Osiris/Horus; others	Once a year a special cow is brought to the bull god Hap/Apis; divine lightning strikes the cow which produces a divine calf; in ritual, women are admitted to see the bull god.
	At the Heliopolis, the sun god, incarnated in the king, mates with the wife of the Pharoah as Horus.
	At the festival of Min, at Koptos, the king and queen mate in front of the bull.
	At Alexandria, Adonis mates with Aphrodite.
Indra	Marries Indrani.
Baal	Shor-El, in bull form, mates with Asherah, mother of the gods; their son Baal mates with Anath.
	At the great festival, unmarried women offer themselves to the god; kings impersonate the lover of the Goddess Anath/Astarte, either as image or represented by priestesses.

Dionysos/Zeus	Amorphous divine male spirit mates with female, both in serpent form (undifferentiated Zagreus, Zeus, Dionysos).
	Pasiphae as cow mates with bull.
	King Minos in bull-skin mates with queen in annual spring ritual.
	Dionysos marries Ariadne on Naxos/Dia island.
	In Anthesteria festival, the Basilinna mates with the god Dionysos in secret rites.
Hephaestos	His wife is 'divine Charis'; 'the lame smith of wide renown, took as his buxom bride Alaia, the youngest of the Graces'; or his wife is Aphrodite.
Asclepios / Aesculapius	Branches of the willow tree with which he is associated were taken to bed by the ladies of Athens in the Thesmophoria fertility festival.
Holy Spirit of god	The holy spirit, father of Jesus, 'came upon Mary'.

SUMER, AKKAD, AND BABYLONIA

Dumuzi / Tammuz

In Sumer, Akkad and Babylonia, Dumuzi-Tammuz, probably the ruler of Erech,[37] one of the many lovers of Innana-Ishtar, dies in autumn, is periodically lost in the underworld, but returns in the spring. Like the verbal sparrings of Mahisa and his ministers with Durga, prior to their marriage rites, Innana and Dumuzi argue:[38] 'From the starting of the quarrel, came the lover's desire.'[39] But unlike Mahisa, on the eve of the New Year, Dumuzi is gladly and royally received into the quarters of the Queen of Heaven and Earth, the 'Awesome Lady... crowned with great horns'.[40] The entire history of the relationship of bull and Goddess is summed up in the beautiful verses describing first their love and then the betrayal of her lover by the Goddess:

> The people will set up my fruitful bed
> They will cover it with plants...
> I will bring there the man of my heart.[41]

During the protracted lovemaking, Dumuzi calls Innana 'sister'; she names him the 'wild bull'[42] and reminds him that 'In battle I am your leader'.[43] The following day, there is a great feast, dancing, music and sacrifices at the great festival.[44] But there is lamenting too because the Goddess betrays, bartering her lover's life for her own.

Innana fastened on Dumuzi the eye of death
She spoke against him the word of wrath
She uttered against him the cry of guilt;
Take him! Take Dumuzi away![45]

Durga's repeated remonstrances, shouting at Mahisa to return to Patala, echo those of ancient Mesopotamia. Innana hands Dumuzi over to the spirits of the underworld, and the hero is thereafter doomed to stay beneath the ground for six months annually. But at his spring festival, to awaken the forces of nature, he is resurrected[46] and remains on earth for the second half of the year. More than fifteen hundred years after these verses were recorded, Herodotus heard about rites during which the king and queen or a hierodule representing the Goddess mated in the sanctified and elaborate bedchamber situated at the height of the sacred monument, the ziggurat:

In the last tower, there is a great temple, and in the temple there stands a great bed, well covered, and by it is set a golden table. But there is no image whatever in the temple, neither does any human being spend the night there, save one woman only, of the natives of the place, whom the god has chosen out of all, as declare the Chaldaean priests of this god.
These same Chaldaeans say—though I myself do not believe their story—that the god is wont to come to this temple and rest on this couch.[47]

Here, the position is reversed; the god-bull Marduk mates with a human female. Until recently in India, the *devadasi* or adolescent girl dedicated to a god's service in the Hindu temple, was married to the god there in a ceremony, and for her entire life, she remained within the temple precincts, performing certain limited ritual functions centering around dancing and singing.[48]

Gilgamesh / Enkidu

Having conquered the dreaded demon Humbaba in the great cedar forest, Gilgamesh cleaned his body and put on royal robes, just as Mahisa did before his meeting with the Goddess. Like Durga, Ishtar plays the role of seducer:

Come to me Gilgamesh, and be my bridegroom; grant me seed of your body, let me be your bride. And you shall be my husband.[49]

But the wise Gilgamesh refuses, anticipating the destructive intentions of this ravishing female, for her marital history is well known:

You have loved the stallion, magnificent in battle, and for him you decreed whip and spur and a thong, to gallop seven leagues by force and to muddy the water before he drinks; and for his mother Silili lamentations.[50]

Durga's invitations to Mahisa may very well echo Ishtar's to Gilgamesh and her many other lovers who were fated to die. Rage at and annihilation of the erstwhile desirable lover are the common reactions of Innana/Ishtar and

Durga, linking them as the symbols invented by ambivalent males. Their
seductive murmurings turned to war cries are sounds heard down the ages.

EGYPT

Imagery expressing the magnetism pulling the bull (as seeder of earth, as
power and beauty, as the sun) toward the cow Goddess, persisted as a
perennial feature in Egyptian religion during historic times. Profuse liturgical
and other textual as well as lithic remains are concerned with the divine,
incarnate in cow and bull, Pharoah and sun.

Osiris/Horus

The cow/sky/Goddess Nut gives birth in the east every morning to the calf
sun. He transverses the day sky and arrives in the west in the evening,
returning to his origins at the end of his life. As her husband, he re-enters the
womb of his mother and is reborn the following morning. Thus he is 'Bull of
his Mother'. The Goddess receives the bull in embrace, but she encourages
him to separate as well.

To the sun in the Old Kingdom:

> Thou art fair, O Re, every day thy mother Nut embraceth thee.[51]

And on to the New Kingdom, to the sun still:

> Adoration of Amunre, Bull of Heliopolis, chief of all the gods, Bull of
> his Mother.... godly bull of the Nine Gods.[52]

Identical words are used to celebrate King Rameses II:

> God, king.... similitude of the Bull of Heliopolis born of Isis, Horus,
> strong bull... bull of rulers.[53]

In these wonderful amalgamations, the bulls all either marry the cow Goddess
or are her sons. King Unas of the fifth dynasty is 'bull of Heaven'. Osiris is
'bull of the underworld'; Amen Ra is 'bull of offering'.[54]

With their centre at Memphis, all the temples of Ptah housed Hap, the
sacred bull whom the Greeks called Apis. He resided in splendid chambers
surrounded by large courts. People brought offerings and made sacrifices and
abided by his auguries. His own group of priests attended to his daily needs,
which included being

> anointed with precious unguents and perfumed with the sweet odours;
> rich beds were also provided for them to lie upon.[55]

Hap/Apis was not alone in the bed, as cows were kept for him, and once a
year a special mate was brought to him,[56] although she died the very day of
their meeting, leaving the bull's mother to share his fine apartments.[57] But

when the bull was old, he was either put to death or he died naturally. Mummification, an ornate funeral with the elaborate mourning ceremonials due to a deity and burial in a permanent stone structure were customary, while the bull's soul went to heaven, where it joined with Osiris.

Today, tourists who walk through the Serapium at Saqqara on the outskirts of Cairo, viewing huge stone coffins in twenty-six separate rooms, if transported in imagination to ancient times will call to mind that from the eighteenth to the Ptolemaic dynasties, these burial centres, surrounded by chapels and shrines, attracted crowds of pilgrims, the sick and the maimed, traders, clerics, and those who came to consult the oracles.[58]

A new calf is born from a mother who is incapable thereafter of bearing offspring and whose insemination is immaculate. It is the result of a great fire which comes down from heaven.

> The Egyptians say that a lightning bolt from heaven has struck the cow, so from it the calf-Apis is born. The calf called Apis has the following marks; he is all black, but has a white triangle on his forehead, and, on his back, the likeness of an eagle. . . .[59]

The calf, born like Mahisa out of the fire, is led by the priests, who

> lead the young ox through the city of Nile and feed him forty days. Then they put him into a barge, wherein is a golden cabin and so transport him as a god to Memphis. During the forty days before mentioned, none but women are admitted to see him, who, being placed in his view, pluck up their coats and expose their persons. Afterwards they are forbidden to come into the sight of this new god.[60]

Diodorus may have added that the women were sacred prostitutes involved in symbolic marriage with the new bull god. At Heliopolis, Mnevis, as incarnation of Ra, and at Hermonthis, Buchis, as incarnation of Ra and Osiris, were the sacred bulls also worshipped as gods.[61]

At the autumn festival of Osiris, the dying season was lamented. The god was carried about and exhibited in the form of a golden ox wearing a coat of black linen. The planting of new seeds occurred during this festival.[62] At Heliopolis, the sun god was incarnated in the king and mated with the wife of the Pharoah as Hathor, who was responsible for human fertility.[63]

The festival calendar of Erdu included thirteen days during which the conquest of Set by Horus was celebrated.[64] Then the Goddess Hathor was transported in a barge from her sanctuary in Denderah to meet Horus. Inscriptions tell that this visit was conducted in order 'to consummate the beauteous embrace with her Horus',[65] indicating a ritual divine marriage. A procession of the divine white bull accompanied by magic rites and chanting was part of the harvest festival of Min, god of reproduction, at Koptos. The king and queen mated in public in front of the bull annually.[66] And Frazer says that according to the Egyptians, 'the monarchs were actually begotten by the god Ammon, who assumed for the time being the form of the reigning king, and in that disguise had intercourse with the queen.'[67]

Whether the god is incarnated in the king, or the king is impersonating the god in the bedchamber with his mortal wife; or when priestesses are consecrated to the bull god in the temple, or during festivals and during visits, when god meets Goddess, the memory of these ancient symbols of mother, cow, son/calf, king and sun god are retained; they are the archetypal references which energize and instil life into a static society.

CANAAN; PHOENICIA; HEBREWS; CHRISTIANS

Baal/Hadad

In Canaan and the Phoenician coastal strip, a prototypal monotheism perceived Shor-El (bull god) as the kindly, great, superior, elder god of rain. In the form of a mighty bull, he united with Asherah-of-the-sea, mother of the gods.[68] But by the second half of the second millennium, as the Jews were returning from Egypt, Shor-El's son/grandson Baal/Hadad/Aliyan, god of lightning, storm, rain and procreation had gained priority of position. He battled with his brother Yam-Nahar, god of waters, and with Mot, god of drought and death. The Goddess Anath, sister/lover of Baal/Hadad and subsequently mother of Aliyan, is warrior, virgin, lady of the skies, fruitful. Her name means womb.[69] While Baal/Hadad and Anath loved one another, and he always put aside other women in her honour,[70] since he loved peace and she loved blood,[71] Anath played the surrogate's role, fighting his battles and providing him with renewed energy when he required it.

In their respective terrific forms, Durga and Anath are twins-in-horror, and their warrior forms can thus be analogized. Both become inebriated with blood and erupt into a violence that knows no restraints, but they are also the Goddesses of love and fertility. Anath is usually depicted nude in the icons and sometimes horned. (In the Bible, she is called 'Ashtoreth of the horns' (Astoreth Karnaim). She even turned into a heifer, just before Baal/Hadad made his journey to Mt Saphon, taking his fertilizing 'wind and cloud and rain with his bucket'.[72] Like the love of her symbolic sister, the Goddess Innana/Ishtar for Dumuzi, and like Durga's intimated affair with Mahisa, the relationship between Anath and Baal/Hadad in bull form, as young and beautiful rain provider, was an exquisite and prolonged romance, sensually described in the texts:

> Aliyan-Baal obeys his father; he loves the heifer in the pasture, the cow in the field; he makes love seventy-seven times, he makes love eighty-eight times.[73]

(Unfortunately for Mahisa and Durga these were merely imaginary pleasures.) The vigorous lovemaking of Anath as cow revived and invigorated the bull god, and she bore a wild steer son (shades of Rambha and Syama), to ensure fertility in future times, in the event that Baal/Hadad did not return from the underworld to which he descends every summer.

If indeed the Ugaritic texts were recited during the New Year rites as many scholars believe, another hierogamy is indicated. Festivals commemorated this: during the vernal festival, in a great temple to Astarte (Anath), on a cliff above the source of the river Adonis near Byblos, Baal (Adonis) was united in sacred marriage to the Goddess. A sacred temple prostitute was brought to a substitute-king, who was then wounded and killed.[74]

The god of Israel of the time of Jesus can be traced directly back to the divine force which appeared to the Hebrews in the desert as thunder and lightning (fire), 'god in the voice of the horn' (Adonai b'kol shofar).[75] In their anxiety, reverting to their only recently abandoned Egyptian bull god, the Israelites, in Egypt bricklayers and construction workers who created a golden calf, were not yet ready to comprehend that deification of the force, vitality, sacred nature and the magic fertility qualities of the bull was in the process of being conjoined to an ethical code embodied in the received commandments. One thousand years later, the monotheistic teachings of the prophets had finally been fixed into a new religious spirit. This construct elevated God on high (El Elyon), who is entirely separated from the temporal world even while he works his ways in history. It had ostensibly eliminated pagan worship, but in fact, Hap, the golden calf, Shor-El and Baal/Hadad/Aliyan were merely submerged. It was this amalgamated deity who 'came upon Mary' as the holy spirit (ruach), preserving the archaic sacred marriage rites of god to a mortal woman, now recreated with an entirely new symbolic interpretation.

CRETE AND GREECE

Zeus/Dionysos

Coeval with the high palace culture in Crete, priests of the primitive hunting society donned the skins of animals in cult ceremonials. They identified with and worshipped a 'lord of wild beasts', a divine male being associated also with plants, wine, the snake and the bull. The Greek god Dionysos, who in the form of a bull was torn to pieces by ecstatic female devotees, is a throwback to the as yet undifferentiated Zeus, Zagreus and Dionysos of Crete.

Ariadne, the Great Goddess who occupied a dominant position in the Cretan pantheon, the mistress of the labyrinth, Goddess of the underworld, but also Goddess of light, was not distinguishable from Rhea and Persephone. In fact, male and female divine spirits were conceived as being of a single primeval animal family. Thus, the conglomerate male spirit visited his mother or daughter in a cave in the form of a snake. This archetypal marriage produced an offspring in the form of a bull, thus incorporating the superior characteristics of both.[76] Like the later Mahisa/Siva infant, born from Siva as buffalo cow, the Cretan issue was simultaneously his own parent and his own child. Later, the snake marriage was abandoned, and the groom, in the form of a bull, came to the bride in the form of a cow. In the myth of Zeus as the white bull who carried off Europa, the daughter of the king of Sidon, a tendency to anthropomorphize can be detected, but the Cretan obsession with the *zoe* (life force) of the bull relentlessly persists.

Their son King Minos married Pasiphae, but her love was offered to the beautiful white bull who arose from the sea. From this union, the Minotaur, half bull, half man, was conceived. Although hidden in the labyrinth, he was greatly feared, so much so that his cannibalistic tendencies had to be appeased with the flesh and blood of Athenian youth. The entire Cretan society was permeated with the life force of the bull, still very much a feared divine symbol. During the spring festival Minos the king, dressed in the skin of a bull, with horns or masks, performed a sacred dance, followed by ritual intercourse under an oak tree with the queen Pasiphae who was dressed as a cow.[77]

While bull symbolism lived on in the imagery of Dionysos, in Greece it was merged with a now concretized mortal figure. Ariadne took shape as the human daughter of King Minos who, with her half brother, the Minotaur, ruled the labyrinthian depths. When the Athenian hero Theseus came to rescue his countrymen, Ariadne fell in love with him, and, for a short while only, she escaped the Dionysian sphere by accompanying her lover to the island of Dia. But there she was abandoned by Theseus and slain by the jealous Goddess Artemis. Dionysos brought Ariadne back to life and took her as wife. On Naxos, a marble gate constructed in the sixth century BC on the site of the marriage of Dionysos to Ariadne still stands. There, as in Crete, the marriage was celebrated in a joyous festival.[78] Tauropolus, the bull, one of their children,[79] is linked with Mahisa, the buffalo.

The sacred marriage rites continued in Greece. During the Anthesteria festival in Attica, the doors of the temple of Dionysos were opened to the public only on the day of the wine pitcher (*choes*). Now, in a mimetic ritual, Ariadne the mortal/goddess was represented by the queen, the Basilinna, who was given in marriage to the god. In an introductory ritual, the statue of (or perhaps a man impersonating the god) was joined in procession by the wife of the archon, or king. Either seated on thrones or on a ship on wheels, together they were carried through the streets, followed by groups of frenzied or excited women and children led by priestesses and musicians playing flutes and trumpets.

Of high station, the Basilinna was required to have been virgin before her temporal marriage to the ruler. She wore rich and costly garments, and on the holy night, she stepped over the threshold of the far apartment in the Boukoleon (the bull's shed). There in divine nuptials, she was wedded to the god in bull's form, in the former old residence of the king, originally the home of the divine bull. The marriage was an ancient religious rite, steeped in the archaic snake and animal unions, a mimetic ritual analogous to the countless prehistoric sacred marriages, designed to arouse the god out of his winter torpor and also to invest devotees with the zoe, the life force immanent in the god, even in his periods of death after dismemberment. His awakening by the queen is a concept not very far removed from the Indian idea that male energy is revived by the female sakti. The union assured the growth of animal and plant life and general prosperity in the coming year. It assumed sacred implications as 'ineffable sacred ceremonies'.[80]

Although it is not known what actually occurred within this temporary sanctuary, the archon's wife may have either been physically mated with a stand-in for the god or with a phallus, as residual archaic symbol, or she entered it alone and proceeded to have mystical conversation with the spirit of god. Outside, the women waited in their homes for the god to appear to each; orgiastic rites accompanied the marriage.

Hephaestos

Hephaestos, the heavenly smith, crafted for himself a magnificent home. He lived there together with his 'divine wife Charis'.[81] He has been paired in marriage also with Alaria, the youngest of the Graces,[82] and with Aphrodite.[83] He even once tried to rape his sister Athene: his seed dropped as he chased her, and from it Ericthonius the snake was born.[84] Mahisa also was born from the dropped semen of a rsi, thinking of his paramour Vetravati.

Asclepios / Aesculapius

As a fertility rite during the orgiastic Athenian Thesmophoria festival, branches of the willow tree, with which the Spartan Asclepios was associated, were taken to bed by the ladies of the city.[85]

CHRISTIAN

Jesus

Holy spirit of god/Mary: the holy spirit, Father of Jesus, 'came upon Mary'[86]

Appendix III Struggle with the Mother

Mahisa is a late version of the ambivalent hero who adores the Goddess but becomes involved in a struggle with her. Of our heroes, only Asclepios seems to have avoided a bitter confrontation with the mother, although his father Apollo before him set his own consort, Coronis, on fire, which may have been good enough reason for Asclepios to avoid such horrid confrontations. As tender healer, his energies were directed elsewhere. But the other heroes had a great deal to contend with, as the mother often erupted into a wild and frightful violence. Anat, Agave and Princess Salome (New Testament) wreaked vengeance, not directly on the hero, but on an *alter ego*.

Common Motifs

Mahisa/Durga	Battles with the Mother Goddess, and she slays him by cutting off his head.
Tiamat–Ummu–Hubur/ Marduk	Because her sons, the gods, betrayed her, Tiamat waged war on them; Marduk conquered her and split open her skull.
Dumuzi–Tammuz/ Innana–Ishtar	When the demons of the underworld refuse to let her ascend, Innana betrays her husband Gilgamesh in exchange for her own life. When Gilgamesh rejects her advances, she persuades her father Anu to create a heavenly bull to kill Gilgamesh, but the bull is defeated.
Osiris–Horus/Isis	During his war with Set, Horus cuts off his mother's head when she sides with his enemy; her head is restored as a cow's head.
Indra/Diti	Enters his mother's womb and cuts her developing embryo into forty-nine pieces.
Baal/Anath	Destroys Baal's enemy brothers. At her festival, the priests emasculate themselves and throw the phallus at the Goddess, reversing the role of the Goddess who decapitates Mahisa.
Dionysos/Semele/ Maenads Pentheus/Agave	According to the will of fate, Zeus (Dionysos) slays Semele with his thunderbolt; the maenads slay the god in the form of a bull; Pentheus, *alter ego* of Dionysos, is decapitated by Agave, his own mother.
Hephaestos/Hera	Takes revenge on his mother, the Goddess Hera, for throwing him off a cliff at infancy; he constructs a special throne to which Hera

	becomes attached, and only Dionysos is able to bring him back, inebriated, to release her.
Asclepios / Coronis	As she has been unfaithful, Apollo, father god to the hero, kills the hero's mother Coronis.
Jesus / Mary John the Baptist / Salome	Princess Salome has John the Baptist, cousin and *alter ego* of the hero, decapitated and his head brought to her on a platter; Jesus turns his back on his mother in favour of the multitude.

SUMER / AKKAD / BABYLONIA

Tiamat versus Marduk

The DM text, which records the struggle of Mahisa with the divine Mother, is a very late version of the paradigmatic legend first recorded in the Babylonian Enuma Elish epic of creation dating to the second half of the second millenium BC. The original primeval mother, whose name was Tiamat,[87] who, like Durga, roared in the beginning, representing the chaos of primeval waters, wages fierce battles against her sons to avenge the murder of the first father Apsu. With the help of her commander-in-chief and recent spouse Kingu, Tiamat created all manner of evil creatures, 'fierce monster-vipers she clothed with terror',[88] mighty tempests and all sorts of weapons. At first her sons believed that through diplomacy they would avoid her attacks, but they soon learned that 'Tiamat our mother has conceived a hatred for us, with all her force she rages full of wrath',[89] so in fear they vowed to trample the neck of their mother underfoot.

At a banquet, the God Marduk is anointed king and charged thus: 'O, Marduk, you are our avenger',[90] 'Go and cut off the life of Tiamat.'[91] Great preparations are made for battle and finally Marduk, who is actually the grandson of Tiamat, faces her on the battlefield:

> Stand! I and you, let us join battle! When Tiamat heard these words, she was like one possessed, she lost her reason. Tiamat uttered wild, piercing cries, she trembled and shook to her very foundations... Then advanced Tiamat and Marduk, the counsellor of the gods.[92]

In this battle, the devouring mother was overcome: 'with his merciless club he smashed her skull,[93] and her warriors he tramples under his feet.'[94]

In ancient Mesopotamia, the god conquers the Goddess, splits open her skull and tramples her warriors underfoot. In India, the Goddess cuts off the head of the demon / god and tramples *him* underfoot.

Innana / Ishtar versus Gilgamesh / Enkidu and Dumuzi / Tammuz

Gilgamesh, king of Uruk, was wise enough to protect himself from the overt seductions of Innana/Ishtar, as her duplicities were well known and legion. The Goddess takes lovers and enjoys them and then either discards them summarily or, still worse, she destroys them. The king recalls:

> You caused your youthful husband Tammuz to weep every year; You made love to the young shepherd, but you beat him and broke his wings. You loved a lion; he was of wondrous strength, but you dug traps for him, seven times and again seven times. For the horse that you loved, you decreed whip, spur and thong... and caused his mother Silili to weep. You beat the shepherd you loved and changed him into a wolf, so that his own shepherd boys drove him off and his dogs bit his skin.[95]

The taunts of the king sent Innana/Ishtar into such a rage that she persuaded her father Anu to create a heavenly bull for the purpose of killing Gilgamesh. Not for naught is the Goddess called 'Lady of Battle'.[96] A great battle ensued between the bull of heaven and Gilgamesh/Enkidu. When the bull was defeated, Innana/Ishtar lamented and violently cursed her foes, which prompted Enkidu to tear off the right thigh from the dead bull and throw it into the face of the Goddess crying: 'As I have done to him I would do the same to you; I would tie his entrails to your side.'[97] For this implied sexual assault, Enkidu suffered the fate of Mahisa; both bull heroes died soon after battle.

Gilgamesh's reference to the betrayal of Dumuzi/Tammuz is about Isis' sojourn in the underworld; there the spirits followed her and demanded that she return forever. She made a contract with them, offering her erstwhile lover, Dumuzi/Tammuz, who would spend as substitute for herself half a year in the underworld.[98] As she was the descendant of Tiamat/Umma-Hubur who had been conquered by Marduk, himself the ancestor of Dumuzi/Tammuz, was there method in her madness?

EGYPT

Isis versus Horus

The Goddess Isis lovingly protected and nourished her infant son Horus; she even brought him back to life, transferring her divine breath into his mouth when he was killed by his uncle Set in the form of a scorpion. Horus grew to manhood, and, to avenge his father's death, entered into a protracted battle; most of the time his mother supported his tremendous efforts. Once, however, when the two contenders, Set and Horus, were in the form of great hippopotami, Isis switched loyalties. It was then that, in a great rage, Horus, without a by-your-leave, cut off his mother's head.[99] In another less sanguinary version, Horus merely tears the royal diadem from the head of Isis.[100] She was brought back to life by Thoth, who furnished her with a bovine head.

An interesting ritual recapitulates the myth at Busiris; a gilded wooden cow which held the image of the beheaded Isis within its inner cavity was presented to the flower pots, the risen god in plant form.[101]

In Egypt, Horus beheads the Mother Goddess who then regains life bearing the head of a cow, while in India, the Goddess, sometimes cow-like, beheads Mahisa who regains life as a god.

CANAAN; PHOENICIA

Anath/Ashtoret versus the brothers of Baal/Hadad/Alyan

Of all these horrific Goddesses, Anath in fact may not have been the worst, but the poets of the Ugaritic texts seemed to enjoy reciting her abominations and depravities, even though the culprit was able to distinguish her enemies from her beloved. She slays Mot, god of the underworld and death:

> Anath seized Mot, the divine son; she cuts him with a sickle, she winnows him with a winnower and scorches him with fire. With a mill, she crushes him and scatters his flesh in the field to be eaten by birds.[102]

The murderous act is a metaphor for dismemberment of the crops at harvest.

After the victory of Yam, the god of waters, Anath gave a great feast for Baal/Hadad and for their enemy brother and his supporters:

> Anath, adorned with henna and rouge and scented, closes the doors of the palace and falls on all who remain of Baal's enemies. She slays guards and warriors alike and girds herself with the heads and hands of the slain; then, wading through blood up to her knees, she drives away also even tottering old men. Proceeding thence to the palace, she joyfully lays about her right and left, smashing the furniture on the heads of her adversaries and slaying guards and warriors until the palace is swimming in blood. She then revives herself by washing in the blood of her victims, distributes their flesh as portions and washes herself clean with the dew.[103]

While Anath does protect her brother/lover loyally, she is even ready to destroy her own father, all for the sake of having a palace built for Baal:

> Anath announces that she intends to go and bid El attend her and to tell him that she will trample him to the ground and make his grey hair run with blood if he does not allow Baal to have a palace and a court.[104]

Finally, in reversal of the theme of Mahisa's decapitation, at her festival priests emasculate themselves and throw the phallus at the Goddess; as we have seen, these were also the sacrifices worshippers offered to Durga. The Ugaritic texts are separated from Indian texts by two millennia and a great distance, but the similarity in the imagery of females battling with a bull is nothing less than startling.

CRETE AND GREECE

Hera/Agave versus Dionysos/Pentheus

The rage of Dionysos stems originally from Hera's malevolence, but in fact all of Thebes suffered from his reprisals. According to Euripides, incarnated as a beautiful youth, Dionysos has arrived in Thebes in order to avenge his mother's death in the lightning fire of Zeus. His methods are as cruel as Hera's, and the punishment is as horrid as the crime. In a subtle play of interlocking innuendos, Dionysos and the king of Thebes, Pentheus, are juxtaposed as opposites, but it soon becomes evident that in regard to family links, role transformations and their similar natures and disposition, they are not entirely differentiated.[105] They are each both persecutor and victim. To which of the two does the Bacchanal refer when she laments: 'Yea, the wild ivy lapt him, and the doomed Wild Bull of Sacrifice before him loomed'?[106]

Speaking of the Bacchic revellers, Pentheus declares: 'It bursts hard on us, like a smothered fire, this frenzy of Bacchic women.'[107] He is as astonished as Mahisa's ministers are when they behold the Indian Goddess; like them, he thinks about waging war and is not entirely innocent of unconscious matricidal motives, for when Dionysos urges him to sacrifice, he sarcastically replies: 'That will I: Yea, sacrifice of women's blood to cry His [Dionysos'] name through all Cithaeron.'[108] It was on this hill that his own mother, at this very moment, was indulging in Dionysian revelries.

When Agave, in her madness, 'set hard against his side her foot',[109] slaying her son and tearing him limb from limb and then holding his head as trophy for all to admire, it is a Dionysian triumph but a tragedy as well, as both the king and the god are victims of the mother's excesses.

When the maenads drink draughts of wine, they become wild and behave with the same irrationalities as Tiamat, Innana/Ishtar, Anath, and like Durga herself.

Aphrodite, Hera versus Hephaestos

The creative forger, the smith god, Hephaestos, also had his struggles with Goddesses. When he was cuckolded by Ares, he hammered out a gossamer net of fine metal which he attached to the marital bed in order to entangle his wife Aphrodite and her lover.[110]

At another time he became furious, remembering that his mother had dropped him when he was an infant child into the ocean, in an attempt to murder him as he had been born lame.[111] Hephaestos forged a mechanical chair; its arms enfolded Hera and imprisoned her there. Only Dionysos was able to free her.[112]

CHRISTIAN

Jesus

Remembering the decapitation of his cousin John by princess Salome, fear of the anger of such a female may have been one reason why Jesus turned his back on his own mother: 'Who is my mother?'[113] he asked, as he spoke to the multitude. Like Siva who is born as Mahisa in the *Kalika Purana*, the Hebrew father god is born as his own son, but since this involves Jesus in a dangerously incestuous situation, his insistence that he is spirit, not flesh, proves to be a convenient defence. The denial of a physical bond with the mother is an attempt to sidestep the crucial source of tension.

what is born of the flesh is flesh
what is born of the spirit is spirit[114]

If he is god, he is not born of mortal woman; or is he?

Appendix IV Death and Resurrection

Common Motifs

Mahisa	Dumuzi–Tammuz	Gilgamesh–Enkidu	Osiris–Horus
1 Is killed at a festival (Navratri) after a probable sacred marriage	Dies after sacred marriage at the festival of the New Year in the month of Tammuz	Because Enkidu rejected the Goddess' advances, she makes him sick, and after twelve days, he dies	He is killed at a banquet
2 At the festival there is music	'To the shrill music of flutes'…		The guests at the banquet are entertained with music
3 At the festival there is lamentation before and after the sacrifice	The women cry for Tammuz; Innana raises a lament for 'my Damu'	Gilgamesh raises a great song of lament for his brother Enkidu	Isis laments the death of Osiris; Osiris is lamented at a great agricultural festival
4 Is decapitated (dismembered)	The galli 'gashed him with axes'		Set dismembers the body of Osiris into fourteen parts
5 His blood falls to the earth	His blood fell to the earth; the sanctum is wiped with his blood		The undecomposed body is buried in fourteen different sites
6 Is eaten			The newborn king, Osiris, is eaten as the new fruits
7 Is resurrected and worshipped as a god; he is Siva	Returns to earth for half the year; 'placed in the hands of the eternal'; in Adapa tablet 3, guards her … portal	Seeks life everlasting, but a snake steals the plant of eternal life, depriving Gilgamesh of his wish	Rises from the underworld first to instruct his son Horus and then to become the judge of the dead, residing in heaven as god
8 As a result of his sacrifice his sins and those of his devotees are forgiven		Orders a statue to be made of the dead Enkidu, simulating afterlife, but 'he will not rise again.'	
9 Is analogized to a plant	Is called 'herb', 'corn', 'willow', 'tamarisk'		Is the seeds and the new plants
10 His death ushers in a millennium, and he is called Saviour			

256

1 Is ejected from heaven after a battle	A substitute is killed after sacred marriage at the festival	Titans tear him into pieces; Bacchantes tear to death a live bull who is the god at Anthesteria festival	Is killed by a thunderbolt	Is killed at Passover festival; a lance pierces his side
2		They dance to the sound of their music	At the festivals there is music	Psalms are sung after the Passover meal
3 Is lamented by his consort Indrani		But there is loud lamentation for the death of Pentheus		The devotees go home beating their breasts; 'daughters of Jerusalem, do not weep for me'
4	Mot 'crushed him like a kid in his mouth'; the Abbirim 'killed him like the bull under the sacrificer's knife'; at Galli festival priests emasculate themselves	The Titans attack and tear into seven or nine pieces the 'horned infant' Dionysos; the phallus is preserved; the Bacchantes tear him to pieces	He is burnt to ashes by the fire of Zeus' thunderbolt	The nails in his hands and feet make holes; the lance makes a wound; Give me your hand, put it into my side' he says to Thomas
5 Writhes like a snake; he becomes tiny and lives within the stalk of a lotus	His redemptive blood runs into the river, turning it red	His redemptive blood falls to the earth; a pomegranate tree arises	The juice of mistletoe berries falls to the earth	The blood from his wounds falls to the earth, and his sweat fell to the ground like great drops of blood.
6	Sacrificial buffalo bulls are killed and eaten	The dismembered body is boiled and eaten by the Titans; Maenads devour the raw flesh and blood of the sacrificed god	The mistletoe (genitals of the oak), Asclepios in vegetative form, is ritually served at Druid festivals	In the Eucharist ritual the bread and wine are the flesh and blood of Jesus
7 Is brought back to heaven and worshipped as god and reunited with Indrani	Anath retrieves his body; he is resurrected; he is reborn as the scarlet poppies; he is god	Is resurrected from the phallus; or Rhea restores the dismembered parts; he is god a god	Later Zeus revives him; the juice of the berries revives the devotee; Asclepios becomes	Is resurrected to sit at the right hand of god; he is god, the son of god
8 He who recites the 'Victory of Indra' of the Mahabharat 'is washed of his evil'	His blood shed when sacrificed is redemptive	The Bacchantes drink the raw blood of the god in order to identify with him	Is the god of healing	The sins of the devotees are forgiven
9 Lives in a lotus stalk in the waters	Grows in the earth as red poppies	A pomegranate tree sprouts where his blood falls; he is the god of wine, the vine	Is mistletoe	Is the vine
10 His devotees will reach heaven			In Rome he comes as the healing Saviour	Is the redeemer and Saviour; his second coming is predicted

Dumuzi / Tammuz

When the Goddess Innana desired to return from her sojourn in the underworld she was forcibly detained there and threatened by the *galli*, creatures or spirits of the nether regions. They offered to take one after the other of her sons in her stead, but she refused and, casting about for a suitable victim, she agreed to ransom her own beloved husband, the shepherd king Dumuzi, with whom she had only recently been engaged in rapturous and prolonged love-making. Like Durga, her later counterpart, Innana's rapid transformations predictably re-enacted archetypal Goddess/male partner patterns. In this case, the demons are merely the substitute perpetrators of the inevitable slaying of the royal lover after sacred marriage. Even though he pleaded with her brothers to rescue him:

> Innana fastened on Dumuzi the eye of death... (1) the galli gashed him with axes (4, 5) seized Dumuzi... They surrounded him... They bound his hands. They bound his neck... the wild bull lives no more... the slain wild bull.[115]

Only after his sister Geshtinanna is called to the underworld for six months of the year as surrogate does Innana announce that 'That day you will be set free.' Then she 'placed Dumuzi in the hands of the Eternal.'[116]

The drama of Innana/Dumuzi/Tammuz was re-enacted in the month of Tammuz. Quoting Berosus, Frazer described the privileges accorded to a human victim prior to his sacrifice in place of the king. To make the substitution credible, a criminal was given leave to sleep with all the concubines of the king for five days after which, during the sacred festival, he was scourged, hanged or impaled.[117] Women wept (3). In other rituals, a sheep was beheaded, the sanctum wiped with the blood, and the carcase carried by priests to the water to rid the victim of its powers.[118]

Even while Innana betrays her lover in the ritual, she raises a lament for 'my Damu', 'to the shrill music of flutes, (3)(2) for a herb that grows not in the bed... for the corn that grows not in the ear, for a great river where no willows grow'(9), and 'for weary children and weary women.'[119]

EGYPT

Osiris / Horus

A sumptuous banquet (1), (2) was the scene of the betrayal of the god/Pharoah Osiris by his evil brother Set. To the assembled guests he promised a reward to the one who would perfectly fit the beautiful, ornate chest which had been set up in the hall for all to test. As Set had previously made sure the chest was constructed according to the measurements of Osiris, as Pharoah lay inside, the king's seventy-two supporters nailed down the lid. Now the chest-become-coffin was thrown into the Nile at the time of inundation. The current bore it into the Mediterranean, and it landed on the shores of Byblos to the north. A protective magic tree grew around it and attracted the attention of the king who commanded that it be cut down, chest and all, and brought as a pillar to his palace.

The grieving (3) sister-wife of Osiris, Isis, wandered in search of him. Finally she arrived at Byblos, rescued the coffin from the pillar and returned with it to Egypt, but the furious Set discovered it, dismembered the undecomposed body of the god, and cast the fourteen pieces in various different sites in Egypt (4). After Isis had conducted the funeral, she created Osiris shrines wherever the parts were buried. His spirit passed into the underworld, the Duat, but he returned from the dead in order to instruct his son Horus who was born posthumously. Horus defeated his evil uncle and reigned as Pharoah for hundreds of years.

Osiris gained a permanent place in heaven, for he rose from the dead to become the king and judge of the dead (7). In another tradition, Thoth, god of wisdom, took the role of the priest who restored Osiris to life by his ceremonial words, or, as Osiris was originally a god/man, he arose himself and was therefore reborn to everlasting life—he was the resurrection and the life (6).[120]

In the great agricultural festivals held in his honour, Osiris' fate was lamented (3) for it was believed that the planted seeds were fragments of his dismembered body and that he was the spirit in the vegetation which was being killed at harvest. But there was also rejoicing, as the new fruits and plants were associated with the coming of the newborn king (6),(9).

Indra

Although the god Indra never actually dies, he does get into all kinds of situations which are tantamount to death. For example, when he struck the Brahman demon Trisiras with his *vajra*, Indra was set on fire by the other's splendour.[121] In his battle with Vrtra he was swallowed:[122]

> The Indra of the Gods went to the end of the worlds, and bereft of consciousness and wits was no longer aware of anything, being pressed down by guilt [for Brahmanicide]. He dwelled concealed in the Waters, writhing like a snake.[123]

His consort Indrani was 'filled with sorrow, ... wailed piteously'[124] and lamented (3). She went on a long journey in search of her lost husband. When finally he was located, in diminished form, he was tiny enough to fit into the stalk of a lotus.[125] But with the help of the priest of the gods, Brihaspati, he resumed his own shape and eventually returned to heaven.[126]

The devotee who reads this story of Indra is

> washed of his evil, wins heaven and rejoices here and hereafter. That

man will be in no danger of enemies, not remain without sons, meet with no calamity, and find a long life, in which he shall meet victory, and no defeat at all.[127]

There were other occasions when Indra almost lost his life. In his battle with Mahisa, he fled the field, leaving everything behind, including his elephant Airavata.[128] Then he and the other gods wandered on earth, bedraggled and weak. When the Devi rescued the gods and slew Mahisa, Indra was again returned to his place in heaven (7).

CANAAN

Baal/Hadad

The hero god Baal is the son of Shor-El (bull god) from whom he inherits control over the rain. He defeats Yam/Nahar, god of the sea, and reigns for half the year. But in the dry season, Mot, god of the underworld, 'crushed him like a kid in his mouth'[129] (1), (4) in the form of a bull. He lifts one section of his mountain home, Saphor, descends to the underworld and 'becomes as the strengthless dead'.[130] Or, when he fought with the Abbirim, creatures with the heads of bulls and human bodies, Baal was killed 'like the bull under the sacrificer's knife' (4), (9).[131] In any case, 'Dead is Aliyan Baal, Perished, the Prince, Lord of Earth!'[132] No rain falls; the earth is cracked and dry. Six months pass and then, with the help of the sun Goddess, Baal's beloved Anath retrieves the body of the god (7). She buries it in Saphon, and as a memorial, she 'slaughters seventy buffaloes' and numerous other sacrificial animals (6). In revenge, she 'cleaves,... winnows, burns..., grinds..., and plants the god of Death, Mot.'[133] When father El dreams of honey and oil, he realizes that Baal has been reborn. He shouts to his wife Asherah:

And lo, the Prince, Lord of Earth exists (7).[134]

Spring returns, the earth is blessed with rain, the plants spring into life—the hero/god lives again (9) (10).

Ritual

During the vernal festival, in a great temple to Astarte (Anath), on a cliff above the source of the river Adonis near Byblos, Baal (Adonis) was united in sacred marriage to the Goddess. A sacred temple prostitute was brought to a king substitute who was then wounded and killed (4). His redemptive blood ran into the river, turning it red (5), watering the earth which gave birth to his resurrected body in the form of fields of scarlet poppies (9).[135]

During other festivals, it was common for priests to emasculate themselves (4), run through the streets dressed in women's clothing, holding the severed organ, and then bury it to ensure fertility.[136]

CRETE AND GREECE

Dionysos

In an archaic myth recorded by the sixth century BC, the life of Dionysos begins in a holocaust of death, for no sooner is he rescued from the flames of his mother's blazing womb and reborn from the thigh of Zeus, after a brief period of enthronement as divine king[137] the 'horned infant' is savagely attacked, torn into seven or nine pieces, boiled and devoured by Titans (1), (4). They are a breed of monsters, reckless divine beings, progeny of the original parents, Gaia and Ouranus, enemies of the branch of the family represented by Zeus.[138]

Fearing that the infant son of Semele and Zeus would threaten her own position of power, and surely out of jealousy of a younger rival, the Goddess Hera, wife of Zeus, aligned herself with the Titans and persuaded them to murder the newborn divine child. The phallus was preserved and from it, the god was resurrected: 'a pomegranate-tree sprouted from the soil (9) where his blood had fallen', or Rhea restored the dismembered parts.[139] Like the vine which bursts into leaf after it is pruned and the grapes have been gathered, Dionysos rose again to life (7), to spread his religion 'even as far as where the distant Ganges washes the sun-stained sides of India'[140] and to 'sit at the right hand of Zeus.'[141] Finally, the god descended to the underworld to rescue his mother, and she took her place among the Olympians.

As for the Titans, Zeus destroyed them with the fire of his lightning, and from the ashes of the conflagration the race of humans arose. The Hera/Titan alliance is a later concretization of the activities of the archaic Great Goddess who slays the sacred king with the thunderbolt in the seventh month of the winter solstice after which the priestesses devour the slain king(6).[142] As mere proxies for the Goddess, the Titans' act repeats the prehistoric pattern.

But in Greece, in a reversal of functions, as symbol of male conquest over the Mother Goddess, Zeus in turn slays the Titans. Because of their association with the Goddess as creatrix, however, the human race is generated, in the same manner that Dionysos and Mahisa are born from the ashes of their Goddess-connected mothers, Semele and Syama.

Ritual

The death and resurrection of the god is the central mimetic ritual in many ancient Greek festivals to Dionysos, during which the Bacchantes, his female devotees, re-enact the murder by Titan and Hera. Under the influence of the god of wine, released entirely from human repressions, and believing that the god resides in the sacrificial victim, the wild women perform the *sparagamos* (1) in order to be renewed by the transformable energies of the god (1). In a resurgence of atavistic prehistoric cannibalism, with their teeth they tear a live victim to pieces, either one of their own children, or an animal, usually a bull. The raw flesh and blood is then ritually devoured (5), but the male phallus is preserved. In a replay of the original event, the victim is himself a substitute for the suffering god, who permits himself to be sacrificed. Thus it is Dionysos the god as bull who is killed, (1) dismembered, (4) and resurrected (7).

And yet perversion is heaped upon perversion as Euripides' *The Bacchae* unfolds. During the madness of the women's revelry, Pentheus, the king of Thebes—his name means 'full of suffering'[143]—is dismembered (4) by his own crazed mother, Agave, devotee of Dionysos and sister to Semele. She and her sisters tear the body of the king to pieces, and under the illusion that she has killed a lion, the mother proudly displays the head of her son for all to see. Kerenyi refers to the common Cretan heritage of Pentheus and his cousin Dionysos:

> Originally the 'man of suffering'—Pentheus... was the god himself. The core of the myth that Greeks found in the Cretan palaces did not change, but changes did occur in the tales that adapted the myth in later times.[144]

O'Flaherty suggests that Pentheus and Dionysos are mirror images in regard to birth, animal associations, androgynous propensities and in the manner each meets his death.[145]

In the story of Mahisa, the same archetypal motifs can be discerned, even while they are expressed in an entirely new context. Semele's (and Syama's) death by fire is a gender reversal of the circumstances of the death of the Titans. As the human race was generated in the ashes of the Titans, the heroes Dionysos and Mahisa arose, each an orphan, from the pyre of the mother. Androgyny, the *sileni* (half-animal, half-human companions of Dionysos), animal transformations, dismemberment and resurrection, which ushers in a world of vegetative and fruitful plenty, are common themes in the Greek and Indian myths. Like Pentheus and Dionysos, Mahisa in demon's clothing is the 'divine sufferer', 'the man of sorrows'. Furthermore, Durga's erotic connections with the hero, the uncontrolled, instantaneous, fluid transformation of emotional states, her intoxication which leads to murder and ravishment, recall the characteristics of the maenads. The image of Agave's appropriation and embrace of the head of the son she has only recently severed is analogous to Durga's compulsive attachment to the head of her victim Mahisa. In these comparable acts, the mother/son relationship is compressed into a metaphor which has retained its validity for millennia. She who gives life requires in turn to have her own regenerative powers recharged.

Asclepios / Aesculapius

The daughter of the centaur Cherion, foster father to Asclepios, prophesied that he would become a god, would die a god and be reborn a god. Born in fire, Asclepios died in fire (4); as god, he appeared as a fiery snake; and an ever-burning lamp (7)[146] in his temple was a dominant feature of his cult. When the physician revived Asclepios and others from death, Hades persuaded Zeus to kill him with his thunderbolt,[147] but later Zeus revived him and set his image among the stars (7).[148]

As the god of healing, Asclepios was the recipient of sacrifices during a three-day period in a prescribed ritual which included abstinence from sexual intercourse and certain foods, but the god's death was not enacted.[149] Graves believes, however, that the name Asclepios is derived from the mistletoe, a parasite which grows on the oak. The 'genitals of the oak' are ritually severed in Druid festivals (1), (5). The juice of the berries rejuvenates the devotee as symbolic of the regenerative blood of the emasculated phallus of the sacrificed oak-hero (6).[150]

By Roman times (according to Ovid), Aesculapius' status as deity was undisputed. The towns on the coast of Epidaurus claimed him as 'a local god who brought prosperity', and the 'god of health' who appears as 'god within the snake', with a crown of fire.

> And here it was the serpent came ashore
> To be the son of Phoebus that he was
> And not a serpent but of godlike features.[151]

CHRISTIAN

Jesus

The stages of the life story of Jesus, with some variations and masking of divergent meanings, recall those of the other heroes, including Mahisa's. Nothing is known about the later childhood of Jesus, but in early manhood, as penitent, in contrition he fasts for forty days in the desert. He returns to oppose the established authorities. By claiming to be the son of god and the one and only path to salvation, he challenges the very essence of the two-thousand-year old ancient heritage: Elohim never manifests, nor ever becomes either flesh or immanent in an idol. Even though Jesus is regarded as a despised and rejected heretic, he attempts to legitimize his divinity by means of control of the phenomena of nature, food proliferations, miracles of healing, magical signs, and promises of the establishment of his kingdom on earth. He also employs violent methods: he employs the whip and advises use of the sword: 'If you have no sword, sell your cloak and buy one.'[152] He threatens vengeance and dire punishment for those who deny his godhood. While he gains popularity amongst the people, he incurs the displeasure of the religious fathers who put him through a series of tests.

Jesus is well aware of the fate of his cousin, his *alter ego*, John the Baptist, which might easily have been his own. In a replay of the archaic Mother Goddess rituals, John had only recently been decapitated (4) for the pleasure of the princess Salome, who desired and received his head on a platter.

Jesus is also ambivalent towards his divine father. At the Passover meal, which has roots in the ancient spring festivals, the Jews ritually partook of the sacrificial lamb and sang psalms (2). Jesus symbolically transforms himself into the lamb of god, *Agnus Dei*. When he offers the bread as his flesh and the wine (6) as his blood, he is consciously offering himself as the god become the victim to be consumed. He is arrested, scourged and sentenced to death by crucifixion (1), (4), (5), all according to the will of god the father. For the ancient father god was accustomed to receive flesh and blood sacrifices at festival time. As paschal lamb, the traditional offering, Jesus serves the god's purpose well. The son wishes to become the father:

'Do you not believe that I am the Father and the Father is in me?'[153] is a thought that cannot be sustained without a great amount of accompanying guilt; it is immediately followed by the self-reassuring statement: 'The father is greater than I.'[154] While the son is to be sacrificed as punishment for forbidden sinful wishes, as he readies himself, he prays to the father in hope of a reprieve, and he goes not like a lamb to the slaughter, but with anger in his heart. To Pilate he replies:

> You would have no power [to crucify me] if it had not been given to you from above; that is why the one who handed me over to you has the greater guilt.[155]

Here Jesus, the rebellious son, rejects his fate while, at the same time, he knows that the sin involved in the original wish to displace the father ultimately will be forgiven only after punishment with death. Yet even at the final moment, he rails against the father: 'Why hast thou forsaken me'?

The arrest is made with swords and clubs. One of his followers cuts off the ear of a servant of the high priest. These violent acts recall the mock battle of the New Year rites, as does the death of the sacrificial victim. Jesus is the age-old pagan sacrificed son/lover/king in the lamb's clothing, playing the divine male role in the immemorial equation. Salome is the obfuscating but direct link with the cults of the neighbouring Mother Goddess.

Jesus is born again (7). Like Osiris, the dismembered but nevertheless undecomposed body retains its life-giving powers. Rising from the grave, Jesus meets his disciples before ascending to heaven. Like the vine, whose roots remain and are perennially brought again to life (9), he prophesizes a second coming, the millennium (10).

Appendix V   Animal Associations

Common Motifs

Mahisa	Buffalo; lion; elephant; sardula
Dumuzi-Tammuz	Bull; snake; gazelle 'Change my hands into the hands of a snake', he cries to Utu
Gilgamesh/Enkidu	Bull
Osiris/Horus	Osiris; bull; 'Come to thy house, beautiful bull'. Lord of Men. Horus; snake; falcon
Indra	Bull
Baal	Bull
Hephaestos	Father is bull, mother is cow.
Asclepios	Golden serpent; in his sanctuary, he is in the form of a snake; he comes to Rome as a golden serpent deity; he is raised by a foster father, a centaur
Jesus	Lamb of god; Agnus Dei

Glossary

abhisheka	ritual bath for the deity
ahamkara	self as separate from others; self centrism
amma	mother; Goddess
ananda	fervent joy as result of bhakti worship
andaya (Kannada)	he, like a man
antarala	vestibule leading to shrine in temple
anubadhya	(cow) to be bound and sacrificed
apsara	heavenly nymph
arati	evening ceremony for the deity with offerings
arhat	ascetic seeking Buddhist knowledge
Astami	eighth day and night of the Navratri festival when the Goddess is Mahisamardini
ashtapada	eight-footed (pregnant) cow
asvamedha	ancient Indian royal horse sacrifice
Asvina	September / October (Hindu calendar)
asura / asuri	demon / demoness
atman	core of the self
avipalli	head sacrifice
balidana	animal sacrifice
bapa	father
basavis	she-buffaloes; here applied to virgin girls
basilinna (Gr.)	wife of archon, the ruler, sometimes called queen
bhajan	devotional song
bhakta	devotee
bhakti	devotion towards the deity without priestly intervention
bhopa	village priest
bhuta	malevolent spirit or godling
bhutanamcha maithunam	sexual coupling for ritual purposes
bilva	a tree (and its fruit), symbolizing the male
bodhana	temporal appearance of a deity; invocation of deity
bodhisattva	compassionate superbeing; potential Buddha

bongas	local deities or spirits
brahmacari	ascetic student who must abstain from sexual relations
bubalis bubalus	large buffalo with long horns
cakra	wheel; Visnu's weapon
Cakravartin	universal king, the wheels of whose chariot move everywhere on earth
Chaitra	March/April of the Hindu calendar
chhalamahisa	in the disguise of a buffalo
chapati	unleavened, flat bread made from wheat flour
choes (Gr.)	wine pitcher
daitya	demon (lit., male offspring of Diti)
daivasuram	battle of gods and demons
daksinayana	period of the southerly course of the sun
danava	demon (lit., sons of Danu)
darshan	blessings during audience with a deity or important person
dasami	tenth day of Navratri festival, also known as Vijaya Dasami
deva	god
devadasi	girl dedicated to service of the deity in Hindu temple
devrsi	local priest, who can exorcise evil spirits from a person or place
dhoti	unstitched cloth worn as lower garment by men
Dussera/Dasahra	Navratri festival, lit., the tenth day; Vijaya Dasami
gai mukha	silver water spout; lit., face of cow
galli	creatures or spirits of the nether regions
gandharva	celestial musician
garbha grha	shrine of a Hindu temple; lit., 'womb-house'
gauda-kona	buffalo husband
gayal	species of Indian ox
ghee	(clarified) butter
ghondhali	non-Brahmin priest, particularly, worshipper of the Goddess
gomedha	cow sacrifice
gotrasya satruh	foe of the family
gramma devata	village goddess
guna	one of three interacting forces: *Sattva*, *rajas*, *tamas*

guru	religious teacher
havan	Brahmanical fire-sacrifice
havi	sacrificial offering
homa kunda	sacrificial pit
Indriya	Indra's physical power
irpalvusthi	annual Toda celebration
ista devata	chosen deity of a devotee
jatas	Siva's strands of knotted hair
jati	sub-caste; community
javari	rye, staple crop of Maharashtra
Kadam	ksatriya dynasty of old
kadamba	species of tree
kama	love; passions; desires
kanya samkranti	day on which sun enters Kanya (Virgo) (September/October)
karakam	a pot; in rituals it symbolizes the Goddess
karma	good or bad results of former actions
karuna	compassion
kirtan	song in praise of Goddess or god, a mixture of prose and poetry
kohala	pumpkin or gourd
kona	buffalo
kote	central square
krttivasas krttivasisvara	one clad in elephant hide; Siva who wears the elephant hide, or any hide
ksatriya	ruler/warrior caste
kum-kum	red powder used for ritual purposes
lila	the play of the Goddess or the god in the world
limbu	lemon
linga	abstract symbol for Siva
linga-sariras	subtle bodies
macchu ghati	a chopper; axe
madiga	outcaste
Magh purnima	full moon night in the month of Magh (January/February)
mahant	head of religious institution
mali	gardener caste
mana	life force
manasic yajna	ascetic exercises of the mind
mandala	circular diagram used for ritual purposes
mandapa	main hall in Hindu temple

mangalpatra	auspicious plate used in worship
mantras	sound vibrations uttered in rituals; mystical formulas
Mara-kona	Goddess of buffaloes
mardini (mardani)	she who kills
mariah	human sacrificial victim
mataji	'honoured mother', appellation for Goddess
maya	the illusory human condition; a Vedantic and theological concept indicating the ephemeral character of the world
maysa	buffalo
mela	festival; gathering; fair
mhas	buffalo
mithan	type of bull found in India
mridanga	type of Indian drum
murti	statue; icon
mutt / math	Hindu religious institution; abode of Sanyasins; centre of religious worship and discourse
naramedha	human sacrifice
Navami	ninth day and night of Navratri
navapatrica	nine plants, which together represent the Goddess on Navratri
Navratri	Hindu festival to the Goddess; literally, nine nights
Nirguna	the Absolute (non-) form of the Goddess; without qualities
paduka, pambada	slaughterer at a sacrificial ceremony
pakora	vegetable fritter
panchagavya	five products of a cow
pancha nada	five rivers of the Indus
pandals	temporary stages built for worship of deity
pandit	Brahmin priest; learned person
paneer	cheese made of curdled milk
par (Heb.)	bull
pasa	weapon, lit., rope
pasubali	animal sacrifice
patala	the nether world
persinir	sacred she-buffaloes
pitrs	ancestors
potraj	buffalo king; in tribal religion, a worshipper of the Goddess

pradaksina	rite of circumambulation
pradaksinam	embryo
pralaya	in the cyclical order of the universe, a state of complete stasis when Visnu sleeps upon the waters which have flooded the earth
prasad	sacred residuals of the offerings to the deity; grace; gift from the deity
pratima	statue when it is the object of worship
puja	ceremonies of worship of the deity
pujari	worshipper priest
puranas	popular Sanskrit texts, eighteen in-number, containing legends, ritual prescriptions, prayers, etc.
purnima	full moon night
purohit	Brahmin priest
Purusha	Supreme Being; also archetypal man
raga	traditional scale or mode in Indian music
rajas, rajasic	expanding horizontal force (guna)
rajasuya	royal sacrificial ceremony
raksas, raksasas	demons
raksaksi	demoness
Raktavija	'blood seed'
rsi	ascetic, holy man
rta	cosmic order
sadhaka	one who seeks divine knowledge
saguna	manifested form of the Goddess
Sakta	cult of the Goddess
sakti	female power or energy
saktis	emanations from the Goddess, her army; wives of gods
samadhi	merging with the Absolute
santa	peaceful (*rasa*)
sanyas	fourth ashrama: ascetic stage of life
sarvapitri amavasya	day for worshipping ancestors
sastras, sastric	sacred texts; revealed scriptures
sattva, sattvic	pure, ascending, light force (*guna*)
satya yuga	golden age
shofar (Heb.)	ram's horn; *b'kol shofar:* in the voice of the horn
shor (Heb.)	bull
siddhi	miraculous powers

simolanghan / silangan	procession across boundary particularly on Vijaya Dasami
sinmal	a flower
sloka	a couplet or quatraine
soma	intoxicating drink of the gods
sopari	betel nut; areca nut
sparagamos (Gr.)	tearing a live victim to pieces
srishanranni	a circle of human heads
sthalapurana	local temple tract
sthanu	post; epithet for Siva
sulagava	spitted cow sacrifice
sulin	trident bearer; epithet for Siva
suras	gods
svastha	emancipation
tahsildar	local government revenue official
tamas, tamasic	negative, destructive, downward-tending force (*guna*)
tamasha	a party, with revelry; a folk entertainment
tapas	ascetic exercises which increase body heat and spiritual power
tapasvin	one who undertakes ascetic exercises
tejas	heat, energy, lustre
ti	enclosed compound for sacred buffaloes
tirth	ablution tank at temple; holy place
todi	human victim, sacrificed by Khonds
triguna	three interacting forces of nature: *sattva, rajas, tamas*
triloka	three worlds: heaven, earth and the nether world
trisula	three-pronged weapon (of Siva and Durga)
tulasi	basil plant; considered to be sacred
Turiya	the Absolute (Goddess); fourth state of consciousness
uttarayanam	period of the northerly course of the sun
urdhavalinga	with phallus erected
vahana	animal vehicle of god or goddess
vajra	Indra's weapon; literally, thunderbolt
varahacarvitakam	the biting of the boar
vibhuti	sacred ashes
Vijaya Dasami	day of victory of Durga over Mahisa; 10th day of Navratri festival

vira	hero; heroic
viraloka	heaven of heroes
virata; visvarupa	cosmic form
virya	valour
yajna	sacrificial ceremony
yajnopavita	sacred thread
yaksas; yaksis	male and female fertility deities or spirits; objects of cult worship
yantra	two-dimensional square and/or circular diagram, used for worship in esoteric sciences
yatra	pilgrimage, festival
yoga	Hindu theistic philosophy and system of bodily exercises
yogi	ascetic; one desiring union with Supreme Reality
zoe (Gr.)	life force

Notes

INTRODUCTION

1. *Rg Ved.*, Bk IV, Hymn 30, v. 8.
2. Ibid., Bk X, Hymn 125, v. 6. Translation and notes, O'Flaherty, 1981, p. 63.
3. Bana, 1896, p. 28, 31.
4. Vakpati, p. xxi.
5. By paying serious attention to the entire body of creative expression, contemporary Indians who are interested in these states might very well find all the pieces of the puzzle exposed to view. They can refocus on to their own rich symbol life, still today operative in the psyche even of urbanized, westernized Indians.
6. For intensive and illuminating studies of the DM and DBP, see Thomas Coburn and C. Mackenzie Brown.
7. Reik, p. 63.
8. O'Flaherty, 1976, p. 59 ff.
9. Shulman, 1980, p. 181.
10. Ibid., p. 318.
11. Shulman, 1986, p. 109.
12. Rank, 1914.
13. DM, Chap. 3, vv. 35–42.
14. O'Flaherty, 1976, 8. 80.
15. Bishop Whitehead's description (at the beginning of the twentieth century) of the various duties of the Madiga and Mala (outcaste) priests, recalls primeval autocthonous rites of the identification of the priest with the sacrificial animal victim: a human substitute for the animal, who is dragged in procession toward the Goddess, is draped with the intestines (of a lamb) with the liver placed in his mouth; or the priest carries the buffalo head on his own, with a new cloth dipped in its blood tied around his neck. Another applies the warm blood of the sacrificed buffalo to his own forehead (Whitehead, 1916, p. 51, 62, 65).
16. Elmore, pp. 123–4.
17. Mitra, S., 1928, pp. 508–9.
18. Shulman, 1985, p. 39.
19. *B.Can.*, 1971, 10: 4; 86: 3.

CHAPTER ONE FAMILY AND SOCIETY IN CONTEMPORARY INDIA

1. This very brief summary, based primarily on my personal observations, is no substitute for the serious sociological studies by Carstairs, Erikson, Lannoy, Kakar, Nandy, and those of a growing group of scholars which provide the basic orientation for an explanation of much of traditional Indian behaviour.

2. On South Indian variations, see Lannoy, p. 87.
3. Kakar, pp. 94–5.
4. Dubois, p. 316.
5. Kakar, p. 301.
6. Ibid., and Obeyeskere, p. 20.
7. *Indian Express*, 22 January 1992.
8. *Mid-Day*, 23 October 1990.

CHAPTER TWO Birth of the Hero

1. *VamP.*, Chap. 18, v. 44; DBP, Bk V, Chap. 2, v. 20.
2. O'Flaherty, 1973, Chap. 2 and 1976, p. 82.
3. *VamP.*, Chap. 18, v. 45.
4. 'Condemned by his fellow deities, Indra sighed a lot, looked anxious, then hid himself in the stalk of a lotus, and he became terribly thin.' In the mean time the gods installed the snake king Nahusha in his place, a case of bad judgement, because he soon demanded Indrani for a wife. Indra had to perform a horse sacrifice to the Goddess before his sin left him, only to be redistributed amongst the 'trees, rivers, mountains, women and the earth' (DBP, Bk VI, Chap. 7, vv. 18–49).
5. *VamP.*, Chap. 18, v. 16.
6. *Rg Ved.*, Bk VIII, Hymn 87, v. 11.
7. Ibid., Bk III, Hymn 31, v. 12.
8. SLA, Vasishtha, Chap. 20, vv. 13–14.
9. Based on the sure belief in after-life, suicide has continually served as a tried and true method to eliminate guilt or take revenge on someone else, or perhaps even as a macabre comment on the absurdity of temporal life, which seems to be the case of a reported suicide in the ninth century: A Muslim observed that a man from a mountain tribe sat on the ground, tied his long hair to a sugarcane plant; he instructed his associates to bend the cane to the ground so that when it snapped up, he would be decapitated (Renaudot in Pinkerton, vol. vii, p. 216).
10. Hertel, quoted in Rank, reprint 1975, p. 66.
11. *In. Vis.*, Chap. 22, vv. 58–61.
12. *VamP.*, Chap. 18, v. 48.
13. *SivP.*, Rudrasamhita (Section 4) Chap. 57.
14. *VamP.*, Chap. 18, vv. 41–52.
15. Ibid., v. 51.
16. Ibid., v. 52.
17. O'Flaherty, 1980, Chap. 3.
18. O'Flaherty, 1973, Chap. 2.
19. O'Flaherty, 1975, pp. 91–4.
20. Ibid., p. 239, from the *SkP.* 3.I.6. 8–48
21. Shulman, 1980, p. 181.
22. *VarP.*, Chap. 28, v. 2.
23. O'Flaherty, 1973, Chap. 2.
24. *VarP.*, Chap. 28, v. 13.
25. Ibid., v. 2 and Chap. 95, v. 4.

26. Ibid., vv. 3–21.
27. *VamP.*, Chap. 18, v. 56.
28. Ibid., v. 58.
29. One wonders what became of Rambha's barren wife.
30. *VamP.*, Chap. 18, v. 60.
31. Ibid., vv. 61–2.
32. DBP, Bk V, Chap. II, vv. 32–50.
33. *KalP.*, Sec. 4, Chap. 62, vv. 140–1.
34. Ibid., v. 142.
35. O'Flaherty, 1976, p. 58.
36. *VamP*, Chap. 18, V. 42.
37. See Jung, 1949, p. 161; O'Flaherty, 1988, p. 81.
38. O'Flaherty, 1976, pp. 331–46.
39. Shulman, 1980, p. 229–30.
40. DBP, Bk V, vv. 32–50.
41. 'This earth is a Mahisi (female buffalo),' SB, Bk VI, Chap. 5, Sec. 3, v. 1.
42. O'Flaherty, 1980, p. 243.
43. *Rg Ved.*, Bk III, Hymn 55, v. 16.
44. Ibid., Bk IV, Hymn 18, v. 10.
45. Ibid., Bk I, Hymn v. 3.
46. *In.Vis.*, 23, 58.
47. Ibid., 60.
48. *Gri.S.*, Bhanhayana, 1, 6, 19.
49. Ibid., 61.
50. Ibid., Gautama, XXII, 18.
51. Ibid., XLV, 19.
52. *In. Vis.*, XLVI, 19.
53. Frazer, 1972, p. 229.
54. Emeneau, 1971, III, 18, v. 43.
55. Ibid., IV, 32, v. 16.
56. Ibid., 33, v. 27.
57. Ibid., 126, v. 23
58. Marshall, p. 128 ff.
59. Rivers, pp. 83–4; Marshall, p. 64.
60. Emeneau, 1971, III, 9, v. 64.
61. Hayavadana Rao, 1922, pp. 141–55.
62. Mukherjea, pp. 247, 254.
63. Nepali, pp. 354–6.
64. *VamP.*, Chap. 18, vv. 61–3.
65. DBP, Bk V, Chap. 2, vv. 32–50.
66. *VamP.*, Chap. 18, v. 61.
67. Ibid., vv. 62–3.
68. Ibid., vv. 64–5.
69. Ibid., v. 66.
70. Ibid., Chap. 20, vv. 36–8.
71. DBP, Bk V, Chap. 2, vv. 32–50.
72. Kerenyi, 1977, pp. 100–1; from the *Artharaveda*; in Keith, ERE, Vol. I, p. 505.
73. Diodorus Sicilus, quoted in Thompson, pp. 33–4.

74. *In.Vis.*, XXV, v. 14.
75. Dubois, p. 360; Aparna Sen's film; *Sati*, 1989.
76. Bushby, p. 15.
77. Colebrook, quoted in Thompson, p. 51.
78. Quoted in Bushby, p. 12.
79. Ibid., p. 15.
80. Ibid., pp. 17–28.
81. Thompson, p. 48.
82. Elmore, pp. 60–2.
83. Conversation with Mulk Raj Anand, 1993.
84. *Indian Express*, 30 March 1990.
85. O'Flaherty, 1980, p. 244.
86. *Rg Ved.*, Bk IV, Hymn 12, v. 6.
87. *Gri.S.*, 1, Sankhavana, 1, 12, 10.
88. Ibid., Paraskara, III, 3, 8.
89. Ibid., III, 10, 49.
90. SBE, SB, Bk XII, Chap. 6, note 2, p. 205.
91. Mitra, Vol. I, reprint, 1960, pp. 363–6.
92. Ibid., p. 358.
93. SB, 4, 5, 1, 5.
94. Ibid., IV, 5, 1, 11.
95. Ibid., 13, 5, 4, 25.
96. *Rg Ved.*, Bk II, Hymn 7, v. 5.
97. SB, Bk IV, Chap. 5, Section 2, v.1.
98. *Tai.S.*, Pt I, III, 3, 10, in Keith, reprint, 1967.
99. *Manu: II, Dulluka Bhatta*, 120 or *Gri.S.*, 1:24, 31 in Mitra, Vol. I, p. 381.
100. Ibid., 32.
101. Ibid.
102. Emeneau, 1971, III, 33, v. 37.
103. Marshall, pp. 174–6; Emeneau, 1971, III, 34, v. 49; Russell, VII, pp. 152, 155.
104. Ibid, pp. 150–1; Marshall, pp. 176–7.
105. Rivers, p. 274.
106. Presler, pp. 33–5.
107. Marshall, pp. 176–7.
108. Mills, p. 184.
109. Elwin, 1955, p. 108.
110. But it would seem Siva is capable of anything. It was not the only time he transformed himself into an animal mother. In Madurai, as sow, he nursed a group of piglets who were in fact twelve boys cursed by a rsi (Harman, p. 58).
111. SBE, *In.Vis.*, Chap. 25, fn, p. 111.
112. *VamP.*, Chap. 18, v. 60.
113. *Khando*, Chap. 5, Sect. 9, v. 2.
114. DBP, Bk V, Chap. 2, vv. 32–50.
115. O'Flaherty, 1980, pp. 25, 28.
116. 'Mr. Rajiv Goswami, who triggered a spate of self-immolations by anti-Mandal students in 1990, was arrested by the police today when he soaked himself with kerosene and threatened to set himself ablaze' (*The Times of India*, 21 September 1993).

117. DBP, Bk V, Chap. 2, vv. 32–50.

CHAPTER THREE THE LABOURS OF MAHISA

1. *VamP.*, Chap. 18, vv. 69–71.
2. See Jung, 1949, p. 85.
3. Money-Kyrle, p. 200.
4. DBP, Bk V, Chap. 2, vv. 3–7.
5. O'Flaherty, 1976, p. 82.
6. DBP, Bk V, Chap. 2, vv. 12–13.
7. Ibid.
8. *VarP.*, Chap. 92, vv. 26–7.
9. DBP, Bk V, Chap. 3, v. 1.
10. Ibid., Bk VI, Chap. 16, vv. 7–22.
11. BP, 4, LM, Chap. 6, v. 37.
12. Ilango-Adigal, Canto 17 (Daniélou), p. 120.
13. Shulman, 1986, pp. 92, 93.
14. Appuswami, 1281, p. 4.
15. BP, 4, LM, Chap. 27, vv.11–12.
16. Long before, Indra had killed *his* father.
17. Shulman, 1986, p. 40.
18. DBP, Bk V, Chap. 3, vv. 1–14.
19. Ibid., Chap. 4, vv. 1–17.
20. Ibid., Chap. 3, vv. 29–53.
21. Ibid. Here Mahisa is close to the mark; when Indra seduced Ahilya, her jealous husband Gautama did indeed slice off Indra's testicles and thus he became impotent (*Ramayana*, as told by O'Flaherty, 1975, pp. 94–6).
22. DBP, Chap. 3, vv. 29–53.
23. Ibid.
24. Ibid.
25. *Rg.Ved.*, Bk I, Hymn 33, v. 12.
26. Stekel, reprint, 1953, Vol. II, p. 179.
27. See O'Flaherty, 1976, pp. 146 ff.
28. Ibid., p. 173.
29. Eliade, 1982, Vol. I, p. 288.
30. Shanti Lal Nagar, 1988, p. 29.
31. O'Flaherty, 1976, p. 136.
32. Ibid., pp. 94–5.
33. Ibid., p. 78.
34. Ibid., pp. 58, 59, 62.
35. Ibid., p. 131.
36. DBP, Bk IV, Chap. 15, vv. 38, 39, 42.
37. Ibid., v. 44.
38. Ibid., vv. 59–64.
39. Ibid., Chap. 14, v. 46. In the contemporary creative imagination, simplistic categorizations of who is evil and who is good are often reversed. In one instance, at a Kathakali performance in Bombay (January 1992), Kalamandalam Gopalakrishnan, as

the god Narasimha, made a magnificent climactic entrance, in horrific form, in a paroxysm of violent rage. In slow and graphic stages he then proceeded to disembowel and consume the intestines of Prahlada's demon father, Hiranya-kasipu, thus symbolizing all that is evil. The demon, on the other hand, was shown as an amusingly mild-mannered prancing, bombastic clown.

40. DBP, Bk IX, Chap. 21, vv. 1–33.
41. Reik, p. 60.
42. DBP, Bk VI, Chap. 9, vv. 32–54.
43. See O'Flaherty, 1976, pp. 102–16.
44. Money-Kyrle, p. 205.
45. DBP, Bk VI, Chap. 4, vv. 1–17.
46. MatP., Chap. 146, vv. 27–37; DBP, Bk III, Chap. 15, vv. 2–29 and Bk IV, Chap. IV, v. 49.
47. Rg.Ved., Bk VIII, Hymn 7, v. 23.
48. Ibid., Bk III, Hymn 55, v. 19.
49. Ibid., Bk VII, Hymn 20, v. 5.
50. Ibid., Hymn 48, v. 4.
51. Ibid., Bk IV, Hymn XVIII, v. 21; translation and notes, O'Flaherty 1981, p. 143.
52. O'Flaherty, 1981, pp. 141–6.
53. VamP., Chap. 20, vv. 26, 27.
54. Rg Ved., Bk IV, Chap. 18, v. 11.
55. Ibid., vv. 1–2, translation and notes, O'Flaherty, 1981, p. 142.
56. SB, Bk V, Chap. 5, Sec. 4, vv. 10, 18.
57. DBP, Bk VI, Chap. 1, vv. 1–12.
58. Rg Ved., Bk IV, Hymn 58, vv. 2, 3.
59. Smith and Doniger (quoting Harivamsa 118.11–39) p. 212.
60. VarP., Chap. 94, vv. 3, 4.
61. DBP, Bk V, Chap. 6, vv. 1–8.
62. Ibid., Chap. 7.
63. B.Can., 42: 2.
64. BP, 4, LM, Chap. 21, vv. 70–2.
65. DBP, Bk V, Chap. 7, vv. 12–22.
66. DM, Chap. 2, v. 3.
67. DBP, BK V, Chap. 7, vv. 4–11
68. Ibid., Bk VII, Chap. 28, vv. 4–45

CHAPTER FOUR The Demon/Deity Spectrum

1. Russell and Lal, Vol. I, pp. 90–2.
2. Arya, p. 144.
3. Hubert and Mauss, p. 62.
4. Conversation with Shiv Bhosale, regarding Savantwadi.
5. Sontheimer, 1976, 1989 edition, pp. 180–4.
6. Ibid., p. 180, fn. p. 76.
7. Ibid., p. 185.
8. Murty and Sontheimer, p. 61.
9. Information supplied by Prof. Doke, Tuljapur College.

10. Ibid.
11. Kosambi, pp. 28, 90.
12. Sontheimer, 1976, 1989 edition.
13. Thanks to R.B. Jamdade for his help. I also consulted Gunther Sontheimer and Suresh Vasant about the location of the Tukai temple.
14. Buchanan, in Pinkerton, Vol. VIII, p. 716.
15. Mukherjea, p. 282.
16. Conversations with U.S. Ramanna, Curator, Folklore Museum, with George Michell, and Manu Shetty; Nima Poovaya-Smith, pp. 113–28.
17. DBP, Bk IX, Chap. 50, vv. 46–100.
18. DM, Chap. 2, vv. 10–13.
19. VarP., Chap. 90, v. 19.
20. DBP, Bk V. Chap. 8, v. 31.
21. KalP., Sec. 4, Chap. 62, v. 54. In fact, at times her name is fire, as at her temple at Uttanhali, Mysore Taluk, where she is Jawala (fire, flame) Tripura Sundari.
22. Ibid., 56.
23. VarP., Chap. 28, vv. 24–5.
24. DBP, Bk IV, Chap. 23, v. 4.
25. Obeyeskere, p. 18.
26. DBP, Bk VII, Chap. 32, v. 2.
27. Ibid., v. 10.
28. Ibid., Bk I, Chap. 5, vv. 51–4; Chap. 7, vv. 27–32.
29. Ibid., vv. 32–51; Bk V, Chap. 10, vv. 1–16; Bk VI, Chap. 14, vv. 7–30.
30. Ibid., Bk I, Chap. 7, vv. 32–51.
31. Ibid., Chap. 8, vv. 31–5.
32. Ibid., Bk VI, Chap. 11, vv. 57–65.
33. Ibid., Bk VIII, Chap. 24, vv. 43–69.
34. Ibid., Bk VII, Chap. 28, vv. 4–15.
35. Ibid., Bk V, Chap. 16, vv. 40–1.
36. Ibid., Bk III, Chap. 12, vv. 83–4.
37. Ibid., Bk V, Chap. 10, v. 2.
38. In the folk tales, a demoness often changes shape. She becomes an ogress, queen or goddess, beautiful but capable of cannibalism or murderous duplicity. Similarly, goddesses take form as kings, kings marry goddesses, queens are warriors and other combinations take place all the time.
39. O'Flaherty, 1980, p. 53.
40. DBP, Bk V, Chap, 26, vv. 31–61.
41. Ibid., v. 17.
42. Ibid., Bk VII, Chap. 33, vv. 21–41.
43. Ibid., vv. 54–6.
44. Jung, reprint 1982, p. 145.
45. Swami Virajananda, p. 110.
46. Rolland, p. 31.
47. Ramakrishna in ibid., p. 33.
48. Quoted in Preston, p. 53.
49. DBP, Bk V, Chap. 9, vv. 23–9.
50. Ibid., Bk III, Chap. 3, vv. 36–7.
51. Ibid., Chap. 4, v. 33.

52. Ibid., Bk I, Chap. 7, vv. 1–26.
53. Ibid., Bk III, Chap. 5, v. 51.
54. Ibid., Chap. 6, v. 2.
55. Ibid., Bk I, Chap. 7, v. 48.
56. Ibid., Chap. 2, vv. 6–10.
57. Ibid., Bk III, Chap. 3, vv. 35–67.
58. Ibid., Chap. 5, vv. 28–31.
59. DM, Chap. I, v. 88.
60. DBP, Bk I, Chap. 4, v. 48
61. Ibid., Bk III, Chap. 4, vv. 1–20.
62. Ibid., Chap. 5, v. 13.
63. Ibid., v. 31.
64. Ibid., v. 39.
65. Ibid., Bk IV, Chap. 20, v. 11.
66. Ibid., vv. 15–16.
67. Ibid., Bk III, Chap. 5, v. 4.
68. Ibid., Chap. 4, v. 9.
69. Ramakrishna, quoted in Rolland, p. 33.
70. Publisher's preface, Sri Sarada Devi, pp. xiii–iv.

CHAPTER FIVE THE MAHISA/DEVI ENCOUNTERS

1. DBP, Bk V, Chap. 9, vv. 32–48 and Chap. 12, vv. 14–30.
2. Ibid.
3. O'Flaherty, 1980, p. 129.
4. Eliade, 1958, pp. 17–18.
5. VamP., Chap. 20, vv. 3–10.
6. VarP., Chap. 92, vv. 32, 33.
7. DBP, Bk V, Chap. 11, vv. 17–30.
8. Ibid.
9. Ibid.
10. 'It is commonly believed that forty drops of butter produce one drop of blood and forty drops of blood produce one drop of semen, hence the loss of semen leads to physical and mental weakness'. Gurmeet Singh, April 1985, pp. 119–122.
11. DBP, Chap. 14, vv. 5–23.
12. Ibid., Bk V, Chap. 9, vv. 49–54.
13. Ibid., Chap. 11, vv. 31–44.
14. Ibid., Chap. 16, vv. 24, 38.
15. Ibid., Chap. 11, vv. 11–16.
16. Ibid., v. 30.
17. Ibid., Chap. 12, vv. 14–30.
18. Ibid., Chap. 11, vv. 31–44.
19. Ibid., Chap. 12, vv. 29–30.
20. Ibid., v. 40.
21. Ibid., Bk V, Chap. 12, vv. 14–30.
22. Ibid., Chap. 31, vv. 34–6.
23. Ibid., Bk I, Chap. 10, vv. 3–37.

24. Ibid.
25. Ibid., Chap. 9, v. 61.
26. *VarP.*, Chap. 92, vv. 1–13.
27. *KalP.*, Section 3, Chap. 60, vv. 54–7.
28. DBP, Bk V, Chap. 10, vv. 1–16.
29. *VamP.*, Chap. 20, v. 23.
30. Ibid., v. 34.
31. DBP, Bk V, Chap. 23, vv. 51–66.
32. Ibid., Chap. 28, vv. 1–5.
33. Campbell, 1973, p. 344.
34. DBP, Bk V, Chap. 10, vv. 29–45.
35. *SkP.*, in O'Flaherty, 1975, p. 247.
36. DBP, Bk V, Chap. 12, vv. 2–13.
37. Ibid., Chap. 10, vv. 53–66.
38. Ibid., Chap. 13, vv. 7–13.
39. *VarP.*, Chap. 28, v. 36.
40. DBP, Bk V, Chap. 12, vv. 12–13.
41. Ibid., Chap. 16, vv. 35–45.
42. Ibid., Chap. 12, vv. 2–13.
43. *B.Can.*, 47:2.
44. DBP, Bk V, Chap. 12, vv. 2–13.
45. Ibid., Chap. 10, vv. 1–16.
46. Ibid.
47. Ibid., Chap. 14, vv. 24–30.
48. Ibid., Chap. 5, vv. 53–66.
49. Leach, Vol. I, p. 168.
50. Samuels, 1985, p. 151.
51. Freud, p. 242.
52. DBP, Bk V, Chap. 16, vv. 35–45.
53. Ibid., Chap. 9, vv. 56–8.
54. Ibid., Chap. 11, vv. 45–51.
55. Shulman, 1985, p. 39.
56. M. S. A. Rao, pp. 66–7.
57. Ghosha, p. 62; Preston, p. 64.
58. Hiltebeitel, 1976, pp. 156–62.
59. DM, Chap. 1, v. 74.
60. Coburn, 1984, p. 125, fn.
61. Agrawala, p. 69.
62. *B.Can.*, 24: 3, 4; Quackenbos, p. 290 fn.
63. Mani, p. 254.
64. DBP, Bk VII, Chap. 29, vv. 74–80.
65. *VarP.*, Chap 28, v. 24.
66. BP, 4, LM, Chap. 12, v. 68–9; Chap. 21, v. 65.
67. Ibid., Chap. 17, v. 3.
68. Ibid., Chap. 29, vv. 53b–55; Chap. 23, vv. 51–3.
69. DM, Chap. 5, v. 51.
70. *VarP.*, Chap. 95, v. 48.
71. *B.Can.*, 26.

72. BP, 4, LM, Chap. 15.
73. DBP, Bk V, Chap. 27, vv. 1–14.
74. B.Can., 14.
75. Hiltebeitel, 1988, p. 74, quoting van den Hoek, 1978.
76. B.Can, 58: 2.
77. Ibid., 20: 2 and 3, p. 286.
78. Ibid., 37: 4.
79. Ibid., 29: 3.
80. Ibid., 74: 3.
81. Ibid., 35: 3.
82. Ibid., 81: 1, 2.
83. Ibid., 14: 3.
84. Ibid., 76: 2.
85. Shulman, 1980, p. 182.
86. O'Flaherty, 1980, p. 85.
87. Shulman, 1980, p. 186.
88. Ibid., p. 183.
89. KalP., Sec. 4, Chap. 62, v. 154.
90. B.Can., 101: 1.
91. Biardeau, p. 130.
92. Beck, 1981, p. 112, 128; see Chap. VI.
93. Gopinath Rao, Vol. II, part 1, p. 60.
94. O'Flaherty, 1976, pp. 224–5.
95. B.Can., 10: 2.
96. DBP, Bk I, Chap. 8, v. 31.
97. SivP., Rudrasamhita, Sec. II, Chap. 26, v. 47.
98. KalP., Sec. 4, Chap. 62, v. 152.
99. O'Flaherty, 1975, pp. 168–73.
100. SivP., Rudrasamhita, Sec. V, Chap. 57, v. 66.
101. Marglin, 1985, pp. 214–15.
102. DBP, Bk V, Chap. 26, vv. 20–2.
103. Ibid., Chap. 16, vv. 1–7.
104. SkP., in O'Flaherty, 1975, p. 246.
105. DBP, Bk V, Chap. 16, vv. 8–38.
106. Ibid.
107. Ibid., vv. 35–45.
108. Ibid.

CHAPTER SIX The Battle

1. Shulman, 1986, p. 124.
2. KalP., Sec. 4, Chap. 62, vv. 84–7.
3. Ibid., vv. 89–90.
4. SivP., Umasamhita, Chap. 46, vv. 54, 56.
5. B. Can., 24: 3.
6. DM, Chap. 2, vv. 59–50.
7. BP, 4, LM, Chap. 16, vv. 3–6.

8. Ibid., v. 31.
9. Ibid., Chap. 17, v. 24.
10. DM, Chap. 2, v. 63.
11. BP, 4, LM, Chap. 28, vv. 57-8.
12. Ibid., vv. 81-4.
13. *VamP.*, Chap. 21, vv. 34, 37.
14. Ibid., v. 17.
15. O'Flaherty, 1980, p. 92.
16. Shulman, 1986, p. 124.
17. Harman, pp. 47, 49.
18. DBP, Bk V, Chap. 11.
19. *B. Can.*, 72: 2.
20. Ibid., 102:4, fn, Jackson translation.
21. BP, 4, LM, Chap. 28, vv. 84, 97.
22. DBP, Bk V, Chap. 24, vv. 41-60.
23. Ibid., Chap. 11, vv. 53-66.
24. KS, Bk II, 7.
25. Ibid., 4.
26. DBP, Bk V, Chap. 18, vv. 26-51.
27. KS, Bk II, 5.
28. DM, Chap. 7, vv. 11, 13.
29. KS, Bk 11, 5.
30. BP, 4, LM, Chap. 20, vv. 2-5.
31. KS, Bk I, 3.
32. BP, 4, LM, Chap. 24, v. 52.
33. *VarP.*, Chap. 96, v. 29.
34. KS, Bk II, 7.
35. *B.Can.*, 82: 2.
36. KS, Bk II, 7.
37. DBP, Bk V, Chap. 18, vv. 6-51.
38. Ibid., Chap. 10, vv. 1-16.
39. Ibid., Bk VIII, Chap. 28, vv. 46-8.
40. KS, Bk II, 4.
41. BP, 4, LM, Chap. 28. vv. 96-7.
42. KS, Bk II, 8.
43. DBP, Bk V, Chap. 11, v. 32.
44. KS, Bk II, 8.
45. DBP, Bk V, Chap. 24, vv. 42-60.
46. *VamP.*, Chap. 20, v. 43.
47. KS, Bk I, 2.
48. BP, 4, LM, Chap. 24, v. 36.
49. *B. Can.*, 53: 1.
50. DM, Chap. 4, v. 13.
51. BP, 4, LM, Chap. 24, vv. 2, 3.
52. *VamP.* Chap. 21, vv. 1, 3.
53. *KalP.*, Sec. 4, Chap. 62, vv. 43-8.
54. DBP, Bk VI, Chap. 17, vv. 49-56 and Chaps. 18, 19.
55. DM, Chap. 8, v. 27.

56. *VamP.*, Chap. 21, vv. 18–20.
57. DM, Chap. 8, vv. 20, 37.
58. Ibid., vv. 19, 36.
59. DBP, Bk V, Chap. 25, v. 6.

CHAPTER SEVEN THE BATTLE AS SACRIFICE: MAHISA AS VICTIM

1. Levi-Strauss, p. 3.
2. Both myth and ritual seem to contradict objections to this point of view. For instance, Oscar Mandel denies that the unconscious really recognizes and thrills to the rehearsal of basic life patterns, and asserts, in regard to tragedy, that 'The origin of an object is not the same thing as its substance. In Hamlet, the Vegetation God is not only transcended but like a snake's skin, moulted, abandoned and forgotten' (Mandel, 1961, pp. 18–19). But this certainly cannot be applied to our myth because its roots are perceptibly and inseparably intertwined with all the branches. It is very old, and gnarled, but very hardy, and defies all efforts to rupture the present from the past.
3. DBP, Bk V, Chap. 11, vv. 53–66.
4. BP, 4, LM, Chap. 28, vv. 45–7.
5. DM, Chap. 7, 23–4.
6. *B.Can.*, 41: 1.
7. Ibid., 96: 1.
8. DBP, Bk V, Chap. 26, vv. 59–61.
9. Ibid., vv. 62–4.
10. *B.Can.*, 43: 1.
11. With reference to the Greek Hippolytus, Farnell remarks: 'Hippolytus was originally a sacred horse, a divinity of the zoolatric or theometric age which preceded anthropomorphism, who, in an annual ritual, was torn to pieces and sacramentally devoured by his devotees, themselves called horses, as being thus assimilated to god; immediately the sacred animal rises again in a new incarnation. Gradually the animal deity becomes humanized' (Farnell, p. 67).
12. Money-Kyrle, p. 205.
13. Hiltebeitel, 1988, Vol. 1, p. 176.
14. SB, Bk I, Chap. 2, Sec. 3, vv. 6, 7.
15. *Rg Ved.*, Bk I, Hymn 24, vv. 13–15.
16. Mitra, reprint, 1969, Vol. II, pp. 71–2; Wilson, pp. 96, 107; DBP, Bk VI, Chap. 12, v. 37, and Chap. 13; ibid., VII, Chaps. 14, 15.
17. *Ramayana*, Balakanda, 35.
18. Katho, I, 1.
19. Ibid., 4.
20. Genesis, Chap. 22, v. 7.
21. See Shulman, 1990, 28: 3, p. 176.
22. Katho, II, 6.
23. Quoted in Mitra, Vol. II, pp. 80–3, from *Taittiriya Brahmana*; see also SB, Bk XIII, 6.2.20.
24. Mitra, Vol. II, pp. 80.
25. BP, 4, LM, Chap. 12, vv. 65–6.

26. *KalP.*, The Rudhiradhyaya, XXIII, v. 9; Blaquière, p. 372.
27. Bose, pp. 67–8. A painting on a mandapa column of the 16th-century Lepaksi temple, Karnataka, depicts the story, with Siva in the role of the holy man. See also Shulman, 1993.
28. von Furer-Haimendorf, 1979, p. 237.
29. James, 1933, p. 34; Frazer, reprint, 1972, pp. 319, 323.
30. In Pinkerton, Vol. VII, p. 216, vv. 541–5.
31. Campbell, R. H., pp. 16–17; Macpherson, pp. 216–74; Satyanarayana, pp. 57, 85–7; Dalton, pp. 285–8; Hopkins, p. 529; for further descriptions see Galt, E., 1898 and 1967.
32. Dalton, p. 115.
33. Mills, pp. 15–16.
34. Hopkins, pp. 527, 535.
35. Satyanarayana, pp. 57, 42.
36. von Furer-Haimendorf, 1945, pp. 206–11.
37. Barua, p. 94.
38. Conversation with Dr Paramashivaya, Mysore University.
39. Kosambi, p. 122; Shrisagar, 1988.
40. *Indian Express*, 14 Nov. 1986.
41. Ibid., 8 Jan. 1986.
42. *KalP.*, Sec. 4, Chap. 61, vv. 16–17.
43. Bhattacharya, 1973, pp. 33–5.
44. Ibid., Drury; O'Flaherty, 1979 and 1980, pp. 149–64; SB, Bk XIII, Chap. 5, Sec. 2, v. 2.
45. *Rg Ved.*, Bk V, Hymn XXIX, vv. 7–8.
46. SB, Bk VI, Chap. 5, Sec. 3, v. 1.
47. Ibid., Bk XIII, Chap. 5, Sec. 2, v. 2.
48. C. Hayavadana Rao, 1921, p. 148.
49. Whitehead, 1916, p. 67.
50. Emeneau, 1971, IV, 34, v. 24, p. 124.
51. Ibid., 118, vv. 7, 13, 15, 20, pp. 397–8.
52. Mills, p. 194; Rivers, pp. 276, 280; Russell, Vol. IV, p. 152.
53. Mills, p. 193.
54. Shaw, p. 44.
55. Whitehead, 1916, p. 47.
56. Mills, pp. 161, 185, 193.
57. *ERE*, Vol. I, p. 505.
58. Dalton, pp. 285–8.
59. Elwin, 1955, p. 89.
60. Shaw, p. 44.
61. Chakrabarty, pp. 99–111.
62. *The Maharashtra Times*, 19 Apr. 1993.
63. Rose, pp. 26–7.
64. Kumar, p. 42.
65. Nepali, pp. 102–51.
66. Rank, 1914, reprint, 1964, p. 94.
67. Freud, in Rieff, p. 155.
68. Vakpati, xxii.

69. *B. Can.*, 51: 1.
70. Bhattacharya, 1974, p. 34.
71. Shulman, 1980, p. 186.
72. DM, Chap. 2, v. 51.
73. Shulman, 1980, p. 179.
74. Reglin, 1936, reprint, 1955, p. 263; see also Kerenyi, 1959.
75. *KalP.*, Sec. 1, Chap. 57, v. 14.
76. Ibid., vv. 19–20.
77. See Whitehead, 1916.
78. Rose, 1986, p. 189.
79. Eliade, 1982, Vol. I, p. 8.
80. Gimbutas, 1974, p. 176.
81. The judgement by Agni that suicide is a sin is borne out neither by Brahmanical prescriptions nor by his own propensity to receive all oblations of human flesh performed by Brahmanas.
82. *VamP.*, Chap. 20, v. 22.
83. DM, Chap. 3, v. 42.
84. Nagaswamy, p. 7.
85. Personal communication, K. V. Soundara Rajan.
86. Ilango-Adigal, Canto 12, vv. 20–50
87. Ibid., Canto 5, v. 78.
88. Vakpati, xxii.
89. Nagaswamy, 1982. For further examples, the reader is referred to Nagaswamy's careful study and to Shulman 1985, pp. 278; 1986, pp. 123 ff.
90. BP, 4, LM, Chap. 22, vv. 43–4.
91. DM, Chap. 2, v. 63.
92. Hiltebeitel, 1988, p. 381.
93. DBP, Bk. VII, Chap. 30, vv. 26–37.
94. Ibid., Bk. I, Chap. 5, vv. 62–8.
95. Ibid., vv. 83–105.
96. Shrisagar (in Marathi).
97. Mills, 1937, p. 161.
98. Elwin, 1955, pp. 384–5.
99. *Indian Express*, 7 April 1987.
100. Campbell, R.H., p. 13.
101. *Mid-Day*, 26 Oct. 1987.
102. BP, 4, LM, Chap. 23, vv. 24–8.
103. DM, Chap. 8, v. 61.
104. *VamP.*, Chap. 29, v. 80.
105. DM, Chap. 7, vv. 53–4; see also DBP, Bk. V, Chap. XXIX, vv. 22–8.
106. DBP, Bk. IX, Chap. 22, vv. 1–75.
107. BP, 4, LM, Chap. 20, vv. 66–7.
108. Ibid., Chap. 22, vv. 79–83.
109. Ibid., Chap. 25, vv. 106–7.
110. Ibid., Chap. 29, vv. 12–13.
111. See O'Flaherty, 1980, pp. 40–3.
112. *B.Can.*, 40, vv. 3, 3.
113. Ibid.; Quackenbos, footnote, p. 305.

114. DBP, Bk. VII, Chap. 33, vv. 21–41.
115. Ibid., Bk. V, Chap. 35, vv. 13–31.
116. *KalP.*, Section I, Chap. 57, vv. 3–6.
117. *Indian Express*, 13 Dec. 1988.
118. *Rg Ved.*, Bk. I, Hymn 162, v. 21.
119. DBP, Bk. III, Chap. 26, vv. 33–4.
120. 'Then the men present come to the buffalo and salute it by bowing down and placing their foreheads on the horns and on the head between the horns.

   The people then group themselves around the buffalo and corpse and cry together, by placing forehead to forehead so that their tears and cries mingle...at a funeral at which the buffalo killed was called Punder, one man would cry, 'O Punder—O, my father' (Rivers, pp. 349–58).
121. SB, 74, 5 ff.
122. Ghurye, p. 240.
123. DBP, Bk. V, Chap. 5, vv. 21–35.
124. Ibid., Chap. 13, vv. 14–25.
125. DM, Chap. 2, v. 54.
126. Ibid., v. 55.
127. DBP, Bk. V, Chap. 26, vv. 62–4.
128. *SivP.*, Umasamhita, Chap. 46, v. 61.
129. DM, Chap. 2, v. 59.
130. DBP, Bk. V, Chap. 17, vv. 52–3.
131. *SivP.*, Umasamhita, Chap. 46, v. 41.
132. DBP, Bk. IX, Chap. 22, vv. 1–75.
133. Ibid., Chap. 28, vv. 55–63.
134. *SivP.*, Umasamhita, Chap. 46, vv. 54, 56.
135. DM, Chap. 2, v. 55.
136. Ibid., v. 34.
137. *KalP.*, Section 4, Chap. 62, v. 107.
138. *VarP.*, Chap. 23, v. 56.
139. DM, Chap. 4, v. 18.
140. DBP, Bk. V, Chap. 19, pp. 2–33.
141. Ibid., vv. 1–33.
142. *KalP.*, Section 4, Chap. 62, vv. 85–6.
143. DBP, Bk. V, Chap. 10, vv. 29–45.
144. Ibid.
145. *KalP.*, Section 4, Chap. 62, vv. 104–5.
146. Ibid., v. 154.
147. Ibid., vv. 107–8.
148. DBP, Bk. V, Chap. 20, vv. 16–50.
149. Ramakrishna quoted in Rolland, 1929, p. 54.
150. Ibid., p. 55.

CHAPTER EIGHT Festival: Myth/Rite Equations

1. Shulman, 1980, p. 317.
2. Kramer, 1969, p. 49.

3. Murray, p. 210.
4. Oppert, p. 465.
5. Thurston, Vol. IV, pp. 416–17.
6. Morab, in Jha, p. 29.
7. Ostor, p. 8.
8. Dalmia, p. 79.
9. Sontheimer, 1976, 1989 edition, Appendix: 'Srinath Maskobha Devacem Charita', pp. 225–30.
10. Richards, p. 117.
11. Obeyesekere, pp. 384–422.
12. Jain Chakresh, Eve's Weekly, Sept. 1989.
13. Whitehead, 1911, pp. 39–42.
14. Beck, 1979, pp. 112, 128.
15. Rao, C.H., Vol. XII, Q.J.M.S., p. 475.
16. Enthoven, pp. 298–9.
17. Ayyar, reprint, 1982, p. 59.
18. Harman, 1989; see also Shulman, 1980; Gatwood.
19. See Whitehead, Shulman, Beck, Ramanujan, Harman, etc.
20. Sundara, A., Department of Archaeology and Museums, Mysore, Karnataka.
21. Mythic Society, Bangalore.
22. Interviews with Sujutha Bijai, Manu Shetty and U.S. Ramanna.
23. Oppert, p. 189, fn, quoting Aurangabad Gazetteer.
24. Personal communication from Davindra Lokhande.
25. Dr A. Jamkedkar kindly informed me about the Mhasoba festival at Nasik.
26. Ghosha, p. 1.
27. KalP., Sec. 4, Chap. 62, v. 6.
28. Quoted in Ghosha, p. 17.
29. DBP, Bk VII, Chap. 37, vv. 11–20.
30. Saletore, Vol. II, pp. 372–86.
31. Brown, p. 167.
32. Brown, Northey and Morris, pp. 75–8; Farwell and conversations with Kirin Manandhar.
33. Preston, Chap. 4.
34. Sircar, p. 50, fn 6.
35. Ghosha, p. 61.
36. Ibid., p. 62.
37. KalP., Sec. 4, Chap. 63, vv. 28–9.
38. Umadikar, p. 23.
39. Amravati District Gazetteer, p. 165.
40. See Ostor, pp. 24–8, 82.
41. Ibid., pp. 24, 35–6.
42. For discussions about Potraj, see Oppert, Whitehead, Shulman, Biardeau, Hiltebeitel, etc.
43. KalP., Sec. 4, Chap. 63, vv. 19–22.
44. Ibid., Sec. 3, Chap. 60, v. 56.
45. Fuller and Logan, p. 90.
46. Harman, p. 75.
47. Ostor, p. 38.

48. *Prayag*, pp. 22–4. This local guidebook should not be confused with the original Tuljapur *Mahatmya*; German translation by Roland Janson.
49. Ostor, p. 64.
50. *KalP.*, Sec. 4, Chap. 62, v. 7.
51. Quoted in Preston, p. 77.
52. Ghosha, p. 81.
53. Ostor, p. 6.

CHAPTER NINE The Life Stages of the Hero: Depictions in Stone

1. See Berkson, 1987.
2. *KalP.*, Sec. 4, Chap. 61, vv. 16–18.

APPENDICES

1. Warner, p. 101.
2. Langdon, p. 97.
3. Wolkstein and Kramer, p. 92.
4. Ibid., p. 86.
5. Ibid., p. 34.
6. Ibid.
7. Kramer, 1969, p. 69.
8. Ibid., p. 54.
9. Wolkstein and Kramer, p. 30.
10. Langdon, p. 349.
11. Quoted in Horne, pp. 190–2.
12. Quoted in Langdon, p. 236.
13. Ibid., p. 115.
14. EG in Sanders, p. 69.
15. Langdon, p. 236.
16. EG in Sanders, p. 19.
17. Ibid., p. 21.
18. Rank, 1914, pp. 26–7; Langdon, p. 234.
19. Muller, W.M., pp. 37–8.
20. Herodotus, Bk II, v. 41.
21. Ibid., Bk II, v. 41.
22. Budge, Vol. II, p. 212.
23. Muller, p. 116.
24. *Rg Ved.*, Bk VII, Hymn 20, v. 5.
25. Ibid., Bk IV, Hymn 18, v. 2, 4, 5, 10.
26. Hesiod, vv. 927–8.
27. Homer, *Iliad*, Bk XVIII.
28. Hesiod, vv. 467; 487–9.
29. Hamilton, pp. 76–8.
30. Kerenyi, 1959, p. 25.
31. Ibid., 1976, p. 274.

32. Frazer, p. 450.
33. Otto, p. 162.
34. Ibid., p. 166.
35. Hamilton, pp. 279–81; Kerenyi, 1976, pp. 106, 111.
36. Graves, I, 50d.
37. Kramer, 1969, p. 57.
38. Ibid., pp. 56; 79–3.
39. Wolkstein and Kramer, p. 34.
40. Ibid., p. 93.
41. Kramer, 1969, p. 77.
42. Ibid., pp. 62, 63, 77–81.
43. Ibid., p. 64.
44. Ibid., pp. 65–6.
45. Wolkstein and Kramer, p. 71.
46. James, 1959, p. 48.
47. Herodotus, Bk I, section 181–2 (trs.) Grene.
48. See Marglin, 1985.
49. EG (6th tablet) in Sanders, p. 85.
50. Ibid., p. 86.
51. Erman, p. 139.
52. Ibid., p. 283.
53. Ibid., p. 258.
54. Budge, Vol. II, pp. 11, 34.
55. Ibid., pp. 258 and 347.
56. Ibid.
57. Ibid.
58. Elgood, p. 136.
59. Herodotus, Bk III, section 28.
60. Diodorus, quoted in Budge, Vol. II, p. 3.
61. Shorter, pp. 112–15.
62. Petrie, p. 31.
63. James, 1958, p. 120.
64. Erman, pp. 214–15.
65. James, 1958, p. 119.
66. Eliade, 1982, Vol. I, p. 98.
67. Frazer, p. 165.
68. Schaeffer, p. 60.
69. Patai, p. 56.
70. Driver, L. 37–46, p. 14.
71. Ibid., 23–36.
72. Ibid., Col. v. 11, 1–7, p. 17.
73. *Ras Sharma* text in Schaeffer, p. 70.
74. Frazer, p. 388.
75. Exodus, 19 vv. 16–21.
76. Kerenyi, 1976, Chap. 3.
77. Conrad, pp. 116–19; Eliade, Vol. I, p. 135; Graves, Vol. I, Section 88: 7, p. 297.
78. Kerenyi, 1976, pp. 122–3.
79. Graves, Vol. I, section 27 i.

80. Kerenyi, 1976, p. 310.
81. Homer, *Iliad*, Bk 18.
82. Hesiod, vv. 945–6.
83. Hamilton, p. 35; Graves, 18, b, c, d.
84. Ibid., 25b.
85. Ibid., 50: 8.
86. *New Testament*, Gospel of St. Matthew 1:18 f.
87. Quotations from Enuma Elish are in Horne, pp. 151–69, EE 1st tablet, 4, 26.
88. Ibid., 117.
89. Ibid., 3rd tablet, 73–4.
90. Ibid., 4th tablet, 14.
91. Ibid., 31.
92. Ibid., 86–9; 94.
93. Ibid., 130.
94. Ibid., 118.
95. EG, sixth tablet.
96. Gudea B, inscription i, Col. viii, in Horne, p. 53.
97. EG, sixth tablet.
98. Wolkstein and Kramer, p. 71.
99. Warner, p. 92 and Frazer, reprint, 1961, Vol. II, p. 88.
100. Budge, p. 125.
101. Frazer, reprint, 1961, p. 88, fn.
102. Quoted in Schaeffer, p. 72.
103. Baal tablets, Col. ii L1 1–16, in Driver, p. 14.
104. Ibid., Col iv 1, 8, v. 16.
105. See O'Flaherty, 1980a, pp. 81–4.
106. Euripides, *The Bacchae*, vv. 1159–60.
107. Ibid., vv. 779–80.
108. Ibid., vv. 796–7.
109. Ibid., v. 1126.
110. Graves, Vol. I, 18b, c, d.
111. Homer, *Iliad*, Bk 18.
112. Graves, Vol. I, 12c.
113. *New Testament*, Gospel of St. Matthew, 13: 48.
114. Ibid., John 3: 6.
115. Wolkstein and Kramer, pp. 71, 86, 87.
116. Ibid., p. 89.
117. Frazer, reprint, 1972, p. 328.
118. James, 1933, p. 109.
119. Quoted in Frazer, reprint, 1972, p. 379.
120. Budge, Vol. II, p. 140.
121. Mhb., Bk V, Chap. 49a, section 9, v. 24.
122. Ibid., v. 46.
123. Ibid., section 10, v. 43.
124. Ibid., section 13, v. 21.
125. Ibid., section 14, v. 10.
126. Ibid., section 16. v. 19.
127. Ibid., section 18, vv. 19–20.

128. DBP, Bk V, Chap. 7, vv. 12–22.
129. Ugaritic Baal tablets, 49, II, 11, in Gordon, p. 9.
130. Ibid., 5, I, Col. vii, 1–17, in Driver, p. 17.
131. Schaeffer, p. 65.
132. Ugaritic Baal tablets, 67, VI, 5, in Gordon, p. 5.
133. Ibid., 49, II, p. 9.
134. Ibid., III, 2.
135. Frazer, reprint, 1972, p. 388.
136. Money-Kyrle, p. 119.
137. Kerenyi, 1976, pp. 262–72.
138. Hesiod, vv. 208–10.
139. Graves, Vol. I, 27a.
140. Ovid, Bk IV, 32–3.
141. Graves, Vol. I, 27k.
142. Ibid., 14. 4.
143. Kerenyi, 1976, p. 70.
144. Ibid., pp. 70–1.
145. O'Flaherty, 1980 (a), pp. 81–4.
146. Burkert, p. 61.
147. Graves, Vol. I, 21n; 101 k; Burkert, p. 201; Euripides, *Alcestis.*
148. Graves, Vol. I, 50g.
149. Burkert, pp. 267–8.
150. Graves, Vol. I, 50: 2.
151. Ovid, Bk XV.
152. *New Testament*, Gospel of St Luke, 22: 7.
153. Ibid., 13: 10.
154. Ibid., 14: 28.
155. Ibid., 19: 28.

Bibliography

PART I   PRIMARY SOURCES

Sanskrit

Brahmanda Purana, Section 4, *Lalita Mahatmya: Ancient Indian Tradition and Mythology Series*, trans. Ganesh Vasudeo Tagore, New Delhi, 1984.

Candisataka: The Sanskrit Poems of Mayura, Including Bana's Candisataka, introduction and trans. George Payn Quackenbos, New York, 1917.

Devi Mahatmyam: Markandeya Purana, trans. F. Eden Pargiter, Varanasi, 1969, trans. Swami Jagadisvarananda, Sri Ramakrishna Math, Madras.

Griha Sutra: Sacred Books of the East, Vols. 29, 30, ed. Max Mueller, trans. Herman Oldenberg; reprint, New Delhi, 1967.

Institutes of Vishnu: Sacred Books of the East, Vol. VII, ed. Max Mueller, trans. Julius Jolly.

Kalika Purana: Worship of the Goddess According to the Kalika Purana, Part I, introduction and trans. Kerel Rijk Van Kooij, Leiden, 1972.

'The *Rudhiradhyaya*, The Blood Chapter of the *Kalika Purana*', *Asiatic Researches*, Vol. V, trans. W. C. Blaquiere, 1797; reprint 1901.

Khandogya Upanisad: Sacred Books of the East, Vol. I, ed. and trans. Max Mueller.

Swami Chinmayananda, *Discourses on the Kathopanishad*, Madras, 1963.

Matsya Purana, trans. a *taluqdar* of Oudh, New Delhi, 1980.

Rig Veda: An Anthology, trans. Wendy Doniger O'Flaherty, Middlesex, 1981.

The Hymn of the Rg Veda, trans. R. T. Griffith, New Delhi, 1986.

Sacred Laws of the Aryas: Sacred Books of the East, Vols. 2, 14, ed. Max Mueller, trans. George Buhler.

Satapatha Brahmana: Sacred Books of the East, five vols., ed. Max Mueller, trans. Julius Eggling.

Siva Purana: Ancient Indian Tradition and Mythology Series, four vols., trans. A board of scholars, reprint, New Delhi 1987.

Srimad Devi Bhagavatam Purana, trans. Swami Vijnanananda, New Delhi, 1986.

Taittiriya Sanhita, trans. A. B. Keith, Cambridge, Mass., 1967.

Vamana Purana, ed. Anand Swarup Gupta, trans. S.M. Mukhopadhyaya, A. Bhattacharya, N. C. Nath and V. K. Verma, C. Varabasum.

Varaha Purana: Ancient Indian Tradition and Mythology Series, Vol. 31, trans. S. Venkitasubramania Iyer, New Delhi, 1985.

Others

Epic of Gilgamesh N. K. Sanders, reprint, Middlesex, 1976 and 1987.

Euripides, *The Bacchae.*

Herodotus, *The History*, introduction and trans. David Grene, 1987.

Hesiod, *Theogeny*, introduction and notes, and trans. Apostolos N. Athanassakis, Baltimore, 1983; reprint 1989.

Homer, *The Iliad.*

The Old Testament.

The New Testament.

Ovid, *The Metamorphoses*, introduction and trans. Horace Gregory, New York, 1958.

PART II   SECONDARY SOURCES

Agarwala, V.S.   1963   *Devi-Mahatmya*: 'The Glorification of the Great Goddess', *All India Kashiraj Trust*, Varanasi

Appuswami, P.N.   1977   *Muttollayiram*, author unknown, Calcutta
(trans.)

Arya, S.P.   1975   *A Sociological Study of Folklore, Kuru Region*, Calcutta

Ayyar, P.V. Jagdisa   1920   *South Indian Festivities*, reprint, New Delhi, 1982

Banabhatta   1896   *The Kadambara of Bana*, trans. C. M. Ridding, London, reprint, 1974

————   1917   *The Sanskrit Poems of Mayura Including Bana's Candisataka*, introduction and trans. George Payn Quackenbos, New York

Banerjea, J. N.   1954   'Some Aspects of Sakti Worship in Ancient India', *Prabuddha Bharata*, 59; March

————   1941   *The Development of Hindu Iconography*, reprint, New Delhi, 1974

Barua, K. L.   1984   'Human Sacrifice in Assam', in *Readings in History and Culture of Assam*, Guwahati

Beck, Brenda   1979   'The Goddess and the Demon: A Local South Indian Festival and its Wider Context', University of British Columbia

————   1986   'Social Dyads in Indic Folktales', in *Another Harmony, New Essays on the Folklore of India*, ed. Stuart Blackburn and A. K. Ramanujan, Bombay

Berkson, Carmel   1978   'Some New Finds at Ramgarth Hill', *Artibus Asiae.*

————   1987   *The Amazon and the Goddess*, Bombay

Bharati Agehnanda   1965   *The Tantric Tradition*, London

Bhattacharyya, N. N.   1973   *History of the Sakta Religion*, New Delhi

————————   1975   *Ancient Rituals and Their Social Contents*, New Delhi

————————   1977   *The Indian Mother Goddess*, New Delhi

————————   1981   *History of the Tantrik Religion*, New Delhi

Biardeau, Madeleine   1981   'L'arbe sami et le buffle sacrificiel', in *Autour de la déesse Hindoue*, Paris

Bose, Tara   1986   *Folk Tales of Gujarat*, New Delhi

Brown, Percy   1912   *Picturesque Nepal*, London

Brubaker, Richard L.   1978   'The Ambivalent Mistress: A Study of South Indian Village Goddesses and the Religious Meaning,' Ph.D. dissertation, University of Chicago

Buchanan, Francis   1808   'A Journey From Madras through the Countries of Mysore, Canara and Malabar', in Pinkerton, John, *General Collection of the Best and Most Interesting Voyages and Travels in All Parts of the World*, London

Budge, E. A. Wallis   1904   *The Gods of the Egyptians*, 2 vols., reprint, New York, 1969

Bushby, Henry   1855   *Widow Burning*, London

Campbell, John   1864   *Wild Tribes of Khondistan*, London

Campbell, Joseph   1959   *The Masks of God: Primitive Mythology*, London

————————   1965   *The Masks of God: Occidental Mythology*, London

————————   1973   *The Hero with a Thousand Faces*, Princeton

Campbell, R. H.   1917   'The Wild Tribes of Vizagapatnam Hill', *Quarterly Journal of the Mythic Society*, Vol. VIII, Oct.

Chakrabarty, Falguni   1987   'Agricultural Rituals of the Santals of Ayodhya Hill', *Man in India*, Pune

Chakravarti, P. C.   1940   *Doctrine of Sakti in Indian Literature*, Calcutta

Chandra, Moti   1973   *Studies in the Cult of the Mother Goddess*, Bombay

Coburn, Thomas B.   1982   'Consort of None, Sakti of All: The Vision of the Devi-Mahatmya', in *The Divine Consort: Radha and the Goddesses of India*, ed. John Stratton Hawley and Donna Marie Wulff, Berkeley

————————   1984   *Devi Mahatmya: The Crystallization of the Goddess Tradition*, New Delhi

Colebrooke, H. T.   1808   'Description of a Species of Ox Named Gayal', in *Asiatic Researches*, Vol. VIII, London

Conard, Jack Randolph   1959   *The Horn and the Sword*, London

Crooke, William   1896   *Tribes and Castes of the Northwestern Provinces and Oudh*, Calcutta

Dalmia, Yashodhara | 1988 | *The Painted World of the Warlis,* New Delhi

Dalton, E. T. | 1872 | *Descriptive Enthnology of Bengal,* reprint, Calcutta, 1973

Datta, V. N. | 1988 | *Sati,* New Delhi

Dhal, Upendra Nath | 1991 | *Mahisasura in Art and Thought,* New Delhi

Divakaran, Odile | 1984 | 'Durga, the Great Goddess: Meanings and Forms in the Early Period', in *Discourses on Siva,* ed. Michael W. Meister, Philadelphia

Driver, G. R. | 1956 | *Canaanite Myths and Legends : Old Testament Studies,* Vol. 3, Edinburgh

Drury, Naama | 1981 | *The Sacrificial Ritual in the* Satapatha Brahmana, New Delhi

Dubois, Abbé | 1816 | *Hindu Manners and Customs,* reprint, Calcutta, 1905

Eisler, Robert | 1951 | *Man Into Wolf,* London

Elgood, P. G. | 1938 | *The Ptolemies of Egypt,* London

Eliade, Mircea | 1958 | *Patterns in Comparative Religion,* Vol. 1, London and New York

———— | 1982 | *A History of Religious Ideas,* Vol. I, Chicago

Elmore, Wilber T. | 1915 | *Dravidian Gods in Modern Hinduism: A Study of the Local and Village Deities of Southern India,* reprint Madras, 1925

Elwin, Verrier | 1949 | *Tribal Myths of Middle India,* Bombay

———— | 1955 | *The Religion of an Indian Tribe,* Bombay

Emeneau, M. B. | 1938 | 'Toda Culture 30 Years After', *Annals of the Bhandarkar Oriental Research Institute,* Vol. 19

———— | 1971 | *Toda Songs,* Oxford

Enthoven, R. E. | 1924 | *The Folklore of Bombay,* Oxford

Erman, Adolph | 1907 | *A Handbook of Egyptian Religion,* London

———— | 1927 | *The Literature of the Ancient Egyptians,* London

Farnell, Lewis | 1921 | *Greek Hero Cults and Ideas of Immoriality,* Oxford

Farwell, Byron | 1985 | *The Gurkhas,* Middlesex

Ferreira, John V. | 1965 | *Totemism in Inida,* Bombay

Frazer, James G. | 1922 | *The Golden Bough,* reprint, New York, 1972

———— | 1922 | *Adonis, Attis, Osiris* (part IV of the *Golden Bough*), Vol. II, reprint, New York, 1972

Fuchs, Stephen | 1973 | *The Aboriginal Tribes of India,* New Delhi, 1982

Freud, S. | 1916 | 'A Connection Between a Symbol and a Symptom', 'Psychoanalyses', in Rieff, Phillip (ed.), *Freud, Character and Culture,* New York, 1963

Fuller, C. J. and Logan, Penny | 1985 | 'The Navratri Festival in Madurai', *Bulletin of the School of Oriental and African Studies,* University of London, Vol. XLVIII, part 1

Gait, E. A.	1898	'Human Sacrifice in Ancient Assam', *Journal of the Royal Asiatic Society of Bengal*, LXVII, Part 2
———————	1911	'Human Sacrifice', *Encyclopedia of Religion and Ethics*, Vol. VI, reprint, London, 1967
Gatwood, Lynn, E.	1985	*Devi and the Spouse Goddess*, New Delhi
Ghosha, Pratapachandra	1871	*Durga Puja*, Calcutta
Ghurye, G. S.	1962	*Gods and Men*, Bombay
Gimbutas, Marija	1974	*The Gods and Goddesses of Old Europe*, London
Gordon, Cyrus H.	1943	*The Loves and Wars of Baal and Anat*, Princeton
Green, Roger L.	1967	*Tales of Ancient Egypt*, Middlesex
Hamilton, Edith	1940	*Mythology*, reprint, Boston, 1969
Harden, Donald	1962	*The Phoenecians*, London
Harman, William	1989	*The Sacred Marriage of a Hindu Goddess*, Indianapolis
Heesterman, J. C.	1957	*The Ancient Indian Royal Consecration*, The Hague
Hiltebeitel, Alf	1976	*The Ritual of Battle*, Ithaca
———————	1988	*The Cult of Draupadi*, Chicago
Hopkins, E. W.	1896	*The Religions of India*, London
———————	1915	*Epic Mythology*, Strasburg
Hubert, Henri and Mauss, Marcel	1964	*Sacrifice, Its Nature and Function*, Chicago
Ilango-Adigal, Prince	1965	*Sillapadikaram: The Anklet Bracelet*, trans. Alain Danielou, London
Israel, Samuel and Sinclair, Toby	1987	*Indian Wildlife, Sri Lanka and Nepal*, Singapore
Iyengar, Sampat	1914	'Bhuta Worship in the West Coast', *Quarterly Journal of the Mythic Society*, Vol. V, #2
Jain, Chakresh	1989	'Lesser Known Festivals of India', *Eve's Weekly*, 30 Sept., Bombay
James, E. O.	1933	*Origins of Sacrifice*, London
———————	1958	*Myth and Ritual in the Ancient Near East*, London
———————	1959	*The Cult of the Mother Goddess*, London
———————	1961	*Seasonal Feasts and Festivals*, London
———————	1962	*Sacrifice and Sacrament*, London
Jones, Ernest	1949	*Hamlet and Oedipus*, New York
Jung, C. G.	1959	'The Psychological Aspects of the Kore', extracted from *Collected Works*, Vol. 9, Princeton, in *Aspects of the Feminine*, Princeton, 1982
Jung, C. G. and Kerenyi, C.	1949	*Essays on a Science of Mythology*, Princeton, 1985

Kakar, Sudhir	1981	*The Inner World*, New Delhi
Kalidas, Raju	1989	'Iconography of Mahisasuramardini: A Probe into Stylistic Evolution', *Acta Orientalia*, Copenhagen, Vol. 50
Kaufman, Yeheskel	1960	*The Religion of Israel*, abridged edition, reprint, New York, 1972
Keith Arthur B.	1911	'Buffalo', *Encyclopedia of Religion and Ethics*, Vol. I, reprint, London, 1967.
————	1914	*Taittiriya Sanhita, Harvard Oriental Series*, two volumes, reprint, New Delhi, 1967
Kerenyi C.	1959	*The Heroes of the Greeks*, reprint, London, 1978
————	1967	*Eleusis*, reprint, New York, 1977
————	1976	*Dionysos*, London
Kipling, John L.	1891	*Beast and Man in India*, London
Kinsley, David	1987	*Hindu Goddesses*, New Delhi
Kirk, G. S.	1974	*The Nature of Greek Myths*, Middlesex
Kosambi, D. D.	1962	*Myth and Reality*, reprint London and Bombay, 1983
Kramer, Samuel Noah	1944	*Sumerian Mythology*, Philadelphia
————	1969	*The Sacred Marriage Rite: Aspects of Faith, Myth and Ritual in Ancient Sumer*, Bloomington
Kramrisch, Stella	1975	'The Indian Great Goddess', in *History of Religions*, 14, # 4, May
Kumar, Pramod	1984	*Folk Icons and Rituals in Tribal Life*, New Delhi
Kumar, Pushpendra	1974	*Sakti Cult in Ancient India*, Varanasi
Langdon, Stephen H.	1931	*The Mythology of All Races (Semitic)*, Vol. V, Boston
Layle, P. G.	1973	*Studies in the Devi Bhagavata*, Bombay
Leach, Maria, ed.	1944	*Standard Dictionary of Folklore, Mythology and Legend*, Vol. I, A-1, New York
Leeming, David	1976	*Mythology*, New York
Levi-Strauss, Claude	1963	*Totemism*, Boston
Lydekker, R.	1912	*The Ox and its Kindred*, London
Maccoby, Hyam	1982	*The Sacred Executioner*, London
Mackenzie Brown, C.	1992	*The Triumph of the Goddess*, New Delhi
Macpherson, S.	1851	'Religion of the Khonds', *Journal of the Royal Asiatic Society of Great Britain and Ireland*, Vol. XIII, part 2
Mahalingam, T.V.	1967	'The Cult of Sakti in Tamilnad' in D.C. Sircar, ed. *The Sakti Cult and Tara*, Calcutta
Government of Maharashtra	1911	*District Gazetteers*, Aurangabad, Amravati, reprint Bombay, 1969.
————	1961	*Fairs and Festivals of Maharashtra*

Mandel, Oscar	1961	*A Definition of Tragedy*, New York
Mani, Vettam	1964	*Puranic Encyclopedia*, reprint, New Delhi, 1974
Marglin, Frédérique Apffel	1985	*Wives of the God-King: The Rituals of the Devadasis of Puri*, New York
Marshall, William C.	1873	*A Phrenologist Among the Todas*, London
Mate, M. S.	1961	*Temples and Legends of Maharashtra*, Bombay
Mills, J. P.	1937	*The Rengma Nagas*, London
Mishra, Vijayakanta	1984	*Mahishasuramardini*, New Delhi
Mitra, Rajendralala	1881	*Indo-Aryans*, two volumes, reprint, New Delhi, 1969
Mitra, Saratchandra	1928	'A Note on the Travesty of an Ancient Indian Myth in a Modern Hindu Ceremony', *Quarterly Journal of the Mythic Society*, Vol. XXIX
Money-Kyrle, R.	1930	*The Meaning of Sacrifice*, London
Morab, S. G.		'Concept of Pilgrimage in Folk Tradition: The Case of the Chamundesvari Ritual Complex', *Dimensions of Pilgrimage: An Anthropological Appraisal*, ed. Makhan Jha, New Delhi
Mukherjea, Charulal	1962	*The Santals*, Calcutta
Muller, W. Max	1958	*The Mythology of All Races, (Egyptian)*, Vol. XII, Boston
Murphy, Dervla	1967	*The Waiting Land*, London
Murray, Gilbert	1935	*Five Stages of Greek Religion*, London
Murty, M.L.K. and Sontheimer, Gunther	1980	'Prehistoric Background to Pastoralism in Southern Deccan', *Anthropos* 75
Nagar, Shanti Lal	1988	*Mahishasuramardini in Indian Art*, New Delhi
Nagaswamy, R.	1982	*Tantric Cult of South India*, New Delhi
Nambiar, P. K. and Kurup, Naryana	1968	*Fairs and Festivals*, Madras
Nepali, Gopal Singh	1965	*The Newars*, Bombay
Neumann, Erich	1954	*The Origins of History and Consciousness*, New York
Norman, Dorothy	1969	*The Hero: Myth, Image, Symbol*, Cleveland
Northey, Major W. B. and Morris, C. J.	1928	*The Gurkhas*, London
Oldfield, H. A.	1818	*Sketches from Nepal*, two volumes, London
Obeyesekere, Gananth	1983	*The Cult of the Goddess Pattini*, Princeton; reprint, New Delhi, 1987
O'Flaherty, Wendy Doniger	1976	*The Origins of Evil in Hindu Mythology*, Berkeley
————	1979	'Sacred Cows and Profane Mares in Indian Mythology', *History of Religions*, Vol. XIX # 1
————	1980	*Women, Androgynes and Other Mythical Beasts*, reprint, Chicago, 1982

	1981	*Rig Veda*, Middlesex
	1988	*Other People's Myths*, New York
Oppert, Gustav	1893	*On the Original Inhabitants of Bharatavarga or India*, reprint, New Delhi, 1972
Ostor, Akos	1980	*The Play of the Gods*, Chicago
Otto, Walter F.	1933	*Dionysos, Myth and Cult*, reprint (2nd ed.) Bloomington and London, 1965
Patai, Raphael	1967	*The Hebrew Goddess*, New York
Payne, Ernest A.	1933	*The Saktas*, Calcutta
Peggs, J.	1828	*The Suttees' Cry to Britain*, London
Petrie, Sir Flinders	1924	*Religious Life in Ancient Egypt*, London
Pinkerton, John	1808	*General Collection of the Best and Most Interesting Voyages and Travels in All Parts of the World*, Vols. VII and VIII, London
Poovaya-Smith, Nima	1992	'Bhuta figures of South Kanara', *Living Wood*, ed. George Michell, MARG Publications.
Potdar, K. R.	1953	*Sacrifice in the Rg Veda*, Bombay
Prater, S. H.	1912	*The Book of Indian Animals*, Bombay, reprint, New Delhi, 1990
Prayag, K. B.	1982	*Tuljapur Mahatmya*, Solapur
Presler, Henry H.	1971	*Primitive Religions in India*, Bangalore
Preston, James J.	1980	*Cult of the Goddess*, New Delhi
Paterson J. D.	1808	'Of the Origin of the Hindu Religion', *Asiatic Researches*, Vol. VIII, London
Raglin, F.R.S.	1906	*The Hero : A Study in Tradition, Myth and Drama*
Rakshit, Indu	1975	'The Concept of Durga Mahishasuramardini and its Iconographic Representation', *Roopa-Lekha*, 41
Ramakrishna Mission	1984	*Sri Sarada Devi: The Great Wonder*, New Delhi, 1984
Rank, Otto	1914	*The Myth of the Birth of the Hero*, reprint, New York, 1964
		The Don Juan Legend, Princeton, reprint, 1975
Rao, Gopinath T.A.	1914	*Elements of Hindu Iconography*, four volumes, Varanasi, reprint 1971
Rao, C. Hayavadana	1922	'Primitive Religion in Mysore', *Quarterly Journal of the Mythic Society*, Vol. XII, Jan.
	1922	'Mysore Castes and Tribes', *Quarterly Journal of the Mythic Society*, Vol. XIII, # 1 Oct.
		'Totemism: Mysore Castes and Tribes', *Quarterly Journal of the Mythic Society*, Vol. XII, Jan.
Rao, M.S.A	1986	'Supernatural Possession in Kerala', *Man in India*, Vol. 66 # 1, March

Reik, Theodore	1958	*Myth and Guilt*, London
Reiniche, M. L.	1987	'Worship of Kaliyamman in Some Tamil Villages: The Sacrifice of the Warrior-Weavers', *Religion and Society in South India*, V. Sudarsen *et al.* ed., New Delhi
Renaudot, Abbé	1808	'An Account of the Travels of Two Mohamedans Through India and China in the Ninth Century', in Pinkerton, Vol. VII
Richards, F. J.	1920	'The Village Deities of Vellore Taluk, North Arcot Dist.', The *Quarterly Journal of the Mythic Society*, Vol. X, # 2, Jan.
Rivers, W.H.R.	1906	*The Todas*, London
Rolland, Romain	1929	*The Life of Ramakrishna*, reprint, Calcutta, 1974
Rose, H.A.	1986	*Hindu Gods and Goddesses*, New Delhi
Russell, R.V. and Lal, R.B.H.	1916	*Tribes and Castes of the Central Provinces of India*, four vols., reprint, New Delhi, 1975
Sahai, Bhagawant	1975	*Iconography of Minor Hindu and Buddhist Deities*, New Delhi
Salatore, B.A.	1932	*Social and Political Life in Vijayanagara Empire*, two vols., Madras
Samuels, Andrew	1985	*Jung and the Post-Jungians*, London
Satyanarayana, K.	1975	*A Study of the History and Culture of the Andhras*, New Delhi
Schaeffer, Claude	1936	*The Cuneiform Texts of Ras Shamra-Ugarit*, The Schweich Lectures of the British Acadamy, London
Sharma, Dashratha	1963	'Verbal Similarities Between the *Durga Sapta Sati* and the *Devi Bhagavata Purana* and Other Considerations Bearing on their Date', *Purana*, Vol. V, # 1, Jan.
Shaw, Lieutenant Thomas	1798	'Hills Near Rajamahal', *Asiatic Researches*, Vol. IV, London
Sheshadri, M.	1963	'Mahishasuramardini: Images, Iconography and Interpretations', *The Half Yearly Journal of the Mysore University*, Vol. XXII, # 2, March
Shirsagar, Mhaskoba Manohar	1984	'*Shrinath Mhaskoba Mahatmya*', Pune, Marathi and Sanskrit; trans. Narendranath B. Patil
Shore, John	1798	'On Some Extraordinary Facts, Customs and Practices of the Hindus', *Asiatic Researches*, Vol. IV, London
Shorter, Alan	1937	*The Egyptian Gods*, London
Shulman, David Dean	1976	'The Murderous Bride: Tamil Versions of the Myth of Devi and the Buffalo-Demon', *History of Religion*, Vol. XVI # 2, Chicago, Nov.

	1980	*Tamil Temple Myths*, Princeton
——————	1985	*The King and the Clown*, Princeton
——————	1986	'Battle as Metaphor in Tamil Folk and Classic Traditions', in *Another Harmony*, ed. S.H. Blackburn and A.K. Ramanujan, New Delhi
——————	1990	*Songs of the Harsh Devotee*, Philadelphia
——————	1993	*The Hungry God*, Chicago
Singh, Gurmeet	1985	'Dhat Syndrome Revisited', *Indian Journal of Psychiatry*, April
Sinha, Jadunath	1966	*Shakta Monism: The Cult of Shakti*, Calcutta
Sircar, D.C.	1967	*The Sakta Cult and Tara*, Calcutta
Smith, Brian K. and O'Flaherty, Wendy Doniger		'Sarifice and Substitution: Ritual Mystification and Mythical Demystification', *Numen*, Vol. XXXVI, Fas. 2
Smith, Brian K.	1989	*Reflections on Resemblance, Ritual and Religion*, New York
Sontheimer, Gunther D.	1976	*Pastoral Deities in Western India*, New York, 1989, trans. Anne Feldman
——————	1987	'Rudra and Khandoba: Continuity', in *Religion and Society in Folk Religion*, Toronto Centre for Asian Studies
Soundara Rajan, K. V.	1963	'The Devi Cult Nucleus at Jagat, Rajasthan', *Vishveshvaranand Indological Journal*, I, part 1, March
Srivastava, M.C.P.	1979	*Mother Goddesses in Indian Art, Archaeology and Literature*, New Delhi
Stein, Burton, ed.	1978	*South Indian Temples*, New Delhi
Stekel, Wilhelm	1929	*Sadism and Masochism*, Vol. I, reprint, New York, 1953; Vol. II, reprint, New York, 1964
——————	1953	*Patterns of Psychosexual Infantilism*, London
Stutley, Margaret	1980	*Ancient Indian Magic and Folklore*, New Delhi
Thompson, Edward	1928	*Suttee*, London
Umadikar, Vasant		*Amravatichi Shri Ambadevi* (Marathi), Nagpur, 1988, trans. Narendranath B. Patil
Underhill, M.M.	1921	*The Hindu Religious Year*, Calcutta
Vakpati	1887	*The Gaudavaho*, ed. S. P. Pandit, Bombay Sanskrit Series, XXXIV–XXI
Van Kooij, K.R.	1972	*Worship of the Goddess According to the Kalika Purana*, Leiden
Vermuele, Emily	1964	*Greece in the Bronze Age*, Chicago
von Furer-Haimendorf, Cristoph	1979	*The Gonds of Andhra Pradesh*, Bombay
——————	1945	*The Reddis of the Bison Hills*, London.
von Stietencron, Heinrich		'Die Göttin Durga Mahishasuramardini,

Mythos, Darstellung und geschichtliche Rolle bei der Hinduisierung Indiens', *Visible Religion*, Vol. II, London

Vernant, Jean-Pierre   1974   *Myth and Society in Ancient Greece*, reprint, London, 1980

Warner, Rex, editor   1975   *Encyclopedia of Mythology*, London

Welbon, Guy and Yocum, Glenn E.   1982   *Religious Festivals in South India and Sri Lanka*, New Delhi

Whitehead, Henry   1916   *The Village Gods of South India*, reprint, New Delhi, 1976

Wilson, H.H.   1850   'On the Sacrifice of Human Beings as an Element of the Ancient Religion of India', *Journal of the Royal Asiatic Society of Great Britain and Ireland*, London

Wolkstein, Diane and Kramer, Samuel Noah   1983   *Inanna, Queen of Heaven*, New York

Wonderlich, Hans Georg   1972   *The Secret of Crete*, Hamburg, English edition, 1976

Yocum, Glenn   1977   'The Goddess in a Tamil Saiva Devotional Text, Manikkavakar's *Tiruvacakam'*, *Journal of the American Academy of Religion*, 45, # 1, supplement (March)

Zimmer, Heinrich   1948   *The King and the Corpse*, Princeton

Index

aboriginal 52, 153; *see also* festival
Absolute, the 4, 82, 95, 107
　　Brahman 156; Goddess as 111, 130
　　See also Purusa
Achichchhtra 222
Aditi
　　Diti's sister, 35; Indra's cow mother
　　abandons him, 42, 235–8; as widow,
　　75; *see also* Indra
Adonai, 246–9
Agave, 25, 254
aggression (ive) 67, 70
　　in battle 139, 145–7; language of
　　Goddess 110, 116, 118
　　See also battle, Goddess, Mahisa, sad-
　　ism
Agarwala, V.S. 123
Agni
　　offers boon, 1, 33; as creative heat, 58;
　　his divine joke, 172; forbids suicide,
　　32; Goddess rejects, 118; preserves
　　infant, 48; Rambha wishes to offer
　　head to, 30; transports devotee's gifts
　　to heaven, 207
agriculture (al)
　　communities, 3, 91; cultivators, 84;
　　cycles, 187; rites 20, 200; settled
　　people, 14
Aihole, 225–6
Airavata, 79
Alaia, 242, 249
Ammon, 245
Anath/Astarte, 241, 146, 250, 252, 253,
　　254
Anatolia, 83
ancestors
　　re-appearance of, 82; worship of, 166,
　　216
Andhakasura, 79, 129
Andhra Pradesh, 52

animal
　　animal/human divine kinship, 83;
　　associated with religious spirit, 85;
　　energy exchange with, 144; as father,
　　53, 83; Goddess: animal headed, 149,
　　behaves like an, 108, 117, 118; calls
　　Mahisa beast, 118; Mistress of Ani-
　　mals, 3, 83, 149, 171; animal nature in
　　humans, 13–15, 144, 247; in children,
　　15; animal/child/adult triad, 15; ani-
　　mal/human/god connections, 41, 82;
　　heroes' association with, 263–4; ani-
　　mal instinct, 109; jungle combats, 133;
　　Pasupati, Lord of, 84; power of, 144;
　　sacrifice of, 162–79; zooanthropic
　　imagery, 148;
　　See also buffalo, bull, cow, Goddess,
　　icon, Todas.
Aphrodite, 242, 249, 254
Apollo, 240, 249
apsara, 69, 79, 114
Apsu, 251
artists, 220–9
　　Yavana, 227
Aruru, 236, 237
Asclepios, 235, 240, 241, 242, 249, 250,
　　254, 257, 263
Assam, 84
astronomical observations, 187
　　See also festival.
asuri, 123, 124
atavism, 39, 73, 164, 171, 175, 261
　　Devi and Mahisa as medium for con-
　　tainment of 179; re-activated erup-
　　tions 164, 181, 189
Athene, 189, 249
atonement
　　achieved through sacrifice, 129; only
　　hope, 180
　　See also sacrifice; denials, lamentations.

305